OXFORD ENGLISH DRAMA

General Editor: Michael Cordner
Associate General Editors: Peter Holland · Martin Wiggins

LONDON ASSURANCE
AND OTHER VICTORIAN COMEDIES

THIS selection of four plays covers the years 1840 to 1908. Focusing on the perennial concerns of love, money, and marriage, each play represents a specifically dramatic approach to these issues central to life in Victorian and Edwardian society. Together, they give an insight into the range of comic modes at the time, from the seriously thoughtful to the brilliantly funny. Only Dion Boucicault is remembered primarily as a playwright in his own right. The other plays highlight aspects of their authors' dramatic talents rendered nearly invisible by the glitter of their fame as novelists, in the case of Bulwer-Lytton and Henry James, or, as with W. S. Gilbert, as the librettist of the unforgettable 'Savoy Operas' with the composer Arthur Sullivan.

KLAUS STIERSTORFER is 'wissenschaftlicher Assistent' in the English Department at the University of Würzburg, Germany. He is the author of *John Oxenford (1812–1877) as Farceur and Critic of Comedy* (1996). His current research is concerned with the development of English literary history.

MICHAEL CORDNER is Reader in the Department of English and Related Literature at the University of York. He has edited George Farquhar's *The Beaux' Stratagem*, the *Complete Plays* of Sir George Etherege, *Four Comedies* of Sir John Vanbrugh, and, for Oxford English Drama, *Four Restoration Marriage Plays* and Sheridan's *The School for Scandal and Other Plays*. He is writing books on *The Comedy of Marriage* and *Shakespeare and the Actor.*

PETER HOLLAND is Professor of Shakespeare Studies and Director of the Shakespeare Institute, University of Birmingham.

MARTIN WIGGINS is a Fellow of the Shakespeare Institute and Lecturer in English at the University of Birmingham.

OXFORD ENGLISH DRAMA

OXFORD WORLD'S CLASSICS

London Assurance and Other Victorian Comedies

EDWARD BULWER-LYTTON
Money

DION BOUCICAULT
London Assurance

W. S. GILBERT
Engaged

HENRY JAMES
The High Bid

Edited by
KLAUS STIERSTORFER
General Editor
MICHAEL CORDNER
Associate General Editors
PETER HOLLAND · MARTIN WIGGINS

OXFORD
UNIVERSITY PRESS

OXFORD

UNIVERSITY PRESS

Great Clarendon Street, Oxford OX2 6DP

Oxford University Press is a department of the University of Oxford.
It furthers the University's objective of excellence in research, scholarship,
and education by publishing worldwide in

Oxford New York

Athens Auckland Bangkok Bogotá Buenos Aires Cape Town
Chennai Dar es Salaam Delhi Florence Hong Kong Istanbul Karachi
Kolkata Kuala Lumpur Madrid Melbourne Mexico City Mumbai Nairobi
Paris São Paulo Shanghai Singapore Taipei Tokyo Toronto Warsaw

with associated companies in Berlin Ibadan

Oxford is a registered trade mark of Oxford University Press
in the UK and in certain other countries

Published in the United States
by Oxford University Press Inc., New York

British Library Cataloguing in Publication Data

Data available

Library of Congress Cataloging in Publication Data

Data available

ISBN–13: 978–0–19–283296–2

4

Typeset in Ehrhardt
by RefineCatch Limited, Bungay, Suffolk
Printed in Great Britain by
Clays Ltd, St Ives plc

CONTENTS

ACKNOWLEDGEMENTS

I WISH to thank the General Editor, Michael Cordner, for his patient assistance and helpful comments on various drafts of the text. I owe a debt of gratitude to Professor Rüdiger Ahrens of Würzburg University, Germany, for granting me a generous allowance of time for research. I gratefully acknowledge James Sharrock's scrupulous checking of the typescript. At OUP, I was able to benefit from Elizabeth Stratford's impressive astuteness in copy-editing and from Judith Luna's readiness to answer any queries whatsoever. Angelika has, as always, been an invaluable help.

INTRODUCTION

THE plays selected for this volume span a period longer than Queen Victoria's reign. Bulwer-Lytton's *Money* (1840) was first produced not long after her accession to the throne in 1837, while Henry James's *The High Bid* (1908) will take the reader well into the Edwardian years, although its initial conception dates from late Victorian times. The four plays are presented together in one volume, as they all characteristically deal with central concerns of nineteenth-century social life. More specifically, they can be read as sharing a common focus on the major themes of love and money, particularly in the institution of marriage. At the same time, each of the plays provides its own variation on these issues, as determined by its author's choice of dramatic mode and genre, but also by the conditions of production at the particular theatre where it was first performed. The volume thus offers the opportunity to explore a palette of views on these vital issues as they evolve through the Victorian era and beyond, and to see how they are interpreted and presented, on a rich and changing stage, by actresses and actors whose art and techniques are reflected in the play texts, and, often enough, as decisive factors in the texts' very conception.

Throughout Victorian times, the 'romantic' view of pure love and sacrosanct marriage with the attendant concepts of clear-cut role-models for all concerned—devoted, protecting male; idealized, vulnerable, and obedient female; dutiful child, generous and wise parent—was part of the official cultural discourse, exemplified by the Queen herself as loving spouse and as faithful 'Widow of Windsor' after the Prince Consort's death in 1861. Walter E. Houghton has given a classic summary of this Victorian view on love:

The whole attitude is exactly what we call Romantic, and it was, in fact, a direct inheritance from Romanticism: partly from its naturalism, which found the instincts good and appealed to the feelings or the heart as the supreme guide to conduct and wisdom; partly from its idealism, whether Platonic or chivalric. The study of Victorian love is the study of how this tradition, embodied mainly in the works of Rousseau, Shelley, and George Sand, was domesticated under the powerful influence of Evangelical and family sentiment, and then emphasized, as a protection against, or a solution for, some major concerns of the time: sensuality, the marriage market, the painful mood of baffled thought, and the decline of religious faith.[1]

As Houghton points out, the Victorian insistence on idealized concepts of love, marriage, and the family must be seen as a reaction to a deep and widespread anxiety, which originated to a large extent from the reverberations of the French Revolution. It is not only the direct, nightmarish fear of similar convulsions happening in Britain, as Houghton explains (pp. 54–8), but, perhaps more importantly, the wider concern of a breakup of the shared social and cultural order which had regulated the individual's passage through life on a communal basis; a breakup, of which the French Revolution and its aftermath were only the final, most potent and immediate symbols to many Victorians' minds.

Common people's values had to be newly defined and reordered, and the theatre provided an important platform in this process. One of theatre's important answers to this challenge was melodrama, a new genre which became popular from the beginning of the nineteenth century onwards. Melodrama was the Romantic response to the decline of the aristocratic genres of tragedy and 'high comedy', and its most immediate conceptual roots can be located in the French Revolution. As Peter Brooks aptly puts it:

assurance must be a central function of melodrama in the post-sacred universe: it relocates and rearticulates the most basic moral sentiments and celebrates the sign of the right. From its very inception during the Revolution—the moment when ethical symbols were patently, convulsively thrown into question—melodrama addressed itself to this relocation and rearticulation of an occulted morality.[2]

Melodrama is a non-realist, expressionistic genre aimed at, again in Brooks's phrase, an 'expressionism of the moral imagination' (p. 55), presenting good and evil, virtue and vice in stark contrast and presenting an almost surrealist vindication of virtue in the face of the dark powers threatening to destroy it. This (re-)assertive mood, both built up and reflected by melodrama, was continually gaining strength after Queen Victoria's accession in 1837 and evolved into a new national and social self-assurance, which expressed itself in such triumphant events as the Great Exhibition of 1851.

[1] Walter E. Houghton, *The Victorian Frame of Mind 1830–1870* (New Haven and London: Yale University Press, 1957, repr. 1987), 375.

[2] Peter Brooks, *The Melodramatic Imagination: Balzac, Henry James, Melodrama, and the Mode of Excess* (New Haven and London: Yale University Press, 1976, repr. 1995), 43.

Both the civil society, as it developed under Queen Victoira's reign, and the dramatic enactments of its core values are major sources from which the four comedies presented in this volume draw their thematic material. They have to be understood against this background of an imminent danger overcome (the Revolution in neighbouring France) and a new-found assurance regarding national identity and social order, as well as the presentations of these common experiences in the theatre. Focusing on love and marriage as key issues, the four plays enact, in their various ways and with various results in mind, a critical investigation of the assumptions underlying the Victorian sense of a well-ordered civil society. The critique they offer is not, however, directed solely at some hard and fast social 'reality'. They must be seen to engage in a critical dialogue with other dramatic modes, most notably melodrama, which both reflect and produce the social reality of which they in fact, as theatrical practice, form a part.

Money

When *Money* was first performed at the Haymarket Theatre on 8 December 1840, Edward Bulwer-Lytton (1803–73) was already a well-known figure, not only in the literary world and the theatre, but also in the sphere of politics. As a novelist, he had first established his fame with *Pelham* (1828), a major specimen of the 'Fashionable novel' or the so-called 'silver-fork school', but his Newgate novels, most famously *Eugene Aram* (1832), were equally celebrated at the time, as were his historical novels, such as *The Last Days of Pompeii* (1834) or *Rienzi* (1835). In the theatre, *Money* was his fifth play to be produced, preceded most notably by the great successes of *The Lady of Lyons* (1838) and *Richelieu* (1839). As a Member of Parliament for St Ives, Huntingdonshire, and then Lincoln, his motion brought forward on 31 May 1832 that a Select Committee be set up to investigate the situation of the theatres had eventually resulted in the abolition of the patent theatres' privileges in the Theatre Regulation Act of 1843. Moreover, Bulwer had been a committed supporter of the far-reaching political and social reform movement of the 1830s, particularly aimed at bringing relief to underprivileged and marginalized social groups, from Catholics and Dissenters to the poor and child labourers.

Readers or spectators of *Money* will, however, quickly notice that this is not primarily a play written to criticize the social injustices in the early Victorian era. There is no doubt that all of the main characters belong to the upper layers of London society; poverty, where it occurs, is relative and of the 'poor cousin' or 'younger son' type, that is, those members of generally well-off families who are not in the direct hereditary line or have fallen on hard times and belong in the 'poor relations' category for other reasons. These persons, Clara and Evelyn as poor cousins of the 'rich' Veseys in our play, are at the mercy of their relatives. Still, the squalor in the living conditions of Mayhew's 'London poor'[3] or Dickens's 'Rookery' (see *Sketches by Boz*, scene xxii) is never a real presence in the play. It only appears at a distance in the form of Mrs Stanton, Evelyn's poor nurse, for whom he tries to raise money. Further persons from the lower social orders who come on stage, such as the various tradesmen or the servants, are all cardbord characters whose stereotypical qualities, especially in the case of the tradesmen, are exploited for comic effect.

Nevertheless, the play is conceived as a severe critique of its contemporaries, and that, it can be argued, mainly on two connected levels. First, the play can be interpreted as a detailed investigation of generally familiar social and moral virtues and vices as they are refracted, prism-like, in the theme of money. The basic structure of the plot is designed for this purpose. The financial fortunes of the poor orphan Evelyn are given several dramatic turns, from his unexpected inheritance of the greater part of his uncle's money, to his (supposed) ruin through gaming, and finally to his 'restoration' to wealth through the revelation of his hoax. This aspect of the play is fairly straightforward and the characters around Evelyn act in predictable ways; mercenary minds reveal themselves in their greed and disappointment at the stipulations of the will, while their attitudes towards Evelyn change with the same volatility as his fortunes. In contrast, Clara, together with Lady Franklin and the honest Graves, stand by Evelyn in poverty and in his pretended dissipation when he is rich. Still, Clara's noble spirit, because of some strange twists of fate and intrigue—that is, through Bulwer's in this respect somewhat artificial and involuted plot—prevents her from accepting Evelyn's hand before the final denouement of the play. Matters are more complex in the constitution of the figure of Evelyn himself. At his first mention in the play, he is characterized as 'a humourist—a cynic' (1.79) by Sir John. This view is confirmed by his first entry, steeped in his philosophical reading and quick to utter his cynical comments, on Sir John's stinginess or on the foppish emptiness of Blount's character. In one sense Evelyn's bitterness, his misanthropy and acidity reminiscent

---

[3] Henry Mayhew, *London Labour and the London Poor* (1851).

of a Shakespearian Timon of Athens or a Thersites in *Troilus and Cressida*, is revealed to be a consequence of his poverty, as he himself confesses in an early soliloquy: 'And thus must I grind out my life forever! I am ambitious, and poverty drags me down! I have learning, and poverty makes me the drudge of fools! I love, and poverty stands like a spectre before the altar!' (1.198–201). When he becomes wealthy, however, his misanthropic bitterness does not wholly disappear. This is partly due to his unhappy love of Clara, without whom money means nothing to him. It is also, however, a reflection of his disillusionment with the majority of the people he meets. Faking his ruin and thus highlighting the threadbare nature of the friendships he has won with his inheritance, Evelyn becomes a guide pointing out to the audience the true natures of the characters who people what Thackeray a few years later called *Vanity Fair* (1847/8).

Here, a further dimension becomes visible beyond the comedy's patently moralistic strain as it exemplifies such general insights as 'money makes the man' (2.1.2–3) and such received wisdom as the unreliability of fair-weather friendships. Such a purely allegorical reading is denied by the play's minutely realistic setting in Bulwer's contemporary London society. The mentioning of real shop and street names, daily newspapers, the very financial detail, government bonds and 'three percents', clearly indicate that this is not, at least not primarily, a reflection on the human condition in general, but an indictment of a specific section of English society. The audience is presented with a panorama of characters who constitute or pretend to belong to the moneyed urban upper class. It is no coincidence that the few sincere persons in the play are, apart from Evelyn and Clara, the only ones who do not seem to worry about money; Lady Franklin is in fact a very rich widow, and Graves, too, is in easy financial circumstances. All the others need to struggle for the necessary funds to keep up appearances. How this is best achieved, by false pretences and advantageous marriages, is vividly represented in Sir John's account of his career to his daughter Georgina in the opening scene of the play. Sir Frederick Blount seems intent on following Sir John's example, while the gambler and possible cardsharper Captain Smooth exemplifies a further, socially accepted way of catering for his pecuniary needs. Here, the real problem is not money in itself, but these persons' greed for it and the egotistic uses to which they intend to put it. The price they pay for it is heavy, however, as they sacrifice the absolute values at the heart of human happiness which Evelyn apostrophizes in his final speech as 'truth and love'. It is therefore no contradiction to the play's general drift when Evelyn and Clara at the happy ending both have their cake and eat it, as they have found each other, but have also their large fortune to enjoy together.

With this ending and for all its realistic concreteness the comedy nevertheless keeps its distance from any social activism. Evelyn's final antidote to 'the humours and the follies, the vanities, deceits and vices' (5.3.317–18) portrayed in the course of the play is not some kind of social reform. His final verdict on party politics is to leave its factitiousness well alone and think of Britain as a unified nation, as that 'Stout Gentleman', John Bull (5.3.310–11). His recourse is to the private happiness of love and true friendship. The effect on society as a whole is indirect and can only be inferred, in so far as the gradual spread of the recognition of these true values could lead to the moral reformation of society as a whole.

These central concerns of the play are, however, evident from its very beginning. False pretences are immediately exposed in Sir John's confessions to Georgina in the first scene, and the reactions at the reading of the will would alone have sufficed to expose the vanities and vices of the various characters. Was a further reiteration of predictably similar experiences in the course of Evelyn's pretended ruin really necessary from a dramatic point of view? This question appears beside the point when the peculiar nature of the comedy is considered. If Peter Brooks's characterization of melodrama as the 'relocation and rearticulation of an occulted morality', as being 'about virtue made visible and acknowledged, the drama of a recognition',[4] is correct, it also goes a long way towards explaining this comedy. It only opens up its true potential when it is understood to work on the 'expressionist' principle shared with melodrama. In the course of the play, the audience is not so much to be taught what vice and virtue truly are; this is all too obvious from the very beginning. Rather, the audience is invited to witness, and to witness empathetically, how this virtue is blocked, suppressed, concealed and how it eventually triumphs in the union of Evelyn and Clara. The play is sentimental in the sense that it does not ask its audience to follow a complex intrigue—the ruse Evelyn uses is, despite his reference to the age-old farcical twist of the 'duper duped' (3.1 and 4.2), not particularly sophisticated or ingenious—nor does it deal with a complex moral problem. Its appeal is to the audience's feelings as they follow the fate of virtue through its tribulations imposed by a depraved world.

[4] Brooks, *Melodramatic Imagination*, 27.

What mainly keeps *Money* within the sphere of comedy and establishes a certain distance to melodrama proper is, however, not its portrayal of virtue, but its treatment of vice. Evelyn and Clara as the virtuous characters in the play are of course surrounded by wickedness and morally doubtful behaviour. Sir John's plotting of his daughter's marriage to his own material gain, or Captain Smooth's setting his traps at the card table and the general greed for money revealed by the various reactions of the potential heirs in the will, are all a dark foil to the sterling qualities portrayed in Clara and Evelyn, in Lady Franklyn and in the crotchety Graves. Stout's apology that it took him 'an hour and a half to beat it into the head of a stupid old widow with nine children that to allow her three shillings a week was against all the rules of public morality' (1.330–3) here remains the offstage background to the action, whereas a typically melodramatic story line might centre on the presentation of the widow's misfortunes. A staple fare in melodrama, the darker shades of black, unmotivated evil, in the tradition of vice figures such as Iago in Shakespeare's *Othello*, do not appear in the same unrelieved intensity in *Money*. The forces opposing the impersonations of virtue in Evelyn and Clara are not of a symbolic, metaphysical nature. Here they are social evils which are clearly pointed out and defined; greed for money, opportunism, rigged elections. As in melodrama, they are eventually overcome by triumphant virtue, but unlike those of melodrama, the evils portrayed here are not unremediable. The fact that they may be ultimately ineradicable does not mean that society in all its spheres, from the family to politics, could not be improved. The play ends on a conciliatory note, and not even Smooth, the gamester, is excluded from the merry tableau with which the comedy ends.

Beyond these very serious issues, the play also contains several instances of comic relief and some humorous episodes. Clearly, these have a significant share in the continuing attractiveness of the play. While the comic elements in melodrama usually work on the principle of stark contrast to the serious part of the play and for that reason tend towards the more rollicking, rumbustious kind of fun typically found in the farces of the time, Bulwer managed to integrate even hilariously comic passages into the play's more serious episodes. Undoubtedly, one of its best moments in this respect is Lady Franklin's slow cajoling of Graves out of the reminiscing about his deceased wife into an unselfconscious enjoyment of a merry song and dance (3.2). The scene's slow crescendo from a few fragmented tunes and first dancing steps into the bacchanalian 'Tum ti-ti-tum' and Scotch reel ending in the abrupt discovery of the frolicking couple is one of the play's highlights.

In the conception of *Money*, Bulwer was quite consciously searching for a new dramatic mode for his contemporary stage, which, according to a widespread feeling, had experienced a steep decline into a heavy reliance on sensationalism, spectacle, and a general pandering to what many perceived as a low or popular taste. What Bulwer wanted to restore was, as he characterized *Money* in a letter to his friend John Forster, 'the old realm of genteel comedy'.[5] As reviewers saw it, Bulwer was indeed successful in rejuvenating English comedy by picking up the development where Richard Brinsley Sheridan, the last British playwright of acknowledged stature, had left off. Notably in *The School for Scandal* (1777), Sheridan had made the attempt, as Charles Lamb put it, 'to join the artifical with the sentimental comedy',[6] thus attempting a compromise for an old theatrical quarrel of the eighteenth century. By fusing the tradition of Restoration wit with eighteenth-century sentiment, Sheridan had, as Lamb saw it with hindsight, overcome the contrast and created a new, mixed genre which profited from the best of both traditions. Lamb's opinion was adopted by John Forster in his review of *Money*, who praised Bulwer for having taken up Sheridan's model. As Forster saw it, however, Bulwer had not simply imitated Sheridan, but could claim the merit of having further adapted this kind of comedy to his own age of increased social consciousness and reform:

the best [comedy] has been that in which the sentiment was most lightly interwoven with the wit and character. This was Sheridan. But even since Sheridan's time our audiences are more in earnest, and require to see fairer play to the truth as well as the falsehood of the society of which they form a portion. Hence the mixed character of the excellent comedy we are noticing.[7]

Bulwer himself had explicitly noted his intention to write a comedy whose earnestness was in keeping with the spirit of its age:

The comedy of a time must be faithful to the character of the time itself. In our own age men are more earnest than in that of the old artificial comedy. No matter in what department, the essence of the drama is still the faithful though idealising representation of life; and in 1840 we know that all life at least is *not*

---

[5] Charles H. Shattuck (ed.), *Bulwer and Macready: A Chronicle of the Early Victorian Theatre* (Urbana, Ill., University of Illinois Press, 1958), 165.

[6] Charles Lamb, 'On the Artificial Comedy of Last Century' in *Elia and The Last Essays of Elia*, ed. Jonathan Bate (Oxford: Oxford University Press, 1987), 165.

[7] John Forster in the *Examiner*, 13 Dec. 1840, 790.

a jest. . . . It is precisely because the present is more thoughtful, that Comedy, in its reflection of the age, must be more faithful to the chequered diversities of existence, and go direct to its end through humours to truth, no matter whether its path lie through smiles or tears.[8]

What made *Money* so successful, then, on the early Victorian stage was its commitment to social and moral improvement while at the same time keeping well aloof from 'low' tastes and pandering to the 'populace', which in political terms meant keeping its distance from any intimations of social radicalism or revolutionary tendencies. The attempt to prove that theatre mattered as a serious, beneficial tool of social improvement can also be identified as a pervasive force in the play's production.

Bulwer's theatrical activities were closely connected to an actor, who continually encouraged and advised him, and for whom many leading parts of his plays were designed: William Charles Macready (1793–1873). Their co-operation can be said to have started in earnest in February 1836, when Macready was invited by Bulwer to call on him at his chambers.[9] Both men were united in their commitment to reinvigorating the English stage which they perceived to be in a dilapidated condition. Where Bulwer brought the successful novelist's ideas for stories and 'poetic' language, Macready contributed his long experience—he had been on the stage since 1810—as actor, but also as manager, for example at Covent Garden from 1837 to 1839. In both functions, Macready was one of the most prominent and influential figures of his time. His acting was in the Romantic tradition, focused on a vivid representation of emotions and passions the intensity of which would be directly communicated to the audience. Although the formalistic conventions in gesture and posture survived from the classicist school of acting, where each state of mind and feeling was assigned a fixed corresponding form in the actor's representation,[10] Macready aspired to fill these empty shells with genuine passion. George Henry Lewes, for example, reported that, in order to work himself into the appropriate frame of mind when playing Shylock in Shakespeare's *Merchant of Venice*, 'Macready, it is said, used to spend some minutes behind the scenes, lashing himself into an imaginary

[8] Edward Bulwer-Lytton, 'Introduction' to *The Dramatic Works of Sir Edward Lytton Bulwer, Bart.* (London, 1841), p. xiii.

[9] The meeting is described in Shattuck (ed.), *Bulwer and Macready*, 18–20.

[10] These conventionalized postures and gestures were variously explained and illustrated in actors' manuals, such as Henry Siddons, *Practical Illustrations of Rhetorical Gesture and Action* (1807), or Leman T. Rede, *The Way to the Stage* (1827).

rage by cursing sotto voce, and shaking violently a ladder fixed against the wall'.[11]

As stage manager, Macready placed the highest demands on the quality of the scenery and the rehearsals of his fellow actresses and actors, even those in minor roles. It is not surprising that this view was not always in tune with the exigencies of keeping a theatre profitable. When Benjamin Webster, manager of the Haymarket Theatre since 1837, showed himself unconvinced of the need to incur the extra expenses in staff, scenery, and costumes expected by Bulwer and Macready for the projected presentation of *Money*, Macready threatened to offer the play to Webster's rival, Madame Vestris, at Covent Garden. In response, the exasperated Webster sent him an acrimonious letter, complaining that 'it would be far better for me to jog on comfortably in my old and humble, but profitable, way, than to endure this continued scene of splendid misery which will probably end in loss'.[12] The dispute was, however, amicably settled, and Bulwer's comedy benefited from the expenditure Macready demanded.

Macready's acting technique in his impersonation of Evelyn and his insistence on a lavish set and costumes had the combined effect of a greater realism in the performance. Bulwer and Macready had joined forces to produce a play where the audience could distinctly discern their own 'reality' on stage. While working on *Money*, for instance, Bulwer asked Macready to inquire of Count d'Orsay, 'whether whist & piquet would be *ever* played in the great Dining-room at Crockford's [Club]',[13] as it is presented in Act 5 of the comedy. With this high degree of verisimilitude and detailed realism of its setting, the play's social and moral criticism, too, could immediately be recognized by the audience as specifically and personally addressed to them and to the world they inhabited in real life.

Money was a huge success and kept its standing on the English stage for the rest of the century. Bulwer had succeeded in infusing a viable, traditional form of comedy with new elements, a considerable portion of which originated in melodrama and which were precisely adapted to the specific taste of his audiences. The appeal to the sentiments and the optimistic call for reform while at the same time opposing any

[11] George Henry Lewes, *On Actors and the Art of Acting* (London, 1875), 40.

[12] Quoted in Alan S. Downer, *The Eminent Tragedian, William Charles Macready* (Cambridge, Mass., Harvard University Press, 1966), 200.

[13] Letter by Bulwer to Macready, 3 Nov. 1840, repr. in Russell Jackson (ed.), *Victorian Theatre. A New Mermaid Background Book* (London: A. & C. Black, 1989), 312.

political partisanship or anything else that might endanger national unity and social peace made the comedy popular with the upwardly mobile middle classes of the Victorian age. The very aspects it shared with melodrama, however, its appeal to the sentiments and its overt moral didacticism, are the main reasons for its fall from grace with twentieth-century theatre directors. Yet, the hope that the play's undoubted potential does not need to be lost for ever is clearly shown in its revivals in recent years.

The Royal Shakespeare Company produced it at The Other Place, Stratford-upon-Avon (11 November 1981), subsequently transferred to London's Pit in the Barbican Theatre (17 June 1982), under the direction of Bill Alexander. Reviewers seemed to be uncertain, however, in what vein to take the performance. The problem, it is clear, was precisely in the play's melodramatic, 'expressionist' qualities which did not come across to the audience and without which its message felt flat and uninspiring. '[N]o depths to be plumbed', wrote Mark Amory in *The Spectator*. 'Serious?', asked Winston Trew in *City Limits*. 'Not really,' he answered himself, 'it's hardly an exploration of the corrupting power of money', which led him on to the logical conclusion: 'Go for the laughs.'[14]

In the Royal National Theatre production of *Money* (3 June 1999), John Caird decided as its director to take the play in all its seriousness. 'He knows that there is no point in mocking the play, or you might as well not do it at all', was John Peter's comment in the *Sunday Times*.[15] John Gross in the *Sunday Telegraph* agreed: 'John Caird . . . has wisely decided to take the more earnest aspects of the plot on their own terms, without sending them up, and to present the satirical elements in the broad and ultimately feel-good spirit of Victorian comedy, without trying to turn Bulwer-Lytton into the Brecht or Edward Bond which he wasn't.' Instead, Caird's serious treatment of the play highlighted the general human weaknesses, but also the redeeming qualities it addresses. This was helped by Rob Howell's powerfully symbolic stage design. Surrounding the golden chairs as the dominant feature of the acting area with old, broken chairs and rubble, Howell drew attention to the circle of poverty in which Sir John's vain intrigues for money and status are acted out, but also, in

---

[14] All reviews on this production are quoted from *London Theatre Record* (16–30 June 1982), 356.

[15] All reviews on this production are quoted from *London Theatre Record* (21 May– 3 June 1999), 705–7.

the broken chairs, the fragility of these pretences. Further depth to Caird's directing and the production as a whole was finally given by Simon Russell Beale's convincing impersonation of Alfred Evelyn's complex character, as perceptively described by Charles Spencer in the *Daily Telegraph*: 'On the surface there is the snide cynicism, mocking intelligence and barbed humour that this actor does so well, but it is accompanied by a sense of desolate hurt and real magnitude of spirit.' The Royal National Theatre's achievement, but also the laughs successfully raised in the earlier Royal Shakespeare Company's production amply show the manifold opportunities and potential Bulwer's comedy still holds in store. It is a worthy candidate for future revivals in the twenty-first century.

London Assurance

Dion Boucicault's *London Assurance* was first performed, a year after *Money*, at Covent Garden on 4 March 1841. It can be seen as another attempt to bring, as Bulwer had put it, 'the old genteel comedy' back to the English stage. Even more directly than *Money*, *London Assurance* assimilated the tradition going back through Sheridan to Restoration comedy. As J. L. Smith has shown in the introduction to his edition,[16] numerous points of reference to earlier plays of this type can be identified. Sir Harcourt Courtly in particular, with his modish mannerisms, ludicrous devotion to his 'toilette' and frenchified speech, seems a linear descendant of Sir Fopling Flutter (George Etherege, *The Man of Mode*, 1676) and his like of a hundred and fifty years before. Furthermore, the comic mode of *London Assurance* is clearly set in the Restoration tradition of laughter and wit. Unlike Bulwer, Boucicault refuses to compromise with the sentimental tradition and, of the four plays presented in this volume, his play is the one most clearly written against the melodramatic contrast; although it does not satirically engage with melodrama, *London Assurance* has melodrama invisibly inscribed in its text as its unspoken 'other', its diagonal opposite. The comedy's tone steers well clear of the sentimental note and moral didacticism which *Money* shares with melodrama. The play's intrigue is not aimed at the final triumph of virtue, but, to say nothing of the piquant brush with adultery in the elopement episode between Sir Harcourt and Lady Gay, ultimately derives

---

[16] James L. Smith (ed. and introd.), *London Assurance*. New Mermaids (London: A. & C. Black, New York: W. W. Norton & Co., 1984), pp. xxv f.

its central interest from the triumph of impecunious, dependent youth over powerful, rich old age in the pursuit of a young lady. The structure of this archetypal comic plot, as for example described by Northrop Frye in his *Anatomy of Criticism* (1957), is as old as Menander. Plautus's use of it in *Asinaria* is a well-known instance, where the old Athenian Demaenetus is conned by his son Argyrippus out of his money and out of the possession of the courtesan Philaenium. Especially in comparison with this antique form of the plot, however, Boucicault's concessions to his own time and audience become evident and the apparent incongruity of the fact that two plays so fundamentally different as *London Assurance* and *Money* could be successful with the same audiences seems less striking.

Grace, the woman courted by the wealthy father and his dependent, impecunious son and heir, is no courtesan as in Plautus but the impeccable daughter of a respectable country squire. The relationship desired of the young lady by both father and son is not reduced to sexual favours, but couched in the legitimate framework of honourable marriage. Where adultery actually appears on the horizon in Sir Harcourt's overtures to Lady Gay, it is, at least on the lady's side, only a ruse, while the gentleman's extramarital affairs would have received a lenient treatment by the Victorian judges of morals, according to the different yardsticks employed to gauge moral integrity of the different sexes. Furthermore, the bare skeleton of the archaic plot is fleshed out by its contemporary English setting. The Harkaways' country house provides local colour with its appending features of love of nature, a passion for hunting, shooting, and a good, solid dinner at an early hour. It is enriched by a choice selection of stock characters of the English comic tradition, of which Sir Harcourt has already been mentioned as a first example. In the Spankers, we further find the virago wife and henpecked husband, gloriously modulated in this play so that both actually come to treasure this type of relationship as a perfect symbiosis, happily suited to their individual needs and temperaments. The homely values of this wholesome country atmosphere are contrasted to Sir Harcourt's profligate urbanity and it is in this country environment, close to nature, where the denouement brings Sir Harcourt's defeat and the triumph of youth over old age and money.

And yet, the play lacks Bulwer's seriousness to convey any specific moral. In the mode of serious comedy which Northrop Frye describes as 'the mythos of spring', there is 'usually a movement from one kind of society to another. . . . At the end of the play the device in the plot that brings hero and heroine together causes a new society to crystallize around the hero'.[17] Compared to this pattern, Charles Courtly as Boucicault's 'young hero' seems oddly anaemic. Similarly, the bookish Grace with her (initially) oddly unromantic views on marriage seems an untypical choice for what would normally be the romantic heroine's position in the comic plot structure. The audience's feelings at the prospect of a new type of society characterized by the country values of the Harkaways, as confirmed against the urban dissoluteness of the Courtlys, can be expected to be half-hearted at best. The lack of audience involvement in this issue is due to the fact that the conflict between town and country, between mercenary profligacy and moral wholesomeness, is not made a central concern of the play. The serious opposition is shown at one remove, so to speak, refracted in a comic mirror. Its main function is not a didactic one, but it primarily provides the machinery for the play's fun. Although 'appearances' (as Bulwer's *Money* was in fact originally entitled) play an important role as well, they are not primarily the false appearances which disguise the recognition of true virtue or which for a while can prevent the detection of false friends. By introducing Charles Courtly under the fake identity of Augustus Hamilton at Oak Hall, Boucicault creates a potential for comic complications, fully realized in the course of the following events. The moral contrast is undercut by the actual presentation of the characters. Sir Harcourt, with his mercenary view of marriage, his readiness to commit adultery, his overriding obsession with appearances, and his 'artificial' life style, by no means comes across as a figure of vice, but serves as a mainstay of the play's comic potential and is certainly one of the most important roles in the cast list. The other important part on which the play's success depends is not his son and opponent in the suit for Grace's hand, but the horsey Lady Gay. She is, to be sure, the main instrument for thwarting Sir Harcourt and thus clearly belongs to the winning side. Still, this lady's tallyhooing hunting slang and manners do not single her out, likeable as her character is, as a didactically serious focus of virtue. She is, as the reviewer of a modern production aptly put it,[18] 'the only real man around' in the play and thus another source of the play's amusing qualities.

To sum up, then, the play's moral structuring is conventional. Youth and beauty win against old age and money. Sir Harcourt even testifies to his conversion in the play's final speech—which no one can

[17] Northrop Frye, *Anatomy of Criticism* (1957, Harmondsworth: Penguin, 1990), 163.
[18] Nicholas De Jongh in the *Guardian*, 15 Dec. 1989.

take very seriously, so inconsistent is it with the speaker's previous behaviour—where he proclaims *Truth* and *Honour* as the real qualities of an English gentleman. But this is not the main point of the comedy. Rather, the traditional plot structure is used as the machinery, pumped for all it is worth, to produce the comic effects. When the play's comic level alone is considered, its balance between town and country, between the Restoration roué Sir Harcourt and Lady Gay's sprightliness, is evenly settled; or, to put it differently, figures in both traditions, those of virtue or of vice, are equally useful for the audience's entertainment.

London Assurance may thus be assigned to the middle ground in the development of Victorian comedy. Although it pays lip service to contemporary moral conventions, it is, on the one hand, a far cry from the didacticism to be found in *Money*. On the other hand, its humorous portrayal of the country-dweller's hunting obsessions and the slight frisson introduced through Lady Gay's feigned escapade, is an equally long distance from a serious questioning of the gentlemanly values which Sir Harcourt praises somewhat too loudly in his final speech. This is further clarified when the play is compared to Oscar Wilde's *The Importance of Being Earnest* (1895), to whose 'Bunburying' Algy young Courtly's incognito excursion into the country and brazenfaced denial of identity look forward. When Wilde in his typically half-serious way described the 'philosophy' behind *The Importance of Being Earnest* in an interview before its first production as that 'we should treat all the trivial things seriously, and all the serious things of life with sincere and studied triviality',[19] he also summed up much of what had constituted Sir Harcourt's credo. Sir Harcourt's answer to Max's 'Does a waspish waist indicate a good heart?' in the rejoinder that '*plain* people always praise the beauties of the *mind*' (1.161–2) is clearly worthy of Algy's Wildean wit. The philosophical implication of this exchange, namely that the preference of content over form may spring from interested motives and that a moral judgement may actually have its roots in a formal aspect (lack of beauty in this case), is not followed up by Boucicault, whereas it will occupy an important position in the Wildean universe. In *The Importance of Being Earnest*, this kind of topsy-turvydom together with Algy's witty paradoxes gather a cumulative force which seriously questions and ultimately subverts the Victorian concepts of both (outward) decorum and (inner) virtue by making them interchangeable. In *London Assurance* they are also

---

[19] Quoted in Harford Montgomery Hyde, *Oscar Wilde* (London, 1975), 177.

identified in a clear juxtaposition, but neither is ultimately vilified or subverted, as in the following exchange between Max and Sir Harcourt:

MAX Damn etiquette! I have seen a man who thought it sacrilege to eat fish with a knife, that would not scruple to rise up and rob his brother of his birthright in a gambling-house. Your thoroughbred, well-blooded heart, will seldom kick over the traces of good feeling. That's my opinion, and I don't care who knows it.

SIR HARCOURT Pardon me, etiquette is the pulse of society, by regulating which the body politic is retained in health. I consider myself one of the faculty in the art. (1.202–9)

Sir Harcourt's concept of etiquette comes close to what Louis Hjelmslev has called the 'content of the form',[20] in so far as he assigns an important function to the form of social interactions which itself is valuable and neccessary for society's 'health', independent of its moral or political content. As the relationship between form and content is established between Max and Sir Harcourt, they are by no means mutually exclusive. If a didactic message were to be sought in Boucicault's comedy, it is surely that both moral content and outward form are important, even if the play's emphasis may be on the former. Although Max's view eventually wins the day, both decorum and virtue have by then fulfilled their primary function in the play by providing the machinery for its fun.

The excellent script, titillating, but not immoral, which made *London Assurance* such a resounding success at the time was written by a newcomer among the playwrights for the London stage. Dionysius Lardner Bou(r)cicault (or 'Boursiquot') (1820–90) had come from Dublin to England, where under the pseudonym of Lee Morton he had started an acting career in 1838 in the provinces and at the same time made his first attempts at playwriting. *London Assurance* was his first major success, followed by a continuous output of eminently presentable plays in a long career, the most memorable of which draw on his country of birth, such as the celebrated *The Colleen Bawn* (1860), *Arrah-na-Pogue* (1864/5), or *The Shaughraun* (1874/5). As Boucicault himself reports, he had, on his arrival in London, forced his way into the manager's room at Covent Garden and, after dining with the manager and two lords, read a tragedy he had brought to make his debut as a dramatist. It was turned down as unsuitable for the stage, but

[20] Louis Hjelmslev, *Prolegomena to a Theory of Language*, tr. F. J. Whitfield (Madison: University of Wisconsin Press, 1961), ch. 13.

Boucicault was able to walk away with a commission to write a five-act comedy instead.[21] There is, however, considerable evidence that this is not the whole story of the comedy's genesis. A sizeable share of Boucicault's comet-like debut with *London Assurance* must in all likelihood go to John Brougham (1810–80), an Irish comedian and himself a successful playwright, with whom Boucicault collaborated on a first draft of the play entitled *Out of Town*. Brougham was, however, bought off and made to relinquish both his claims to joint authorship for Boucicault's benefit, and to the part of Dazzle, which he had written for himself, in favour of Charles Mathews, the manager.

Boucicault's hit comedy was thus crucially influenced not only by Brougham's contribution in its first draft, but also by the management and stage company of the theatre at which it was first presented. Charles Mathews and Madame Vestris had moved from the management of the Olympic to Covent Garden in 1839 which they held until 1842. Taking leading parts themselves, they had a stock company under contract, consisting partly of actors, like John Brougham, whom they had brought over from the Olympic. The stock company system was common to most London theatres at the time. It meant that, rather than hire actors for each new production, each theatre, or sometimes a group of theatres, would have a number of actors on its books, each of whom was a specialist in a certain 'line of business'. Thus, there would be a tragedian, a young lover, a light comedian, a low comedian and so forth. In addition to that, each of the actors might have his own idiosyncratic style of acting, due to his particular physiognomy, voice, or personal taste. With such a fixed group of actors at their disposal, the theatre's management would then offer a repertory of plays, with frequently changing bills and periodical resumptions of older productions, depending on their success. In preparation for production under these conditions, a script therefore could, where it had not already been written with a particular company in mind, undergo major alterations to suit a company's specific needs.

Thus Charles Mathews's choice of the role of Dazzle, which Brougham had intended for himself, led, as Smith (p. xx) describes, to the transfer of the name Dazzle from the lover (now called Charles

handwritten margin note: fits into idea of stereotypes in comedy

---

[21] Boucicault reports this in a lecture at Hope Chapel, New York, 27 Dec. 1853, as given in *New York Daily Times*, 29 Dec. 1853, 2, repr. in appendix A of *London Assurance*, ed. James L. Smith, 127 f.

Courtly) to the lover's assistant (originally given the Irish name of Ignatius). Obviously, the manager's decision also helps to explain the relative prominence of the part of the lover's assistant (the witty servant of Plautine comedy) as compared to a relatively colourless juvenile lead in James Anderson's Charles Courtly, as well as the fact that the play's title, *London Assurance*, was now derived from Mathews's part. The version of Dazzle as presented in the play's first performance was then quite in keeping with Mathews's profile as an actor. He was perhaps the very opposite of what Macready stood for. Where the latter found his real talents in the depiction of passion in tragedy, Mathews lacked precisely this romantic immersion into emotional states. George Henry Lewes describes him as 'utterly powerless in the manifestation of all the powerful emotions: . . . He cannot even laugh with animal heartiness. He sparkles, he never explodes.'[22] With that, Mathews not only pointed the way to the more restrained style of acting characteristic of the later nineteenth century; he was also admirably suited for the part of Dazzle, the cool young spark with an intrepid 'London assurance'. The actor's weak point, namely his difficulty in appearing credible in scenes of high emotion, was thus turned into a virtue for this specific part.

Sir Harcourt's age of 63, to give a further example, almost matched that of his impersonator, William Farren (1786–1861), who had before played Lord Ogleby in the elder George Colman's and David Garrick's *The Clandestine Marriage*, and stayed in this line also in his Shakespearian roles of Sir Andrew Aguecheek and Malvolio (*Twelfth Night*). Similarly Mrs Nisbett's famous silvery peals of laughter influenced the conception of the merry Lady Gay, whose love for horses had been prefigured in Mrs Nisbett's earlier impersonation of Neighbour Constance in Sheridan Knowles's *The Love Chase* (Smith, p. xvii).

What Macready and Bulwer had to wheedle out of Benjamin Webster at the Haymarket in setting and stage props for the production of *Money*, Madame Vestris lavished, as was her wont, on the staging of *London Assurance*. The Harkaways' mansion of Oak Hall lived up to its name in the stately presence it was given on the Covent Garden stage. The *Theatrical Journal* (13 March 1841) described it as 'a mansion, in the midst of a park of stately oaks, with tasteful flowers, plots, and parterres in the foreground, the glass folding doors and richly curtained windows [of which] are so arranged as to afford an excellent view of the interior, and there we descry furniture and articles of

---

[22] Lewes, *On Actors and the Art of Acting*, 63.

recherché, displayed in the most chaste and costly style'. It turned out to be Vestris's and Mathews's most successful play at Covent Garden and had run to 69 performances by the end of the season in June 1841. Like Bulwer's *Money*, it held the stage throughout the nineteenth century, but was only rarely staged after the turn of the century. Apart from a few exceptions, such as performances at a charity matinée in the presence of the King and Queen at the St James's on 27 June 1913 and at the Malvern Festival on 5 August 1932, it was only from the 1970s onwards that the comedy experienced a kind of revival. It started in 1970 with Ronald Eyre's adaptation and direction of the play for the famous RSC production, and retained its force in Sam Mendes's lavish production for the Chichester Festival on 12 July 1989, which subsequently moved to the Haymarket Theatre in London. Whereas the RSC production received universal praise, Mendes's directing led to mixed, and indeed partly contradictory reactions. While Hugo Williams, in the *Sunday Correspondent* (24 December 1989) felt that Eddington's Sir Harcourt was 'over-played to a turn', Charles Spencer in the *Daily Telegraph* (15 December 1989) thought his performance to be 'oddly underpowered, soliciting too hesitantly for laughs, and one longs for the fruity relish which Donald Sinden must have brought to the role with the RSC'. Similarly, James Tweed in *What's On* (3 January 1990) commented that '[p]erformances are uniformly splendid, though Angela Thorne [as Lady Gay], in particular, lights up the stage every time she appears', whereas Jim Hiley (*Listener*, 4 January 1990) felt that 'Thorne is miscast, but the rest of the performers appear splendidly at home', and Clive Hirschhorn (*Sunday Express*, 17 December 1989) further elaborated that 'Angela Thorne's Lady Gay is appropriately robust but lacks the eccentricity Elizabeth Spriggs brought to the role in the famous 1972 [*sic*] RSC production'. Apart from illustrating the theatre critics' personal preferences, this may be an indication that Mendes's production as a whole failed to signal with sufficient clarity how he wanted it to be understood. With its hilariously funny characters and bouts of laughter the play has the mettle for a rollicking farce. If this mode is chosen by a director, however, an overemphasis on the star roles of Sir Harcourt or Lady Gay wears thin over the entire length of three acts. In this case, the other variants of comic business in the smaller, albeit equally well-designed parts may need to be given greater weight, such as the servant roles of Pert and Cool, and the particularly rewarding part of the lawyer Meddle, who with great relish offers his backside to be kicked at the prospect of the damages he will then be able to claim.

The alternative way, perhaps, of looking at the comedy is by placing stronger emphasis on its more serious implications. The contrast of form and content, of appearance and essence, is one of the themes which can be explored through their comic presentation, as is the possibility of pointing out deeper levels in the main characters' profiles, such as the 'vulnerable, sad, decaying man beneath the figurehead' discovered by Benedict Nightingale in Donald Sinden's Sir Harcourt (*New Statesman*, 10 July 1970). To make a production fully consistent along one of these lines and accordingly guide the audience to a sustained reading may be one of the challenges directors of this most rewarding comedy have to face.

Engaged

The William Schwenck Gilbert we meet as the author of *Engaged* (Haymarket 3 October 1877) is perhaps the less widely known side of the world-famous lyricist of the Savoy Operas such as *H.M.S. Pinafore* (1878) or *The Pirates of Penzance* (1879) on which he collaborated with Arthur Sullivan as composer. These operas' very splendour, very much alive to the present day, has had the effect of obscuring in the course of time Gilbert's merits as a dramatist in his own right; or, as a reviewer of a modern production of *Engaged* wittily put it, '[t]hose who always believed Gilbertansullivan was one person would be surprised to learn that W. S. Gilbert was a noted and prolific dramatist before he ever teamed up with Arthur Sullivan'.[23] Gilbert had been in the playwriting business since the mid-1860s, at first specializing in the comic genres of burlesque and farce. Among the latter, his rendering of Eugène Labiche's *Chapeau de Paille d'Italie* (1851) as *The Wedding March* (Court 15 November 1873) is particularly noteworthy. It successfully brought to the London stage a play which clearly reached, albeit in a farcical mode, the outer limits of what was considered morally acceptable at the time. It featured an adulterous lady who is in danger of discovery, because her straw hat is eaten by the protagonist's horse on his wedding day, a circumstance which draws further complications in its train. *The Wedding March* was also a fine specimen of the clockwork precision of plot construction in the French tradition of the well-made play, which Gilbert may also have imbibed from his mentor, T. W. Robertson, together with a taste for the social setting of

[23] Peter Elliott in the *Standard*, quoted in *London Theatre Record*, 30 July–17 August 1983, 598.

Robertson's so-called cup-and-saucer drama. In plays[24] like *Society* (1865), *Caste* (1867), or *School* (1869), Thomas William Robertson (1829–71) had provided a critique of contemporary society. He ensured the direct appeal of his satire to his audiences by setting his plays in faithfully realistic domestic interiors of Victorian London, and by creating characters who expressed themselves in what was felt to be the true language spoken at the time, although it may appear stilted to today's audiences. Robertson in turn had served his apprenticeship as prompter with Madame Vestris and Charles Mathews in the 1850s at the Lyceum. This personal link going back from Gilbert through Robertson to Madame Vestris represents a major line of the growing tradition of realism on the London stage, together with an increasingly careful production in terms of stage management, casting, and rehearsals.

And there is a third face to the theatrical Gilbert, perhaps the one most buried in oblivion today. Apart from his comic plays and Savoy librettos full of satire and wit, it is surprising to note that Gilbert also had a liking for the melodramatic and sentimental. Examples are *Charity* (1874), *Sweethearts* (1874), or *Brantinghame Hall* (1888), and particularly *Dan'l Druce* (1876) which had a run of 119 performances in London and was itself burlesqued in Arthur Clements's somewhat flat *Dan'l Tra-duced, Tinker*.[25] What Clement failed to do in his burlesque on Gilbert's own sentimental comedy, however, Gilbert himself triumphantly achieved in *Engaged*, where he burlesqued a whole range of conventions and stereotypes to be found in melodrama and the sentimental, moralizing type of comedy which still continued as staple fare on his contemporary stage.

Much of the plot and setting of *Engaged* are taken straight from the Romantic tradition. A lonely railway line through sparsely populated areas of the Scottish Borderlands made famous as the setting of Sir Walter Scott's Waverly novels; local colours heightened by the introduction of cottagers with Scottish dialect and manners; the natural honesty and sincerity of feelings of love and filial duty among the Borderland 'natives'; the railway 'accident' evoking intimations of tales of highwaymen and famous robberies; an eloped couple on the

---

[24] See e.g. *T. W. Robertson: Six Plays*, introd. Michael R. Booth (Ashover: Amber Lane Press, 1980) and Daniel Barrett, *T. W. Robertson and the Prince of Wales's Theatre* (New York: Peter Lang, 1995).

[25] See Jane W. Stedman, *W. S. Gilbert: A Classic Victorian and His Theatre* (Oxford: Oxford University Press, 1996), 141–3.

way to Gretna Green; talk of duelling; and the list could be continued. With this romantic machinery as his starting point, Gilbert then piles on the parodic devices in thick layers. The borderland natives living an innocent and contented country life in their simple cottage turn out to be in the habit of poaching; they operate an illicit whisky still and cause criminal damage to the nearby railway-line. In order to understand the nature of Gilbert's distinctive brand of burlesque, a comparison with Boucicault's methods in *London Assurance* proves revealing. Indeed, such a comparison is invited by the fact that, much like Boucicault, both Gilbert's town and country folk come in for a similar share of satire when they first appear on the stage. Thus, the play's very first dialogue between Angus and Maggie derives its fun from a strategy very similar to the one Boucicault used in portraying the Harkaway household. Clearly recognizable country manners, based on natural honesty and a 'gude hairt', are rendered amusing by their presentation in a mildly parodic way. Angus's over-indulgence in tears and Maggie's naïvety are on approximately the same parodic level as Grace's bookishness or Lady Gay's yoiking obsession with horses. Equally, the caricature in the first dialogue between Belvawney and Miss Treherne is on a par with the characterization of Sir Harcourt, when Belvawney for example recapitulates the railway accident in his attempt to comfort Miss Treherne with whom he has eloped: 'It was in truth a weird and gruesome accident. The line is blocked, your parasol is broken and your butterscotch trampled in the dust, but no serious harm is done' (1.116–19). But Gilbert's comedy does not stop there. While the audience is settling back to have a good laugh at a farcical comedy of the *London Assurance* type, Gilbert's burlesque has only reached its first stage. The stereotypes of country simplicity and dandified city manners are portrayed in this amusingly comic way only to be radically exploded afterwards. Witness Gilbert's first, masterly orchestrated crescendo in the description of Angus's 'honest way to make a living'. After Mrs Macfarlane's assurance that Angus is 'a prosperous, kirk-going man' and therefore a suitable son-in-law, Angus tearfully sets out to confirm her good opinion: 'Yes, I'm a fairly prosperous man. What wi' farmin' a bit land, and gillieing odd times, and a bit o' poachin' now and again; and what wi' my illicit whusky still; and throwin' trains off the line, that the poor distracted passengers may come to my cot, I've mair ways than one of making an honest living' (1.46–50). To finish off the impact of this turn in the comic mode, Mrs Macfarlane, far from upbraiding him for his confession to a steeply climactic series of unlawful activities, upbraids him for a laxness she thinks she has recently perceived in his most criminal line of business, that of train derailing.

A similar effect is achieved by the parody of romantic courtship in Cheviot's dazzling multiplication of passionate confessions of love. There is a humorous start of the *London Assurance* type, as it is revealed that Cheviot had actually been at the point of asking his uncle Symperson for his daughter's hand, when the train accident happened. While Cheviot's flightiness on the matter is first indicated by the fact that he completely forgot about it afterwards, however, his prospective father-in-law evidently had more important reasons to come back to the topic at the very next opportunity:

SYMPERSON Cheviot, my dear boy, at the moment of the accident you were speaking to me on a very interesting subject.

CHEVIOT Was I? I forget what it was. The accident has knocked it clean out of my head.

SYMPERSON You were saying that you were a man of good position and fortune; that you derived £2000 a year from your bank; that you thought it was time you settled. You then reminded me that I should come into Belvawney's £1000 a year on your marriage, and I'm not sure, but I rather think you mentioned, casually, that my daughter Minnie is an Angel of Light.

CHEVIOT True, and just then we went off the line. To resume: Uncle Symperson, your daughter Minnie is an Angel of Light, a perfect being, as innocent as a new-laid egg. (1.223–45)

The uncle's mercenary motives are as stunning as the ease with which Cheviot is able to take up his passionate suit. Again, Gilbert's parodic roller-coaster picks up speed after that. Not only will Cheviot shortly repeat his suit to two further women, Maggie and Miss Treherne, both already engaged to other men and complete strangers to Cheviot; he will also be equally successful in it, buying Maggie off for two pounds and gaining the hand of Miss Treherne, who had left her first fiancé alone at the altar on their wedding-day to elope with Belvawney, but now feels unable to marry Belvawney when that gentleman turns out to be penniless.

Gilbert is able to keep up this bristling fun by a machine-like logic in his plot construction. He takes his characters through an increasingly dense tangle of complications which mainly spring from the fact that Cheviot becomes engaged to three different women at the same time. These land Cheviot in the most awkward situations, until he is on the verge of losing all three, of which he bitterly complains to Symperson: 'Symperson, I never loved three girls as I loved those three—never! never!' (3.202–3). As he thinks his situation is desperate, Cheviot informs his uncle of his plans to commit suicide. In one of the play's comic highlights, Symperson, who would greatly profit from Cheviot's death, goes on to discuss with him the pros and cons of several methods to end his life, actually dispersing Cheviot's apprehensions and showing practicable solutions rather than trying to prevent him from the act. In Symperson's absence, however, Cheviot changes his mind, and the scene's climax is reached when Symperson re-enters wearing all the apparel of mourning, only to notice to his surprise that Cheviot is still alive. Symperson is furious:

Why, sir, this is confounded trifling. I don't understand this line of conduct at all. You threaten to commit suicide; your friends are dreadfully shocked at first, but eventually their minds become reconciled to the prospect of losing you. They become resigned, even cheerful; and when they have brought themselves to this Christian state of mind, you coolly inform them that you have changed your mind and mean to live. It's not business, sir, it's not business. (3.331–8)

Again, the comedy's theme revolves around 'appearances' and what they hide. This time, however, the play discovers that all the noble appearances presented are façades. For all the variety of outward show and protestations, each and everyone in the play is discovered to be hiding the same primary motive underneath: money. The title of Bulwer's play would therefore fit Gilbert's even better. While Bulwer's comedy enters into a discussion of the good and bad uses to which money can be put, Gilbert brings it out as the object of greed behind all other pretensions. Here, money has become the universally signified, the only possible interpretation of any outward sign in human behaviour and speech, however noble or naturally honest it may seem. As opposed to *Money*, the appearances treated in *Engaged* are exclusively of a noble kind, all of which are then shown to be false, hiding base motives of greed. This time, no positive surprises are in store for the audience, as experienced in *Money* when the sombre Graves not only revealed the frolicsome nature hidden beneath this façade through Lady Franklin's mediation, but also turned out to be a friend in need to Evelyn. In *Engaged*, people are the same everywhere, only appearances differ. While the English town-dwellers arriving from London put up a show of passionate devotion and romantic courtship, their Scottish counterparts are revealed to be doing the same with their sentimental simplicity and original goodness. Both groups, it does not take long to find out, use these cultural stereotypes to hide their keenness on the 'main chance' and financial advantage, which they all alike share. Even the traditional topos dividing the young lovers as romantic and idealistic from the older generation as material-minded and economically realistic is deflated in the same way. The respective, stereotyped appearances are hilariously exploded when Minnie answers to her father's inquiry about her settlement early in Act 2, that, as she saw things 'in her silly childish way' and 'foolish little noddle', she would 'fall in with Cheviot's views in everything *before* marriage' while expecting a dramatic inversion of this situation after the knot is tied (2.62–4). 'Young lovers' in this play are, behind their romantic façades, quite as scheming and greedy as their parents hope they should be. Is this, then, the work of a misanthropist?

Although the 110 performances the play had as its first run speak for its success, many reviewers[26] were shocked by its apparent lack of mercy implied in its demonstration of the same base motives underlying all of its characters' actions. Thus, the critic of the *Morning Advertiser* (6 October 1877) thought it was 'a violent burlesque upon everyday existence and a fantastic mockery of life as we know it'. Another typical reaction in this vein was expressed in the *Sunday Times* (7 October 1877): 'Carried away by his cleverness, Mr. Gilbert has forgotten to make any appeal to sympathy . . . In *Engaged* Mr. Gilbert is more cold-bloodedly cynical than any human being has ever shown himself in the drama. Thus, though as an intellectual exercise his new play is admirable, we doubt whether it will ever be thoroughly and lastingly popular.' Similarly, the *Figaro* (10 October 1877) indirectly admitted the play's comic potential, but thought that the 'laughter, extorted from his audience in spite of their [i.e. the audience's] sense of honour or of decency, however loud and hearty it may sound in his [i.e. Gilbert's] ears', was not worth the cost: 'From beginning to end of this nauseous play not one of the characters ever says a single word or does a single action that is not inseparable from the lowest moral degradation . . .'

Meanwhile, far from intending a straightforward, moralizing

---

[26] For an anthology of its contemporary reviews see the 'Appendix. Criticism of *Engaged*' in Michael Booth (ed.), *Nineteenth-Century Plays*, 5 vols. (Oxford: Oxford University Press, 1969–76), iii. 385–94. The following quotations of contemporary reviews are taken from this source.

indictment of the general depravity of his fellow countrymen or humanity in general, Gilbert had of course aimed the main thrust of his satire at the respective stage conventions of romantic love, sentimental confessions of honour and friendship, and the myth of the wholesomeness and simplicity of those living in the country. The people in his play do not, after all, speak, respectively, in the everyday language of the Scottish countryside or the London drawing-room, but in the conventionalized speech specified for the various situations in the poetry, fiction, and drama of the time. Few commentators saw this with the same clarity as the critic writing in the *Saturday Review* (13 October 1877). Although dismissive of the play for technical reasons, he thought it was 'a long-drawn-out skit upon the false stage sentiment which may be found . . . in almost every stage play in which sentiment plays a part'. He saw it as Gilbert's 'joke of making everybody turn the usual sentiments of the stage into practical ridicule'.

Why was it, then, that Gilbert's persiflage of romantic stage conventions provoked such responses from some of the reviewers? The *Figaro* critic, already quoted above, attempted an answer by suggesting that 'the representation of the characters, admitting them to be caricatures, is so free from any exaggeration or extravagance, that to ordinary people they can appear nothing but real types of human nature'. Because the stage conventions of realism Gilbert employed for his satire signalled to the audiences that they were to take the performance as a representation of real life, so this argument runs, the misunderstanding was bound to happen. Had Gilbert wanted to satirize and correct aspects of the stage to which he objected, he should have used, in this critic's opinion, a dramatic mode which would have allowed his audiences to recognize that the characters they saw on stage were not to be taken for real, but were burlesque impersonations of the vices of the contemporary stage; he should have stuck, in other words, to the farcical and burlesque tradition of his early years. These traditional burlesques had been clearly recognizable as such, from the play's title and billing, the fancy costumes and make-up of the actors, and other conventions which Gilbert had in fact spelt out in Norma's final speech in his parody *Norma, the Pretty Druidess* (1869):

> [T]he piece is common-place, grotesque,
> A solemn folly—a proscribed burlesque!
> So for burlesque I plead. Forgive our rhymes;

> Forgive the jokes you've heard five thousand times;
> Forgive each breakdown, cellar-flap, and clog,
> Our low-bred songs—our slangy dialogue;
> And, above all—oh, ye with double barrel—
> Forgive the scantiness of our apparel![27]

The fact that Gilbert deviated from this tradition reaching back to the Duke of Buckingham's *The Rehearsal* (1671), Henry Fielding's *Tom Thumb* (1730), or Sheridan's *The Critic* (1779) made *Engaged* a novelty at the time. It is also possible to argue, however, that this change was not only due to the different burlesque strategy employed in *Engaged*, but, equally importantly, to a parodic attack on a dramatic mode which had only come into being in the middle decades of the nineteenth century. Where some of the play's critics condemned it for setting, inconsistently, an outrageous burlesque within a realistic framework, this was precisely the point at which Gilbert could be seen to aim his satire in the plays he parodied. There, too, the conventions of realism, as gradually introduced under such managements as Madame Vestris's at the Olympic and the Lyceum or the Bancrofts' at the Prince of Wales's Theatre, provided the setting for melodramatic action or fustian, moralizing speeches by improbably idealized characters with equal incongruity. It was this incongruity of the perfect integrity and nobleness of the romantic heroes and heroines taken for real that Gilbert lambasted in his burlesque. By holding up an inverting mirror and exposing the ridiculousness of the assumption that each and everyone we meet is ultimately motivated by greed, Gilbert implicitly ridicules the opposite assumption that people could be idealized as creatures of unalloyed virtue.

What is more, the fact that Gilbert's burlesque of a certain kind of drama was mistaken for a derogatory comment on human nature in real life in a sense proved his point. The fact that audiences and reviewers could mistake stage character for real human nature amply showed the necessity of his critical treatment of the respective conventions. The circumstance that Victorian audiences directly applied stage 'reality' to their own lives need not, however, suggest so much a naïvity in their reception as it conversely highlights the degree to which Victorians' lives were in reality governed by the kind of 'romantic' or idealizing conventions presented on stage; the high

---

[27] Quoted in Michael Booth, *Prefaces to English Nineteenth-Century Theatre* (Manchester: Manchester University Press, [1981]), 175.

degree, in other words, to which their real lives were in fact theatrical.[28]

Thus, Gilbert's *Engaged* does contain a form of social critique after all. Its trajectory is, however, more complex than the mere suggestion of the depravity of human nature, as some critics thought. Its point is directed at the specific form of type-casting and role-modelling which was not only common in the theatrical traditions of melodrama and sentimental comedy—aspects of Bulwer's *Money* would thus fall within the range of Gilbert's burlesque—but pervaded the real lives of his contemporaries. Summing up his analysis of Oscar Wilde's *The Importance of Being Earnest*, Russell Jackson writes: '*The Importance of Being Earnest* does not return its characters . . . to the security of their accustomed life: it liberates them.'[29] Not only did Gilbert's *Engaged* directly influence a number of lines and scenes in Wilde's most famous play,[30] but it can be argued to share its overall intended effects in Jackson's sense. It is aimed at liberating its audiences from conventions which, for their very claim to truth and reality, are particularly difficult to expose as social constructs. Although they provide a superficial security through a fixed code of social behaviour, they also stir up a constraining unease at a deeper level.

With its particular brand of parody so deeply rooted in contemporary Victorian culture, *Engaged* shares the fate of all satire; it only survives either if the circumstances against which it had originally been directed continue to obtain, or if the play has merits which still make its performance rewarding to an audience which does not share any longer this specific cultural background. In terms of a modern production of *Engaged*, directors will thus need to decide whether to bring its satirical point up to date or to present it as a play with a

[28] Commenting on the Victorians' fears of performance, which could also be seen as the basis of the severe stricture against *Engaged*, Nina Auerbach writes in *Private Theatricals: The Lives of the Victorians* (Cambridge, Mass., and London: Harvard University Press, 1990), 114: 'I suggest that the source of Victorian fears of performance lay not on the stage, but in the histrionic artifice of ordinary life. Playing themselves continually, convinced of the spiritual import of their lives, Victorian men and women validated those lives with the sanction of nature but feared that nature was whatever the volatile self wanted it to be. The theater was a visible reminder of the potential of good men and women to undergo inexplicable changes. Its menace was not its threat to the integrity of sincerity, but the theatricality of sincerity itself. The specter that audiences called the actor performed lives they recognized as their own.'

[29] Oscar Wilde, *The Importance of Being Earnest*, ed. Russell Jackson, New Mermaids (London: A. & C. Black, New York: W. W. Norton, 1988, repr. 1992), p. xxxvi.

[30] On the relationship between the two plays see Lynton Hudson, *The English Stage, 1850–1950* (London, Harrap, 1951), 101–5.

timeless theatrical, and perhaps also topical, value. Perhaps from an unclear conception of this clear choice to be made, recent attempts to revive the play have been at best only moderate successes. When the Royal National Theatre staged it on 6 August 1975 under Michael Blakemore's direction, Irving Wardle commented on it in *The Times* (7 August 1975) under the title 'Bomb-shell under Victorian hypocrisy turns out a damp squib', taking issue with the unwieldy plot structure. Robert Cushman in the *Observer* (17 August 1975), at least obliquely noted that the point of the play was burlesque, not to convey a moral: 'Probably he [i.e. Gilbert] meant every unflattering word of *Engaged*, but there is a facetiousness, even an archness, about those words that separates him from the great misanthropists. The dialogue is conceived as a parody of some other unwritten play; it has an effervescent spirit but no body.' A production by an actors' co-operative at the Arts Theatre in August 1983 fared slightly better. Antony Thorncroft in the *Financial Times* described it as 'a stylish work, well worth reviving',[31] but was contradicted by Kenneth Hurren in the *Guardian*, who found the reasons for another 'exhumation' of the play after the one at the Royal National Theatre in 1975 'generally inscrutable' because of its dated appeal: 'Over 100 years on, the satire seems as dated as it is primitive.' It is revealing that one of the few outright praises came from John Connor in *City Limits*, who saw the play's main point in 'a farcical attack on the marriage institution', but also liked its technical craftsmanship: 'Gilbert, unaccompanied by Sullivan turns out to be a funny and direct writer with a penchant for corny one-liners. Indeed, compared to the standard British farce of recent years, it is really something of a treasure. Society is sent up rather than women.' The prospects of the future stage career of this play need not, however, be as uncertain as the lukewarm reception of these two productions seems to suggest. The two traditions it mainly attacks are stereotyped romantic love and the myth of unspoilt country living, not only in Scotland. These are certainly very much alive today, albeit less prominent in the theatre than in popular fiction as well as in film and television soaps (which to a certain extent have taken the place occupied by the theatre in Victorian times). Thus, finding a way to revitalize Gilbert's parodic thrust could promise as much fun to today's audiences as was experienced by those Victorian spectators who understood its main objective.

[31] The following reviews of this production quoted from *London Theatre Record*, 30 July–12 August, 1983, 598 f.

The High Bid

Henry James's *The High Bid* was first performed at the Royal Lyceum Theatre in Edinburgh on 26 March 1908. It had, in all, five matinée performances when it came to London, at Herbert Beerbohm Tree's His Majesty's Theatre on 18, 19, 23, 25, and 26 February 1909. Despite a very positive press at the time, this stage record can be described as at best a very modest success. For Henry James himself, it was much more than that. It was the much-needed balm for a quintessential dramatist whose wounds from the traumatic failure of his efforts as a playwright in the 1890s had remained fresh all this time. The story is well known, and need only briefly be recalled.

From his childhood to his dying day, James was never far from the theatre. As a stage-struck theatregoer, his travels had made him familiar with many of the great theatrical houses in Europe and on the American East Coast. Although his boyhood dreams of becoming an actor did not materialize, he did establish a reputation as a serious, perceptive theatre critic, writing reviews for many of the major newspapers and journals of the day.[32] As a playwright, he started in earnest with *The American*, which opened at the Opera Comique in the Strand on 16 September 1891 after a successful trial run in the provinces. It came off well and the 1890s promised to bring James's hopes as a dramatist to fruition, not least motivated by the expectation of swifter financial gain than his novelistic activities yielded at this time. However, as James was to learn in the next few years, the reality of the managers' offices and green-rooms was quite different from the artistic ideals cultivated in the auditorium. Haggling with managers and the direct exposure to what he considered the low tastes of the greater part of the audience soon developed into a nightmarish experience, deeply depressing to James. It culminated on the first night of his *Guy Domville* at the St James's Theatre (5 January 1895), when George Alexander, its manager and star actor who had played the leading part, took him in front of the curtain and James was greeted, apart from supportive applause from the small coterie of his admirers, by a concert of catcalls and whistles.

Despite this fiasco, James though obviously bruised was not beaten, since, on meeting a sympathetic Ellen Terry only a few days later, he agreed to write a short play for her approaching American tour. The

---

[32] For a selection of James's theatre criticism see for example Allan Wade (ed.), *The Scenic Art: Notes on Acting and Drama by Henry James* (London: Hart-Davis, 1949).

one-act piece he produced was entitled *Summersoft*. It contains the core of the story later expanded to three acts in *The High Bid*. James posted it to Terry from Torquay in August 1895,[33] but the play was never staged. Three years later James demanded the manuscript back and turned it into a short story, *Covering End*.[34] Now both Alexander and Johnston Forbes-Robertson suddenly voiced great interest in its potential for the stage, but James categorically declined. It took eight years before James consented to listen to Forbes-Robertson's renewed request, 'for the lust of a little possible gold',[35] as he put it, and in October 1907 he set out to turn the short story into the three-act *High Bid*. Today the works of this second and final phase in James's career as a playwright, which ended with *The Outcry* in 1909 (produced posthumously in 1917), are usually noted as the fertile ground for James's mature novels, whose technique shows a strong tincture of drama, notably in the use of the scenario as a core device of their structural composition. Working on a new novel, James would, as his notebook sketches[36] show, first devise scenes and plot complications, and then go on to elaborate them in the narrative voices of his charac-ters. Thus, the notebook sketch of *The Wings of the Dove* (1902)[37] clearly gives the impression of a playscript of a slightly melodramatic flavour, very much along the lines of James's actual playtexts. Turning then to the novel itself, it will be noted that this 'dramatic' element is submerged in James's probing language which, as Malcolm Bradbury has so aptly put it, 'is not what we see through; it is what we see with'.[38] Nevertheless, the novel's dramatic beginnings remain present as the hidden backbone keeping together James's complex explor-ations of the vicissitudes of language which, for him, become syn-onymous to the vicissitudes of human existence.

It is not only the novels, however, which are illuminated by a con-sideration of James's dramatic concepts, but the plays, too, can be better understood when seen in the light of his novelistic enterprise.

[33] See *The Complete Notebooks of Henry James*, ed. Leon Edel and Lyall H. Powers (New York and Oxford: Oxford University Press, 1987), 407.

[34] Published, together with *The Turn of the Screw*, as *The Two Magics* (1898).

[35] Quoted by Leon Edel, 'Editor's Foreword' to *The High Bid*, *The Complete Plays of Henry James*, ed. Edel (New York and Oxford: Oxford University Press, 1990), 549.

[36] See *The Complete Notebooks of Henry James*.

[37] See *The Complete Notebooks of Henry James*, 102–7.

[38] Malcolm Bradbury, *The Modern British Novel* (Harmondsworth: Penguin, 1994), 32.

James's variations on the mode of melodrama, it can be argued, form a particularly interesting area where both spheres, the novelistic and the dramatic, intersect. One such way of looking at James's mature novels is to see them as taking traditional melodrama as their starting point, but then pushing its conventions to their outer limits and beyond. Peter Brooks gives a succinct summary of this view:

> The heightening of experience and the intensification of choice are motivated by the desire of the novelist, and those characters who act as his 'centers of consciousness', to find, to see, to articulate and eventually to dramatize in their actions moral problems seized in their essence, as pure imperatives and commitments. This must not be construed to mean that characters are themselves integral, representative of pure moral conditions, black and white. . . . It is rather that characters, whatever their nuances, make reference to such absolutes, recognize, more or less clearly, their existence and force, and in their worldly actions gesture toward them. The movement of the typical Jamesian plot from complex and often obscure interrelationship to crisis imaged as revelation signals his need to disengage from the complications of reality a final confrontation, however nuanced, of moral integers.[39]

Why was that a programme which worked so well in James's novels but seemed capable of only a very precarious life on stage? It is true that not all the plays to be seen on the London stage at the turn of the century were blunt melodrama or raucous farce; the translations of Henrik Ibsen's plays notably contained a high level of social complexity infused into the machinery of the well-made play. Nevertheless it is possible to argue that audiences were largely unprepared for James's type of drama that was so heavily reliant on finely tuned sensitivities on their part; the ear for the nuance in every word and the eye for the slightest gesture which James's plays seemed to demand to an increasing degree. Compare for example Boucicault's Sir Harcourt, with his caricatured expressiveness, his overacted mannerisms, and his 'ogling' in the tradition of the Restoration stage fops, to the Jamesian character presentation through stage directions such as Prodmore's speaking 'with an appropriate smile and a gathering-in of his fingers as to present a flower' (1.743–4) or Chivers's 'staring through a dimness that presently glimmers' (1.748–9).

Yet, more fundamental issues appear to be at stake as well. In a letter to Robert Louis Stevenson, James expressed his conviction of a natural affinity to the drama: 'I feel as if I had at last found my form—my real one—that for which pale fiction is an ineffectual substitute'. He

[39] Brooks, *Melodramatic Imagination*, 159.

here repeats once again the word 'pale' as an attribute of fiction which he had used a few days before in a letter to William James,[40] and in his first article on the theatre (1872) he had expounded this view by defining an acted play as 'a novel intensified; it realizes what the novel suggests'.[41] In the face of James's comparative failure in the theatre and his enduring success as a novelist, it may be necessary to turn this estimation around. It was not the glaring light of the stage, but the dim light of the reading room which eventually seemed to prove most congenial with his art. The delicate tinctures and fine lines of his novels represent so well the many shades of good and evil in his characters which the reader must learn to follow in all their nuances to understand the complex involutions, in the guise of which the most fundamental moral choices come upon us in the Jamesian world. His novelistic technique, which for that reason depended so much on hints, allusions, and writing 'between the lines', suffered when transferred to actors of flesh and blood and exposed to the demands of concreteness of a stage performance.

The script of *The High Bid* is a good example of James's aspiration to exactness in all the gradations of dramatic expression. It will immediately be observed that, compared to the three earlier plays in this volume, the stage directions have become much more extensive. This is partly due to the fact that the texts were intended for a reading public as well as for presentation on stage. Demand for printed versions of the plays seen on stage had been rising and royalties from the copyright to publish the plays had in fact begun to make a substantial contribution towards the playwright's income. Moreover, the bulging stage directions in *The High Bid* also reflect a development gaining momentum in the later nineteenth century, when dramatic authors, far from providing only an outline of a dialogue which was to be fleshed out by the histrionic experience of actors and stage managers, were increasingly legislating for the type of production and acting they envisioned, thus integrating all dimensions of theatrical expression.

For Henry James, this opened a way of introducing his nuances and ambiguities on a metalevel into the playtext. What actors were to intimate to a perceptive audience was to be couched in a sophisticated array of implied meaning, tone, gesture, and movements on stage,

---

[40] Both passages are quoted by Edel, 'Henry James: The Dramatic Years', in *Complete Plays* (see n. 35), 50.

[41] Quoted in Jean Chothia, *English Drama of the Early Modern Period 1890–1940*, Longman Literature in English Series (Harlow: Longman, 1996), 181.

which finds its minute description in the stage directions. The weight of this expressiveness on any section of spoken dialogue, be it ever so small, can be overwhelming. Thus, speaking about Captain Yule, Cora has the following line in Act 2: 'If he does care he'll propose', which is answered by Mrs Gracedew by 'He does care! He'll propose'. The actors speaking these short sentences are, however, to convey a great complexity of meaning:

CORA (*before her across the interval; unconscious of any irony and of the effect she produces; and almost as if entertaining Mrs Gracedew's suggestion, conclusive, logical, fatal*) If he does care he'll *propose*.

MRS GRACEDEW (*catching sight of Yule at top of stairs, just as she had shortly before, from opposite side of stage, caught sight of Cora; and making out from this fact of his rapid return that her own ardour has practically worked upon him, has taken such effect that he now comes down to act; but passing swiftly across to let the girl have it, in a quick whisper*) He *does* care! He'll *propose*.
(2.662–70)

The use of such comprehensive directions, together with James's extensive italicizing to mark the position of stress in the syntactic structures is about as far as the art of fine-tuning a script could be taken. The main thrust of this oversaturation with meaning is obvious. Readers of the playscript are called upon, as they are in his novels, to do their utmost in an interpretative effort which should respond to the whole spectrum of finely graded meaning. The feeling that this effort can never be conclusive, but must remain a perpetual challenge to look and look again, is further heightened by a subcurrent of tentativeness infused in the explicitness of the directions by the frequent use of the qualifiers 'as', 'as with', or 'as if'. This can also be read as casting a shade of doubt on the very comprehensiveness of the directions themselves, while it can equally be interpreted as a scepticism about the painstakingly built façades which the characters present to each other and to the audience. No doubt, this is art in the best Jamesian vein.

When it comes to its presentation in the theatre, however, the complexity of James's meanings is reduced by one level. On stage, all the niceties and ambiguities of the Jamesian text are first of all harnessed into a clearly defined shape through their interpretation by the actor. Thus an important level of the indefiniteness on which James's mature novels thrive is lost. Although the gesture itself can of course be acted to appear ambiguous, the interpretation of its frequently polyvalent description will have been carried out for the audience by the actor and cast into the clearly defined form which he actually presents on stage.

Having lost this particular level of ambiguity in the reception process, the play may, in terms of its sophistication, indeed appear 'pale' when compared to his greatest novels. As the theatrical venture it is conceived to be, *The High Bid* nevertheless poses an inspiring challenge to actors and audiences alike. The big Jamesian theme of the precariousness of human perception and the knowledge we can gain through the use of language becomes focused in the actors' craftsmanship. It is up to them alone to express the artful opaqueness of the Jamesian universe of meaning. It is here that the complexity of *The High Bid* is to be realized and then developed in its presentation, and it is here, too, that James's technique profitably draws on the melodramatic tradition, but also diverges from it.

In its overall impression, *The High Bid* can indeed be read as a mixture of Jamesian sophistication and the straightforwardness of a melodramatic setup. As in Bulwer's *Money*, the audience is never in any doubt from the start which values are upheld and which views are rejected. The negative side is obviously represented by Prodmore. His machiavellian ruse is designed further to buttress his already powerful position, based on the dictates of the market and his successful speculations, by acquiring in Captain Yule a son-in-law for his somewhat unwieldy daughter and through Yule's name an aristocratic veneer for his pedigree. On the positive side, the house in its historical importance and the traditions it epitomizes is enthusiastically championed by Mrs Gracedew. But here the similarities end. Although the question of the right moral choice is a theme that *The High Bid* shares with *Money*, James's options are not the obvious crossroads between good and evil offered by traditional melodrama. Yule is caught in a cleft stick, with positive values on both sides of the balance. Will he be true to his political convictions or to his ancestral inheritance? The choice is complicated in the plot structure, in so far as it is only his conscience which speaks for his radical ideals and there is no one else on stage who endorses his views in this matter. Otherwise, all persons around him speak in favour of the manorial home, albeit for very different reasons. This is what makes Yule's choice at first so difficult. When he finally decides for the house after a real process of growing insight on his part, he not only confirms the positive values so convincingly attached to it by Mrs Gracedew. At the same time he has to shoulder a heavy load of negative 'side effects': he betrays his ideal of political integrity; he consents to marry for opportunistic if not mercenary reasons; and he confirms, by accepting Prodmore's conditions and playing his game, his cynical view of a world where the power of money rules supreme and where the father even sees his own daughter primarily as an important investment whose profits he now wants to reap (see 1.404–15). Most of these dilemmas are subsequently resolved through Mrs Gracedew's 'high bid', with Prodmore leaving the house and the play for good (3.435). Still, the play's focus throughout is really on Yule's gradually growing insight into the overriding value of his ancestral home and the history it incorporates as the greater and timeless good he is meant to hold in trust. This insight, as well as the moral integrity and altruistic goodness behind Mrs Gracedew's enthusiasm and Yule's growing realization of his love for her is what the play slowly unfolds to a perceptive audience.

The High Bid thus shares with Bulwer's *Money* (and with melodrama in general) an obvious black-and-white contrast in its set of values, epitomized by the opposition between Mrs Gracedew and Prodmore. This clear-cut division is not, however, reflected in the way the moral choices present themselves to Captain Yule. The final triumph with which the play ends comes about as the result of several processes of recognition. These are not only brought about on the side of Captain Yule who discovers his love for his historic house as well as for its most committed supporter, Mrs Gracedew, but also on the side of the audience. After the basic situation, including Prodmore's plan and the choice to be faced by Captain Yule, is made clear to the audience at the beginning of the play, they are then at leisure to observe how persons on stage slowly unravel the intricacies of Prodmore's plot and Yule's dilemma; how they react to it; and how they communicate it to each other, often in roundabout ways, sensitively circling around each other's supposed meanings. Here James's style and language are particularly demanding in their suggestiveness and indeterminacy. The following questions in one of Mrs Gracedew's rare monologues can also be read as a guideline for the type of reflections expected on the audience's part throughout the play:

Why didn't he tell me *all*? But (*throwing up her arms and letting them fall at her sides as in supreme renouncement*) it was none of my business! (*Yet it continues to hold her*) What does he mean to do? (*Then as answering herself*) What should he do but what he *has* done? And (*following up this sense of it*) what *can* he do, when he's so deeply committed, when he's practically engaged, when he's just the same as married—and as *buried*? (2.916–22)

Like the audience, Mrs Gracedew knows all about Captain Yule's dilemma from Cora. What she does not know, however, is why Yule did not want to tell her about it. Thus the main interest for her, as for the audience watching the play, is not so much the basic plot complication, which is made fairly obvious, but the way it makes people interact with each other. This interaction happens in James's finely tuned language, in which the complexity of the sentence structure mirrors the complexity of the situations in which the characters are caught. In a traditional comedy or farce, Mr Prodmore would have been beaten by some kind of counter-intrigue against his plot to ensnare Captain Yule for his purposes. In this case, however, his main opponent is Mrs Gracedew who succeeds in gaining people's confidences and eventually directing events her way. Mrs Gracedew succeeds, not by tricks and ruses—here she is even victimized by ending up paying Prodmore's usurous price for the house—but by her quick wit and general perceptiveness. Of all the persons on stage, she is the best and most alert interpreter of other people's meanings and innuendos. The stage directions she is given in her dialogues clearly point in this direction. Thus, talking to Captain Yule, we find her '*down on him like a flash*'; '*already all there*'; '*Then, as if herself answering her questions, seeing it clear, triumphantly making it sure*' (2.293, 367, 385–6); or, in her 'high-bid' discussion with Prodmore: '*absolute, distinct, clear as a bell*'; '*sharp, downright*'; or '*all considerate, all perceptive, as taking in this*' (3.137, 150, 186–7). The heroine as reader of other people's minds could be an apt summary of James's Mrs Gracedew, around whom his play revolves. Mrs Gracedew will thus be the key part in the play's cast. The actress's ability to display Mrs Gracedew's perceptiveness and clarity as against the opacity, from her point of view, of the other persons' communications; and the resulting process of Mrs Gracedew's piecing together the picture of the situation bit by bit while indeed actively shaping and constructing it at the same time, will be a touchstone for any production of *The High Bid*.

Here, perhaps, was one of the weak points of a much-discussed production of the play at the Criterion Theatre, starting on 29 December 1970 after opening at Guildford in October, when the flamboyant Eartha Kitt had the part of Mrs Gracedew. Irving Wardle of *The Times* (30 December 1970) seemed to put his finger on the problem when he wrote: 'the production itself falls, with an even more resounding thump as usual, into the trap of treating Jamesian dialogue as an unfortunate liability.' John Barber[42] was more explicit:

[42] John Barber, 'The Criterion Theatre', *Daily Telegraph*, 29 Dec. 1970.

I cannot persuade myself, however, that the play was quite a happy choice for her. Certainly, she is never off the stage, and it is a kind of pleasure to see so flamboyant a performance—such a swirling of shawls, such a twirling of arms, and swinging beads, accompanied by so extensive a repertoire of erotic low gurgles and melodious coos. But none of this has much to do with James's quiet ironies and veiled cruelties.

Compared to the Criterion production, the play's earlier performance at the Mermaid Theatre (16 October 1967), directed by Bernard Miles and with Fenella Fielding as Mrs Gracedew, was considerably more successful. Here, as J. C. Trewin put it in the *Illustrated London News* (28 October 1967), 'the very commas are considered, and it is lucky that the Mermaid has speakers who can deal with them'. Similarly, Harold Hobson in the *Sunday Times* (27 October 1967) described his experience as a member of the Mermaid audience:

One begins by feeling an inclination to laugh at James, at his inability to make any of his characters, whatever they may be . . . speak in any but the most complicated grammatical constructions inlaid with baroque incrustations. It is something of a ridiculous shock . . . But the shock diminishes, and a certain pleasure develops, as the impossible offence is repeated. For, beneath the courtesies, and the shy touches of self-conscious slang, one perceives that something is being said, and that what is being said is not only interesting, but challenging.

Just as his novels are not material for an easy read just before dropping off to sleep, Henry James's *The High Bid* may thus never be a play for the light entertainment on a nice evening out. For those who care to look and listen, *The High Bid* is packed with pleasant ironies, sparkling language, and humorous touches, but it will always remain one of the more sophisticated pleasures for actors and audiences alike.

Taking a final overview of the four plays presented in this volume, their various ways of critically exploring aspects of their contemporary culture can be further specified. *Money* and *The High Bid* are the two plays which take the approach of serious comedy. The virtues held high and confirmed in these two plays are endangered by the encroachments of the hegemonic claims of financial interest, which are contrasted to the protagonists' insistence on values which transcend both the orientation towards personal gain and even the immediate concerns of party politics. It is interesting to note that the positive values propounded in the two plays are in each case decisively supported by forces from outside of England itself. In *Money*, the inheritance and the healthy opinions on whom best to bestow it come from an uncle who has lived the greater part of his life in colonial India (and presumably acquired his wealth there). The money which saves Captain Yule's manor house for him is provided by an American widow, who also knows best of all how to appreciate its worth through her acquired taste. It is as if the colonial past (in the American Mrs Gracedew) and present (the uncle in colonial India) had come back not only with its wealth but with a lucidity in the perception of traditional values which English society itself was, in the authors' views, about to lose. Impulses of renovation and reform can also be discerned in *London Assurance* and *Engaged*, both of which contain strong elements of farce and are based on comic modes of outright fun and laughter. Boucicault achieves his specific tone by drawing on the conventions of sentimental comedy as well as of the witty urbanity of the Restoration tradition, mildly satirizing them both for comic effect. Gilbert, finally, produces an outright burlesque of the stage conventions of romantic love, truth, and honour so pompously held high, in particular in Victorian melodrama and kindred genres, thereby simultaneously questioning the formulaic professions of these values in his audience's real lives. Taken together, the four plays provide an eloquent testimony of the richness of the Victorian stage in general, but also of its complex negotiations with the social reality of its time.

NOTE ON THE TEXTS

INSTABILITY is one of the important characteristics of playscripts in general as they develop from production to production, and even through individual performances. In the nineteenth century these processes of the texts' development involved authors, stage managers, prompters, and the actors themselves, all honing and adapting the script for each new production, but also during the run of a play. What is more, even prompt books give us no definite picture of the actual performance, as the extent or quality of rehearsal could vary widely. Actors' improvisations could make up a substantial part of the text spoken at any particular performance. Far from giving the appearance of monolithic sanctity which the canonized 'classics', especially, have acquired in twentieth-century mainstream theatre, playscripts could change significantly over the course of time; they might mature, but they could also get out of focus or lose the stringency and coherence of the author's original intention.

Generally speaking, the period spanned by the plays collected in this edition is characterized by a development towards the director's theatre evolving in the early twentieth century, where the director would be in charge of the play's presentation on stage but would not normally infringe on the integrity of the playscript's text at his own discretion. Changes that suggested themselves in the course of rehearsals now tended to be made by the playwrights themselves, instead of actors rewriting their roles to their liking or stage managers taking the liberty of rearranging the whole play whenever they felt it suited them. In the following choice of copy texts, the editorial policy tries to take account of the scripts' specific origins, but also of the expected interests of today's readers.

In the case of *Money*, Macready, as well as later actors and managers, was of course instrumental in shaping the play during its long stage life. The alterations made when compared to the first editions of 1840 are, however, essentially cuts to give the piece greater smoothness and speed. In his edition of the play, Michael Booth has collated these later versions, highlighting particularly the Routledge edition of 1874, which he considers 'the most authentic of the acting editions; that is, closest to the performance text of *Money* as it emerged after much cutting and altering during its first long run at the Haymarket'.[1] In order to avoid repetition, but also because the original, full-length version would be of interest to those looking for Bulwer's original conception of the characters and because the later cuts do not contribute any fundamental alteration to the play's overall thematic pattern or tone of speech, the early edition published by Saunders and Otley is used as the basis for the text presented in this volume. In this version, therefore, the attempt to present a text close to the nineteenth-century performance realities is not compromised, while at the same time the interest of Bulwer's original conception of his characters is respected. *Money* actually ran through four editions in 1840, and a further three in 1841. A 'first edition' is no longer readily available,[2] if indeed it ever existed, so the version presented in the following is based on the copies of the 'second' and the 'fourth' edition held in the British Library, the differences between the two being minuscule and indicated in the notes where necessary. *Money* was continually reprinted throughout the nineteenth century, reflecting its popularity in the theatre and among readers alike.

In his edition of *London Assurance* in the 'New Mermaids' series (London: A. & C. Black, New York: W. W. Norton & Co., 1984), James L. Smith[3] opted for the first edition and against Lacy's Acting Edition, since he considers the latter's revisions 'certainly the product of inventive performers', while 'there is no evidence that Boucicault had anything to do with them' (p. xlii). Smith has a point, in so far as Boucicault was one of the very pioneers who spearheaded the attempted reduction of the actors' leeway by careful rehearsals and imposing tighter central control on productions. His successful fight for a greater share in the profits for the author would also result in a rise in the playwright's authority over the playscript. On the one hand, the editorial choice of a version as close as possible to the author's original seems therefore well justified in his case. On the other hand,

[1] M. R. Booth, *Nineteenth-Century Plays*, 5 vols. (Oxford, 1969–76), iii. 163–238, and 160 f.

[2] Neither the British Library in London nor the Bodleian Library, Oxford, hold a copy of a 'first edition', neither is it listed in the *National Union Catalogue*. The practice to call the first imprint the 'second edition' was not uncommon, albeit not the rule, at the time, as a bookseller's device to make the book appear very popular from the start.

[3] Smith's annotations are of exemplary scrupulousness and I would like to acknowledge here summarily my indebtedness for much enlightenment on a number of obscure references and connotations. In notes to the play where this is the case I explicitly do so by adding '(Smith)'.

however, these reforms in which Boucicault was to have such an important share really belong to the time after his return from America in 1860 and later. At the time of *London Assurance*, his first play to be accepted for a London performance, written at Mathews's request, he was still a newcomer who relied on the stage manager's advice—to say nothing of Henry Brougham's collaboration—even in the creative process before handing his script in to the theatre (Smith, 7). It appears therefore equally fair to maintain that, having come into being as a product of a collaboration and having gone through the able hands of the company under the Vestris–Mathews management at Covent Garden, the text of Lacy's Acting Edition of 1858, chosen here, can be considered the more mature and authentic product in terms of the idiosyncracies of the Victorian theatre at the time. 'Most of the changes' in Lacy, as Smith himself observes, 'improve the text' (p. xlii), and it is this version which is printed here. With it, we come closest to the shape of the comedy as it presented itself to audiences during the overwhelming success of its first run at Covent Garden. In this context, finally, the alterations in later editions are of little value and will not be included.

Of the three printed contemporary versions of *Engaged* (1877), French's Acting Edition (vol. 117; no. 1748) is almost identical to the 1877 edition (London: printed for private circulation), which differs from the version in *Original Plays*, Second Series (London: Chatto and Windus, 1881) in mainly two points: its stage directions are more extensive and its punctuation seems to follow more closely the rhythm of speech than syntactical considerations. On these grounds, the 1877 edition is reproduced here. It is evident that, in contrast to *Money* or *London Assurance*, the play's early textual history is much more stable. Even the differences to be found in the Lord Chamberlain's manuscript,[4] albeit somewhat more remarkable, confirm this impression. It contains a number of passages which were subsequently cut, quite obviously with a view to a smoother performance on stage. The discarded passages are mainly wordy speeches which, in the production,

---

[4] Licensing Laws in the 19th cent. stipulated that new plays, and new matter added to existing plays, had to be presented to the Lord Chamberlain's office and were read by the Examiner of Plays for approval. These powers of censorship were absolute and were founded on the Licensing Act of 1737, revised in the Theatres Act of 1843. Censorship through the Lord Chamberlain's office only ended with the Theatres Act of 1968. The manuscripts handed in to the Examiner of Plays were collected and the greater part of this collection has found its way into the British Library in London, where it can be consulted.

proved dispensable. In one or two instances, however, these speeches are of a colourful volubility, such as Cheviot's detailed description of a breakfast, so that they have been added in an appendix. All those interested in the opportunities offered by a modern revision of the play are here directed to the adaptation by George Rowell and Kenneth Mobbs under the title *Engaged! or Cheviot's Choice* (London: Chappel & Co, [1963]).

Henry James's *The High Bid*, written in 1907, was not printed at the time of its first performance in 1908, but survived in a number of typescript copies listed by Leon Edel[5] who edited the play for its first publication in 1949. Instead of rendering the longer version of the Lord Chamberlain's copy, he decided to give the result of the cuts and alterations indicated in Johnston Forbes-Robertson's copy at the Houghton Library as it was 'the text as actually performed on the stage in 1909, which James had approved'.[6] As Edel notes, some of the inserts in this copy are in Forbes-Robertson's hand, which shows that the actor clearly exerted considerable influence on the script's fate in rehearsal. In comparison, the longer Lord Chamberlain's copy shows James's more novelistic tendency, enhanced by the later addition of the role of 'Young Man' in Act 1 containing a description of Cora. By contrast, the later copies reflect the necessities of stage production. As James's fame rests so much on his talents as a novelist, the play's earliest version can be expected to be of interest to many readers and, as it has never been printed, it is reproduced here with the addition of the 'Young Man' part. Again, the later alterations in the Forbes-Robertson copy are mainly cuts of passages or phrases which were considered inefficient or simply tedious in performance. They do not substantially affect the play's structure or thematic framework. The most conspicuous examples are indicated in the annotations.

In general, it has been the present editor's preference wherever possible to avoid creating new hybrid texts by compiling existing editions of a given play into a newly integrated version. Where variants of the copy texts are given, they are clearly marked as such. As a rule, the original texts have been rendered as conservatively as possible. In line with series policy, obvious mistakes in spelling or punctuation have been silently corrected, and obsolete spellings and punctuation have been modernized.

---

[5] *The Complete Plays of Henry James* ed. Leon Edel (1949; New York and Oxford: Oxford University Press, 1990), 822.
[6] Ibid. 820.

Finally, the indications of the characters' relative positions on stage, as well as of their entrances and exits have been largely standardized in the stage directions. The system used in the process follows George Rowell's thoughtful glossary in his anthology of nineteenth-century plays.[7] Thus, L for 'left' and R for 'right' are to be understood from the actor's point of view. LIE refers to the entrance nearest to the audience on, again from the actor's position, the left-hand side of the stage. C is 'centre', LC 'left of centre', LUE is 'left upper entrance', that is, the one furthest away from the audience, 'up' the stage. Where entrances and exits are through a door in the backdrop of the stage, i.e. the 'wall' at the back, facing the audience, they are marked as 'at back' with their respective positions from left to right. Actors going 'up' move away from the audience, while they approach the footlights when they come 'down', the terms originating from the time when the use of raked or sloping stages was common, so that the back of a stage would actually be higher up than its front end. The somewhat archaic stage direction 'without' has been replaced by 'offstage' throughout the texts; similarly, *omnes* has been translated into 'all'. Square brackets have been used to indicate editional stage directions; original stage direction are in parentheses.

[7] George Rowell, 'Glossary of Stage Terms' in his *Nineteenth-Century Plays* (Oxford and New York: Oxford University Press, 1953, 2nd edn. 1972, 8th impression 1988), pp. xiii f.

SELECT BIBLIOGRAPHY

THE comprehensiveness of the two nineteenth-century volumes (iv and v) of Allardyce Nicoll's *A History of English Drama*, 6 vols. (Cambridge: Cambridge University Press, 2nd edn. 1952–9) make it still a standard work and starting point for research in the drama and theatre of this period. Useful general introductions of a more recent date are vol. vi of *The Revels History of Drama in English* (London: Methuen, 1975); George Rowell, *The Victorian Theatre* (1955, 2nd edn. London: Oxford University Press, 1967); Michael R. Booth, *Prefaces to English Nineteenth-Century Theatre* (Manchester: Manchester University Press, 1981) and *Theatre in the Victorian Age* (Cambridge: Cambridge University Press, 1991). Surveys of research are to be found in Michael R. Booth, 'A Defence of Nineteenth-Century English Drama', *Educational Theatre Journal*, 26 (1974), 5–13, Victor Emeljanow, 'Victorian Drama and Theatre', *The Year's Work in English Studies*, 73 (1992), and Michael R. Booth, 'Studies in Nineteenth-Century British Theatre 1980–1989', *Nineteenth Century Theatre*, 20 (1992), 46–59, but also in David Mayer, 'Recent Studies in Victorian Society and Culture', *Nineteenth Century Theatre*, 19 (1991), 139–44. On the theatres in London, Raymond Mander and Joe Mitchenson's *The Theatres of London* (London: Rupert Hart-Davis, 1961, 2nd edn. 1963) and *The Lost Theatres of London* (London: Rupert Hart-Davis, 1968) give a good survey, with further insights provided by Richard Southern, *The Victorian Theatre* (Newton Abbot: David & Charles, 1970) and Victor Glasstone, *Victorian and Edwardian Theatres* (London: Thames and Hudson, 1975). On the art of Victorian acting, George Taylor's *Players and Performances in the Victorian Theatre* (Manchester and New York: Manchester University Press, 1989) sets the standard. Russell Jackson (ed.), *Victorian Theatre*, Mermaid Background Book (London: A. & C. Black, 1989), is a most helpful source book on many important aspects of theatre and acting. John Russell Stephens, *The Censorship of English Drama 1824–1901* (Cambridge: Cambrige University Press, 1980) provides useful information on the development of the legal conditions under which authors and theatre managers had to work. Anthony Jenkins includes Bulwer's *Money* in a close reading of what he considers hallmarks in *The Making of Victorian Drama* (Cambridge: Cambridge University Press, 1991). For the dramatic and theatrical context of Henry James's *The High Bid*, the Longman Literature in English Series offers a good survey with many bibliographical clues in Jean Chothia, *English Drama of the Early Modern Period 1890–1940*, Longman Literature in English Series (Harlow: Longman, 1996). The volume *English Drama: Romantic and Victorian, 1789 to 1890* in this series is in preparation.

Literary biographies of Edward Bulwer-Lytton, such as Allan Conrad Christensen, *Edward Bulwer-Lytton: The Fictions of New Regions* (Athens Ga.: University of Georgia Press, 1976), and James L. Campbell, *Edward Bulwer-Lytton* (Boston: Twayne Publishers, 1986), are mainly focused on his career as a novelist, but may be consulted as giving a background to his dramatic career.

Dion Boucicault's motley life story is presented by Robert Goode Hogan, *Dion Boucicault* (New York: Twayne, 1969) and in Richard Fawkes's eminently readable *Dion Boucicault: A Biography* (London and New York: Quartet Books, 1979). David Krause's *The Dolmen Boucicault* (Dublin: Dolmen Press, 1964), still a standard edition, is also worth investigating.

Following Hesketh Pearson's earlier *Gilbert: His Life and Strife* (London: Methuen, 1957), William Schwenk Gilbert's life and work has now been excellently documented in Jane W. Stedman, *W. S. Gilbert: A Classic Victorian and His Theatre* (Oxford: Oxford University Press, 1996). This book's 'Select Bibliography' (pp. 351–60) is most helpful and comprehensive. Andrew Goodman, *Gilbert and Sullivan's London* (Tunbridge Wells: Spellmount Ltd., 1982) is useful for specific background information.

The studies on Henry James are, of course, much more numerous than any on the first three authors. Nevertheless, Leon Edel's extensive work on James's biography is of course the classic to begin with. His *Henry James: A Life* (London: Flamingo, 1996) is a conflation of these longer works into a still substantial single volume. Edel's and Dan H. Lawrence's *A Bibliography of Henry James*: (Oxford: Clarendon Press, 3rd edn. 1982) is very helpful. A succinct portrait of James's career in the theatre can be found in Leon Edel's 'Introductory Essay' to his edition of *The Complete Plays of Henry James* (New York and Oxford: Oxford University Press, 1990), 19–69, entitled 'Henry James: The Dramatic Years'. For the time of origin of James's *The High Bid*, Michael Egan, *Henry James: The Ibsen Years* (London: Vision, 1972) is also very informative. The standard work on the melodramatic vein in James's work is Peter Brooks, *The Melodramatic Imagination: Balzac, Henry James, Melodrama, and the Mode of Excess*

(New Haven and London: Yale University Press, 2nd edn. 1995). Nevertheless, Leo B. Levy, *Versions of Melodrama: A Study of the Fiction and Drama of Henry James, 1865–1897* (Berkeley: University of California Press, 1957) is still worth consulting.

CHRONOLOGIES OF THE AUTHORS

Edward George Earle Bulwer-Lytton (1803–1873)

1822   Enters Trinity Hall, Cambridge.

1827   Marries Rosina Doyle Wheeler.

1828   *Pelham* Bulwer's first success as a novelist.

1831–41   Member of Parliament for St Ives, Huntingdonshire, then Lincoln.

1834   *The Last Days of Pompeii* (novel).

1836   Separation from his wife.

1837   *The Duchess de la Vallière* performed at Covent Garden.

1838   *The Lady of Lyons* performed at Covent Garden.

1839   *Richelieu* performed at Covent Garden, *The Sea-Captain* at the Haymarket.

1840   *Money* performed at the Haymarket.

1842   *Zanoni* (novel).

1851   *Not So Bad As We Seem*, comedy, performed at the Haymarket.

1852–66   Conservative Member of Parliament for Hertfordshire.

1866   Raised to peerage as Baron Lytton.

1869   *The Rightful Heir* performed at the Lyceum.

1871   *The Coming Race* (science fiction fantasy).

1877   *The House of Darnley* performed at the Court Theatre.

1885   *Junius Brutus* performed at the Princess'.

Dionysius Lardner Bou(r)cicault (1820–1890)

1838   First appearances as actor (under pseudonym Lee Morton) in the English provinces.

1841   *London Assurance* performed at Covent Garden as Boucicault's London debut as playwright.

1844   First of many journeys to Paris.

         Used Up, comedietta in collaboration with Charles Mathews, performed at Haymarket.

1845   Marriage to rich widow, Anne Guiot, who dies in the same year.

1847   *The School for Scheming*, comedy, performed at Haymarket.

1850   House dramatist to Charles Kean at the Princess'.

1852   *The Corsican Brothers* and *The Vampire* performed at the Princess'.

1853   Private declaration of marriage.

1853–60   First of several tours in America, with Agnes Robertson.

1857   *The Poor of New York* performed at Wallack's, New York; at the Princess', London, on 1 August 1864 as *The Streets of London*.

1859   *The Octoroon; or, Life in Louisiana* performed at Winter Garden, New York; first London performance at the Adelphi, 18 November 1861.

        Birth of a son by Agnes Robertson, Darley George, himself to become an actor and dramatist.

1860   *The Colleen Bawn* performed at Laura Keene's, New York (28 March) and at the Adelphi, London (10 September).

1864   *Arrah-na-Pogue* performed in Manchester; 7 November 1864 in Dublin; 21 March 1865 at the Princess', London.

1867   Birth of daughter by Agnes Robertson, Nina, to become an actress.

1874   *The Shaughraun* performed at Wallack's, New York; 4 September 1875 at Drury Lane, London.

1876   *Forbidden Fruit* performed at Wallack's, New York; 22 October 1877 in Liverpool; 3 July 1880 at Adelphi, London.

1885   Tours to Australia and New Zealand.

1888   Marriage to Louise Thorndike.

William Schwenck Gilbert (1836–1911)

1855   Enters department of general literature and science at King's College, London.

1857   Graduates BA from London University.

1857–62   Clerk in the education department of the Privy Council.

1863   Called to the Bar.

1866   *Dulcamara*, which Gilbert had written on T. W. Robertson's encouragement, produced at St James's as his first play, followed by several light burlesques.

1867   Marries Lucy Blois Turner (no children).

1869   *Bab Ballads.*

1871   *Thespis; or, The Gods Grown Old* performed at the Gaiety; first in the long series of Gilbert's collaborations with the composer Arthur Sullivan.

1873   *The Wedding March* performed at the Court Theatre.

1877   *Engaged* performed at Haymarket.

1878   *H.M.S. Pinafore* (with Sullivan) performed at the Opera Comique.

1879   *The Pirates of Penzance* (with Sullivan) performed at Fifth Avenue, New York; 1880 at Opera Comique, London.

1885   *The Mikado* (with Sullivan) performed at the Savoy.

1889   Opening of the Garrick Theatre, which Gilbert has built from the proceeds of his plays.

1896   *The Grand Duke* performed at Savoy; last collaboration with Arthur Sullivan.

1907   Gilbert knighted.

1911   *The Hooligans*, Gilbert's last play.

Henry James (1843–1916)

1860   Art studies at Newport.

1862–3 Law School at Harvard University.

1875–6 Spends a year in Paris meeting prominent literary figures of the day.

1875   *Roderick Hudson* serialized in the *Atlantic Monthly*; then published in 1876.

1877   Moves to London.

1878   Breakthrough as writer with 'Daisy Miller'.

1881   *Portrait of a Lady*.

1890   *The Tragic Muse* (novel on theatre).

1891   *The American* performed at Winter Gardens, Southport, then Opera Comique, London.

1894   *Theatricals* (*Tenants* and *Disengaged*) published, but not performed.

1895   *Theatricals* (Second Series: *The Album* and *The Reprobate*) published, but not performed; *Guy Domville* 'disaster' at St James'. Writes *Summersoft* for Ellen Terry.

1897   *What Maisie Knew*.

1898   Moves to Lamb House, Rye, Sussex. *The Turn of the Screw* published together with *Covering End* as *The Two Magics*.

1902   *The Wings of the Dove*.

1903   *The Ambassadors*.

1904   *The Golden Bowl*.

1905   Revisits America.

1908   *The High Bid* performed in Edinburgh; 1909 to His Majesty's Theatre.

1911   *The Saloon* produced by Gertrude Kingston at the Little Theatre in John Adam Street, London.

1915   Becomes a naturalized British citizen.

1916   Awarded the Order of Merit.

1917   *The Outcry* produced by the Stage Society.

MONEY

EDWARD BULWER-LYTTON

DEDICATED

To JOHN FORSTER, Esq.,°

AUTHOR OF

THE LIVES OF STATESMEN OF THE COMMONWEALTH.°

A SLIGHT MEMORIAL

OF SINCERE RESPECT AND CORDIAL FRIENDSHIP;

ALTHOUGH

(FOR WE ARE ALL HUMAN!)

HE HAS IN ONE INSTANCE

AND BUT ONE,

SUFFERED HIS JUDGMENT

TO BE MISLED

BY TOO GREAT A REGARD

FOR

'MONEY'!°

London,
   Nov., 1840

CHARACTERS OF THE PLAY

MEN

Lord Glossmore°	Mr Vining
Sir John Vesey, Bart., Knight of the Guelph; F.R.S., F.S.A.°	Mr Strickland
Sir Frederick Blount	Mr Lacy
Stout	Mr D. Rees
Graves°	Mr Webster
Evelyn	Mr Macready
Captain Dudley Smooth°	Mr Wrench
Sharp,° *Lawyer*	Mr Waldron
Toke, *Evelyn's Butler*	Mr Oxberry
Frantz, *Tailor*	Mr O. Smith
Tabouret,° *Upholsterer*	Mr Howe
Macfinch, *Jeweller and Silversmith*	Mr Gough
Macstucco,° *Architect*	Mr Mathews
Kite,° *Horse-dealer*	Mr Santer
Crimson,° *Portrait-painter*	Mr Gallot
Grab,° *Publisher*	Mr Caulfield
Patent, *Coach-builder*	Mr Clarke

At least three Members, one of them 'old', and one Servant of the *** Club,° a Servant at Sir John Vesey's house and two Servants at Evelyn's house; a bailiff; a footman.

WOMEN

Lady Franklin,° *half-sister to* Sir John Vesey	Mrs Glover
Georgina, *daughter to* Sir John	Miss Horton
Clara, *companion to* Lady Franklin, *cousin to* Evelyn	Miss Faucit

Scene, London, 1840

1.

A drawing-room in Sir John Vesey's house; folding-doors at the back, which open on another drawing-room; a table, R, with newspapers, books, etc.; a sofa writing-table,° L

Sir John Vesey, Georgina

SIR JOHN (*reading a letter edged with black*) Yes, he says at two precisely. 'Dear Sir John, as since the death of my sainted Maria,'— Hum, that's his wife; she made him a martyr, and now he makes her a saint!

GEORGINA Well, as since her death?— 5

SIR JOHN (*reading*) 'I have been living in chambers,° where I cannot so well invite ladies. You will allow me to bring Mr Sharp, the lawyer, to read the will of the late Mr Mordaunt (to which I am appointed executor) at your house, your daughter being the nearest relation. I shall be with you at two precisely. Henry Graves.' 10

GEORGINA And you really feel sure that poor Mr Mordaunt has made me his heiress?

SIR JOHN Ay, the richest heiress in England. Can you doubt it? Are you not his nearest relation? Niece by your poor mother, his own sister. All the time he was making this enormous fortune in India 15 did we ever miss sending him little reminiscences of our disinterested affection? When he was last in England and you only so high, was not my house his home? Didn't I get a surfeit° out of complaisance to his execrable curries and pilaus?° Didn't he smoke his hookah,° nasty old—that is, poor dear man—in my best 20 drawing-room? And did you ever speak without calling him your 'handsome uncle'? For the excellent creature was as vain as a peacock—

GEORGINA And so ugly—

SIR JOHN The dear deceased! Alas, he *was*, indeed, like a kangaroo in 25 a jaundice!° And *if*, after all these marks of attachment, you are *not* his heiress, why then the finest feelings of our nature, the ties of blood, the principles of justice, are implanted in us in vain.

GEORGINA Beautiful, sir. Was not that in your last speech at the Freemasons' Tavern° upon the great Chimney-sweep Question?° 30

SIR JOHN Clever girl! What a memory she has! Sit down, Georgy. Upon this most happy—I mean, melancholy—occasion, I feel that

I may trust you with a secret. You see this fine house, our fine
servants, our fine plate, our fine dinners: everyone thinks Sir John
Vesey a rich man.   35

GEORGINA And are you not, Papa?

SIR JOHN Not a bit of it; all humbug, child, all humbug, upon my
soul! As you hazard a minnow to hook in a trout, so one guinea
thrown out with address° is often the best bait for a hundred.
There are two rules in life: *First*, men are valued not for what they   40
are, but what they *seem* to be. *Secondly*, if you have no merit or
money of your own, you must trade on the merits and money of
other people. My father got the title by services in the army and
died penniless. On the strength of his services I got a pension of
four hundred pounds a year; on the strength of four hundred   45
pounds a year I took credit for eight hundred pounds; on the
strength of eight hundred pounds a year I married your mother
with ten thousand pounds; on the strength of ten thousand pounds
I took credit for forty thousand pounds and paid Dicky Gossip
three guineas a week to go about everywhere calling me 'Stingy   50
Jack'.

GEORGINA Ha! ha! A disagreeable nickname.

SIR JOHN But a valuable reputation. When a man is called stingy, it is
as much as calling him rich; and when a man's called rich, why he's
a man universally respected. On the strength of my respectability I   55
wheedled a constituency,° changed my politics, resigned my seat to
a minister, who, to a man of such stake in the country, could offer
nothing less in return than a patent office° of two thousand pounds
a year. That's the way to succeed in life. Humbug, my dear, all
humbug, upon my soul!   60

GEORGINA I must say that you—

SIR JOHN Know the world, to be sure. Now, for your fortune, as I
spend all that I have, I can have nothing to leave you. Yet, even
without counting your uncle, you have always passed for an heiress
on the credit of your expectations from the savings of 'Stingy Jack'.   65
The same with your education. I never grudged anything to make a
show. Never stuffed your head with histories and homilies; but you
draw, you sing, you dance, you walk well into a room; and that's the
way young ladies are educated nowadays in order to become a pride
to their parents and a blessing to their husband—that is, when they   70
have caught him. Apropos of a husband: you know we thought of
Sir Frederick Blount.

GEORGINA Ah, Papa, he is charming.

6

SIR JOHN He *was so*, my dear, before we knew your poor uncle was
dead; but an heiress such as you will be should look out for a   75
duke.—Where the deuce° is Evelyn this morning?

GEORGINA I've not seen him, Papa. What a strange character he is. So
sarcastic, and yet he can be agreeable.

SIR JOHN A humorist,° a cynic! One never knows how to take him.
My private secretary, a poor cousin, has not got a shilling, and yet,   80
hang me if he does not keep us all at a sort of a distance.

GEORGINA But why do you take him to live with us, Papa, since
there's no good to be got by it?

SIR JOHN There you are wrong. He has a great deal of talent: prepares
my speeches, writes my pamphlets, looks up my calculations. My   85
report on the last Commission° has got me a great deal of fame and
has put me at the head of the new one. Besides, he *is* our cousin. He
has no salary. Kindness to a poor relation always tells well in the
world, and benevolence is an useful virtue, particularly when you
can have it for nothing. With our other cousin, Clara, it was differ-   90
ent. Her father thought fit to leave me her guardian, though she had
not a penny; a mere useless encumbrance. So, you see, I got my
half-sister, Lady Franklin, to take her off my hands.

GEORGINA How much longer is Lady Franklin's visit to be?

SIR JOHN I don't know, my dear; the longer the better, for her hus-   95
band left her a good deal of money at her own disposal. Ah, here
she comes.

Enter Lady Franklin and Clara

SIR JOHN My dear sister, we were just loud in your praises. But how's
this? Not in mourning?

LADY FRANKLIN Why should I go into mourning for a man I never   100
saw?

SIR JOHN Still, there may be a legacy.

LADY FRANKLIN Then there'll be less cause for affliction. Ha! ha! my
dear Sir John, I'm one of those who think feelings a kind of property and never take credit for them upon false pretences.   105

SIR JOHN (*aside*) Very silly woman! [*Aloud*] But, Clara, I see you are
more attentive to the proper decorum. Yet you are very, *very*, VERY
distantly connected with the deceased. A third cousin, I think.

CLARA Mr Mordaunt once assisted my father, and these poor robes
are all the gratitude I can show him.   110

SIR JOHN Gratitude! Humph! [*Aside*] I am afraid the minx has got
expectations.

LADY FRANKLIN So, Mr Graves is the executor; the will is addressed

to him? The same Mr Graves who is always in black, always lament-
ing his ill fortune and his sainted Maria, who led him the life of a   115
dog?

SIR JOHN The very same. His liveries are black, his carriage is black,
he always rides a black galloway, and, faith, if he ever marry again, I
think he will show his respect to the sainted Maria by marrying a
black woman.   120

LADY FRANKLIN Ha! ha! We shall see. (*Aside*) Poor Graves, I always
liked him. He made an excellent husband.

Enter Evelyn; seats himself and takes up a book, unobserved

SIR JOHN What a crowd of relations this will brings to light: Mr
Stout, the political economist, Lord Glossmore—

LADY FRANKLIN Whose grandfather kept a pawnbroker's shop, and   125
who, accordingly, entertains the profoundest contempt for everything popular, parvenu and plebeian.

SIR JOHN Sir Frederick Blount—

LADY FRANKLIN Sir Fwedewick Blount, who objects to the letter R
as being too wough and therefore dwops its acquaintance. One of   130
the new class of prudent young gentlemen, who, not having spirits
and constitution for the hearty excesses of their predecessors,
entrench themselves in the dignity of a lady-like languor. A man of
fashion in the last century was riotous and thoughtless; in this he is
tranquil and egotistical. He never does anything that is silly, or says   135
anything that is wise. I beg your pardon, my dear; I believe Sir
Frederick is an admirer of yours, provided, on reflection, he does
not see 'what harm it could do him' to fall in love with your beauty
and expectations. Then, too, our poor cousin the scholar,—Oh, Mr
Evelyn, there you are!   140

SIR JOHN Evelyn! The very person I wanted. Where have you been all
day? Have you seen to those papers? Have you written my epitaph
on poor Mordaunt? Latin, you know! Have you reported my speech
at Exeter Hall?° Have you looked out the debates on the Customs?°
And, oh, have you mended up all the old pens in the study?   145

GEORGINA And have you brought me the black floss silk?° Have you
been to Storr's° for my ring? And, as we cannot go out on this
melancholy occasion, did you call at Hookham's° for the last H.B.°
and the *Comic Annual*?°

LADY FRANKLIN And did you see what was really the matter with my   150
bay horse? Did you get me the opera box? Did you buy my little
Charley his peg-top?°

EVELYN (*always reading*) Certainly, Paley° is right upon that point;

for, put the syllogism thus—(*looking up*) Ma'am, sir, Miss Vesey—
you want something of me? Paley observes that to assist even the   155
undeserving tends to the better regulation of our charitable feelings. No apologies, I am quite at your service.

SIR JOHN Now he's in one of his humours!

LADY FRANKLIN You allow him strange liberties, Sir John.

EVELYN You will be the less surprised at that, madam, when I inform   160
you that Sir John allows me nothing else. I am now about to draw
on his benevolence.

LADY FRANKLIN I beg your pardon, sir, and like your spirit. Sir John,
I'm in the way, I see; for I know your benevolence is so delicate that
you never allow anyone to detect it! (*Walks aside*)   165

EVELYN I could not do your commissions today. I have been to visit a
poor woman, who was my nurse and my mother's last friend. She is
very poor, *very* sick, dying, and she owes six months' rent!

SIR JOHN You know I should be most happy to do anything for yourself. But the nurse! (*Aside*) Some people's nurses are always ill!   170
[*Aloud*] There are so many impostors about! We'll talk of it tomorrow. This most mournful occasion takes up all my attention. (*Looking at his watch*) Bless me! So late! I've letters to write and—none of
the pens are mended?

    Exit Sir John Vesey

GEORGINA (*taking out her purse*) I think I will give it to him. And yet,   175
if I don't get the fortune after all! Papa allows me so little! Then I
must have those earrings. (*Puts up the purse*) Mr Evelyn, what is the
address of your nurse?

EVELYN (*writes and gives it*) She has a good heart with all her foibles!
Ah! Miss Vesey, if that poor woman had not closed the eyes of my   180
lost mother, Alfred Evelyn would not have been this beggar to your
father.

    Clara looks over the address

GEORGINA I will certainly attend to it, (*aside*) if I get the fortune.

SIR JOHN (*calling offstage*) Georgy, I say.

GEORGINA Yes, Papa.   185

    *Exit Georgina. Evelyn has seated himself at the table, R, and
    leans his face on his hands*

CLARA His noble spirit bowed to this! Ah, at least here I may give him
comfort. (*Sits down to write*) But he will recognise my hand.

LADY FRANKLIN What bill are you paying, Clara? Putting up a banknote?

CLARA Hush! O Lady Franklin, you are the kindest of human beings.   190

This is for a poor person. I would not have her know whence it came, or she would refuse it. Would you?—No, he knows *her* handwriting also!

LADY FRANKLIN Will I what? Give the money myself? With pleasure! Poor Clara. Why this covers all your savings, and I am so rich!   195

CLARA Nay, I would wish to do all myself! It is a pride, a duty; it is a joy; and I have so few joys! But, hush! This way.

> *Clara and Lady Franklin retire into the inner room and converse in dumb show*°

EVELYN And thus must I grind out my life forever! I am ambitious, and poverty drags me down! I have learning, and poverty makes me the drudge of fools! I love, and poverty stands like a spectre before   200
the altar! But, no, no. If, as I believe, I am but loved again, I will— will—what?—turn opium-eater and dream of the Eden I may never enter!

LADY FRANKLIN (*to Clara*) Yes, I will get my maid to copy and direct this. She writes well and *her* hand will never be discovered. I will   205
have it done and sent instantly.

> *Exit Lady Franklin. Clara advances to the front of the stage and seats herself. Evelyn reading. Enter Sir Frederick Blount*

BLOUNT No one in the woom! Oh, Miss Douglas! Pway don't let me disturb you. Where is Miss Vesey—Georgina? (*Taking Clara's chair as she rises*)

> *Evelyn, looking up, gives Clara a chair and re-seats himself*

EVELYN (*aside*) Insolent puppy!   210

CLARA Shall I tell her you are here, Sir Frederick?

BLOUNT Not for the world—vewy pwetty girl this companion!

CLARA What did you think of the Panorama° the other day, cousin Evelyn?

EVELYN (*reading*)   215

> 'I cannot talk with civet° in the room,
> A fine puss gentleman that's all perfume!'°

Rather good these lines.

BLOUNT Sir!

EVELYN (*offering the book*) Don't you think so?—Cowper.   220

BLOUNT (*declining the book*) Cowper!

EVELYN Cowper.

BLOUNT (*shrugging his shoulders, to Clara*) Stwange person, Mr Evelyn! Quite a chawacter! Indeed the Panowama gives you no idea of Naples—a delightful place. I make it a wule to go there evewy   225
second year. I am vewy fond of twavelling. You'd like Wome; bad

inns, but vewy fine wuins. Gives you quite a taste for that sort of thing!

EVELYN (*reading*)

  'How much a dunce that has been sent to roam,   230
  Excels a dunce that has been kept at home.'°

BLOUNT (*aside*) That fellow Cowper says vewy odd things! Humph! It is beneath me to quawwell. (*Aloud*) It will not take long to wead the will, I suppose. Poor old Mordaunt. I am his nearest male welation. He was vewy eccentwic. By the way, Miss Douglas, did you wemark   235 my cuwicle?° It is bwinging cuwicles into fashion. I should be most happy if you would allow me to dwive you out. Nay, nay, I should, upon my word. (*Trying to take her hand*)

EVELYN (*starting up*) A wasp! A wasp! Just going to settle. Take care of the wasp, Miss Douglas!   240

BLOUNT A wasp! Where? Don't bwing it this way? Some people don't mind them! I've a particular dislike to wasps; they sting damnably!

EVELYN I beg pardon, it's only a gadfly.

  Enter Servant

SERVANT Sir John will be happy to see you in his study, Sir Frederick.

  Exit Servant

BLOUNT Vewy well. Upon my word, there is something vewy nice   245 about this girl. To be sure, I love Georgina; but if this one would take a fancy to me (*thoughtfully*)—Well, I don't see what harm it could do me! *Au plaisir!*°

  Exit Sir Frederick Blount

EVELYN Clara!

CLARA Cousin!   250

EVELYN And you too are a dependant!

CLARA But on Lady Franklin, who seeks to make me forget it.

EVELYN Ay, but can the world forget it? This insolent condescension, this coxcombry of admiration, more galling than the arrogance of contempt! Look you now, robe beauty in silk and cashmere,° hand   255 virtue into her chariot, lackey their caprices, wrap them from the winds, fence them round with a golden circle, and virtue and beauty are as goddesses, both to peasant and to prince. Strip them of the adjuncts, see beauty and virtue poor, dependent, solitary, walking the world defenceless; oh, *then*, the devotion changes its   260 character, the same crowd gather eagerly around; fools, fops, libertines, not to worship at the shrine, but to sacrifice the victim!

CLARA My cousin, you are cruel!

EVELYN Forgive me! There is a something, when a man's heart is

better than his fortunes, that makes even affection bitter. Mortifica- 265
tion for myself, it has ceased to chafe me. I can mock where I once
resented. But *you*, YOU, so delicately framed and nurtured; one
slight to you, one careless look, one disdainful tone, makes me feel
the true curse of the poor man. His pride gives armour to *his own*
breast, but it has no shield to protect another! 270

CLARA But I, too, have pride of my own. I, too, can smile at the
pointless insolence.

EVELYN [*aside*] Smile, and he took your hand! [*Aloud*] Oh, Clara, you
know not the tortures that I suffer hourly! When others approach
you, young, fair, rich, the sleek darlings of the world, I accuse you 275
of your very beauty, I writhe beneath every smile that you bestow.
No, speak not! My heart has broke its silence, and you shall hear the
rest. For you I have endured the weary bondage of this house, the
fool's gibe, the hireling's sneer, the bread, purchased by toils, that
should have led me to loftier ends. Yes, to see you, hear you, breathe 280
the same air, be ever at hand, that if others slighted, from one at
least you might receive the luxury of respect. For this, for this I
have lingered, suffered and forborne. Oh, Clara! We are orphans
both, friendless both. You are all in the world to me. Turn not
away; my very soul speaks in these words: *I love you!* 285

CLARA No, Evelyn, Alfred, no! Say it not, think it not! It were
madness.

EVELYN Madness! Nay, hear me yet. I am poor, penniless, a beggar for
bread to a dying servant. True! But I have a heart of iron! I have
knowledge, patience, health, and my love for you gives me at last 290
ambition! I have trifled with my own energies till now, for I despised all things till I loved thee! With you to toil for, your step to
support, your path to smooth, and I, I, poor Alfred Evelyn, promise at last to win for you even fame and fortune! Do not withdraw
your hand, *this* hand, shall it not be mine? 295

CLARA Ah, Evelyn! Never, never!

EVELYN Never!

CLARA Forget this folly! Our union is impossible and to talk of love
were to deceive both!

EVELYN (*bitterly*) Because I am poor! 300

CLARA And *I too*! A marriage of privation, of penury, of days that
dread the morrow! I have seen such a lot! Never return to this
again.

EVELYN Enough, you are obeyed. I deceived myself. Ha! ha! I fancied
that I, too, was loved. I, whose youth is already half gone with care 305

and toil, whose mind is soured, whom nobody *can* love, who ought
to have loved no one!

CLARA (*aside*) And if it were only *I* to suffer, or perhaps to starve! Oh,
what shall I say? [*Aloud*] Evelyn, cousin?

EVELYN Madam.   310

CLARA Alfred, I, I—

EVELYN Reject me!

CLARA Yes! It is past!
    Exit Clara

EVELYN Let me think. It was yesterday her hand trembled when mine
touched it. And the rose I gave her, yes, she pressed her lips to it   315
once when she seemed as if she saw me not. But it was a trap, a
trick, for I was as poor then as now. This will be a jest for them all!
Well, courage! It is but a poor heart that a coquette's contempt can
break! And now that I care for no one, the world is but a great
chess-board and I will sit down in earnest and play with fortune!   320
    Enter Lord Glossmore, preceded by Servant

SERVANT I will tell Sir John, my lord!
    Exit Servant. Evelyn takes up the newspaper

GLOSSMORE [*aside*] The secretary. Hum! [*Aloud*] Fine day, sir. Any
news from the East?

EVELYN Yes! All the wise men° have gone back there!

GLOSSMORE Ha, ha! Not all, for here comes Mr Stout, the great   325
political economist.
    Enter Stout

STOUT Good morning, Glossmore.

GLOSSMORE [*Aside*] *Glossmore!* The parvenu!

STOUT Afraid I might be late. Been detained at the vestry.° Astonish-
ing how ignorant the English poor are! Took me an hour and a half   330
to beat it into the head of a stupid old widow with nine children
that to allow her three shillings a week was against all the rules of
public morality!

EVELYN Excellent! Admirable! Your hand, sir!

GLOSSMORE What! You approve such doctrines, Mr Evelyn? Are old   335
women only fit to be starved?

EVELYN Starved! Popular delusion! Observe, my lord, to squander
money upon those who starve is only to afford encouragement to
starvation!

STOUT A very superior person that!   340

GLOSSMORE Atrocious principles! Give me good old times when it
was the duty of the rich to succour the distressed.

EVELYN On second thoughts, *you* are right, my lord. I, too, know a
poor woman, ill, dying, in want. Shall *she*, too, perish?

GLOSSMORE Perish! Horrible! In a Christian country. Perish! Heaven   345
forbid!

EVELYN (*holding out his hand*) What, then, will you give her?

GLOSSMORE Ehem! Sir, the parish ought to give.

STOUT No! No, no. Certainly not! (*With great vehemence*)

GLOSSMORE No, no! But I say yes, yes! And if the parish refuse to   350
maintain the poor, the only way left to a man of firmness and
resolution, holding the principles that I do, and adhering to the
constitution of our fathers, is to force the poor *on* the parish by
never giving them a farthing oneself.

　　　Enter Sir John Vesey, Sir Frederick Blount, Lady
　　　Franklin, Georgina

SIR JOHN How d'ye do! Ah! How d'ye do, gentlemen? This is a most   355
melancholy meeting! The poor deceased! What a man he was!

BLOUNT I was chwistened Fwedewick after him. He was my first
cousin.

SIR JOHN And Georgina his own niece, next of kin! An excellent man,
though odd. A kind heart, but no liver! I sent him twice a year   360
thirty dozen of the Cheltenham waters.° It's a comfort to reflect on
these little attentions at such a time.

STOUT And I, too, sent him the *Parliamentary Debates*° regularly,
bound in calf. He was my second cousin, sensible man, and a fol-
lower of Malthus.° Never married to increase the surplus popula-   365
tion and fritter away his money on his own children. And now—

EVELYN He reaps the benefit of celibacy in the prospective gratitude
of every cousin he had in the world!

LADY FRANKLIN Ha! ha! ha!

SIR JOHN Hush! hush! Decency, Lady Franklin; decency!   370
　　　Enter Servant

SERVANT Mr Graves, Mr Sharp.

SIR JOHN Oh, here's Mr Graves. That's Sharp, the lawyer, who
brought the will from Calcutta.

　　　[*Exit Servant.*] *Enter Graves and Sharp*

CHORUS OF SIR JOHN, GLOSSMORE, BLOUNT, STOUT Ah, sir! Ah,
Mr Graves!   375

　　　Georgina holds her handkerchief to her eyes

SIR JOHN A sad occasion!

GRAVES But everything in life is sad. Be comforted, Miss Vesey. True,
you have lost an uncle. But I, I have lost a wife. Such a wife! The

first of her sex—and the second cousin of the defunct! Excuse me,
Sir John, at the sight of your mourning my wounds bleed afresh.   380
    Servants hand round wine and sandwiches   *Vironie - all after*
                                                 the money
SIR JOHN Take some refreshment, a glass of wine.
GRAVES Thank you. [*Aside*] Very fine sherry! [*Aloud*] Ah, my poor
sainted Maria! Sherry was *her* wine. Everything reminds me of
Maria! Ah, Lady Franklin, *you* knew her. Nothing in life can charm
me now. (*Aside*) A monstrous fine woman that!   *disingenuous*   385
SIR JOHN And now to business. Evelyn, you may retire.
SHARP (*looking at his notes*) Evelyn, any relation to Alfred Evelyn?
EVELYN The same.
SHARP Cousin to the deceased, seven times removed. Be seated, sir;
there may be some legacy, though trifling. All the relations, how-   390
ever distant, should be present.
LADY FRANKLIN Then Clara is related. I will go for her.
    Exit Lady Franklin
GEORGINA Ah, Mr Evelyn; I hope you will come in for something. A
few hundreds, or even more.
SIR JOHN Silence! Hush! Whugh! Ugh! Attention!   395
    While the lawyer opens the will, re-enter Lady Franklin and
    Clara
SHARP The will is very short, being all personal property. He was a
man that always came to the point.
SIR JOHN I wish there were more like him! (*Groans and shakes his*
head)
    Chorus° groan and shake their heads
SHARP (*reading*) 'I, Frederick James Mordaunt, of Calcutta, being, at   400
the present date, of sound mind, though infirm body, do hereby
give, will and bequeath, imprimis,° to my second cousin, Benjamin
Stout, Esq., of Pall Mall,° London,—
    Chorus exhibit lively emotion — *building up tension*
being the value of the *Parliamentary Debates*, with which he has
been pleased to trouble me for some time past, deducting the   405
carriage thereof, which he always forgot to pay, the sum of fourteen
pounds, two shillings, four pence'.
    Chorus breathe more freely
STOUT Eh, what! Fourteen pounds? Oh, hang the old miser!
SIR JOHN Decency, decency! Proceed, sir.
SHARP 'Item. To Sir Frederick Blount, Baronet, my nearest male   410
relative—'
    Chorus exhibit lively emotion

BLOUNT Poor old boy!

Georgina puts her arm over Blount's chair

SHARP 'Being, as I am informed, the best-dressed young gentleman in
London, and in testimony to the only merit I ever heard he possessed, the sum of five hundred pounds to buy a dressing-case.'   415

*Chorus breathe more freely; Georgina catches her father's eye
and removes her arm*

BLOUNT (*laughing confusedly*) Ha! ha! ha! Vewy poor wit, low! Vewy,
vewy low!

SIR JOHN Silence, now, will you?

SHARP 'Item. To Charles Lord Glossmore, who asserts that he is my
relation, my collection of dried butterflies and the pedigree of the   420
Mordaunts from the reign of King John.'

Chorus as before

GLOSSMORE Butterflies! Pedigree! I disown the plebeian!

SIR JOHN (*angrily*) Upon my word, this is too revolting! Decency! Go
on.

SHARP 'Item. To Sir John Vesey, Baronet, Knight of the Guelph,   425
F.R.S., F.S.A., etc. –'

Chorus as before

SIR JOHN Hush! *Now* it is really interesting!

SHARP 'Who married my sister and who sends me every year the
Cheltenham waters, which nearly gave me my death, I bequeath—
the empty bottles.'   430

SIR JOHN Why, the ungrateful, rascally, old—

CHORUS Decency, Sir John, decency!

SHARP 'Item. To Henry Graves, Esq., of the Albany°—'

Chorus as before

GRAVES Pooh, gentlemen. My usual luck. Not even a ring, I dare swear!

SHARP 'The sum of five thousand pounds in the three per cents.'°   435

LADY FRANKLIN I wish you joy!

GRAVES Joy, pooh! Three per cents! Funds sure to go! Had it been
land, now, though only an acre! Just like my luck.

SHARP 'Item. To my niece Georgina Vesey—'

Chorus as before

SIR JOHN Ah, now it comes!   440

SHARP 'The sum of ten thousand pounds India stock,° being, with
her father's reputed savings, as much as a single woman ought to
possess.'

SIR JOHN And what the devil, then, does the old fool do with all his
money?   445

CHORUS Really, Sir John, this is too revolting. Decency! Hush!

SHARP 'And, with the aforesaid legacies and exceptions, I do will and bequeath the whole of my fortune, in India stock, bonds,° exchequer bills,° three per cents, consols,° and in the Bank of Calcutta° (constituting him hereby sole residuary legatee and joint executor with the aforesaid Henry Graves, Esq.), to Alfred Evelyn, now or formerly of Trinity College, Cambridge—'

    Universal excitement

'Being, I am told, an oddity, like myself, the only one of my relations who never fawned on me, and who, having known privation, may the better employ wealth.' And now, sir, I have only to wish you joy, and give you this letter from the deceased. I believe it is important.

EVELYN (*crossing over to Clara*) Ah, Clara, if you had but loved me!

CLARA (*turning away*) And this wealth, even more than poverty, separates us forever!
    All crowd round to congratulate Evelyn

SIR JOHN (*to Georgina*) Go, child, put a good face on it. He's an immense match! [*To Evelyn*] My dear fellow, I wish you joy. You are a great man now, a very great man!

EVELYN (*aside*) And *her* voice alone is silent!

GLOSSMORE If I can be of any use to you—

STOUT Or I, sir—

BLOUNT Or I ? Shall I put you up at the clubs?°

SHARP You will want a man of business. I transacted all Mr Mordaunt's affairs.

SIR JOHN Tush, tush! Mr Evelyn is at home *here*. Always looked on him as a son! Nothing in the world we would not do for him! Nothing!

EVELYN Lend me ten pounds for my old nurse!
    Chorus put their hands into their pockets

    [*Curtain*]°

2.1

An anteroom in Evelyn's new house. At one corner, behind a large screen, Mr Sharp writing at a desk, books and parchments before him. Mr Crimson, the portrait-painter; Mr Grab, the publisher; Mr MacStucco, the architect; Mr Tabouret, the upholsterer; Mr MacFinch, the silversmith; Mr Patent, the coachmaker; Mr Kite, the horse-dealer; and Mr Frantz, the tailor. Servants in livery cross to and fro the stage

PATENT (*to Frantz, showing a drawing*) Yes, sir; this is the Evelyn vis-à-vis! No one more the fashion than Mr Evelyn. Money makes the man,° sir.

FRANTZ But de tailor, de schneider,° make de gentleman! It is Mr Frantz, of St James's,° who take his measure and his cloth and who make de fine handsome noblemen and gentry, where de faders and de mutters make only de ugly little naked boys!

MACSTUCCO He's a mon o' teeste, Mr Evelyn. He taulks o' buying a veela, just to pool dune and build oop again. Ah, Mr MacFinch, a design for a piece of pleete, eh!

MACFINCH (*showing the drawing*) Yees, sir, the shield o' Alexander the Great, to hold ices and lemonade! It will coost two thousand pound!

MACSTUCCO And it's dirt cheap. Ye're Scotch, arn't ye?

MACFINCH Aberdounshire! Scraitch me and I'll scraitch you!°
Door at the back thrown open. Enter Evelyn

EVELYN A levee,° as usual. Good day. Ah, Tabouret, your designs for the draperies. Very well. And what do you want, Mr Crimson?

CRIMSON Sir, if you'd let me take your portrait, it would make my fortune. Everyone says you're the finest judge of paintings.

EVELYN Of paintings! paintings! Are you sure I'm a judge of paintings?

CRIMSON Oh, sir, didn't you buy the great Correggio° for four thousand pounds?

EVELYN True. I see. So four thousand pounds makes me an excellent judge of paintings. I'll call on you, Mr Crimson, good day. Mr Grab—oh, you're the publisher who once refused me five pounds for my poem? You are right, it was sad doggerel.

GRAB Doggerel! Mr Evelyn, it was sublime! But times were bad then.

EVELYN Very bad times with me.

GRAB But now, sir, if you give me the preference, I'll push it, sir, I'll
push it! I only publish for poets in high life, sir; and a gentleman of
your station ought to be pushed! Five hundred pounds for the
poem, sir!

EVELYN Five hundred pounds when I don't want it, where five
pounds once would have seemed a fortune.

> 'Now I am rich, what value in the lines!
> How the wit brightens,—how the sense refines!'
> *Turns to the rest, who surround him*

KITE Thirty young horses from Yorkshire, sir!

PATENT (*showing drawing*) The Evelyn vis-à-vis!

MACFINCH (*showing salver*) The Evelyn salver!

FRANTZ (*opening his bundle, and with dignity*) Sare, I have brought de
coat, de great Evelyn coat.

EVELYN Oh, go to, that is, go home! Make me as celebrated for vis-à-
vis, salvers, furniture and coats, as I already am for painting and
shortly shall be for poetry. I resign myself to you. Go!

> *Exeunt Grab, Frantz, Kite, MacFinch, MacStucco, Patent,*
> *Tabouret, Crimson. Enter Stout*

EVELYN Stout, you look heated!

STOUT I hear you have just bought the great Groginhole° property.

EVELYN It is true. Sharp says it's a bargain.

STOUT Well, my dear friend Hopkins, member for Groginhole, can't
live another month. But the interests of mankind forbid regret for
individuals! The patriot° Popkins intends to start for the boro'° the
instant Hopkins is dead!° Your interest° will secure his election!
Now is your time! Put yourself forward in the march of enlightenment! By all that is bigoted here comes Glossmore!

> *Enter Lord Glossmore; Sharp still at his desk*

GLOSSMORE So lucky to find you at home! Hopkins, of Groginhole, is
not long for this world. Popkins, the brewer, is already canvassing
underhand, so very ungentlemanlike! Keep your interest for young
Lord Cipher, a most valuable candidate. This is an awful moment:
the *Constitution* depends on his return! Vote for Cipher!

STOUT Popkins is your man!

EVELYN (*musingly*) Cipher and Popkins, Popkins and Cipher!
Enlightenment and Popkins, Cipher and the Constitution!° I *am*
puzzled! Stout, I am not known at Groginhole.

STOUT Your *property*'s known there!

EVELYN But purity of election, independence of votes—

19

STOUT To be sure: Cipher bribes *abominably*. Frustrate his schemes, preserve the liberties of the borough, turn every man out of his house° who votes against enlightenment and Popkins!

EVELYN Right! Down with those who take the liberty to admire any liberty except *our* liberty! That *is* liberty!   70

GLOSSMORE Cipher has a stake in the country, will have fifty thousand pounds a year. Cipher will never give a vote without considering beforehand how people of fifty thousand pounds a year will be affected by the motion.

EVELYN Right. For, as without law there would be no property, so to   75
be the law for property is the only proper property of law! That *is* law!

STOUT Popkins is all for economy. There's a sad waste of the public money. They give the Speaker° five thousand pounds a year, when I've a brother-in-law who takes the chair at the vestry and who   80
assures me confidentially he'd consent to be Speaker for half the money!

GLOSSMORE Enough, Mr Stout. Mr Evelyn has too much at stake for a leveller.°

STOUT And too much sense for a bigot.   85

EVELYN Mr Evelyn has no politics at all! Did you ever play at *battledore?*°

BOTH Battledore?

EVELYN Battledore! That is a contest between two parties. Both parties knock about something with singular skill, something is kept   90
up, high, low, here, there, everywhere, nowhere! How grave are the players! How anxious the bystanders! How noisy the battledores! But when this something falls to the ground, only fancy; it's nothing but cork and feather! Go, and play by yourselves, I'm no hand at it!   95

STOUT (*aside*) Sad ignorance! Aristocrat!

GLOSSMORE [*aside*] Heartless principles! Parvenu!

STOUT Then you don't go *against* us? I'll bring Popkins tomorrow.

GLOSSMORE Keep yourself free till I present Cipher to you.

STOUT I must go to inquire after Hopkins. The return of Popkins will   100
be an era in history.
    Exit Stout

GLOSSMORE I must be off to the club. The eyes of the country are upon Groginhole. If Cipher fail, the constitution is gone!
    Exit Lord Glossmore

EVELYN Both sides alike! Money *versus* Man! Sharp, come here. Let

me look at you! You are my agent, my lawyer, my man of business. I   105
believe you honest. But what *is* honesty? Where does it exist? In
what part of us?

SHARP In the heart, I suppose, sir.

EVELYN Mr Sharp, it exists in the breeches' pocket! Observe, I lay
this piece of yellow earth° on the table, I contemplate you both; the   110
man there, the gold here! Now, there is many a man in those streets
honest as you are, who moves, thinks, feels and reasons as well as we
do; excellent in form,° imperishable in soul; who, if his pockets
were three days empty, would sell thought, reason, body and soul
too, for that little coin! Is that the fault of the man? No! it is the   115
fault of mankind! God made man. Behold what mankind have
made a god! When I was poor I hated the world. Now I am rich I
despise it! Fools, knaves, hypocrites! By the by, Sharp, send a hundred pounds to the poor bricklayer whose house was burnt down
yesterday.   120

    Enter Graves

Ah, Graves, my dear friend! What a world this is! A cur of a world,
that fawns on its master and bites the beggar! Ha! ha! It fawns on
me now, for the beggar has bought the cur!

GRAVES It is an atrocious world! But astronomers say that there is a
travelling comet which must set it on fire one day, and that's some   125
comfort!

EVELYN Every hour brings its gloomy lesson. The temper sours, the
affections wither, the heart hardens into stone! Zounds, Sharp!
What do you stand gaping there for? Have you no bowels?° Why
don't you go and see to the bricklayer?   130

    Exit Sharp

EVELYN Graves, of all my new friends—and their name is legion—
you are the only one I esteem; there is sympathy between us, we
take the same views of life. I am cordially glad to see you!

GRAVES (*groaning*) Ah! Why should you be glad to see a man so
miserable?   135

EVELYN Because I am miserable myself!

GRAVES You! Pshaw! *You* have not been condemned to lose a wife!

EVELYN But, plague on it, man, I may be condemned to take one! Sit
down and listen. I want a confidant! Left fatherless, when yet a boy,
my poor mother grudged herself food to give me education. Some-   140
one had told her that learning was better than house and land.
That's a lie, Graves.

GRAVES A scandalous lie, Evelyn!

EVELYN On the strength of that lie I was put to school, sent to college,
a sizar.° Do you know what a sizar is? In pride he is a gentleman, in   145
knowledge he is a scholar and he crawls about, amidst gentlemen
and scholars, with the livery of a pauper on his back! I carried off
the great prizes, I became distinguished, I looked to a high degree,
leading to a fellowship; that is, an independence for myself, a home
for my mother. One day a young lord insulted me, I retorted, he   150
struck me, refused apology, refused redress. I was a sizar! A pariah!
A thing to *be* struck! Sir, I was at least a man and I horsewhipped
him in the hall before the eyes of the whole college! A few days and
the lord's chastisement was forgotten. The next day the sizar was
expelled, the career of a life blasted. That is the difference between   155
rich and poor. It takes a whirlwind to move the one, a breath may
uproot the other! I came to London. As long as my mother lived I
had one to toil for; and I did toil, did hope, did struggle to be
something yet. She died and then, somehow, my spirit broke. I
resigned myself to my fate. The Alps above me seemed too high to   160
ascend. I ceased to care what became of me. At last I submitted to
be the poor relation, the hanger-on and gentleman-lackey of Sir
John Vesey. But I had an object in that. There was one in that house
whom I had loved at the first sight.

GRAVES And were you loved again?   165

EVELYN I fancied it and was deceived. Not an hour before I inherited
this mighty wealth, I confessed my love and was rejected because I
was poor. Now, mark: You remember the letter which Sharp gave
me when the will was read?

GRAVES Perfectly. What were the contents?   170

EVELYN After hints, cautions and admonitions, half in irony, half
in earnest (Ah, poor Mordaunt had known the world!), it
proceeded—but I'll read it to you: [*Reads letter*] 'Having selected
you as my heir, because I think money a trust to be placed where it
seems likely to be best employed, I now—not impose a condition,   175
but ask a favour. If you have formed no other and insuperable
attachment, I could wish to suggest your choice. My two nearest
female relations are my niece Georgina and my third cousin, Clara
Douglas, the daughter of a once dear friend. If you could see in
either of these one whom you could make your wife, such would be   180
a marriage that, if I live long enough to return to England, I would
seek to bring about before I die.' My friend, this is not a legal
condition, the fortune does not *rest* on it. Yet, need I say that my
gratitude considers it a moral obligation? Several months have

22

elapsed since thus called upon. I ought now to decide. You hear the   185
names. Clara Douglas is the woman who rejected me!

GRAVES But now she would accept you!

EVELYN And do you think I am so base a slave to passion that I would
owe to my gold what was denied to my affection?

GRAVES But you must choose one, in common gratitude. You *ought* to   190
do so, yes, there you are right. Besides, you are constantly at the
house. The world observes it. You must have raised hopes in one of
the girls. Yes, it is time to decide between her whom you love and
her whom you do not!

EVELYN Of the two, then, I would rather marry where I should exact   195
the least. A marriage, to which each can bring sober esteem and
calm regard, may not be happiness, but it may be content. But to
marry one whom you could adore and whose heart is closed to you,
to yearn for the treasure and only to claim the casket, to worship the
statue that you never may warm to life, oh, such a marriage would   200
be a hell the more terrible because paradise was in sight.

GRAVES Georgina is pretty, but vain and frivolous. (*Aside*) But he has
no right to be fastidious. He has never known Maria! (*Aloud*) Yes,
my dear friend, now I think on it, you *will* be as wretched as myself!
When you are married we will mingle our groans together!   205

EVELYN You may misjudge Georgina. She may have a nobler nature
than appears on the surface. On the day, but before the hour, in
which the will was read, a letter, in a strange or disguised hand,
signed 'From an unknown friend to Alfred Evelyn', and enclosing
what to a girl would have been a considerable sum, was sent to a   210
poor woman for whom I had implored charity and whose address I
had given only to Georgina.

GRAVES Why not assure yourself?

EVELYN Because I have not dared. For sometimes, against my reason,
I have hoped that it might be Clara! (*Taking a letter from his bosom*   215
and looking at it) No, I can't recognise the hand. Graves, I detest
that girl!

GRAVES Who? Georgina?

EVELYN No. Clara! But I've already, thank heaven, taken some
revenge upon her. Come nearer. (*Whispers*) I've bribed Sharp to say   220
that Mordaunt's letter to me contained a codicil leaving Clara
Douglas twenty thousand pounds.

GRAVES And didn't it? How odd, then, not to have mentioned her in
his will.

EVELYN One of his caprices. Besides, Sir John wrote him word that   225

Lady Franklin had adopted her. But I'm glad of it. I've paid the money. She's no more a dependant. No one can insult her now. She owes it all to me and does not guess it, man, does not guess it! Owes it to me, me whom she rejected, me, the poor scholar! Ha! ha! There's some spite in that, eh?   230

GRAVES You're a fine fellow, Evelyn, and we understand each other. Perhaps Clara may have seen the address and dictated this letter after all!

EVELYN Do you think so? I'll go to the house this instant!

GRAVES Eh? Humph! Then I'll go with you. That Lady Franklin is a   235
fine woman! If she were not so gay, I think I could—

EVELYN No, no. Don't think any such thing. Women are even worse than men.

GRAVES True. To love is a boy's madness!

EVELYN To feel is to suffer!   240

GRAVES To hope is to be deceived.

EVELYN I have done with romance!

GRAVES Mine is buried with Maria!

EVELYN If Clara did but write this!—

GRAVES Make haste, or Lady Franklin will be out!—A vale of tears, a   245
vale of tears!

EVELYN A vale of tears, indeed!

Exeunt Graves, Evelyn. Re-enter Graves for his hat

GRAVES And I left my hat behind me! Just like my luck! If I had been bred a hatter, little boys would have come into the world without heads.

Exit Graves

[*Curtain*]

2.2

Drawing-rooms at Sir John Vesey's, as in 1.

Lady Franklin, Clara, Servant

LADY FRANKLIN Past two and I have so many places to go to. Tell Philipps I want the carriage directly, instantly.

SERVANT I beg pardon, my lady. Philipps told me to say the young horse had fallen lame and could not be used today.

Exit Servant

LADY FRANKLIN Well, on second thoughts, that is lucky. Now I have   5
an excuse for not making a great many tedious visits. I must borrow
Sir John's horses for the ball tonight. Oh, Clara, you must see my
new turban from Carson's; the prettiest thing in the world, and so
becoming!

CLARA Ah, Lady Franklin, you'll be so sorry, but—but—   10

LADY FRANKLIN But what?

CLARA Such a misfortune! Poor Smith is in tears. I promised to break
it to you. Your little Charley had been writing his copy and spilt the
ink on the table; and Smith, not seeing it and taking out the turban
to put the pearls in it as you desired, she—she—   15

LADY FRANKLIN Ha! ha! Laid it on the table and the ink spoilt it. Ha!
ha! How well I can fancy the face she made! Seriously, on the
whole, it is fortunate, for I think I look best, after all, in the black
hat and feathers.

CLARA Dear Lady Franklin, you really have the sweetest temper!   20

LADY FRANKLIN I hope so, for it's the most becoming turban a
woman can wear! Think of that when you marry. Oh, talking of
marriage, I've certainly made a conquest of Mr Graves.

CLARA Mr Graves! I thought he was inconsolable.

LADY FRANKLIN For his sainted Maria! Poor man! Not contented   25
with plaguing him while she lived, she must needs haunt him now
she is dead.

CLARA But why does he regret her?   *satirical.*

LADY FRANKLIN Why? Because he has everything to make him
happy. Easy fortune, good health, respectable character. And since   30
it is his delight to be miserable, he takes the only excuse the world
will allow him. For the rest, it's the way with widowers, that is,
whenever they mean to marry again. But, my dear Clara, you seem
absent, pale, unhappy; tears too?

CLARA No, no; not tears. No!   35

LADY FRANKLIN Ever since Mr Mordaunt left you twenty thousand pounds everyone admires you. Sir Frederick is desperately
smitten.

CLARA (with disdain) Sir Frederick!

LADY FRANKLIN Ah! Clara, be comforted. I know your secret. I am   40
certain that Evelyn loves you.

CLARA He did. It is past now. He misconceived me when he was poor
and, now he is rich, it is not for me to explain.

LADY FRANKLIN My dear child, happiness is too rare to be sacrificed
to a scruple. Why does he come here so often?   45

confusion - source of comedy

CLARA Perhaps for Georgina!

> *Enter Sir John Vesey and turns over the books etc., on the table,*
> *as if to look for the newspaper*

LADY FRANKLIN Pooh! Georgina is my niece. She is handsome and accomplished, but her father's worldliness has spoilt her nature. She is not worthy of Evelyn! Behind the humour of his irony there is something noble, something that may yet be great. For his sake as well as yours, let me at least— 50

CLARA Recommend me to his pity! Ah, Lady Franklin! If he addressed me from dictation, I should again refuse him. No, if he cannot read my heart, if he will not *seek* to read it, let it break unknown.

LADY FRANKLIN You mistake me, my dear child. Let me only tell him that you dictated that letter, that you sent that money to his old nurse. Poor Clara! It was your little all. He will then know, at least, if avarice be your sin. 55

CLARA He would have guessed it, had *his* love been like *mine*.

LADY FRANKLIN Guessed it? Nonsense! The handwriting unknown to him, every reason to think it came from Georgina. 60

SIR JOHN (*aside*) Hum! Came from Georgina!

LADY FRANKLIN Come, *let* me tell him *this*. I know the effect it would have upon his choice.

CLARA Choice! Oh, that humiliating word! No, Lady Franklin, no! Promise me! 65

LADY FRANKLIN But—

CLARA No! Promise. Faithfully, sacredly.

LADY FRANKLIN Well, I promise.

CLARA You know how fearful is my character. No infant is more timid. If a poor spider cross the floor, you often laugh to see me grow pale and tremble; and yet I would lay this hand upon the block, I would walk barefoot over the ploughshare of the old ordeal° to save Alfred Evelyn one moment's pain. But I have refused to share his poverty and I should die with shame if he thought I had now grown enamoured of his wealth. My kind friend, you will keep your promise? 70 75

LADY FRANKLIN Yes, since it must be so.

CLARA Thanks. I—I—forgive me—I am not well.

> *Exit Clara*

LADY FRANKLIN What fools these girls are! They take as much pains to lose a husband as a poor widow does to get one! 80

SIR JOHN Have you seen the *Times* newspaper? Where the deuce is the newspaper? I can't find the *Times* newspaper!

LADY FRANKLIN I think it is in my room. Shall I fetch it?

SIR JOHN My dear sister. You're the best creature. Do!   85

    Exit Lady Franklin

Ugh! You unnatural conspirator against your own family! What
can this *letter* be? Ah! I recollect something.

    Enter Georgina

GEORGINA Papa, I want—

SIR JOHN Yes, I know what you want well enough! Tell me, were you
aware that Clara had sent money to that old nurse Evelyn bored us   90
about the day of the will?

GEORGINA No! He gave me the address, and I promised, if—

SIR JOHN Gave you the *address*? That's lucky! Hush!

    Enter Servant

SERVANT Mr Graves, Mr Evelyn.

    Enter Graves and Evelyn. Exit Servant

LADY FRANKLIN (*returning*) Here is the newspaper.   95

GRAVES Ay, read the newspapers! They'll tell you what this world is
made of. Daily calendars of roguery and woe! Here, advertisements
from quacks, money-lenders, cheap warehouses and spotted boys
with two heads. So much for dupes and impostors! Turn to the
other column, police reports, bankruptcies, swindling, forgery and   100
a biographical sketch of the snub-nosed man who murdered his
own three little cherubs at Pentonville.° Do you fancy these but
exceptions to the *general* virtue and health of the nation? Turn to
the leading article and your hair will stand on end at the horrible
wickedness or melancholy idiotism of that half of the population   105
who think differently from yourself. In my day I have seen already
eighteen crises,° six annihilations of agriculture and commerce,
four overthrows of the Church and three last, final, awful and
irremediable destructions of the entire Constitution!° And that's a
newspaper!   110

LADY FRANKLIN Ha! ha! Your usual vein! Always so amusing and
good-humoured!

GRAVES (*frowning and very angry*) Ma'am, good-humoured!

LADY FRANKLIN Ah! You should always wear that agreeable smile.
You look so much younger, so much handsomer, when you smile!   115

GRAVES (*softened*) Ma'am—[*Aside*] A charming creature, upon my
word!

LADY FRANKLIN You have not seen the last H.B.? It is excellent. I
think it might make you *laugh*. But, by the by, I don't think you can
laugh.   120

27

GRAVES Ma'am, I have not laughed since the death of my sainted Ma—

LADY FRANKLIN Ah! and that spiteful Sir Frederick says you never laugh, because—But you'll be angry?

GRAVES Angry! Pooh! I despise Sir Frederick too much to let any-   125
thing he says have the smallest influence over me! He says I don't laugh, because—

LADY FRANKLIN You have lost your front teeth!

GRAVES Lost my front teeth! Upon my word! Ha! ha! ha! That's too good. Capital! Ha! ha! ha! (*Laughing from ear to ear*)   130

LADY FRANKLIN Ha! ha! ha!

> *Graves and Lady Franklin retire to the table in the inner drawing-room*

EVELYN (*aside*) Of course Clara will not appear! Avoids me as usual! But what do I care? What is she to me? Nothing! I'll swear this is her glove! No one else has so small a hand. She'll miss it—so—so! Nobody's looking. I'll keep it, just to vex her.   135

SIR JOHN (*to Georgina*) Yes, yes, leave me to manage. You took his portrait, as I told you.

GEORGINA Yes, but I could not catch the expression. I got Clara to touch it up.

SIR JOHN That girl's always in the way!   140

> *Enter Captain Dudley Smooth*

SMOOTH Good morning, dear John. Ah, Miss Vesey, you have no idea of the conquests you made at Almack's° last night!

EVELYN (*examining him curiously while Smooth is talking to Georgina*) And that's the celebrated Dudley Smooth!

SIR JOHN More commonly called Deadly Smooth! The finest player   145
at whist, écarté,° billiards, chess and piquet,° between this and the Pyramids. The sweetest manners! Always calls you by your Christian name. But take care how you play at cards with him!

EVELYN He does not cheat, I suppose?

SIR JOHN Hist! *No!* But he always *wins*! Eats up a brace of lords and a   150
score or two of guardsmen every season and runs through a man's fortune like a course of the Carlsbad° waters. He's an uncommonly clever fellow!

EVELYN Clever? Yes! When a man steals a loaf, we cry down the knavery. When a man diverts his neighbour's mill-stream to grind   155
his own corn, we cry up the cleverness! And everyone courts Captain Dudley Smooth!

SIR JOHN Why, who could offend him? The best-bred, civilest

creature—and a dead shot! There is not a cleverer man in the three
kingdoms.   160

EVELYN A study, a study! Let me examine him! Such men are living
satires on the world.

SMOOTH (*passing his arm caressingly over Sir John's shoulder*) My dear
John, how well you are looking! A new lease of life! Introduce me to
Mr Evelyn.   165

EVELYN Sir, it's an honour I've long ardently desired.

> *Evelyn and Smooth bow and shake hands. Enter Sir Frederick*
> *Blount*

BLOUNT How d'ye do, Sir John. Ah, Evelyn, I wished so much to see
you!

EVELYN 'Tis my misfortune to be so visible!

BLOUNT A little this way. You know, perhaps, that I once paid my   170
addwesses to Miss Vesey; but since that vewy eccentwic will Sir
John has shuffled me off and hints at a pwior attachment—(*aside*)
which I know to be false.

EVELYN A prior attachment!

> *Enter Clara*

[*Evelyn sees her; aside*] Ha! Clara! [*Aloud*] Well, another time, my   175
dear Blount.

BLOUNT Stay a moment. I want you to do me a favour with regard to
Miss Douglas!

EVELYN Miss Douglas!

BLOUNT Yes. You see, though Georgina has great expectations and   180
Stingy Jack will leave her all that he has, yet she has only her legacy
of ten thousand pounds at the moment; no doubt closely settled on
herself too. Clawa has twenty thousand pounds. And, I think,
Clawa always liked me a little.

EVELYN You! I dare say she did!   185

BLOUNT It is whispered about that you mean to pwopose to Georgina. Nay, Sir John more than hinted that was her pwior
attachment!

EVELYN Indeed!

BLOUNT Now, as you are all in all with the family, if you could say a   190
word for me to Miss Douglas, I don't see what harm it could do me!
(*Aside*) I will punish Georgina for her pwerfidy.

EVELYN 'Sdeath, man! Speak for yourself! You are just the sort of
man for young ladies to like. They understand you. You're of their
own level. Pshaw! You're too modest. You want no mediator!   195

BLOUNT My dear fellow, you flatter me. I'm well enough in my way.

But you, you know, would cawwy evewything before you! You're so
confoundedly wich!

EVELYN (*turning to Clara*) Miss Douglas, what do you think of Sir
Frederick Blount? Observe him. He is well dressed, young, toler-   200
ably handsome (*Blount bowing*), bows with an air, has plenty of
small talk, everything to captivate. Yet he thinks that if he and I
were suitors to the same lady, I should be more successful because I
am richer? What say you? Is love an auction? And *do* women's
hearts go to the highest bidder?   205

CLARA   Their hearts? No!

EVELYN   But their hands, yes! You turn away. Ah, you dare not answer
that question!

GEORGINA (*aside*) Sir Frederick flirting with Clara? I'll punish him
for his perfidy. [*Aloud*] *You* are the last person to talk so, Mr Eve-   210
lyn! You, whose wealth is your smallest attraction. You, whom
everyone admires; so witty, such taste, such talent! Ah, I'm very
foolish!

SIR JOHN (*clapping him on the shoulder*) You must not turn my little
girl's head. Oh, you're a sad fellow! Apropos, I must show you   215
Georgina's last drawings. She has wonderfully improved since you
gave her lessons in perspective.

GEORGINA   No, Papa. No! Pray, no! Nay, don't!

SIR JOHN   Nonsense, child! It's very odd, but she's more afraid of *you*
than of anyone!   220

SMOOTH (*to Blount, taking snuff*) He's an excellent father, our dear
John, and supplies the place of a mother to her.

> Turns away to Lady Franklin and Graves. Eveyln and
> Georgina seat themselves and look over the drawings; Sir John
> leans over them; Sir Frederick converses with Clara, Evelyn
> watching them

EVELYN   Beautiful! A view from Tivoli.° [*Aside*] Death! She looks
down while he speaks to her! [*Aloud*] Is there a little fault in that
colouring? [*Aside*] She positively blushes! [*Aloud*] But this Jupiter is   225
superb. [*Aside*] What a damned° coxcomb it is! (*Rising*) Oh, she
certainly loves him. I, too, can be loved elsewhere. I, too, can see
smiles and blushes on the face of another!

GEORGINA   Are you not well?

EVELYN   I beg pardon. Yes, you are indeed improved! Ah, who's so   230
accomplished as Miss Vesey?

> Takes up the drawings. Pays her marked attention in dumb show°

CLARA   Yes, Sir Frederick, the concert was very crowded! [*Aside*] Ah, I

[handwritten: comedy in the Lords]

see that Georgina consoles him for the past! He has only praises for her, nothing but taunts for me!

BLOUNT I wish you would take my opewa-box next Saturday. 'Tis the best in the house. I'm not wich, but I spend what I have on myself! I make a point to have evewything the best in a quiet way. Best opewa-box, best dogs, best horses, best house of its kind. I want nothing to complete my estabishment but the best wife! 235

CLARA (*abstractedly*) That will come in good time, Sir Frederick. 240

EVELYN [*aside*] Oh, it will come, will it? Georgina refused the trifler. *She* courts him. (*Taking up a portrait; [aloud]*) Why, what is this? My own—

GEORGINA You must not look at that, you must not indeed. I did not know it was there! 245

SIR JOHN Your own portrait, Evelyn. Why, child! I was not aware you took likenesses? That's something new! Upon my word, it's a strong resemblance.

GEORGINA Oh, no. It does not do him justice. Give it to me. I will tear it. (*Aside*) That odious Sir Frederick! 250

EVELYN Nay, you shall not.

CLARA So, so, he loves her then! Misery, misery! But he shall not perceive it! No, no, I can be proud, too. Ha! ha! Sir Frederick, excellent, excellent, you are so entertaining. Ha! ha! (*Laughs hysterically*) 255

EVELYN Oh, the affectation of coquettes. They cannot even laugh naturally! *[handwritten: → provoking them in situation]*

> Clara looks at him reproachfully and walks aside
> with Sir Frederick

But where is the new guitar you meant to buy, Miss Vesey? The one inlaid with tortoiseshell? It is near a year since you set your heart on it and I don't see it yet! 260

SIR JOHN (*taking him aside confidentially*) The guitar—Oh, to tell you a secret: She applied the money I gave her for it to a case of charity several months ago, the very day the will was read. I saw the letter lying on the table, with the money in it. Mind, not a word to her. She'd never forgive me! 265

[handwritten: planting the scheme to assure Georgias success]

EVELYN Letter! Money! What was the name of the person she relieved? Not Stanton?

SIR JOHN I don't remember indeed.

EVELYN (*taking out the letter*) This is not her hand!

SIR JOHN No! I observed at the time it was not her hand, but I got out from her that she did not wish the thing to be *known* and had 270 employed someone else to copy it. May I see the letter? Yes, I think this is the wording. But I did not mean to tell you what case of charity it was. I promised Georgy I would not. Still, how did she know Mrs Stanton's address? You never gave it to me!   275

EVELYN I gave it to her, Sir John.

CLARA (*at a distance*) Yes, I'll go to the opera, if Lady Franklin will. Do go, dear Lady Franklin! On Saturday, then, Sir Frederick.

EVELYN Sir John, to a man like me, this simple act of unostentatious generosity is worth all the accomplishments in the world. A good   280 heart, a tender disposition, a charity that shuns the day, a modesty that blushes at its own excellence, an impulse towards something more divine than Mammon: Such are the true accomplishments which preserve beauty forever young. Such I have sought in the partner I would take for life. Such I have found, alas, not where I   285 had dreamed! Miss Vesey, I will be honest. I say, then, frankly—(*as Clara approaches, raising his voice and looking fixedly at her*) I have loved another, deeply, truly, bitterly, *vainly*! I cannot offer to you, as I did to her, the fair first love of the human heart, rich with all its blossoms and its verdure. But if esteem, if gratitude, if an earnest   290 resolve to conquer every recollection that would wander from your image; if these can tempt you to accept my hand and fortune, my life shall be a study to deserve your confidence.

    Clara stands motionless, clasping her hands, and then
    slowly seats herself

SIR JOHN The happiest day of my life!

    Clara falls back in her chair

EVELYN (*darting forward; aside*) She is pale. She faints! What have I   295 done? Oh, heaven! Clara!

CLARA (*rising with a smile*) Be happy, my cousin, be happy! Yes, with my whole heart I say it: Be happy, Alfred Evelyn!

[*Curtain*]

3.1

The drawing-rooms in Sir John Vesey's house

Sir John Vesey, Georgina

SIR JOHN And he has not pressed you to fix the wedding-day?

GEORGINA No; and since he proposed he comes here so seldom and
seems so gloomy. Heigho! Poor Sir Frederick was twenty times
more amusing.

SIR JOHN But Evelyn is fifty times as rich!   5

GEORGINA Sir Frederick *dresses* so well!

SIR JOHN You'll have magnificent diamonds! But a word with you: I
saw you yesterday in the square with Sir Frederick; that must not
happen again. When a young lady is engaged to one man, nothing
is so indecorous as to flirt with another. It might endanger your   10
marriage itself. Oh, it's highly indecorous!

GEORGINA Don't be afraid, Papa—he takes up with Clara.

SIR JOHN Who? Evelyn?

GEORGINA Sir Frederick. Heigho!—I hate artful girls.

SIR JOHN The settlements will be splendid! If anything happens,   15
nothing can be handsomer than your jointure.°

GEORGINA My own kind Papa, you always put things so pleasantly.
But do you not fear lest he discover that Clara wrote the letter?

SIR JOHN No; and I shall get Clara out of the house. But there is
something else that makes me very uneasy. You know that no   20
sooner did Evelyn come into possession of his fortune than he
launched out in the style of a prince. His house in London is a
palace, and he has bought a great estate in the country. Look how
he lives! Balls, banquets, fine arts, fiddlers, charities, and the devil
to pay!   25

GEORGINA But if he can afford it—

SIR JOHN Oh, so long as he stopped *there*, I had no apprehension; but
since he proposed for you he is more extravagant than ever. They
say he has taken to gambling, and he is always with Captain
Smooth. No fortune can stand deadly Smooth! If he gets into a   30
scrape he may fall off from the settlements.° We must press the
marriage at once.

GEORGINA Heigho! Poor Frederick! You don't think he is *really*
attached to Clara?

SIR JOHN Upon my word I can't say. Put on your bonnet and come to   35
Storr and Mortimer's to choose the jewels.

GEORGINA The jewels!—Yes—The drive will do me good. So you'll
send away Clara?—She's so very deceitful.

SIR JOHN Never fear.—Yes—Tell her to come to me.

Exit Georgina

Yes, I must press on this marriage. Georgina has not wit enough to   40
manage him—at least till he's her husband, and then all women
find it smooth sailing. This match will make me a man of prodigious importance! I suspect he'll give me up her ten thousand
pounds. I can't think of his taking to gambling, for I love him as a
son—and I look on his money as my own.   45

Enter Clara

SIR JOHN Clara, my love!

CLARA Sir—

SIR JOHN My dear, what I am going to say may appear a little rude
and unkind, but you know my character is frankness. To the point,
then. My poor child, I'm aware of your attachment to Mr Evelyn—   50

CLARA Sir! *My attachment?*

SIR JOHN It is generally remarked. Lady Kind says you are falling
away.° My poor girl, I pity you. I do indeed! Now, there's that letter
you wrote to his old nurse. It has got about somehow, and the world
is so ill-natured. I don't know if I did right; but, after he had   55
proposed to Georgy—of course not before!—I thought it so
unpleasant for you, as a young lady, to be suspected of anything
forward with respect to a man who was not attached to you, that I
rather let it be supposed that Georgy *herself* wrote the letter.

CLARA Sir, I don't know what right you had to—   60

SIR JOHN That's very true, my dear; and I've been thinking since
that I ought perhaps to tell Mr Evelyn that the letter was yours.
Shall I?

CLARA No, sir. I beg you will not. I—I—° (*Weeps*)

SIR JOHN My dear Clara, don't take on. I would not have said this for   65
the world, if I was not a little anxious about my own girl. Georgina
is so unhappy at what everyone says of your attachment—

CLARA Everyone? Oh, torture!

SIR JOHN That it preys on her spirits. It even irritates her temper!
You see, though the marriage will take place almost immediately,   70
Mr Evelyn does not come so often as he ought. In a word, I fear
these little jealousies and suspicions will tend to embitter their
future union. I'm a father, forgive me.

CLARA Embitter their union! Oh, never! What would you have me do, sir?   75

SIR JOHN Why, you're now independent. Lady Franklin seems resolved to stay in town. Surely she can't mean to take her money out of the family by some foolish inclination for Mr Graves! He's always purring and whining about the house, like a black cat in the megrims.° What think you, eh?   80

CLARA Sir, it was of myself, my unhappy self, you were speaking.

SIR JOHN [aside] Sly! [Aloud] True, true! What I meant to say was this. Lady Franklin persists in staying here. You are your own mistress. Mrs Carlton, aunt to my late wife, is going abroad for a short time and would be delighted if you would accompany her.   85

CLARA It is the very favour I would have asked of you. (Aside) I shall escape at least the struggle and the shame. [Aloud] When does she go?

SIR JOHN In five days. Next Monday. You forgive me?

CLARA Sir, I thank you.   90

SIR JOHN (drawing the table) Suppose, then, you write a line to her yourself and settle it at once?

Enter Servant

SERVANT The carriage, Sir John. Miss Vesey is quite ready.

SIR JOHN Wait a moment. Shall I tell Evelyn you wrote the letter?

CLARA No, sir, I implore you.   95

SIR JOHN But it would be awkward for Georgy, if discovered.

CLARA It never shall be.

SIR JOHN Well, well, as you please. I know nothing could be so painful to a young lady of pride and delicacy. James, if Mr Serious, the clergyman, calls, say I am gone to the great meeting at Exeter Hall.° If Lord Spruce calls, say you believe I'm gone to the   100
rehearsal° of Cinderella.° Oh, and if MacFinch should come—MacFinch, who duns me three times a week—say I've hurried off to Garraway's° to bid for the great Bulstrode estate. Just put the Duke of Lofty's card° carelessly on the hall table. And, I say, James,   105
I expect two gentlemen a little before dinner; Mr Squab, the radical, and Mr Qualm of the great Marylebone Conservative Association.° Show Squab into the study and be sure to give him the Weekly True Sun, Qualm into the back parlour with The Times and the Morning Post.° One must have a little management   110
in this world. All humbug! All humbug, upon my soul!

Exeunt Sir John Vesey and Servant

CLARA (folding the letter) There, it is decided! A few days and we are parted forever! A few weeks and another will bear his name, his wife! Oh, happy fate! She will have the right to say to him, though the whole world should hear her, 'I am thine!' And I embitter their lot. I am the cloud upon their joyous sunshine! And yet, O Alfred, if she loves thee, if she knows thee, if she values thee and, when thou wrong'st her, if she can forgive, as I do, I can bless her, when far away, and join her name in my prayers for thee! 115

EVELYN (*offstage*) Miss Vesey just gone? Well, I will write a line. 120
    Enter Evelyn

EVELYN (*aside*) So, Clara! [*Aloud*] Do not let me disturb you, Miss Douglas.

CLARA (*going*) Nay, I have done.

EVELYN I see that my presence is always odious to you. It is a reason why I come so seldom. But be cheered, madam. I am here but to fix 125 the day of my marriage, and I shall then go into the country, till— till—In short, this is the last time my visit will banish you from the room I enter.

CLARA (*aside*) The last time! And we shall then meet no more! And to part thus forever, in scorn, in anger. I cannot bear it! (*Approaching 130 him.* [*Aloud*]) Alfred, my cousin, it is true this may be the last time we shall meet. I have made my arrangements to quit England.

EVELYN To quit England?

CLARA But, before I go, let me thank you for many a past kindness, which it is not for an orphan easily to forget. 135

EVELYN (*mechanically*) To quit England!

CLARA I have long wished it, but enough of me. Evelyn, now that you are betrothed to another; now, without recurring to the past; now, without the fear of mutual error and mistake; something of our old friendship may at least return to us. And if, too, I dared, I have that 140 on my mind which only a friend, a sister, might presume to say to you.

EVELYN (*moved*) Miss Douglas, Clara, if there is aught I could do. If, while hundreds, strangers, beggars, tell me that I have the power, by opening or shutting this worthless hand, to bid sorrow rejoice or 145 poverty despair; if—if my life, my heart's blood, could render to *you* one such service as my gold can give to others—why, speak! And the past you allude to, yes, even that bitter past, I will cancel and forget!

CLARA (*holding out her hand*) We are friends, then! You are again my 150 cousin! My brother!

EVELYN (*dropping her hand*) Brother! Ah! Say on!

CLARA I speak, then, as a sister—herself weak, inexperienced, ignorant, nothing—*might* speak to a brother, in whose career she felt the
ambition of a man. Oh, Evelyn! When you inherited this vast   155
wealth I pleased myself with imagining how you would wield the
power delegated to your hands. I knew your benevolence, your
intellect, your genius! The ardent mind couched beneath the cold
sarcasm of a long-baffled spirit!° I saw before me the noble and
bright career open to you at last, and I often thought that, in after   160
years, when far away—as I soon shall be—I should hear your name
identified, not with what fortune can give the base, but with deeds
and ends to which, for the *great*, fortune is but the instrument. I
often thought that I should say to my own heart, weeping proud
and delicious tears: 'And once this man loved me!'   165

EVELYN No more, Clara! Oh, heavens! No more!

CLARA But *has* it been so? Have you been true to your own self?
Pomp, parade, luxuries, pleasures, follies! All these might dis-
tinguish others, they do but belie the ambition and the soul of
Alfred Evelyn! Oh, pardon me. I am too bold. I pain, I offend you.   170
Ah, I should not have dared thus much had I not thought, at times,
that—that—

EVELYN That these follies, these vanities, this dalliance with a loftier
fate, were your own work! You thought that, and you were right!
Perhaps, indeed, after a youth steeped to the lips in the hyssop and   175
gall° of penury; perhaps I might have wished royally to know the
full value of that dazzling and sterile life which, from the last step
in the ladder, I had seen indignantly and from afar. But a month, a
week, would have sufficed for that experience. Experience! Oh, how
soon we learn that hearts are as cold and souls as vile, no matter   180
whether the sun shine on the noble in his palace, or the rain drench
the rags of a beggar cowering at the porch. The extremes of life
differ but in this. Above, *vice* smiles and revels, below, *crime* frowns
and starves. But you, did not you reject me because I was poor?
Despise me if you please! My revenge might be unworthy. I wished   185
to show you the luxuries, the gaud,° the splendour I thought you
prized, to surround you with the attributes your sex seems most to
value the station that, had you loved me, it should have been yours
to command. But vain, vain alike my poverty and my wealth! You
loved me not in either and my fate is sealed!   190

CLARA A happy fate, Evelyn! You love!

EVELYN And at last I am beloved. (*After a pause and turning to her
abruptly*) Do you doubt it?

37

CLARA No, I believe it firmly! (*Aside*) Were it possible for her not to
love him?   195

EVELYN Georgina, perhaps, is vain and light and—

CLARA No, think it not! Once removed from the worldly atmosphere
of her father's counsels, and you will form and raise her to your
own level. She is so young yet. She has beauty, cheerfulness and
temper. The rest you will give, if you will but yet do justice to your   200
own nature. And now, that there is nothing unkind between us, not
even regret and surely (*with a smile*) not revenge, my cousin, you
will rise to your nobler self, and so, farewell!

EVELYN No, stay—one moment. You still feel interest in my fate!
Have I been deceived? Oh, why, why did you spurn the heart whose   205
offerings were lavished at your feet? Could you still—still—? Distraction, I know not what I say! My honour pledged to another, my
vows accepted and returned! Go, Clara, it is best so! Yet you will
miss someone, perhaps, more than me, someone to whose follies
you have been more indulgent, someone to whom you would   210
permit a yet tenderer name than that of brother!

CLARA (*aside*) It will make him, perhaps, happier to think it! [*Aloud*]
Think so, if you will! But part friends.

EVELYN Friends, and that is all! Look you, this is life! The eyes that
charmed away every sorrow, the hand whose lightest touch thrilled   215
to the very core, the presence that, like moonlight, shed its own
hallowing beauty over the meanest things; a little while, a year, a
month, a day and we smile that we could dream so idly. All, all, the
sweet enchantment, known but once, never to return again, vanished from the world! And the one who forgets the soonest, the one   220
who robs your earth forever of its summer, comes to you with a
careless lip, and says: 'Let us part friends!' Go, Clara, go, and be
happy if you can!

CLARA (*weeping*) Cruel, cruel, to the last! Heaven forgive you, Alfred!
      Exit Clara

EVELYN Soft! Let me recall her words, her tones, her looks. *Does she*   225
love me? She defends her rival. She did not deny it when I charged
her with attachment to another. And yet—and yet—there is a voice
at my heart which tells me I have been the rash slave of a jealous
anger. But I have made my choice. I must abide the issue!
      Enter Graves, preceded by Servant

SERVANT Lady Franklin is dressing, sir.   230

GRAVES Well, I'll wait.
      Exit Servant

She was worthy to have known the lost Maria! So considerate to ask me hither. Not to console me, *that* is impossible, but to indulge the luxury of woe. It will be a mournful scene. (*Seeing Evelyn*) Is that you, Evelyn? I have just heard that the borough of Groginhole is vacant at last. Why not stand yourself? With your property you might come in without even a personal canvass.   235

EVELYN I, who despise these contests for the colour of a straw, this everlasting litigation of authority *versus* man, I to be one of the wranglers? Never!   240

GRAVES You are quite right, and I beg your pardon.

EVELYN (*aside*) And yet Clara spoke of ambition. She would regret me if I could be distinguished. (*Aloud*) To be sure, after all, Graves, corrupt as mankind are, it is our duty to try at least to make them a little better. An Englishman owes something to his country.   245

GRAVES He does, indeed! (*Counting on his fingers*) East winds, fogs, rheumatism, pulmonary complaints and taxes—(*Evelyn walks about in disorder*) You seem agitated. A quarrel with your intended? Oh, when you've been married a month, you won't know what to do without one!   250

EVELYN You are a pleasant comforter.

GRAVES Do you deserve a comforter? One morning you tell me you love Clara, or at least detest her, which is the same thing (poor Maria often said she detested *me*), and that very afternoon you propose to Georgina!   255

EVELYN Clara will easily console herself, thanks to Sir Frederick!

GRAVES He is young!

EVELYN Good looking!

GRAVES A coxcomb!   260

EVELYN And therefore irresistible!

GRAVES Nevertheless Clara has had the bad taste to refuse him. I have it from Lady Franklin, to whom he confided his despair in re-arranging his neckcloth.

EVELYN My dear friend, is it possible?   265

GRAVES But what then? You *must* marry Georgina, who, to believe Lady Franklin, is sincerely attached to—your fortune. Go and hang yourself, Evelyn. You have been duped by them.

EVELYN By them, bah! If deceived, I have been my own dupe. Is it not a strange thing that in matters of reason, of the arithmetic and logic of life, we are sensible, shrewd, prudent men? But touch our hearts, move our passions, take us for an instant from the hard safety of   270

39

worldly calculation, and the philosopher is duller than the fool! *Duped*, if I thought it!

GRAVES To be sure! You tried Clara in your *poverty*. It was a safe experiment to try Georgina in your *wealth*.   275

EVELYN Ha! That is true, very true. Go on.

GRAVES You'll have an excellent father-in-law. Sir John positively weeps when he talks of your income!

EVELYN Sir John, possibly, but Georgina?   280

GRAVES Plays affection to you in the afternoon, after practising first with Sir Frederick in the morning.

EVELYN On your life, sir, be serious. What do you mean?

GRAVES That in passing this way I see her very often walking in the square with Sir Frederick.   285

EVELYN Ha! Say you so?

GRAVES What then? Man is born to be deceived. You look nervous, your hand trembles. That comes of gaming.° They say at the clubs that you play deeply.

EVELYN Ha! ha! Do they say that? A few hundreds lost or won, a   290 cheap opiate, anything that can lay the memory to sleep. The poor man drinks and the rich man gambles. The same motive to both! But you are right. It is a base resource. I will play no more.

GRAVES I am delighted to hear it, for your friend, Captain Smooth, has ruined half the young heirs in London. To play with him is to   295 advertise yourself a bankrupt. Even Sir John is alarmed. I met him just now in Pall Mall. He made me stop and implored me to speak to you. By the by, I forgot. Do you bank with Flash, Brisk, Credit and Co.?

EVELYN So, Sir John is alarmed? (*Aside*) Gulled by this cogging char-   300 latan? Aha! I may beat him yet at his own weapons! [*Aloud*] Humph! Bank with Flash! Why do you ask me?

GRAVES Because Sir John has just heard that they are in a very bad way and begs you to withdraw anything you have in their hands.

EVELYN I'll see to it. So Sir John is *alarmed* at my gambling?   305

GRAVES Terribly! He even told me he should go himself to the club, this evening, to watch you.

EVELYN To watch me! Good. I will be there.

GRAVES But you will promise not to play.

EVELYN Yes, to play. I feel it is impossible to give it up!   310

GRAVES No, no! 'Sdeath, man! Be as wretched as you please, break your heart, that's nothing! But damme, take care of your pockets!

EVELYN I will be there. I will play with Captain Smooth. I will lose as

[handwritten: planning on losing it all to make a point about there being more than money in society]

much as I please, thousands, millions, billions; and if he presume to
spy on my losses, hang me if I don't lose Sir John himself into the   315
bargain! (*Going and returning*) I am so absent!° What was the bank
you mentioned! Flash, Brisk and Credit. Bless me, how unlucky!
And it's too late to draw out today. Tell Sir John, I'm very much
obliged to him, and he'll find me at the club any time before day-
break hard at work with my friend Smooth!   320

    Exit Evelyn

GRAVES He's certainly crazy! But I don't wonder at it. What the
approach of the dog-days° is to the canine species, the approach of
the honeymoon is to the human race.

    Enter Servant

SERVANT Lady Franklin's compliments. She will see you in the
boudoir, sir.   325

GRAVES In the *boudoir*! Go, go. I'll come directly. — *[handwritten: comical given his outer appearance]*

    Exit Servant

My heart beats. It must be for grief. Poor Maria! (*Searching his
pockets for his handkerchief*) Not a white one, just like my luck. I call
on a lady to talk of the dear departed and I've nothing about me but
a cursed gaudy, flaunting, red, yellow and blue abomination from   330
India, which it's even indecent for a disconsolate widower to
exhibit. Ah! Fortune never ceases to torment the susceptible. The
boudoir! Aa! ha! The *boudoir*!

    Exit Graves   *[handwritten: → humourous climatic end to the scene]*

[*Curtain*]

3.2

    A boudoir in the same house

LADY FRANKLIN Now, if my scheme does but succeed! I can't help
laughing to think of it!—Mum!° Here he comes! *[handwritten: getting the better of the men]*

    Enter Graves

GRAVES (*sighing*) Ah, Lady Franklin!

LADY FRANKLIN (*sighing*) Ah, Mr Graves! (*They seat themselves*)
Pray excuse me for having kept you so long. Is it not a charming   5
day?

GRAVES An east wind, ma'am! But nothing comes amiss to you! It's a
happy disposition! Poor Maria! *She*, too, was naturally gay.

(margin handwritten note: indulging Graves' ego / note)

LADY FRANKLIN Yes, she was gay. So much life, and a great deal of spirit.   10

GRAVES Spirit? Yes! Nothing could master it. She *would* have her own way! Ah, there was nobody like her!

LADY FRANKLIN And then, when her spirit was up, she looked so handsome! Her eyes grew so brilliant!

GRAVES Did not they? Ah! ah! ha! ha! ha! And do you remember her   15
pretty trick of stamping her foot? The tiniest little foot. I think I see her now. Ah, this conversation is very soothing.

LADY FRANKLIN How well she acted in your private theatricals!

GRAVES You remember her Mrs Oakly in *The Jealous Wife*?° Ha! ha!
How good it was! Ha! ha!   20

LADY FRANKLIN Ha! ha! Yes, in the very first scene, when she came out with (*mimicking*) 'Your unkindness and barbarity will be the death of me!'°

GRAVES No, no! That's not it! More energy. (*Mimicking*) 'Your unkindness and barbarity will be the DEATH of me!' Ha! ha! I ought   25
to know how she said it, for she used to practise it on me twice a day. Ah! Poor dear lamb! (*Wipes his eyes*)

LADY FRANKLIN And then she sang so well! Was such a composer! What was that little French air she was so fond of?

GRAVES Ha! ha! Sprightly! Was it not? Let me see, let me see.   30

LADY FRANKLIN (*humming*) Tum ti-ti tum-ti-ti-ti. No, that's not it.

GRAVES (*humming*) Tum ti-ti-tum ti-ti-tum-tum-tum.

BOTH Tum ti-ti-tum ti-ti-tum-tum-tum. Ha! ha!

GRAVES (*throwing himself back*) Ah! What recollections it revives! It is too affecting.   *dramatic irony*   35

(margin handwritten note: manipulates him for her own gains)

LADY FRANKLIN (*aside*) Now, if I could but get him to dance with me, we should end with being partners for life. (*Aloud*) It *is* affecting, but we are all mortal. (*Sighs*) And at your Christmas party, at Cyprus Lodge, do you remember her dancing the Scotch reel° with Captain Macnaughten.   40

GRAVES Ha! ha! ha! To be sure, to be sure.

LADY FRANKLIN Can you think of the step? Somehow thus, was it not? (*Dancing*)

GRAVES No, no, quite wrong! Just stand there. Now then. (*Humming the tune*) La, la-la-la. La, la, etc. (*They dance*) That's it, excellent,   45
admirable!

LADY FRANKLIN (*aside*) Now it's coming.

> *Enter Sir John Vesey, Sir Frederick Blount, Georgina. They stand amazed. Lady Franklin continues to dance*

GRAVES Bewitching, irresistible! It's Maria herself that I see before
me! Thus, thus, let me clasp—Oh, the devil! Just like my luck!
(*Stopping opposite Sir John*)   50
        Lady Franklin runs off — playing with societies ideals
SIR JOHN Upon *my* word, Mr Graves! about relationships should
GEORGINA, BLOUNT Encore, encore! Bravo, bravo! work
GRAVES It's all a mistake! I—I—Sir John. Lady Franklin, you see—that
is to say—I—Sainted Maria! You are spared, at least, this affliction!
GEORGINA Pray go on!   55
BLOUNT Don't let us interwupt you.
GRAVES Interrupt me! I must say that this rudeness, this gross
impropriety, to pry into the sorrows of a poor bereaved sufferer,
seeking comfort from a sympathizing friend,—but such is human
nature!   60
GEORGINA But, Mr Graves! (*Following him*)
GRAVES Heartless!
BLOUNT My dear Mr Graves! (*Following him*)
GRAVES Frivolous!
SIR JOHN Stay and dine! (*Following him*)   65
GRAVES Unfeeling!
ALL Ha! ha! ha!
GRAVES Monsters! Good day to you.°
        Exit Graves, followed by Sir John Vesey and the others

[*Curtain*]

3.3

The interior of ***'s Club; ° *night; lights, etc. Small sofa-
tables, with books, papers, tea, coffee, etc. Several members
grouped by the fireplace; one member with his legs over the back
of his chair; another with his legs over his table; a third with his
legs on the chimney-piece. To the left, and in front of the stage, an
old member reading the newspaper, seated by a small round table;
to the right a card-table, before which Captain Dudley Smooth is
seated and sipping lemonade; at the bottom of the stage another
card-table*

Lord Glossmore, Stout
GLOSSMORE You don't often come to the club, Stout?

STOUT No, time is money. An hour spent at a club is unproductive capital. *[handwritten: Flat characters presented without]*

OLD MEMBER (*reading the newspaper*) Waiter! The snuff-box.

>   *Waiter brings it*

GLOSSMORE So, Evelyn has taken to play?° I see Deadly Smooth, 'hushed in grim repose, awaits his evening prey.'° Deep work tonight, I suspect, for Smooth is drinking lemonade. Keeps his head clear. Monstrous clever dog!

>   *Enter Evelyn; salutes and shakes hands with different members in passing up the stage*

EVELYN How d'ye do, Glossmore? How are you, Stout? *You* don't play, I think! Political economy° never plays at cards, eh? Never has time for anything more frivolous than rents and profits, wages and labour, high prices and low, Corn Laws, Poor Laws,° tithes, currency, 'dot and go one',° rates, puzzles, taxes, riddles and botheration! Smooth is the man. Aha! Smooth. Piquet, eh? You owe me my revenge!

>   *Members touch each other significantly; Stout walks away with the snuff-box; Old Member looks at him savagely*

SMOOTH My dear Alfred, anything to oblige.

>   *Evelyn and Smooth seat themselves*

OLD MEMBER Waiter! The snuff-box.

>   *Waiter takes it from Stout and brings it back to Old Member. Enter Sir Frederick Blount*

BLOUNT So, so! Evelyn at it again, eh, Glossmore?

GLOSSMORE Yes, Smooth sticks to him like a leech. Clever fellow, that Smooth!

BLOUNT Will you make up a wubber?°

GLOSSMORE Have you got two others?

BLOUNT Yes, Flat and Green.

GLOSSMORE Bad players.

BLOUNT I make it a wule to play with bad players; it is five per cent, in one's favour. I hate gambling. But a quiet wubber, if one is the best player out of four, can't do any harm.

GLOSSMORE Clever fellow, that Blount!

>   *Blount takes up the snuff-box and walks off with it. Old Member looks at him savagely. Blount, Lord Glossmore, Flat and Green make up a table at the bottom of the Stage*

SMOOTH A thousand pardons, my dear Alfred, ninety repique,° ten cards! Game!

5

10

15

20

25

30

[margin handwritten notes: "using his gambling to illuminate the character", "envying how to profit from the situation"]

44

EVELYN (*passing a note to him*) Game! Before we go on, one question. This is Thursday. How much do you calculate to win of me before Tuesday next?

SMOOTH *Ce cher Alfred!*° He is so droll!

EVELYN (*writing in his pocket-book*) Forty games a night, four nights, 35 minus Sunday, our usual stakes—that would be right, I think!

SMOOTH (*glancing over the account*) Quite. If I win all, which is next to impossible.

EVELYN It shall be possible to win twice as much, on one condition. Can you keep a secret? 40

SMOOTH My dear Alfred, I have kept myself! I never inherited a farthing. I never spent less than four thousand pounds a year. And I never told a soul how I managed it. — *gaining a position in society*

EVELYN Hark ye, then. A word with you—(*Evelyn and Smooth whisper*) *from having*

OLD MEMBER Waiter! The snuff-box. *money* 45

 Waiter takes it from Blount and brings it back to Old Member.
 Enter Sir John Vesey

EVELYN You understand?

SMOOTH Perfectly. Anything to oblige.

EVELYN (*cutting*) It is for you to deal. (*They go on playing*)

SIR JOHN (*groaning*) There's my precious son-in-law that is to be, *only concerned for his own interests.* 50 spending *my* consequence° and making a fool of himself. (*Takes up the snuff-box; Old Member looks at him savagely*)

BLOUNT I'm out. Flat, a pony on the odd twick.° That's wight. (*Coming up, counting his money*) Well, Sir John, you don't play?

SIR JOHN Play? No! Confound him. Lost again!

EVELYN Hang the cards! Double the stakes! 55

SMOOTH Just as you please. Done!

SIR JOHN Done, indeed!

OLD MEMBER Waiter! The snuff-box.

 Waiter takes it from Sir John

BLOUNT I've won eight points and the bets. I never lose. I never play in the Deadly Smooth set! (*Takes up snuff-box; Old Member as before*) 60

SIR JOHN (*looking over Smooth's hand and fidgeting backwards and forwards*) Lord have mercy on us! Smooth has seven for his point!° What's the stakes?

EVELYN Don't disturb us. I only throw out four.° Stakes, Sir John? *playing hint at his own game.* Immense! Was ever such luck? Not a card for my point. Do stand 65 back, Sir John. I'm getting irritable!

OLD MEMBER Waiter! The snuff-box. → *adds to the tension.*

 Waiter brings it back

45

BLOUNT One hundred pounds on the next game, Evelyn?

SIR JOHN Nonsense, nonsense, don't disturb him! All the fishes come
to the bait. Sharks and minnows all nibbling away at my son-in-law!   70

EVELYN One hundred pounds, Blount? Ah! the finest gentleman is
never too fine a gentleman to pick up a guinea. Done! Treble the
stakes, Smooth!

SIR JOHN I'm on the rack! (*Seizing the snuff-box*) Be cool, Evelyn!
Take care, my dear boy! Now don't ye, now don't!   75

EVELYN What? What? You have four queens! Five to the king.° Confound the cards! A fresh pack. (*Throws the cards behind him over Sir
John*)

OLD MEMBER Waiter! The snuff-box.

>   *Different members gather round*

FIRST MEMBER I never before saw Evelyn out of temper. He must be   80
losing immensely!

SECOND MEMBER Yes, this is interesting!

SIR JOHN Interesting! There's a wretch!

FIRST MEMBER Poor fellow! He'll be ruined in a month!

SIR JOHN I'm in a cold sweat.   85

SECOND MEMBER Smooth is the very devil.

SIR JOHN The devil's a joke to him!

GLOSSMORE (*slapping Sir John on the back*) A clever fellow, that
Smooth, Sir John, eh? (*Takes up the snuff-box; Old Member as
before*) A hundred pounds on this game, Evelyn?   90

EVELYN (*half turning round*) You! Well done, the Constitution! Yes,
one hundred pounds!

OLD MEMBER Waiter! The snuff-box.

STOUT *I think I'll* venture! Two hundred pounds on this game,
Evelyn?   95

EVELYN (*quite turning round*) Ha! ha! ha! Enlightenment and the Constitution on the same side of the question at last! O, Stout, Stout!
Great happiness of the greatest number,° greatest number, number
one! Done, Stout! Two hundred pounds! Ha! ha! ha! I deal, Stout.
Well done, political economy. Ha! ha! ha!   100

SIR JOHN Quite hysterical, drivelling! Aren't you ashamed of yourselves? His own cousins! All in a conspiracy, a perfect gang of them.

>   *Members indignant*

STOUT (*to Members*) Hush! He's to marry Sir John's daughter.

FIRST MEMBER What, Stingy Jack's? Oh!

CHORUS OF MEMBERS Oh! oh!   105

OLD MEMBER Waiter! The snuff-box.

fained air- knowing
how reputation is worth

EVELYN (*rising in great agitation*) No more, no more. I've done! Quite
enough. Glossmore, Stout, Blount, I'll pay you tomorrow. I—I—
Death! This is ruinous! (*Seizes the snuff-box; Old Member as before*)

SIR JOHN *Ruinous?* I dare say it is! What has he lost? What *has* he lost, 110
Smooth? Not much? Eh? Eh?

All gather round Smooth

SMOOTH Oh, a trifle, dear John! Excuse me! We never tell our win-
nings. (*To Blount*) How d'ye do, Fred? (*To Glossmore*) By the by,
Charles, don't you want to sell your house in Grosvenor Square?°
Twelve thousand pounds, eh?   115

GLOSSMORE Yes, and the furniture at a valuation.° About three thousand pounds more.

SMOOTH (*looking over his pocketbook*) Um! Well, we'll talk of it.

SIR JOHN [*aside*] Twelve and three—Fifteen thousand pounds. What
a cold-blooded rascal it is! [*Aloud*] Fifteen thousand pounds,   120
Smooth?   *only interested in money.*

SMOOTH Oh, the house itself is a trifle, but the establishment; I'm
considering whether I have enough to keep it up, my dear John.

OLD MEMBER Waiter, the snuff-box! (*Scraping it round, and with a wry
face*) And it's all gone! (*Gives it to the Waiter to fill*)   125

SIR JOHN (*turning round*) And it's all gone! → *snuff running parallel*
                                                  to money

EVELYN (*starting up and laughing hysterically*) Ha! ha! All gone? Not a
bit of it. Smooth, this club is so noisy. Sir John, you are always in
the way. Come to my house! Come! Champagne and a broiled bone.
Nothing venture, nothing have! The luck must turn, and, by Jupi-   130
ter, we'll make a night of it!

SIR JOHN A night of it!!! For heaven's sake, *Evelyn*! EVELYN!! Think
what you are about! Think of Georgina's feelings! Think of your
poor lost mother! Think of the babes unborn! Think of—   *construct a new appearance in society*

EVELYN I'll think of nothing! Zounds! You don't know what I have   135
lost, man. It's all your fault, distracting my attention! Pshaw!
pshaw! Out of the way, do! Come, Smooth. Ha! ha! A night of it,
my boy, a night of it!

Exeunt Captain Dudley Smooth and Evelyn

SIR JOHN (*following*) You must not, you shall not! Evelyn, my dear
Evelyn! He's drunk, he's mad! Will no one send for the police?   140

MEMBERS Ha! ha! ha! Poor old Stingy Jack! → *reputation being*

OLD MEMBER (*rising for the first time and in a great rage*) Waiter. The
snuff-box!   *destroyed.*

[*Curtain*]

4.1

The anteroom in Evelyn's house, as in 2.1.

Tabouret, MacFinch, Frantz and other tradesmen

TABOURET (*half whispers*) So, I hear that Mr Evelyn is turned gamester! There are strange reports about today. I don't know what to
make of it! We must look sharp, Mr MacFinch, we poor tradesmen,
and make hay while the sun shines.°

MACFINCH I wuish these geeming-houses were aw at the deevil! It's a   5
sheam and a sin for gentlemen to gang and ruin themselves, when
we honest tradesmen could do it for them with sae muckle advantage to the arts and coummerce o' the country.

All shake their heads approvingly. Enter Captain Dudley
Smooth from the inner room, with a pocketbook and pencil
in his hand

SMOOTH (*looking round*) Hum! ha! Fine pictures! (*Feeling the curtains*)
The new-fashioned velvet, hem! Good-proportioned rooms! Yes,   10
this house is better than Glossmore's!—Oh, Mr Tabouret, the
upholsterer! You furnished these rooms! All of the best, eh?

TABOURET Oh! The *very* best! Mr Evelyn is not a man to grudge
expense, sir!

SMOOTH He is not indeed. You've been paid, I suppose, Tabouret?   15

TABOURET No, sir, no. I never send in my bills when a customer is
rich. (*Aside*) Bills are like trees and grow by standing.

SMOOTH Humph! Not *paid*? Humph!

All gather round

MACFINCH I dinna like that hoomph, there's something vara suspeecious abun' it.   20

TABOURET (*to the tradesmen*) It's the great card-player, Captain
Smooth. Finest player in Europe. Cleaned out the Duke of Silly
Val. Uncommonly clever man!

SMOOTH (*pacing about the room*) Thirty-six feet by twenty-eight. Um!
I think a bow-window *there* would be an *improvement*. Could it be   25
done easily, Tabouret?

MACFINCH If Mr Evelyn wuishes to pool about his house, there's no
mon like my friend Mr MacStucco.

SMOOTH Evelyn? I was speaking of *myself*. Mr MacStucco? Humph!

TABOURET Yourself? Have you bought the house, sir?   30

48

SMOOTH *Bought* it? Hum! Ha! It depends. So you've not been paid
yet? Um! Nor you, nor you, nor you? Hum? Ah!

TABOURET No, sir! What *then*? No fear of Mr Evelyn! Ha! ha!

ALL (*anxiously*) Ha! ha! What then?

MACFINCH Ah, sir, what then? I'm a puir mon with a family: this way, 35
Captain! You've a leetle account in the buiks;° an' we'll e'en wipe it
out altogether, gin you'll say what you mean by that Hoom ha!

SMOOTH MacFinch, my dear fellow, don't oblige me to cane you; I
would not have Mr Evelyn distressed° for the world. Poor fellow!
He holds very bad cards. So you've not been paid yet? Don't send 40
in your bills on any account. Mind! Yes, I don't dislike the house
with some alteration. Good day to you. Hum! Ha!

    Exit Captain Dudley Smooth, looking about him, examining
    the chairs, tables, etc.

TABOURET Plain as a pikestaff! Staked his very house on an odd trick!

    Enter Sharp from the inner room, agitated and in a hurry

SHARP O Lord! O Lord! Who'd have thought it? Cards are the devil's
book! John! Thomas! Harris! (*Ringing the bell*) 45

    Enter Two Servants

Tom, take this letter to Sir John Vesey's. If not at home, find him. He
will give you a cheque. Go to his banker's and get it cashed
instantly. Quick, quick off with you!

TABOURET (*seizing Servant*) What's the matter? What's the matter?
How's Mr Evelyn? 50

SERVANT Bad, very bad! Sat up all night with Captain Smooth!

    First Servant runs off

SHARP (*to the other Servant*) Yes, Harris, your poor master! O dear! O
dear! You will take this note to the Belgian minister, Portland
Place.° Passport for Ostend! Have the travelling carriage ready at a
moment's notice! 55

MACFINCH (*stopping Servant*) Passport! Harkye, my mon. Is he gaun
to pit the saut seas between us and the siller?

SERVANT Don't stop me. Something wrong in the chest—change of
air—late hours—and Captain Smooth!

    Exit Servant

SHARP (*walking about*) And if the bank should break! If the bank *is* 60
broke, and he can't draw out! Bound to Smooth!

TABOURET Bank! What bank?

SHARP Flash's bank! Flash, brother-in-law to Captain Smooth! What
have *you* heard? Eh? Eh?

TABOURET That there's an awful run on it! 65

49

SHARP I must be off. Go, go, you can't see Mr Evelyn today!

TABOURET My account, sir!

MACFINCH I've a muckle bairns and a sma' bill!

FRANTZ O Sare, de great gentlemen always tink first of de tailor!

SHARP Call again, call again at Christmas. The bank, the cards; the   70
cards, the bank! O dear! O dear!

> *Exit Sharp*

TABOURET The bank!

MACFINCH The passport!

FRANTZ And all dat vill be seen of de great Evelyn coat is de back of
it. *Donner und Hagel!°* I vil arrest him. I vil put de salt on de tail   75
of it!

TABOURET (*aside*) I'll slip down to the city and see how the bank goes!

MACFINCH (*aside*) I'll e'en gang to my coosin the la'yer. [*Aloud*]
Nothing but peetience for us, Mr Tabouret.

TABOURET Ay, ay, stick by each other, share and share alike, that's my   80
way, sir.

ALL Share and share alike.

> *Exeunt all. Enter Servant, Lord Glossmore and Sir*
> *Frederick Blount*

SERVANT My master is not very well, my lord; but I'll let him know.

> *Exit Servant*

GLOSSMORE I'm very curious to learn the result of his gambling tête-
à-tête.   85

BLOUNT Oh, he's so howwidly wich, he can afford even a tête-à-tête
with Deadly Smooth!

GLOSSMORE Poor old Stingy Jack. Why, Georgina was *your* intended.

BLOUNT Yes; and I really like the girl, though out of pique I pwoposed to her cousin. But what can a man do against money?   90

> *Enter Evelyn*

If we could start fair, you'd see whom Georgina would pwefer. But
she's sacwificed by her father! She as much as told me so!

EVELYN So, so, gentlemen, we've a little account to settle. One hundred each.

BOTH Don't talk of it.   95

EVELYN Well, I won't! (*Taking Blount aside*) Ha! ha! You'd hardly
believe it, but I'd rather not pay you just at present; my money is
locked up, and I must wait, you know, for the Groginhole rents. So!
Instead of owing you one hundred pounds, suppose I owe you *five*?
You can give me a cheque for the other four. And, harkye! Not a   100
word to Glossmore.

BLOUNT Glossmore! The gweatest gossip in London! I shall be
delighted! (*Aside*) It never does harm to lend to a wich man; one
gets it back somehow. [*Aloud*] By the way, Evelyn, if you want my
gwey cab-horse, you may have him for two hundred pounds, and   105
that will make seven!

EVELYN (*aside*) That's the fashionable usury. Your friend does not
take interest. He sells you a horse. (*Aloud*) Blount, it's a bargain.

BLOUNT (*writing the cheque and musingly*) No. I don't see what harm it
can do me. That off leg must end in a spavin.°   110

EVELYN (*to Glossmore*) That hundred pounds I owe you is rather
inconvenient at present; I've a large sum to make up for the
Groginhole property. Perhaps you would lend me five or six
hundred more, just to go on with?

GLOSSMORE Certainly! Hopkins is dead. Your interest for Cipher   115
would—

EVELYN Why, I can't promise *that* at this moment. But as a slight
mark of friendship and gratitude, I shall be very much flattered if
you'll accept a splendid grey cab-horse I bought today. Cost two
hundred pounds!   120

GLOSSMORE Bought *today*! Then I'm safe. My dear fellow! You're
always so princely!

EVELYN Nonsense! Just write the cheque. And, harkye, not a syllable
to Blount!

GLOSSMORE Blount? He's the town-crier! (*Goes to write*)   125

BLOUNT (*giving Evelyn the cheque*) Wansom's,° Pall Mall East.

EVELYN Thank you. So you *proposed* to Miss Douglas!

BLOUNT Hang it, yes! I could have sworn that she fancied me. Her
manner, for instance, that very day you pwoposed for Miss Vesey,
otherwise Georgina—   130

EVELYN Has only half what Miss Douglas has.

BLOUNT You forget how much Stingy Jack must have saved! But I
beg your pardon.

EVELYN Never mind. But not a word to Sir John, or he'll fancy I'm
ruined.   135

GLOSSMORE (*giving the cheque*) Ransom's, Pall Mall. Tell me, did you
win or lose last night?

EVELYN Win! Lose! Oh! No more of that, if you love me. I must send
off at once to the banker's. (*Looking at the two cheques*)

GLOSSMORE (*aside*) Why, he's borrowed from Blount, too!   140

BLOUNT (*aside*) That's a cheque from Lord Glossmore!

EVELYN Excuse me. I must dress. I have not a moment to lose. You

remember you dine with me today. Seven o'clock. You'll meet
Smooth. (*With tears in his voice*) It may be the last time I shall ever
welcome you here! My—what am I saying? Oh, merely a joke!   145
Good-bye, *good*-bye.

> *Shaking them heartily by the hand and exit by the inner room*

BLOUNT Glossmore!

GLOSSMORE Blount!

BLOUNT I am afraid all's not wight!

GLOSSMORE I incline to your opinion!   150

BLOUNT But I've sold my gwey cab-horse.

GLOSSMORE Grey cab-horse! You! What is he really worth now?

BLOUNT Since he is sold, I will tell you. Not a sixpence!

GLOSSMORE Not a sixpence! He gave it to me!

> *Evelyn at the door, giving directions to a Servant in dumb show*

BLOUNT That was devilish unhandsome! Do you know, I feel nervous!   155

GLOSSMORE Nervous? Let us run and stop payment of our cheques.

> *Evelyn shuts the door, and Servant runs across the stage*

BLOUNT Hollo,° John! Where so fast?

SERVANT (*in great haste*) Beg pardon, Sir Frederick, to Pall Mall East.
Messrs Ransom.

> *Exit Servant*

BLOUNT (*solemnly*) Glossmore, we are floored!   160

GLOSSMORE Sir, the whole town shall know of it!

> *Exeunt Sir Frederick Blount and Lord Glossmore. Enter Toke
> and Footman*

TOKE Come, come, stir yourselves! We've no time to lose. This room
is to be got ready for the shawls. Mrs Crump and the other ladies of
our household are to wait here on the women before they go up to
the drawing-room. Take away that desk, don't be lazy! And give me   165
the newspaper.

> *Toke seats himself; the Servants bustle about*

Strange reports about my patron! And the walley is gone for the
passport!

> *Enter Frantz with a bundle*

FRANTZ Mr Toke, my goot Mr Toke, I've brought you von leetel
present.   170

TOKE John and Charles, vanish!

> *Exeunt Servants*

I scorns to corrupt them 'ere working classes!

FRANTZ (*producing a pair of smallclothes, which Toke examines*) Your
master is von beggar! He vants to run avay; ve are all in de same

vat-you-call-it—de same leetel nasty boat, Mr Toke! Just let my   175
friend Mr Clutch up through the area° and I vill arrest him dis very
day.

TOKE I accept the abridgments°. But you've forgotten to line the
pockets!°

FRANTZ Blesh my soul, so I have! (*Giving a note°*)   180

TOKE The area gate shall be left undefended. Do it quietly, no *claw*,°
as the French say.

FRANTZ Goot Mr Toke. Tomorrow I vill line de oter pocket.
        Exit Frantz

TOKE My patron does not give me satisfaction!
        Enter Footman

FOOTMAN What chandeliers are to be lighted, Mr Toke? It's getting   185
late.

TOKE Don't disturb me. I'm rum-mynating! Yes, yes, there's no
doubt of it! [*To Footman*] Charles, the area gate is open?

FOOTMAN And all the plate in the pantry! I'll run and—

TOKE Not a step! Leave it open.   190

FOOTMAN But—

TOKE (*with dignity*) It's for the sake of wentilation!
        Exeunt all

[*Curtain*]

4.2

A splendid saloon in Evelyn's house

Evelyn, Graves, Stout°

GRAVES You've withdrawn your money from Flash and Brisk?

EVELYN No.

GRAVES No! Then—
        Enter Sir John Vesey, Lady Franklin and Georgina

SIR JOHN You got the cheque for five hundred pounds safely? Too
happy to—   5

EVELYN (*interrupting him*) My best thanks! My warmest gratitude! So
kind in you! So seasonable, that five hundred pounds; you don't
know the value of that five hundred pounds. I shall never forget
your nobleness of conduct.

53

ironic given his real motives

SIR JOHN Gratitude! Nobleness! (*Aside*) I can't have been taken in?   10

EVELYN And in a moment of such distress!

SIR JOHN (*aside*) Such distress! He picks out the ugliest words in the whole dictionary!

EVELYN I've done with Smooth. But I'm still a little crippled, and you must do me *another* favour. I've only as yet paid the deposit of ten   15
per cent for the great Groginhole property. I am to pay the rest this week, nay, I fear, tomorrow. I've already sold out of the funds. The money lies at the bankers', and of course I can't touch it. For if I don't pay by a certain day, I forfeit the estate and the deposit.

SIR JOHN What's coming now, I wonder?   20

EVELYN Georgina's fortune is ten thousand pounds. I always meant, my dear Sir John, to present you with that little sum.

SIR JOHN Oh, Evelyn! Your generosity is positively touching! (*Wipes his eyes*)

EVELYN *But* the news of my losses has frightened my tradesmen! I   25
have so many heavy debts at this moment that—that—that—. But I see Georgina is listening and I'll say what I have to say to her.

SIR JOHN No, no. No, no. Girls don't understand business!

EVELYN The very reason I speak to her. This is an affair, not of business, but of *feeling*. Stout, show Sir John my Correggio.   30

SIR JOHN (*aside*) Devil take his Correggio! The man is born to torment me!

EVELYN My dear Georgina, whatever you may hear said of me, I flatter myself that you feel confidence in my honour.

GEORGINA Can you doubt it?   35

EVELYN I confess that I am embarrassed° at this moment; I have been weak enough to lose money at play, and there are other demands on me. I promise you never to gamble again as long as I live. My affairs can be retrieved, but for the first few years of our marriage it may be necessary to retrench.   40

GEORGINA Retrench!

EVELYN To live perhaps altogether in the country.

GEORGINA Altogether in the country!

EVELYN To confine ourselves to a modest competence.

GEORGINA Modest competence! I knew something horrid was   45
coming!

EVELYN And now, Georgina, you may have it in your power at this moment to save me from much anxiety and humiliation. My money is locked up. My debts of honour must be settled. You are of age. Your ten thousand pounds in your own hands—   50

Stout listening as well as Sir John — *realising how far he's gone.*

SIR JOHN [*aside*] I'm standing on hot iron!

EVELYN If you could lend it to me for a few weeks.—You hesitate! Oh! Believe the honour of the man you will call your husband before all the calumnies of the fools whom we call the world! Can you give me this proof of your confidence? Remember, without confidence, 55 what is wedlock?

SIR JOHN (*aside to her*) No! (*Aloud, pointing his glass at the Correggio*) Yes, the picture may be fine.

STOUT But you don't like the subject?

GEORGINA (*aside*) He may be only trying me! Best leave it to Papa.   60

EVELYN Well— *suspecting other motives.*

GEORGINA You—you shall hear from me tomorrow.
    [*Enter Blount*]
    (*Aside*) Ah, there's that dear Sir Frederick! (*Goes to Blount*)
    *Enter Lord Glossmore and Captain Dudley Smooth; Evelyn
    salutes them, paying Smooth servile respect*

LADY FRANKLIN (*to Graves*) Ha! ha! To be so disturbed yesterday, was it not droll?   65

GRAVES Never recur to that humiliating topic.

GLOSSMORE (*to Stout*) See how Evelyn fawns upon Smooth! *ironic given the way that they*

STOUT How mean in him! *Smooth*, a professional gambler, a fellow *lead their life* who lives by his wits! I would not know such a man on any account!

SMOOTH (*to Glossmore*) So Hopkins is dead. You want Cipher to come 70 in for Groginhole, eh?

GLOSSMORE What! Could *you* manage it?

SMOOTH *Ce cher Charles!* Anything to oblige!

STOUT [*aside*] Groginhole! What can he have to do with Groginhole?
    [*Aloud*] Glossmore, present me to Smooth.   75

GLOSSMORE What! The gambler, the fellow who lives by his wits? *dramatic irony*

STOUT Why, his wits seem to be an uncommonly productive capital! I'll introduce myself. How d'ye do, Captain Smooth? We have met at the club, I think. I am charmed to make your acquaintance in private. I say, sir, what do you think of the affairs of the nation? 80 Bad! Very bad! No enlightenment! Great fall-off in the revenue! No knowledge of finance! There's only one man who can save the country, and that's *Popkins*! — *humorous in the way he constantly*

SMOOTH Is he in parliament, Mr Stout? What's your Christian name, *drives us politics* by the by?   85

STOUT Benjamin. No, constituencies are so ignorant, they don't understand his value. He's no orator. In fact, he stammers so much.

But devilish profound. Could not we ensure him for Groginhole?

SMOOTH My dear Benjamin, it's a thing to be thought on.

EVELYN (*advancing*) My friends, pray be seated. I wish to consult you. 90
This day twelvemonths I succeeded to an immense income, and as,
by a happy coincidence, on the same day I secured your esteem, so
now I wish to ask you if you think I could have spent that income in
a way more worthy your good opinion.

GLOSSMORE Impossible! Excellent taste, beautiful house! 95

BLOUNT Vewy good horses—(*aside to Glossmore*) especially the gwey
cab!

LADY FRANKLIN Splendid pictures!

GRAVES And a magnificent cook, ma'am!

SMOOTH (*thrusting his hands in his pockets*) It's my opinion, Alfred— 100
and I'm a judge—that you could not have spent your money better!

ALL (*except Sir John*) Very true!

EVELYN What say *you*, Sir John? You may think me a little extravagant. But you know that in this world the only way to show oneself
thoroughly respectable is to make a thoroughly respectable show. 105

SIR JOHN Certainly, certainly! No, you could not have done better.
(*Aside*) I don't know what to make of it.

GEORGINA Certainly. (*Coaxingly*) Don't retrench, my dear Alfred!

GLOSSMORE Retrench! Nothing so plebeian!

STOUT Plebeian, sir! Worse than plebeian! It is against all the rules of 110
public morality. Everyone knows, nowadays, that extravagance is a
benefit to the population; encourages art, employs labour and
multiplies spinning-jennies°.

EVELYN You reassure me! I own I did think that a man worthy of
friends so sincere might have done something better than feast, 115
dress, drink, play—

GLOSSMORE Nonsense! We like you the better for it. (*Aside*) I wish I
had my six hundred pounds back, though.

EVELYN And you are as much my friends now as when you offered me
ten pounds for my old nurse. 120

SIR JOHN A thousand times more so, my dear boy!

All approve. Enter Sharp

SMOOTH But who's our new friend?

EVELYN Who! The very man who first announced to me the wealth
which you allow I have spent so well. But what's the matter, Sharp?
(*Sharp whispering [to] Evelyn*) 125

EVELYN (*aloud*) The bank's *broke*!

SIR JOHN Broke! What bank?

EVELYN Flash, Brisk and Co.

GLOSSMORE (*to Smooth*) And Flash was your brother-in-law. I'm very
sorry.   130

SMOOTH (*taking snuff*) Not at all, Charles. I did not bank there.

SIR JOHN But I warned you. You withdrew?

EVELYN Alas! No!

SIR JOHN Oh! Not much in their hands?

EVELYN Why, I told you the purchase-money for Groginhole was at   135
my bankers'. But no, no, don't look so frightened! It was not placed
with Flash. It is at Hoare's.° It is, indeed. Nay, I assure you it is! A
mere trifle at Flash's, upon my word, now! Tomorrow, Sharp, we'll
talk of this! One day more, one day, at least, for enjoyment!

SIR JOHN Oh! A pretty enjoyment!   140

BLOUNT And he borrowed seven hundred pounds of me!

GLOSSMORE And six hundred pounds of me!

SIR JOHN And five hundred pounds of me!

STOUT Oh! A regular Jeremy Diddler!°

SMOOTH (*to Sir John*) John, do you know, I think I would take a   145
handsome offer for this house just as it stands; furniture, plate,
pictures, books, bronzes and statues! *— adding to Evelyn's act.*

SIR JOHN Powers above!

STOUT (*to Sir John*) I say, you have placed your daughter in a very
unsafe investment. What then? A daughter's like any other capital.   150
Transfer the stock in hand to t'other speculation. *attitudes to women*

SIR JOHN (*going to Georgina*) Ha! I'm afraid we've been very rude to *show them*
Sir Frederick. A monstrous fine young man!   *as objects*

    Enter Toke   *allowing Georgina the end she wanted for*

TOKE (*to Evelyn*) Sir, I beg your pardon, but Mr MacFinch insists on *purely*
my giving you this letter instantly.   *financial*   155

EVELYN (*reading*) How! Sir John, this fellow, MacFinch, has heard of *reasons*
my misfortunes and insists on being paid. A lawyer's letter, quite
insolent! *— exaggeration in tone — comic as it doesn't*

TOKE And, sir, Mr Tabouret is below and declares he won't stir till *fit the*
he's paid.   *situation*   160

EVELYN Won't stir till he's paid! What's to be done, Sir John?
Smooth, what *is* to be done? *—*

SMOOTH If he won't stir till he's paid, make him up a bed, and I'll
take him in the inventory as one of the fixtures, Alfred!

EVELYN It is very well for you to joke, Mr Smooth. But—   165

    Enter Sheriff's Officer, giving paper to Evelyn and whispering

EVELYN What's this? Frantz, the tailor. Why, you impudent

[margin handwritten annotations: element of theatricality in his behaviour and words]

57

scoundrel! Faith! This is more than I bargained for. Sir John, I'm arrested.

STOUT (*slapping Sir John on the back with glee*) He's arrested, old gentleman! But I didn't lend him a farthing.

EVELYN And for a mere song, one hundred and fifty pounds! Sir John, pay this fellow, will you? Or bail me, or something, while we go to dinner!

SIR JOHN Pay, bail, I'll be damned if I do! Oh, my five hundred pounds! My five hundred pounds! Mr Alfred Evelyn, I want my five hundred pounds!

GRAVES I'm going to do a very silly thing. I shall lose both my friend and my money. Just like my luck! Evelyn, go to dinner. I'll settle this for you.

LADY FRANKLIN I love you for that!

GRAVES Do you? Then I am the happiest—Ah! Ma'am, I don't know what I am saying!

Exeunt Graves and Sheriff's Officer

EVELYN (*to Georgina*) Don't go by these appearances! I repeat, ten thousand pounds will more than cover all my embarrassments. I shall hear from you tomorrow?

GEORGINA Yes, yes!

EVELYN But you're not going? You, too, Glossmore? You, Blount? You, Stout? You, Smooth?

SMOOTH No. I'll stick by you, as long as you've a guinea to stake!

GLOSSMORE Oh, this might have been expected from a man of such ambiguous political opinions!

STOUT Don't stop me, sir. No man of common enlightenment would have squandered his substance in this way. Pictures and statues! Bah!°

EVELYN Why, you all said I could not spend my money better! Ha! ha! ha! The absurdest mistake! You don't fancy I'm going to prison? Ha! ha! Why don't you laugh, Sir John? Ha! ha! ha!

SIR JOHN Sir, this horrible levity! Take Sir Frederick's arm, my poor injured, innocent child! Mr Evelyn, after this extraordinary scene, you can't be surprised that I—I—Zounds! I'm suffocating!

SMOOTH But, my dear John, they've no right to arrest the dinner!

STOUT (*aside*) But the election at Groginhole is tomorrow. This news may not arrive before the poll closes! (*Rushing to Evelyn*) Sir, Popkins never bribes. But Popkins will bet you one thousand pounds that he don't come in for Groginhole.

GLOSSMORE This is infamous, Mr Stout! Cipher is a man who scorns every subterfuge! (*Aside to Evelyn*) But, for the sake of the Constitution, name your price.

EVELYN I know the services of Cipher. I know the profundity of Popkins. But it's too late, the borough's engaged!   210

    [*Enter Toke*]

TOKE Dinner is served.

GLOSSMORE (*pausing*) Dinner!

STOUT Dinner! It's a very good smell!

EVELYN (*to Sir John*) Turtle and venison too!

    They stop irresolute

EVELYN That's right. Come along. But, I say, Blount, Stout, Glossmore, Sir John; one word first: Will you lend me ten pounds for my old nurse?   215

    Exeunt all, indignantly

SMOOTH AND EVELYN Ha! ha! ha! → *signals to the audience the false nature of events*

    [*Curtain*]

[handwritten annotation: dever human]

5.1

*** 's Club*

Captain Dudley Smooth, Lord Glossmore, other members

GLOSSMORE Will his horses be sold, think you?

SMOOTH Very possibly, Charles! A fine stud. Hum! ha! Waiter, a glass
of sherry!

GLOSSMORE They say he must go abroad!

SMOOTH Well! It's the best time of year for travelling, Charles.　　　　5

GLOSSMORE We are all to be paid today, and that looks suspicious!

SMOOTH Very suspicious, Charles! Hum! Ah!

GLOSSMORE My dear fellow, you must know the rights of the matter.
I wish you'd speak out. What have you really won? Is the house
itself gone?　　　　10

SMOOTH The house itself is certainly not gone, Charles, for I saw it
exactly in the same place this morning at half past ten. It has not
moved an inch!

Waiter gives a letter to Glossmore

GLOSSMORE (*reading*) From Groginhole, and express! What's this? I'm
amazed!!! (*Reading*) They've actually at the eleventh hour started　　15
Mr Evelyn. And nobody knows what his politics are! We shall be
beat! The constitution is gone! Cipher! Oh! This is infamous in
Evelyn! Gets into parliament just to keep himself out of the Bench.°

SMOOTH He's capable of it!

GLOSSMORE Not a doubt of it, sir! Not a doubt of it!　　　　20

Enter Sir John Vesey and Sir Frederick Blount, talking

SIR JOHN My dear boy, I'm not flint! I am but a man! If Georgina
really loves you—and I am sure that she *does*—I will never think of
sacrificing her happiness to ambition. She is yours. I told her so this
very morning.

BLOUNT [*aside*] The old humbug!　　　　25

SIR JOHN She's the best of daughters! The most obedient artless
creature! Oh! She's been properly brought up. A good daughter
makes a good wife. Dine with me at seven and we'll talk of the
settlements.

BLOUNT Yes, I don't care for fortune; but—　　　　30

SIR JOHN Her ten thousand pounds will be settled on herself. That of
course.°

BLOUNT *All* of it, sir? Weally I—

SIR JOHN What *then*, my dear boy? I shall leave you both all I've laid
by. Ah! You know I'm a close° fellow! 'Stingy Jack', eh? After all,   35
worth makes the man! *still using deception to keep position in*

SMOOTH And the more a man's worth, John, the worthier man he *society*
must be!

Exit Captain Dudley Smooth

BLOUNT (*aside*) Yes, he has no other child! She *must* have all his
savings. I don't see what harm it could do me. Still that ten thou-   40
sand pounds, I want that ten thousand pounds. If she would but
run off now, one could get rid of the settlements.

Enter Stout, wiping his forehead, and takes Sir John aside

STOUT Sir John, we've been played upon! My secretary is brother to
Flash's head clerk. Evelyn had not three hundred pounds in the
bank!   45

SIR JOHN Bless us and save us! You take away my breath! But then—
Deadly Smooth—the arrest—the—Oh, he must be done up!°

STOUT As to Smooth, he'd 'do anything to oblige'. All a trick, depend
on it! Smooth has already deceived me, for before the day's over
Evelyn will be member for Groginhole. I've had an express from   50
Popkins. He's in despair! Not for *himself*, but for the *country*, Sir
John. What's to become of the country?

SIR JOHN But what could be Evelyn's *object*?   *expected to be involved in*

STOUT *Object?* Do you look for an object in a whimsical creature like   *politics*
that? A man who has not even any political opinions! Object! Per-   55
haps to break off his match with your daughter! Take care, Sir   *position*
John, or the borough will be lost to your family!

SIR JOHN Aha! I begin to smell a rat! But it's not too late yet.

STOUT My interest in Popkins made me run to Lord Spendquick, the
late proprietor of Groginhole. I told him that Evelyn could not pay   60
the rest of the money; and *he* told me that—

SIR JOHN What?

STOUT Mr Sharp had just paid it him. There's no hope for Popkins!
England will rue this day!

SIR JOHN *Georgina* shall lend him the money! *I'll* lend him. Every   65
man in my house shall lend him. I feel again what it is to be a
father-in-law! (*Aside*) But stop, I'll be cautious. Stout may be on his
side. A trap—not likely. But I'll go first to Spendquick myself.
[*Aloud, to Blount*] Sir Frederick, excuse me. You can't dine with me
today. And, on second thoughts, I see that it would be very unhand-   70
some to desert poor Evelyn now he's down in the world. Can't

think of it, my dear boy, can't think of it. Very much honoured and
happy to see you as a friend. [*Calling*] Waiter! My carriage! [*Aside*]
Um! What, humbug *Stingy Jack*, will they? Ah! A good joke,
indeed!   75

    Exit Sir John Vesey

BLOUNT Mr Stout, what have you been saying to Sir John? Something against my character, I know you have. Don't deny it. Sir, I
shall expect satisfaction!°

STOUT Satisfaction, Sir Frederick! As if a man of enlightenment had
any satisfaction in fighting! Did not mention your name. We were   80
talking of Evelyn. Only think! He's no more ruined than you are.

BLOUNT Not wuined? Aha, now I understand! So, so! Stay, let me see.
She's to meet me in the square! (*Pulls out his watch; a very small
one*)

STOUT (*pulling out his own; a very large one*) I must be off to the   85
vestry.

BLOUNT Just in time! Ten thousand pounds! Gad, my blood's up and
I won't be tweated in *this* way, if he were fifty times Stingy Jack!

    Exit Sir Frederick Blount

[*Curtain*]

5.2

The drawing-rooms in Sir John Vesey's house

Lady Franklin, Graves

GRAVES Well, well, I am certain that poor Evelyn loves Clara still. But
you can't persuade me that she cares for him.

LADY FRANKLIN She has been breaking her heart ever since she
heard of his distress. Nay, I am sure she would give all she has could
it save him from the consequences of his own folly.   5

GRAVES (*half aside*) She would only give him his own money, if she
did. I should like just to sound her.

LADY FRANKLIN (*ringing the bell*) And you shall. I take so much interest in her that I forgive your friend everything but his offer to
Georgina.   10

    Enter Servant

Where are the young ladies?

SERVANT Miss Vesey is, I believe, still in the square. Miss Douglas is just come in, my lady.

LADY FRANKLIN What, did not she go out with Miss Vesey?

SERVANT No, my lady. I attended her to Drummond's, the banker.   15

Exit Servant

LADY FRANKLIN Drummond's!

Enter Clara

Why, child, what on earth could take you to Drummond's at this hour of the day?

CLARA (*confused*) Oh, I—that is—I—Ah, Mr Graves! How is Mr Evelyn? How does he bear up against so sudden a reverse?   20

GRAVES With an awful calm. I fear all is not right here! (*Touching his head*) The report in the town is, that he must go abroad instantly, perhaps today!

CLARA Abroad! Today!

GRAVES But all his creditors will be paid, and he only seems anxious to know if Miss Vesey remains true in his misfortunes.   25

CLARA Ah! He loves her so *much*, then!

GRAVES Um! That's more than I can say.

CLARA She told me, last night, that he said to the last that ten thousand pounds would free him from all his liabilities. That was the sum, was it not?   30

GRAVES Yes, he persists in the same assertion. Will Miss Vesey lend it?

LADY FRANKLIN (*aside*) If she does I shall not think so well of her poor dear mother, for I am sure she'd be no child of Sir John's!

GRAVES I should like to convince myself that my poor friend has nothing to hope from a woman's generosity.   35

LADY FRANKLIN Civil! And are men, then, less covetous?

GRAVES I know one man, at least, who, rejected in his poverty by one as poor as himself, no sooner came into a sudden fortune than he made his lawyer invent a codicil which the testator never dreamt of,   40 bequeathing independence to the woman who had scorned him.

LADY FRANKLIN And never told her?

GRAVES Never! There's no such document at Doctors' Commons,° depend on it! You seem incredulous, Miss Clara! Good day!

CLARA (*following him*) One word, for mercy's sake! Do I understand   45 you right? Ah, how could I be so blind! Generous Evelyn!

GRAVES *You* appreciate, and *Georgina* will desert him. Miss Douglas, he loves you still. [*Aside*] If that's not just like me! Meddling with other people's affairs, as if they were worth it. Hang them!

Exit Graves

CLARA Georgina will desert him. Do you think so? (*Aside*) Ah, he will   50
soon discover that she never wrote that letter!

LADY FRANKLIN She told me, last night, that she would never see
him again. To do her justice, she's less interested than her father
and as much attached as she can be to another. Even while engaged
to Evelyn she has met Sir Frederick every day in the square.   55

CLARA And he is alone, sad, forsaken, ruined. And I, whom he
enriched; I, the creature of his bounty; I, once the woman of his
love; I stand idly here to content myself with tears and prayers! Oh,
Lady Franklin, have pity on me, on him! We are both of kin to him,
as relations we have both a right to comfort! Let us go to him.   60
Come!

LADY FRANKLIN No! It would scarcely be right. Remember the
world. I cannot.

CLARA All abandon him. Then I will go alone!

LADY FRANKLIN You! So proud, so sensitive!   65

CLARA Pride, when he wants a friend?

LADY FRANKLIN His misfortunes are his own fault. A gambler!

CLARA Can you think of his faults now? *I* have no right to do so. All I
have, all, his gift! And I never to have dreamed it!

LADY FRANKLIN But if Georgina does indeed release him, if she has   70
already done so, what will he think? What but—

CLARA What but, that if he love me still, I may have enough for both,
and I am by his side! But that is too bright a dream. He told me I
might call him brother! Where, now, should a sister be? But—
but—I—I—I tremble! If, after all—if—if—In one word, am I too   75
bold? The world, my conscience can answer *that*. But do you think
that *he* could despise me?

LADY FRANKLIN No, Clara, no! Your fair soul is too transparent for
even libertines to misconstrue. Something tells me that this meeting may make the happiness of both! You cannot go alone. My   80
presence justifies all. Give me your hand. We will go together!

Exeunt Lady Franklin and Clara

[*Curtain*]

5.3

A room in Evelyn's house

EVELYN Yes, as yet, all surpasses my expectations. I am sure of
Smooth. I have managed even Sharp. My election will seem but an
escape from a prison. Ha! ha! True, it cannot last long. But a few
hours more are all I require, and for that time at least I shall hope to
be thoroughly ruined.   5

Enter Graves

Well, Graves, and what do people say of me?

GRAVES Everything that's bad!

EVELYN Three days ago I was universally respected. I awake this
morning to find myself singularly infamous. Yet I'm the same man.

GRAVES Humph! Why gambling—   10

EVELYN Cant! It was not criminal to gamble. It was criminal to lose.
Tut! Will you deny that, if I had ruined Smooth instead of myself,
every hand would have grasped mine yet more cordially and every
lip would have smiled congratulation on my success? Man, man!
I've not been rich and poor for nothing! The vices and the virtues   15
are written in a language the world cannot construe. It reads them
in a vile translation, and the translators are—*failure* and *success*! You
alone are unchanged.

GRAVES There's no merit in that. I am always ready to mingle my
tears with any man. (*Aside*) I know I'm a fool, but I can't help it.   20
[*Aloud*] Hark ye, Evelyn! I like you. I'm rich, and anything I can do
to get you out of your hobble° will give me an excuse to grumble for
the rest of my life. There, now it's out.

EVELYN (*touched*) There's something good in human nature after all!
My dear friend, did I want your aid I would accept it, but I can   25
extricate myself yet. Do you think Georgina will give me the same
proof of confidence and affection?

GRAVES Would you break your heart if she did not?

EVELYN It is in vain to deny that I still love Clara. Our last conversation renewed feelings which would task all the energies of my soul   30
to conquer. What then? I am not one of those, the Sybarites° of
sentiment, who deem it impossible for humanity to conquer love.
Who call their own weakness the voice of a resistless destiny. Such
is the poor excuse of every woman who yields her honour, of every
adulterer who betrays his friend. No! The heart was given to the   35
soul as its ally, not as its traitor.

GRAVES What do you tend to?°

EVELYN This: If Georgina still adhere to my fortune (and I will not
put her to too harsh a trial), if she can face the prospect, not of ruin
and poverty, for reports wrong me there, but of a moderate   40
independence; if, in one word, she love me for myself, I will shut
Clara forever from my thought. I am pledged to Georgina and I will
carry to the altar a soul resolute to deserve her affection and fulfil
its vows.

GRAVES And if she reject you?   45

EVELYN (*joyfully*) If she do, I am free once more! And then, then I will
dare to ask, for I can ask without dishonour, if Clara can explain the
past and bless the future!

> *Enter Servant with a letter*

EVELYN (*after reading it*) The die is cast, the dream is over! Generous
girl! Oh, Georgina! I will deserve you yet.   50

GRAVES Georgina, is it possible?

EVELYN And the delicacy, the womanhood, the exquisite grace of this!
How we misjudge the depth of the human heart! How, seeing the
straws on the surface, we forget that the pearls may lie hid below!° I
imagined her incapable of this devotion.   55

GRAVES And *I too*!

EVELYN It were base in me to continue this trial a moment longer. I
will write at once to undeceive that generous heart. (*Writing*)

GRAVES [*aside*] I would have given a thousand pounds, if that little
jade Clara had been beforehand. But just like my luck! If I want a   60
man to marry one woman, he's sure to marry another on purpose to
vex me!

> *Evelyn rings the bell. Enter Servant*

EVELYN Take this instantly to Miss Vesey. Say I will call in an hour.

> *Exit Servant*

And now Clara is resigned forever! Why does my heart sink within
me? Why, why, looking to the fate to come, do I see only the   65
memory of what has been?

GRAVES You are re-engaged then to Georgina?

EVELYN Irrevocably.

> *Enter Servant*°

SERVANT Lady Franklin; Miss Douglas.

> *Enter Lady Franklin and Clara. Exit Servant*

LADY FRANKLIN My dear Evelyn, you may think it strange to   70
receive such visitors at this moment. But, indeed, it is no time for
ceremony. We are your relations. It is reported you are about to

66

leave the country. We come to ask frankly what we can do to serve you?

EVELYN Madam—I—   75

LADY FRANKLIN Come, come, do not hesitate to confide in us. Clara is less a stranger to you than I am. Your friend here will perhaps let me consult with him. (*Aside to Graves*) Let us leave them to themselves.

GRAVES You're an angel of a widow, but you come too late, as what-   80
ever is good for anything generally does. — *cynical world view*

They retire into the inner room, which should be partially open

EVELYN Miss Douglas, I may well want words to thank you. This goodness, this sympathy—

CLARA (*abandoning herself to her emotion*) Evelyn! Evelyn! Do not talk thus! Goodness! Sympathy! I have learned *all*, *all*! It is for *me* to   85
speak of *gratitude*! What! Even when I had so wounded you, when you believed me mercenary and cold, when you thought that I was blind and base enough not to know you for what you are; even *at that time* you thought but of my happiness, my fortune, my fate! And to you, you, I owe all that has raised the poor orphan from   90
servitude and dependence! While your words were so bitter, your deeds so gentle! Oh, noble Evelyn, this, then, was your revenge!

EVELYN You owe me no thanks. That revenge was sweet! Think you it was nothing to feel that my presence haunted you, though you knew it not? That in things, the pettiest as the greatest, which that   95
gold could buy, the very jewels you wore, the very robe in which, to other eyes, you might seem more fair, in all in which you took the woman's young and innocent delight, *I* had a part, a share? That even if separated forever, even if another's, even in distant years, perhaps in a happy home, listening to sweet voices, that might call   100
you 'mother'; even then should the uses of that dross bring to your lips one smile. That smile was mine, due to me, due, as a sacred debt, to the hand that you rejected, to the love that you despised!

CLARA Despised! See the proof that I despised you! See, in this hour, when they say you are again as poor as before, I forget the world,   105
my pride, perhaps too much my sex. I remember but your sorrow, I am here!

EVELYN (*aside*) O, heaven! Give me strength to bear it! (*Aloud*) And is this the same voice that, when I knelt at your feet, when I asked but *one day* the hope to call you mine, spoke only of poverty and   110
answered, '*never*'?

CLARA Because I had been unworthy of your love if I had ensured your misery. Evelyn, hear me! My father, like you, was poor, generous; gifted, like you, with genius, ambition; sensitive, like you, to the least breath of insult. He married, as you would have done, married one whose only dower was penury and care! Alfred, I saw that genius the curse to itself! I saw that ambition wither to despair! I saw the struggle, the humiliation, the proud man's agony, the bitter life, the early death! And heard over his breathles clay my mother's groan of self-reproach! Alfred Evelyn, now speak! Was the woman you loved so nobly to repay you with such a doom?

EVELYN Clara, we should have shared it!

CLARA Shared? Never let the woman who really loves comfort her selfishness with such delusion! In marriages like this the wife cannot share the burden. It is he, the husband, to provide, to scheme, to work, to endure, to grind out his strong heart at the miserable wheel! The wife, alas, cannot share the struggle, she can but witness the despair! And, therefore, Alfred, I rejected you.

EVELYN Yet you believe me as poor now as I was then.

CLARA But *I* am not poor; *we* are not so poor! Of this fortune, which is all your own—if, as I hear, one half would free you from your debts, why, *we have the other half still left*, Evelyn! It is humble, but it is not penury.

EVELYN Cease, cease. You know not how you torture me. Oh, that when hope was possible! Oh, that you had bid me take it to my breast and wait for a brighter day.

CLARA And so have consumed your life upon a hope perhaps delayed till age; shut you from a happier choice, from fairer fortunes; shackled you with vows that, as my youth and its poor attributes decayed, would only have irritated and galled; made your whole existence one long suspense! No, Alfred, even *yet* you do not know me!

EVELYN Know you! Fair angel, too excellent for man's harder nature to understand! At least it is permitted me to revere. Why were such blessed words not vouchsafed to me before? Why, why come they now, too late? Oh, heaven, too late!

CLARA Too late! What, then, have I said?

EVELYN Wealth! What is it without you? *With* you, I recognise its power; to forestall your every wish, to smooth your every path, to make all that life borrows from grace and beauty your ministrant and handmaid. And then, looking to those eyes, to read there the treasures of a heart that excelled all that kings could lavish. Why

that were to make gold indeed a god! But vain, vain, vain! Bound by
every tie of faith, gratitude, loyalty and honour, to another! 155

CLARA Another! Is she, then, true to your reverses? I did not know
this, indeed, I did not! And I have thus betrayed myself! O, shame!
he must despise me now!

>   *Enter Sir John Vesey; at the same time Graves and Lady*
>   *Franklin advance from the inner room*

SIR JOHN (*with dignity and frankness*) Evelyn, I was hasty yesterday.
You must own it natural that I should be so. But Georgina has been 160
so urgent in your defence, that—(*as Lady Franklin comes up to
listen*) sister, just shut the door, will you? That I cannot resist her.
What's money without happiness? So give me your security, for she
insists on lending you the ten thousand pounds.

EVELYN I know; and have already received it. 165

SIR JOHN Already received it! Is he joking? Faith, for the last two days
I believe I have been living amongst the Mysteries of Udolpho!°
Sister, have you seen Georgina?

LADY FRANKLIN Not since she went out to walk in the square.

SIR JOHN (*aside*) She's not in the square nor the house. Where the 170
deuce can the girl be?

EVELYN I have written to Miss Vesey. I have asked her to fix the day
for our wedding.

SIR JOHN (*joyfully*) Have you? Go, Lady Franklin, find her instantly.
She must be back by this time. Take my carriage, it is but a step. 175
You won't be two minutes gone. (*Aside*) I'd go myself, but I'm
afraid of leaving him a moment while he's in such excellent
dispositions.

LADY FRANKLIN (*repulsing Clara*) No, no. Stay till I return.

>   *Exit Lady Franklin*

SIR JOHN And don't be downhearted, my dear fellow; if the worst 180
come to the worst, you will have everything I can leave you. Meantime, if I can in any way help you—

EVELYN Ha! You! *You*, too? Sir John, you have seen my letter to Miss
Vesey? (*Aside*) Or could she have learned the truth before she ventured to be generous? 185

SIR JOHN No, on my honour. I only just called at the door on my way
from Lord Spend—that is, from the City°. Georgina was out. Was
ever anything so unlucky?

VOICES (*offstage*) Hurrah, hurrah! Blue° forever!

SIR JOHN What's that? 190

>   *Enter Sharp*

SHARP Sir, a deputation from Groginhole. Poll closed in the first hour.° You are returned! Hollow,° sir, hollow!

EVELYN And it was to please Clara!

SIR JOHN Mr Sharp, Mr Sharp, I say, how much has Mr Evelyn lost by Messrs Flash and Co.?   195

SHARP Oh, a great deal, Sir, a great deal.

SIR JOHN (*alarmed*) How! A great deal!

EVELYN Speak the truth, Sharp, concealment is all over.

SHARP Two hundred and twenty three pounds, six shillings, three pence. A great sum to throw away.   200

GRAVES Ah, I comprehend now! Poor Evelyn, caught in his own trap!

SIR JOHN Eh! What, my dear boy? What? Ha! ha! All humbug, was it? All humbug, upon my soul! So, Mr Sharp, isn't he ruined after all? Not the least, wee, rascally, little bit in the world, ruined?

SHARP Sir, he has never even lived up to his income.   205

SIR JOHN Worthy man! I could jump up to the ceiling! I am the happiest father-in-law in the three kingdoms. [*Knock heard*] And that's my sister's knock too.

CLARA Since I was mistaken, cousin; since now you do not need me, forget what has passed. My business here is over. Farewell!   210

EVELYN Could you but see my heart at this moment, with what love, what veneration, what anguish it is filled, you would know how little, in the great calamities of life, fortune is really worth. And must we part now, *now*, when—when—[*weeps*] I never wept before, since my mother died!   215

> *Enter Lady Franklin and Georgina, followed by Sir Frederick*
> *Blount, who looks shy and embarrassed*

GRAVES Georgina herself. Then there's no hope.

SIR JOHN What the deuce brings that fellow Blount here? Georgy, my dear Georgy, I want to—

EVELYN Stand back, Sir John.

SIR JOHN But I must speak a word to her, I want to—   220

EVELYN Stand back, I say, not a whisper, not a sign. If your daughter is to be my wife, to *her* heart only will I look for a reply to *mine*.

LADY FRANKLIN (*to Georgina*) Speak the truth, niece.

EVELYN Georgina, it is true, then, that you trust me with your confidence, your fortune. Is it also true that, when you did so, you   225
believed me ruined? O pardon the doubt! Answer as if your father stood not there. Answer me from that truth the world cannot yet have plucked from your soul. Answer as if the woe or weal of a life trembled in the balance. Answer as the woman's heart, yet virgin

and unpolluted, *should* answer to one who has trusted to it his all! 230

GEORGINA What can he mean?

SIR JOHN (*making signs*, [*aside*]) She won't look this way, she won't, hang her. [*Aloud*] HEM!

EVELYN You falter. I implore, I adjure you, answer! 235

LADY FRANKLIN The truth!

GEORGINA Mr Evelyn; your fortune might well dazzle me, as it dazzled others. Believe me, I sincerely pity your reverses.

SIR JOHN Good girl. You hear her, Evelyn?

GEORGINA What's money without happiness? 240

SIR JOHN Clever creature! My own sentiments!

GEORGINA And so, as our engagement is now annulled, Papa told me so this very morning, I have promised my hand where I have given my heart—to Sir Frederick Blount.

SIR JOHN I told you, I? No such thing, no such thing. You frighten 245 her out of her wits. She don't know what she's saying.

EVELYN Am I awake? But this letter, this letter, received today—

LADY FRANKLIN (*looking over the letter*) Drummond's! From a banker!

EVELYN Read, read. 250

LADY FRANKLIN 'Ten thousand pounds just placed to your account, from the same unknown friend to Alfred Evelyn.' Oh, Clara, I know now why you went to Drummond's this morning!

EVELYN Clara! What! And the former one with the same signature, on the faith of which I pledged my hand and sacrificed my heart— 255

LADY FRANKLIN Was written under my eyes and the secret kept that—

EVELYN Look up, look up, Clara. I am free! I am released! You forgive me? You love me? You are mine! We are rich, rich! I can give you fortune, power. I can devote to you my whole life, thought, heart, 260 soul. I am all yours, Clara, my own, my wife!

SIR JOHN A pretty mess you've made of it, to humbug your own father! And you, too, Lady Franklin. I am to thank you for this!

LADY FRANKLIN You've to thank me that she's not now on the road to Scotland° with Sir Frederick. I chanced on them by the Park just 265 in time to dissuade and save her. But, to do her justice, a hint of your displeasure was sufficient.

GEORGINA (*half sobbing*) And you know, Papa, you said this very morning that poor Frederick had been very ill used and you would settle it all at the club. 270

BLOUNT Come, Sir John, you can only blame yourself and Evelyn's cunning device! After all I'm no such vewy bad match, and as for the ten thousand pounds.—

EVELYN I'll double it. Ah, Sir John, what's money without happiness?

SIR JOHN Pshaw, nonsense, stuff! Don't humbug me. 275

LADY FRANKLIN But if you don't consent, she'll have no husband at all.

SIR JOHN Hum! There's something in that. (*Aside to Evelyn*) Double it, will you? Then settle it all *tightly* on her. Well, well, my foible is not avarice. Blount, make her happy. Child, I forgive you. (*Pinching* 280 *her arm*) Ugh, you fool!

GRAVES (*to Lady Franklin*) I'm afraid it's catching. What say you? I feel the symptoms of matrimony creeping all over me. Shall we? Eh? Shall we? Frankly, now, frankly—

LADY FRANKLIN Frankly, now, there's my hand, on one condition: 285 that we finish our reel on the wedding-day.

GRAVES Accepted. Is it possible? Sainted Maria! Thank heaven you are spared this affliction.

Enter Captain Dudley Smooth

SMOOTH How d'ye do, Alfred? I intrude, I fear! Quite a family party. 290

BLOUNT Wish us joy, Smooth. Georgina's mine, and—

SMOOTH And our four friends there apparently have made up another rubber. John, my dear boy, you look as if you had something at stake on the odd trick.

SIR JOHN Sir, you're very—Confound the fellow! And he's a dead 295 shot too!

Enter Stout and Lord Glossmore hastily, talking with each other

STOUT I'm sure he's of our side. We've all the intelligence.

GLOSSMORE I'm sure he's of ours if his fortune is safe, for we've all the property.

STOUT Just heard of your return, Evelyn! Congratulate you. The 300 great motion of the session° is fixed for Friday. We count on your vote. Progress with the times!

GLOSSMORE Preserve the Constitution!

STOUT Your money will do wonders for the party! Advance!

GLOSSMORE The party respects men of your property! Stick fast! 305

EVELYN I have the greatest respect, I assure you, for the worthy and intelligent flies upon both sides of the wheel;° but whether we go too fast or too slow does not, I fancy, depend so much on the flies as on the Stout Gentleman who sits inside and pays the post-boys.°

Now all my politics as yet is to consider what's best for the Stout   310
Gentleman!

SMOOTH Meaning John Bull.° *Ce cher* old John!

STOUT I'm as wise as I was before.

GLOSSMORE Sir, he's a trimmer!°

EVELYN Ah, Clara, you—you have succeeded where wealth had   315
failed! You have reconciled me to the world and to mankind. My
friends, we must confess it. Amidst the humours and the follies, the
vanities, deceits and vices that play their part in the great comedy
of life, it is our own fault if we do not find such natures, though rare
and few, as redeem the rest, brightening the shadows that are flung   320
from the form and body of the *time* with glimpses of the everlasting
holiness of truth and love.

GRAVES But for the truth and the love, when found, to make us toler-
ably happy, we should not be without—

LADY FRANKLIN Good health—   325

GRAVES Good spirits—

CLARA A good heart—

SMOOTH An innocent rubber—

GEORGINA Congenial tempers—°

BLOUNT A pwoper degwee of pwudence—   330

STOUT Enlightened opinions—

GLOSSMORE Constitutional principles—

SIR JOHN Knowledge of the world—

EVELYN And—plenty of Money!

[*Curtain*]

LONDON ASSURANCE

DION BOUCICAULT

PREFACE

There is a species of literary modesty observed by authors of the present day—I mean, that of prefacing their works with an apology for taking the liberty of inflicting them upon the patient public. Many require no such plea, but the following pages are too full of flagrant faults to pass from me without some few words of extenuation.

The management of Covent Garden Theatre requested me to write a comedy—a modern comedy:° I feared that I was unequal to the task; but by the encouragement and kindness of Mr Charles Mathews° I was induced to attempt it. Once begun, the necessity of excessive rapidity became evident; and, on the spur of the moment, I completed this work in thirty days. I had no time to revise or correct—the ink was scarcely dry before it was in the theatre and accepted. I am aware that it possesses all the many faults, incongruities and excrescences of a hastily written performance. It will not bear analysis as a literary production. In fact, my sole object was to throw together a few scenes of a dramatic nature; and, therefore, I studied the stage rather than the moral effect. I attempted to instil a pungency into the dialogue, and to procure vivid tones by a strong antithesis of character. The moral which I intended to convey is expressed in the last speech of the comedy; but as I wrote *currente calamo*° I have doubtless through the play strayed far wide of my original intent.

Let me take this opportunity of stating the facts attending my reception at Covent Garden Theatre, as it may also hold out encouragement to the faint hearts of many entering the perilous shoals of dramatic literature.

In the beginning of last November° I entered this establishment under the assumed name of Lee Moreton.° I was wholly unknown to any person therein. I received every mark of kindness and attention on the part of the management, and was cordially welcomed on all sides; my productions° were read without loss of time; and the rapidity with which this play was produced, together with the unsparing liberality of its appointments,° give ample proof that the field is open to all comers.

London Assurance was made to order, on the shortest possible notice. I could have wished that my first appearance before the public° had not been in this out-of-breath style; but I saw my opportunity at hand: I knew how important it was not to neglect the chance of production; the door was open—I had a run for it, and here I am.

How shall I return thanks adequate to the general sympathy and hearty goodwill I have received at the hands of the mass of talent congregated in this piece?

Mr W. Farren's personation of *Sir Harcourt* made me regret that I had not the part to rewrite. The *ci-devant jeune homme*°—the veteran *roué*°—consummate vanity—blunt, lively perception, redolent with the very essence of etiquette—the exquisite—the vane of the *beau monde*°—were consummated in his appearance; before a word was uttered, he more than shared the creation of the character.

Mr Harley in *Meddle* was, as Mr Harley is universally acknowledged to be—irresistible.

Who could view the quiet, deliberate impertinence, the barefaced impudence of *Dazzle*, reflected in Mathews, without the reiterated roars of laughter which attended nearly every word he uttered! Passages which I never intended as hits° were loaded, primed and pointed with an effect as unexpected to me as it was pleasing.

Mr Bartley as *Max* gave a tone and feeling to the country squire, both fresh and natural. To this gentleman I am under the greatest obligation for the numerous and valuable suggestions which he tendered; and to him I must attribute, to a great extent, the success of the piece.

I have to offer my most sincere thanks to Mr Anderson, for the kind manner in which he accepted the part of *Courtly*; the prominence which it held in the representation was wholly attributable to his excellent impersonation.

What can I say to Mr Keeley? Praise would be superfluous. His part had one fault in his hands: it was not long enough. (*Mem.*° To correct that another time.)

Out of the trivial character of *Cool* Mr Brindal produced effects wholly unexpected. Let him not imagine that by mentioning him last° I prize him least.

Mrs Nisbett did not enact, she was *Lady Gay Spanker*, the substance of my thoughts. She wore the character with grace and ease, divesting it of any coarseness yet enjoying all its freedom. She dashed in like a flash of lightning and was greeted with a thunder of applause. What can I say of this laughing, frolic° creature? Has Momus° a wife? If he has not, let him make haste.

Mrs Humby, with her usual good nature, undertook a very paltry

page or two, grinding blunt humour into the keenest edge with a
power which she alone possesses.

To those who have witnessed this play, I need not describe my 80
gratitude to Mrs C. Mathews; to those who have not seen it, I must
express my inability of expression. I am well aware that to her judgement, taste and valuable suggestions with regard to alterations of
character, situation, dialogue, expunging passages and dilating others,
to her indefatigable zeal, I owe my position. All this being independ- 85
ent of the participation in the performance, would it not be vanity
in me to add a mite of praise to that which has been showered round
her throughout her life? Detail were vain. No one could guess my
countless obligations, had they not witnessed the conferring of them.

For the success of this play I have to thank a most indulgent audi- 90
ence, an ultra-liberal management, an unrivalled cast; but little, very
little, is due to

the public's
humble servant,
D.L.B.

CHARACTERS OF THE PLAY

FIRST PERFORMED AT THE THEATRE ROYAL, COVENT GARDEN,
ON THURSDAY, MARCH 4, 1841

Sir Harcourt Courtly°	Mr W. Farren	*names echo*
Max Harkaway°	Mr Bartley	*certain features*
Charles Courtly	Mr Anderson	*of the characters*
Mr [Adolphus] Spanker°	Mr Keeley	*—see notes*
[Richard] Dazzle°	Mr Charles Mathews	
Mark Meddle°	Mr Harley	
Cool, [Sir Harcourt's] valet	Mr Brindal	
Simpson, butler [at Oak Hall]	Mr Honner	
Martin	Mr Ayliffe	
James	Mr Collett	
Mr Solomon Isaacs°	Mr W. H. Payne	
Servants	Mr Ireland, Mr Gardiner	

Lady Gay Spanker	Mrs Nisbett
Grace Harkaway	Madame Vestris
Pert°	Mrs Humby

The scene lies in London and Gloucestershire in 1841
Time: three days
Time of representation: 2 hours 50 minutes
Costumes of the day; striking and very fashionable

1.

An ante-room in Sir Harcourt Courtly's house in Belgrave Square,° doors, R, L and C.° Four neat chairs, table

Enter Cool, R°

COOL Half past nine, and Mr Charles has not yet returned: I am in a fever of dread. If his father happen to rise earlier than usual on any morning, he is sure to ask first for Mr Charles. Poor deluded old gentleman. He little thinks how he is deceived.

Enter Martin, lazily, L2E

Well, Martin, he has not come home yet?   5

MARTIN No; and I have not had a wink of sleep all night. I cannot stand this any longer. I shall give warning.° This is the fifth night Mr Courtly has remained out, and I am obliged to stand at the hall window to watch for him.

COOL You know if Sir Harcourt was aware that we connived at his   10
son's irregularities, we should all be discharged.

MARTIN I have used up all my common excuses on his duns. 'Call again', 'Not at home' and 'Send it down to you' won't serve any more; and Mr Crust, the wine merchant, swears he will be paid.   15

COOL So they all say. Why, he has arrests° out against him already. I've seen the fellows watching the door—(*Loud knock and ring heard, L*) There he is just in time. Quick, Martin, for I expect Sir Harcourt's bell every moment—(*Small bell rings, R*) and there it is.

Exit Martin, slowly, R

Thank heaven! He will return to college tomorrow, and this heavy   20
responsibility will be taken off my shoulders. A valet is as difficult a post to fill properly as that of prime minister.

Exit Cool, C

COURTLY (*offstage, L*) Hollo!

DAZZLE (*offstage*) Steady!

Enter Charles Courtly and Dazzle, L

COURTLY Hollo-o-o——   25

DAZZLE Hush! What are you about, howling like a Hottentot?° Sit down there and thank heaven you are in Belgrave Square instead of Bow Street.°

COURTLY D-D-Damn Bow Street.

DAZZLE Oh, with all my heart! You have not yet seen as much of it as   30
I have.

COURTLY I say—let me see—what was I going to say? Oh, look
here—(*He pulls out a large assortment of knockers, bell-pulls, etc.,
from his pocket*) There! Damme! I'll puzzle° the postmen; I'll
deprive them of their right of disturbing the neighbourhood. That   35
black lion's head did belong to old Vampire, the money-lender, this
bell-pull to Miss Stitch, the milliner.

DAZZLE And this brass griffin—

COURTLY That! Oh, let me see—I think, I twisted that off our own
hall-door as I came in, while you were paying the cab.   40

DAZZLE What shall I do with them?

COURTLY Be kind to 'em. Pack 'em in a small hamper and send 'em to
the sitting magistrate with my father's compliments. In the meantime come into my room, and I'll astonish you with some Burgundy.

    Charles Courtly and Dazzle rise. Enter Cool, C

COOL (*R*) Mr Charles—   45

COURTLY (*c*) Out! Out! Not at home to any one.

COOL And drunk—

COURTLY As a lord.

COOL If Sir Harcourt knew this he would go mad; he would discharge
me.   50

COURTLY You flatter yourself; that would be no proof of his insanity.
(*To Dazzle, L*) This is Cool, sir, Mr Cool. He is the best liar
in London. There is a pungency about his invention and an
originality in his equivocation that is perfectly refreshing.

COOL (*aside*) Why, Mr Charles, where did you pick him up?   55

COURTLY You mistake; he picked *me* up.

    Bell rings, R

COOL Here comes Sir Harcourt. Pray do not let him see you in this
state.

COURTLY State! What do you mean? I am in a beautiful state.

COOL I should lose my character.   60

COURTLY That would be a fortunate epoch in your life, Cool.

COOL Your father would discharge me.

COURTLY How dare you get drunk, sir?

COOL Retire to your own room, for heaven's sake, Mr Charles.

COURTLY I'll do so for my own sake. (*To Dazzle*) I say, old fellow,   65
(*staggering*) just hold the door steady while I go in.

DAZZLE This way. Now then! Take care!

    Dazzle helps Charles Courtly into the room, R. Enter Sir

*Harcourt Courtly in an elegant dressing-gown and Greek skull-
cap and tassels° etc., etc., R*

SIR HARCOURT (*c*) Cool, is breakfast ready?

COOL (*R*) Quite ready, Sir Harcourt.

SIR HARCOURT Apropos, I omitted to mention that I expect Squire   70
Harkaway to join us this morning, and you must prepare for my
departure to Oak Hall immediately.

COOL Leave town in the commencement of the season,° Sir
Harcourt? So unprecedented a proceeding.

SIR HARCOURT It is. I confess it. There is but one power could effect   75
such a miracle—that is, divinity.

COOL How!

SIR HARCOURT In female form, of course. Cool, I am about to present
society with a second Lady Courtly; young, blushing eighteen;
lovely, I have her portrait; rich, I have her banker's account; an   80
heiress and a Venus!

COOL Lady Courtly could be none other.

SIR HARCOURT Ha! ha! Cool, your manners are above your station.
Apropos, I shall find no further use for my brocaded dressing-
gown.°   85

COOL I thank you, Sir Harcourt; might I ask who the fortunate lady
is?

SIR HARCOURT Certainly. Miss Grace Harkaway, the niece of my old
friend Max.

COOL Have you never seen the lady, sir?   90

SIR HARCOURT Never. That is, yes—eight years ago. Having been, as
you know, on the Continent for the last seven years, I have not had
the opportunity of paying my *devoirs.*° Our connection and
betrothal was a very extraordinary one. Her father's estates were
contiguous to mine. Being a penurious, miserly, ugly old scoundrel,   95
he made a market of° my indiscretion and supplied my extravagance with large sums of money on mortgages, his great desire
being to unite the two properties. About seven years ago he died,
leaving Grace, a girl, to the guardianship of her uncle, with this
will: If on attaining the age of nineteen she would consent to marry   100
me, I should receive those deeds and all his property as her dowry;
if she refused to comply with this condition, they should revert to
my heir presumptive or apparent.° She consents.

COOL Who would not?

SIR HARCOURT I consent to receive her fifteen thousand pounds a   105
year.

84

COOL (*aside*) Who would not?

SIR HARCOURT So prepare, Cool, prepare. (*Crosses to R*) But where is
my boy? Where is Charles?

COOL Why—Oh, he is gone out, Sir Harcourt; yes, gone out to take a   110
walk.

SIR HARCOURT Poor child! A perfect child in heart; a sober placid
mind; the simplicity and verdure of boyhood kept fresh and unsul-
lied by any contact with society. Tell me, Cool, at what time was he
in bed last night?   115

COOL Half past nine, Sir Harcourt.

SIR HARCOURT Half past nine! Beautiful! What an original idea!
Reposing in cherub slumbers, while all around him teems with
drinking and debauchery. Primitive sweetness of nature! No pilot-
coated, bearskinned brawling.°   120

COOL Oh, Sir Harcourt!

SIR HARCOURT No cigar smoking—

COOL Faints at the smell of one.

SIR HARCOURT No brandy-and-water bibbing—

COOL Doesn't know the taste of anything stronger than barley-water.   125

SIR HARCOURT Never heard the clock strike twelve, except at noon.
In fact, he is my son and became a gentleman by right of paternity.
He inherited my manners.

Enter Martin, L

MARTIN Mr Harkaway.

Enter Max Harkaway, L

MAX Squire Harkaway, fellow, or Max Harkaway, another time.   130

Martin bows and exit, L

Aha! ha! Sir Harcourt, I'm devilish glad to see ye. Gi' me your fist.
Dang it, but I'm glad to see ye! Let me see—six, seven years or
more, since we have met. How quickly they have flown.

SIR HARCOURT (*throwing off his studied manner*) Max, Max! Give me
your hand, old boy. (*Aside*) Ah! He is glad to see me; there is no   135
fawning pretence about that squeeze. (*Aloud*) Cool, you may retire.

Exit Cool, R

MAX Why, you are looking quite rosy.

SIR HARCOURT Ah, ah, rosy! Am I too florid?

MAX Not a bit; not a bit.

SIR HARCOURT I thought so. (*Aside*) Cool said I had put too much on.   140

MAX (*L*) How comes it, Courtly, that you manage to retain your
youth? See, I'm as grey as an old badger, or a wild rabbit, while you
are as black as a young rook. I say, whose head grew your hair, eh?

SIR HARCOURT Permit me to remark that all the beauties of my person are of home manufacture. Why should you be surprised at my   145
youth? I have scarcely thrown off the giddiness of a very boy;
elasticity of limb; buoyancy of soul. Remark this position. (*Throws
himself into an attitude*) I held that attitude for ten minutes at Lady
Acid's last *reunion*,° at the express desire of one of our first
sculptors, while he was making a sketch of me for the Apollo.°   150

MAX (*aside*) Making a butt of thee for their gibes.

SIR HARCOURT Lady Sarah Sarcasm started up and, pointing to my
face, ejaculated, 'Good gracious! Does not Sir Harcourt remind
you of the countenance of Ajax, in the Pompeian portrait?'°

MAX Ajax. Humbug!   155

SIR HARCOURT You are complimentary.

MAX I'm a plain man and always speak my mind. What's in a face or
figure? Does a Grecian nose entail° a good temper? Does a waspish
waist indicate a good heart? Or do oily, perfumed locks necessarily
thatch a well-furnished brain?   160

SIR HARCOURT It's an undeniable fact; *plain* people always praise the
beauties of the *mind*.

MAX Excuse the insinuation; I had thought the first Lady Courtly had
surfeited you with beauty.

SIR HARCOURT No; she lived fourteen months with me and then   165
eloped with an intimate friend. Etiquette compelled me to challenge the seducer. So I received satisfaction—and a bullet in my
shoulder at the same time. However, I had the consolation of knowing that he was the handsomest man of the age. She did not insult
me by running away with a damned ill-looking scoundrel.   170

MAX That certainly was flattering.

SIR HARCOURT I felt so, as I pocketed the ten thousand pounds'
damages.°

MAX That must have been a great balm to your sore honour.

SIR HARCOURT It was. Max, my honour would have died without it;   175
for in that year the wrong horse won the Derby°—by some mistake.
It was one of the luckiest chances, a thing that does not happen
twice in a man's life; the opportunity of getting rid of his wife and
his debts at the same time.

MAX Tell the truth, Courtly! Did you not feel a little frayed in your   180
delicacy? Your honour, now? Eh?

SIR HARCOURT Not a whit. Why should I? I married *money* and I
received it, virgin gold! My delicacy and honour had nothing to do
with hers. The world pities the bereaved° husband, when it should

congratulate. No, the affair made a sensation and I was the object.° 185
Besides, it is vulgar to make a parade of one's feelings, however
acute they may be. Impenetrability of countenance is the sure sign
of your highly-bred man of fashion.

MAX So, a man must therefore lose his wife and his money with a
smile—in fact, everything he possesses but his temper. 190

SIR HARCOURT Exactly—and greet ruin with '*vive la bagatelle*!'° For
example, your modish beauty never discomposes the shape of her
features with convulsive laughter. A smile rewards the *bon mot*° and
also shows the whiteness of her teeth. She never weeps impromptu;
tears might destroy the economy° of her cheek. Scenes are vulgar, 195
hysterics obsolete. She exhibits a calm, placid, impenetrable lake,
whose surface is reflection, but of unfathomable depth; a statue,
whose life is hypothetical and not a *primâ facie* fact.° (*Crosses to L*)

MAX Well, give me the girl that will fly at your eyes in an argument
and stick to her point like a fox to his own tail.° 200

SIR HARCOURT But, etiquette! Max, remember etiquette.

MAX Damn etiquette! I have seen a man who thought it sacrilege to
eat fish with a knife,° that would not scruple to rise up and rob his
brother of his birthright in a gambling-house. Your thoroughbred,
well-blooded heart, will seldom kick over the traces of good feeling. 205
That's my opinion, and I don't care who knows it.

SIR HARCOURT Pardon me, etiquette is the pulse of society, by regulating which the body politic is retained in health. I consider myself
one of the faculty° in the art.

MAX Well, well; you are a living libel upon common sense, for you are 210
old enough to know better.

SIR HARCOURT Old enough! What do you mean? Old! I still retain all
my little juvenile indiscretions, which your niece's beauties must
teach me to discard. I have not sown my wild oats yet.

MAX Time you did, at sixty-three. 215

SIR HARCOURT Sixty-three! Good Gracious! Forty, 'pon my life!
Forty, next March.

MAX Why, you are older than I am.

SIR HARCOURT Oh! You are old enough to be my father.

MAX Well, if I am, I am; that's etiquette, I suppose. Poor Grace! How 220
often I have pitied her fate. That a young and beautiful creature
should be driven into wretched splendour, or miserable poverty!

SIR HARCOURT Wretched! Wherefore? Lady Courtly wretched!
Impossible!

MAX Will she not be compelled to marry you, whether she likes you or 225

providing a commentary on the marriage system.

87

not? A choice between you and poverty. (*Aside*) And hang me if it isn't a tie! [*Aloud*] But why do you not introduce your son Charles to me? I have not seen him since he was a child. You would never permit him to accept any of my invitations to spend his vacation at Oak Hall. Of course, we shall have the pleasure of his company now.   230

SIR HARCOURT He is not fit to enter society yet. He is a studious, sober boy.

MAX Boy! Why, he's five and twenty.

SIR HARCOURT Good gracious! Max, you will permit me to know my own son's age. He is not twenty.   235

MAX I'm dumb.

SIR HARCOURT You will excuse me while I indulge in the process of dressing.° Cool!

> *Enter Cool, R*

Prepare my toilet.

> *Exit Cool, L*

That is a ceremony which, with me, supersedes all others. I con-   240
sider it a duty which every gentleman owes to society, to render himself as agreeable an object as possible; and the least compliment a mortal can pay to nature, when she honours him by bestowing extra care in the manufacture of his person,° is to display her taste to the best possible advantage; and so, *au revoir*.   245

> *Exit Sir Harcourt Courtly, RC*

MAX (*sits R of table*) That's a good soul! He has his faults, and who has not? Forty years of age! Oh, monstrous! But he does look uncommonly young for sixty, spite of his foreign locks and complexion.

> *Enter Dazzle, R2E*

DAZZLE Who's my friend with the stick and gaiters,° I wonder? One of the family—the governor,° maybe.   250

MAX Who's this? (*Rises*) Oh, Charles, is that you, my boy? How are you? (*Aside*) This is the *boy*.

DAZZLE [*aside*] He knows me. He is too respectable for a bailiff.° (*Aloud*) How are you?

MAX Your father has just left me.   255

DAZZLE (*aside*) The devil he has, he's been dead these ten years. Oh! I see, he thinks I'm Courtly. (*Aloud*) The honour you would confer on me, I must unwillingly disclaim; I am not Mr Courtly.

MAX I beg pardon; a friend, I suppose?

DAZZLE Oh, a most intimate friend, a friend of years, distantly related   260
to the family, one of my ancestors married one of his. (*Aside*) Adam and Eve.

88

MAX Are you on a visit here?

DAZZLE Yes. Oh yes. (*Aside*) Rather a short one, I'm afraid.

MAX (*aside*) This appears a dashing kind of fellow, and he is a friend of   265
Sir Harcourt's. I'll invite him to the wedding. (*Aloud*) Sir, if you are
not otherwise engaged, I shall feel honoured by your company at
my house, Oak Hall, Gloucestershire.

DAZZLE Your name is—

MAX Harkaway, Mr Harkaway.   270

DAZZLE Harkaway—let me see; I ought to be related to the Harkaways, somehow.

MAX A wedding is about to come off. Will you take a part on the
occasion?

DAZZLE With pleasure; any part but that of the husband.   275

MAX Have you any previous engagement?

DAZZLE I was thinking—eh! Why, let me see. (*Aside*) Promised to
meet my tailor and his account tomorrow. However, I'll postpone
that. (*Aloud*) Have you good shooting?

MAX Shooting! Why, there's no shooting at this time of the year.°   280

DAZZLE Oh! I'm in no hurry. I can wait till the season, of course. I was
only speaking precautionally. You have good shooting.

MAX The best in the country.

DAZZLE Make yourself comfortable! Say no more, I'm your man. Wait
till you see how I'll murder your preserves.°   285

MAX Do you hunt?

DAZZLE Pardon me, but will you repeat that? (*Aside*) Delicious and
expensive idea!

MAX You ride?

DAZZLE Anything! Everything! From a blood° to a broomstick! Only   290
catch me a flash of lightning, and let me get on the back of it, and
dam'me if I wouldn't astonish the elements.

MAX Ha! ha!

DAZZLE I'd put a girdle round about the earth, in very considerably
less than forty minutes.°   295

MAX Ah! ah! We'll show old Fiddlestrings° how to spend the day. He
imagines that nature, at the earnest request of fashion, made summer days long for him to saunter in the park, and winter nights,
that he might have good time to get cleared out° at hazard or at
whist.° Give me the yelping of a pack of hounds before the shuf-   300
fling of a pack of cards. What state° can match the chase in full cry,
each vying with his fellow which shall be most happy? A thousand
deaths° fly by unheeded in that one hour's life of ecstasy. Time is

outrun, and nature seems to grudge our bliss in making the day so short. 305

DAZZLE No, for then rises up the idol of my great adoration.

MAX Who's that?

DAZZLE The bottle, that lends a lustre to the soul. When the world puts on its nightcap and extinguishes the sun, then comes the bottle. Oh, mighty wine! Don't ask me to apostrophise. Wine and 310 love are the only two indescribable things in nature; but I prefer the wine, because its consequences are not entailed,° and are more easily got rid of.

MAX How so?

DAZZLE Love ends in matrimony, wine in soda water. 315

MAX Well, I can promise you as fine a bottle as ever was cracked.

DAZZLE Never mind the bottle, give me the wine. Say no more, but, when I arrive, just shake one of my hands and put the key of the cellar into the other, and if I don't make myself intimately acquainted with its internal organisation—well, I say nothing, time 320 will show.

MAX I foresee some happy days.

DAZZLE And I some glorious nights.

MAX It mustn't be a flying visit.

DAZZLE I despise the word; I'll stop a month with you. 325

MAX Or a year or two.

DAZZLE I'll live and die with you.

MAX Ha! ha! Remember, Max Harkaway, Oak Hall, Gloucestershire.

DAZZLE I'll remember. Fare ye well. (*Max is going, R*) I say, holloa! Tallyho-o-o-o! 330

MAX Yoicks! Tallyho-o-o-o!°

Exit Max Harkaway, L

DAZZLE There I am, quartered for a couple of years at the least. The old boy wants somebody to ride his horses, shoot his game and keep a restraint on the morals of the parish: I'm eligible. What a lucky accident to meet young Courtly last night! Who 335 could have thought it? Yesterday I could not make certain of a dinner, except at my own proper peril.° Today I would flirt with a banquet.°

Enter Charles Courtly, R2E

COURTLY What infernal row was that? Why, (*seeing Dazzle*) are you here still? 340

DAZZLE Yes. Ain't you delighted? I'll ring and send the servant for my luggage.

90

COURTLY The devil you will! Why, you don't mean to say you seriously intend to take up a permanent residence here? (*He rings bell*)

DAZZLE Now, that's a most inhospitable insinuation.   345

COURTLY Might I ask your name?

DAZZLE With a deal of pleasure. Richard Dazzle, late of the
Unattached° Volunteers, vulgarly entitled the 'Dirty Buffs'.°
    [*Enter Martin, L*]

COURTLY Then, Mr Richard Dazzle, I have the honour of wishing
you a very good morning. Martin, show this gentleman the door.   350

DAZZLE If he does, I'll kick Martin out of it. [*To Martin*] No offence.
    Exit Martin, L

Now, sir, permit me to place a dioramic view of your conduct before
you. After bringing you safely home this morning; after indulgently
waiting whenever you took a passing fancy to a knocker or bell-pull;
after conducting a retreat that would have reflected honour on   355
Napoleon,° you would kick me into the street, like a mangy cur:
and that's what you call gratitude. Now, to show you how superior I
am to petty malice, I give you an unlimited invitation to my
house—my country house—to remain as long as you please.

COURTLY Your house!   360

DAZZLE Oak Hall, Gloucestershire. Fine old place; for further particulars see road-book;° that is, it *nominally* belongs to my old
friend and relation, Max Harkaway; but I'm privileged—capital old
fellow—say, shall we be honoured?

COURTLY Sir, permit me to hesitate a moment. (*Aside*) Let me see. I   365
go back to college tomorrow, so I shall not be missing. Tradesmen
begin to dun.
    *A noise off L between Martin and Isaacs; Cool has entered, C,
    crosses and goes off, L*
I hear thunder; here is shelter ready for me.
    Enter Cool, L

COOL Oh, Mr Charles, Mr Solomon Isaacs is in the hall and swears he
will remain till he has arrested you!   370

COURTLY Does he! Sorry he is so obstinate. Take him my compliments, and I will bet him five to one he will not.

DAZZLE Double or quits, with my kind regards.

COOL But, sir, he has discovered the house in Curzon Street.° He
says, he is aware the furniture, at least, belongs to you, and he will   375
put a man in° immediately.

COURTLY That's awkward. What's to be done?

DAZZLE Ask him whether he couldn't make it a woman?   *witty comedy*

91

COURTLY I must trust that to fate.

DAZZLE I will give you my acceptance,° if it will be of any use to you;   380
it is of none to me.

COURTLY No, sir; but in reply to your most generous and kind invitation, if you be in earnest, I shall feel delighted to accept it.

DAZZLE Certainly.

COURTLY Then, off we go, through the stables, down the mews, and   385
so slip through my friend's fingers.

DAZZLE But, stay, you must do the polite.° Say farewell to him before
you part. Hang it, don't cut him.

COURTLY You jest!

DAZZLE Here, lend me a card. (*Courtly gives him one*) Now, then.   390
(*Writes. [To Cool]*) Our respects to Mr Isaacs—sorry to have been
prevented from seeing him. Ha! ha!

COURTLY Ha! ha!

DAZZLE We'll send him up some game.°

COURTLY [*to Cool*] Don't let my father see him.   395
    Exeunt Charles Courtly and Dazzle, R

COOL What's this? (*Reading*) 'Mr Charles Courtly, P.P.C.,° returns
thanks for obliging enquiries.'
    Exit Cool, L°

[*Curtain*]

2.

The lawn before Oak Hall, a fine Elizabethan mansion; a drawing-room is seen through large French windows at the back. Statues, urns and garden-chairs about the stage

Enter Pert through window, LUE, to James who is discovered°

PERT James, Miss Grace desires me to request that you will watch at the avenue and let her know when the squire's carriage is seen on the London road.

JAMES I will go to the lodge.

Exit James, LIE

PERT How I do long to see what kind of a man Sir Harcourt Courtly   5
is. They say he is sixty; so he must be old and consequentially ugly. If I were Miss Grace I would rather give up all my fortune and marry the man I liked than go to church with a stuffed eel-skin.° But taste is everything. She doesn't seem to care whether he is sixty or sixteen; jokes at love; prepares for matrimony as she would for   10
dinner; says it is a necessary evil, and what can't be cured must be endured. Now, I say this is against all nature; and she is either no woman, or a deeper one than I am, if she prefers an old man to a young one.

Enter Grace Harkaway through window, LUE

Here she comes, looking as cheerfully as if she was going to marry   15
Mr Jenks—my Mr Jenks, whom nobody won't lead to the halter° till I have that honour.

GRACE Well, Pert, any sign of my uncle yet?

PERT *(L)* No, Miss Grace; but James has gone to watch the road.

GRACE In my uncle's letter, he mentions a Mr Dazzle, whom he has   20
invited, so you must tell Mrs Howton to prepare a room for him. He is some friend of my husband that-is-to-be, and my uncle seems to have taken an extraordinary predilection for him. Apropos! I must not forget to have a flower for the dear old man when he arrives.   25

PERT The dear old man! Do you mean Sir Harcourt?

GRACE Law,° no! My uncle, of course. *(Plucking flowers from bed, R)* What do I care for Sir Harcourt Courtly?

PERT Isn't it odd, Miss, you have never seen your intended, though it has been so long since you were betrothed?   30

93

GRACE Not at all. Marriage matters are conducted nowadays in a most mercantile manner; consequently a previous acquaintance is by no means indispensable. Besides, my *prescribed* husband has been upon the Continent for the benefit of his—property! They say a southern climate is a great restorer of consumptive estates.°   35

PERT Well, Miss, for my own part I should like to have a good look at my bargain before I paid for it; 'specially when one's life is the price of the article. But why, ma'am, do you consent to marry in this blind-man's-buff sort of manner? What would you think if he were not quite so old?   40

GRACE I should think he was a little younger.

PERT Well, *I* should like him all the better.

GRACE That wouldn't I. A young husband might expect affection and nonsense, which 'twould be deceit in me to render; nor would he permit me to remain with my uncle. Sir Harcourt takes me with the encumbrances on his estate, and I shall beg to be left among the rest of the live-stock. (*Crosses,* L)   45

PERT Ah, Miss! But some day you might chance to stumble over *the* man. What could you do then?   50

GRACE Do! Beg *the* man's pardon, and request *the* man to pick me up again.

PERT Ah! You were never in love, Miss?

GRACE No! Nor ever will be till I am tired of myself and common sense. Love is a pleasant scapegoat for a little epidemic madness. I must have been inoculated in my infancy, for the infection passes over poor me in contempt.   55

Enter James, L

JAMES Two gentlemen, Miss Grace, have just alighted.

GRACE Very well, James.

Exit James, L

Pert, remember, this as a maxim; a woman is always in love with one of two things.   60

PERT What are they, Miss?

GRACE A man, or herself—and I know which is the most profitable.

Exit Grace Harkaway, 2LUE

PERT I wonder what my Jenks would say, if I was to ask him. Law! Here comes Mr Meddle, his rival 'contemporary solicitor'° as he calls him; a nasty, prying, ugly wretch. What brings him here? He comes puffed with some news. (*Retires*)   65

Enter Mark Meddle, with a newspaper, L I E

MEDDLE I have secured the only newspaper in the village; my character° as an attorney-at-law depended on the monopoly of its information. I took it up by chance, when this paragraph met my astonished view: (*Reads*) 'We understand that the contract of marriage, so long in abeyance on account of the lady's minority,° is about to be celebrated at Oak Hall, Gloucestershire, the well-known and magnificent mansion of Maximilian Harkaway, Esq., between Sir Harcourt Courtly, Baronet, of fashionable celebrity, and Miss Grace Harkaway, niece to Mr Harkaway. The preparations are proceeding on the good old English style.' Is it possible! I seldom swear except in a witness box, but, damme, had it been known in the village, my reputation would have been lost, my voice in the parlour of The Red Lion mute, and Jenks, a fellow who calls himself a lawyer, without more capability than a broomstick and as much impudence as a young barrister after getting a verdict° by mistake, why, he would actually have taken the Reverend Mr Spout by the button,° which is now my sole privilege. Ah! Here is Mrs° Pert; couldn't have hit upon a better person. I'll cross-examine her: lady's maid to Miss Grace, confidential purloiner of second-hand silk—a *nisi prius*° of her mistress. Ah, sits on the woolsack° in the pantry and dictates the laws of kitchen etiquette.° Ah! Mrs Pert, good morning, permit me to say,—and my word as a legal character° is not unduly considered°—I venture to affirm that you look a—quite like the—a—

PERT (*L*) Law! Mr Meddle.

MEDDLE (*L*) Yes, that's it—exactly like the Law.

PERT Ha! Indeed, complimentary, I confess; like the law; tedious, prosy, made up of musty paper. You shan't have a long suit of me.° Good morning! (*Going*)

MEDDLE Stay, Mrs Pert; don't calumniate my calling, or disseminate vulgar prejudices.

PERT Vulgar! You talk of vulgarity to me; you, whose sole employment is to sneak about like a pig snouting out the dust-hole of society and feeding upon the bad ends° of vice; you, who live upon the world's iniquity; you miserable specimen of a bad six-and-eightpence.° (*Following him round to R*)

MEDDLE (*L*) But, Mrs Pert—

PERT (*RC*) Don't 'but' me, sir. I won't be butted° by any such low fellow.

MEDDLE This is slander; an action will lie.°

PERT Let it lie; lying is your trade. I'll tell you what, Mr Meddle; if I

had my will I would soon put a check on your prying propensities.
I'd treat you as the farmers do the inquisitive hogs.   110

MEDDLE How?

PERT I would ring your nose.° *comical in its ridiculousness.*
    Exit Pert into house, LUE

MEDDLE Not much information elicited from that witness. Jenks is at
the bottom of this. I have very little hesitation in saying Jenks is
a libellous rascal; I heard reports that he was undermining my   115
character here through Mrs Pert. Now I'm certain of it; assault is
expensive; but I certainly will put by a small weekly *stipendium*,°
until I can afford to kick Jenks.

DAZZLE (*outside, L*) Come along; this way!

MEDDLE Ah! Whom have we here? Visitors; I'll address them.   120
    Enter Dazzle, L

DAZZLE Who's this, I wonder; one of the family? I must know him.°
(*To Meddle*) Ah! How are ye?

MEDDLE Quite well. Just arrived!—Ah!—Um!—Might I request the
honour of knowing whom I address?

DAZZLE Richard Dazzle, Esquire; and you—   125

MEDDLE Mark Meddle, attorney-at-law.
    Enter Charles Courtly, L

DAZZLE What detained you?

COURTLY My dear fellow, I have just seen such a woman!

DAZZLE (*aside to Courtly*) Hush! (*Aloud*) Permit me to introduce you
to my very old friend, Meddle. He's a capital fellow; know him.   130

MEDDLE (*R*) I feel honoured. Who is your friend?

DAZZLE Oh, he? What, my friend? Oh! Augustus Hamilton.

COURTLY How d'ye do? (*Meddle attempts to shake hands—looking off*)
There she is, again!

MEDDLE (*looking off, LUE*) Why, that is Miss Grace.   135

DAZZLE (*LC*) Of course, Grace.

COURTLY (*C*) I'll go and introduce myself.
    Dazzle stops him

DAZZLE (*aside*) What are you about? Would you insult my old friend
Puddle by running away? (*Aloud*) I say, Puddle, Mud-Puddle,° just
show my friend the lions,° while I say how d'ye do to my young   140
friend, Grace. (*Aside [to Meddle]*) Cultivate his acquaintance.
    Exit Dazzle, LUE. Courtly looks after him

MEDDLE Mr Hamilton, might I take the liberty? | *word play*

COURTLY (*looking off*) Confound the fellow!

MEDDLE Sir, what did you remark?

COURTLY [*aside*] She's gone! [*Aloud*] Oh, are you here still, Mr   145
Thingomerry Puddle?

MEDDLE Meddle, sir, Meddle, in the list of attorneys.

COURTLY Well, Muddle or Puddle, or whoever you are, you are a bore.

MEDDLE (*aside*) How excessively odd! Mrs Pert said I was a pig; now
I'm a boar; I wonder what they'll make of me next.   150

COURTLY Mr Thingamy, will you take a word of advice?

MEDDLE Feel honoured.

COURTLY Get out.

MEDDLE Hollo! Do you mean to—I don't understand.

COURTLY Delighted to quicken your apprehension. You are an ass,   155
Puddle.

MEDDLE Ha, ha! Another quadruped! Yes; beautiful! (*Aside*) I wish
he'd call me something libellous; but that would be too much to
expect. (*Aloud*) Anything else?

COURTLY Some miserable pettifogging scoundrel!   160

MEDDLE Good! Ha! ha!

COURTLY What do you mean by laughing at me?

MEDDLE Ha! ha! ha! Excellent! Delicious!

COURTLY Mr—are you ambitious of a kicking?

MEDDLE Very, very. Go on, kick, go on!   165

COURTLY (*looking off*) Here she comes! I'll speak to her.

MEDDLE But, sir—sir—

COURTLY Oh, go to the devil!

Charles Courtly runs off, LUE

MEDDLE There, there's a chance lost. Gone! I have no hesitation in
saying that in another minute I should have been kicked, literally   170
kicked; a legal luxury! Costs, damages and actions rose up like sky-
rockets in my aspiring soul; with golden tails reaching to the infin-
ity of my hopes. (*Looking*) They are coming this way, Mr Hamilton
in close conversation with Lady Courtly that-is-to-be. Crim.
con.°—Courtly versus Hamilton,—damages problematical—   175
Meddle, chief witness for Plaintiff—guinea a day—professional
man! I'll take down their conversation verbatim.

*Meddle retires, R2E. Enter Grace Harkaway, followed by
Courtly from LUE*

GRACE (*R*) Perhaps you would follow your friend into the dining-
room. Refreshment after your long journey must be requisite.

COURTLY (*L*) Pardon me, madam; but the lovely garden and the love-   180
liness before me is better refreshment than I could procure in any
dining-room.

GRACE Ha! Your company and compliments arrive together.

COURTLY I trust that a passing remark will not spoil so welcome an
introduction as this by offending you.   185

GRACE I am not certain that anything you could say would offend me.

COURTLY I never meant—

GRACE I thought not. In turn pardon me, when I request you will
commence your visit with this piece of information; I consider
compliments impertinent and sweetmeat° language fulsome.   190

COURTLY I would condemn my tongue to a Pythagorean silence° if I
thought it could attempt to flatter.

GRACE It strikes me, sir, that you are a stray bee from the hive of
fashion. If so, reserve your honey for its proper cell. A truce to
compliments. You have just arrived *from town*, I apprehend?   195

COURTLY This moment I left mighty London, under the fever of a
full season, groaning with the noisy pulse of wealth and the giddy,
whirling brain of fashion. Enchanting, busy London! How have I
prevailed on myself to desert you! Next week the new ballet comes
out; the week after comes Ascot,° oh!   200

GRACE How agonising must be the reflection.

COURTLY Torture! Can you inform me how you manage to avoid
suicide here? If there was but an opera, even within twenty miles.
We couldn't get up a rustic ballet among the village girls? No? Ah.

GRACE I am afraid you would find that difficult. How I contrive to   205
support life I don't know. It is wonderful, but I have not precisely
contemplated suicide yet, nor do I miss the opera.

COURTLY How can you manage to kill time?

GRACE I can't. Men talk of killing time, while time quietly kills them.
I have many employments; this week I devote to study and various   210
amusements, next week to being married, the following week to
repentance perhaps.

COURTLY Married!

GRACE You seem surprised. I believe it is of frequent occurrence in
the metropolis, is it not?   215

COURTLY Oh, yes, I believe they do it, there. Might I ask to whom?

GRACE I have never seen him yet, but he's a gentleman who has been
strongly recommended to me for the situation° of husband.

COURTLY What an extraordinary match! Would you not consider it
advisable to see him, previous to° incurring the consequence of   220
such an act?

GRACE You must be aware that fashion says otherwise. The gentleman
swears eternal devotion to the lady's fortune, and the lady swears

she will outvie him still. My lord's horses and my lady's diamonds
shine through a few seasons, until a seat in Parliament, or the 225
Continent, stares them in the face;° then, when thrown upon each
other for resources of comfort, they begin to quarrel about the
original conditions of the sale.

COURTLY Sale! No, that would be degrading civilisation into Turkish
barbarity. 230

GRACE Worse, sir, a great deal worse; for there at least they do not
attempt concealment of the barter, but here, every London ball-
room is a marriage mart. Young ladies are trotted out, while the
mother, father, or chaperone plays auctioneer and knocks them
down to the highest bidder. Young men are ticketed up with their 235
fortunes on their backs, and love, turned into a dapper shopman,°
descants on the excellent qualities of the material.

COURTLY Oh! That such a custom could have ever emanated from the
healthy soil of an English heart!

GRACE It never did, like most of our literary dandyisms and dandy 240
literature,° it was borrowed from the French.

COURTLY You seem to laugh at love.

GRACE Love! Why, the very word is a breathing satire upon man's
reason, a mania, indigenous to humanity, nature's jester, who
plays off° tricks upon the world and trips up common sense. 245
When I'm in love I'll write an almanac for very lack of wit,
prognosticate the sighing season, when to beware of tears: 'about
this time, expect matrimony to be prevalent!' Ha! ha! Why should
I lay out° my life in love's bonds upon the bare security of a
man's word? 250

Enter James, L

JAMES The squire, madam, has just arrived and another gentleman
with him.

Exit James, L

GRACE (*aside*) My intended,° I suppose.

COURTLY I perceive you are one of the railers against what is termed
the follies of high life. 255

GRACE No, not particularly; I deprecate all folly. By what prerogative
can the West End mint° issue° absurdity which, if coined in the
East, would be voted vulgar.

COURTLY By a sovereign° right, because it has fashion's head upon its
side,° and that stamps it current.° 260

GRACE Poor Fashion, for how many sins hast thou to answer?

COURTLY Is this idol of the world so radically vicious?

99

GRACE No, the root is well enough, as the body was, until it had outgrown its native soil; but now, like a mighty giant lying over Europe, it pillows its head in Italy, its heart in France, leaving the heels alone for poor little England.   265

COURTLY Pardon me, madam, you wrong yourself to rail against your own inheritance, the kingdom to which loveliness and wit attest your title.

GRACE A mighty realm, forsooth,° with milliners for ministers, a cabinet of coxcombs,° envy for my homage, ruin for my revenue, my right of rule depending on the shape of a bonnet or the sit of a pelisse,° with the next grand noodle as my heir-apparent. Mr Hamilton, when I am crowned, I shall feel happy to abdicate in your favour.   275

  Grace Harkaway curtseys and exit into house, LUE

COURTLY What did she mean by that? Hang me if I can understand her. She is evidently not used to society. Ha! Takes every word I say for infallible truth; requires the solution of a compliment, as if it were a problem in Euclid.° She said she was about to marry, but I rather imagine she was in jest. 'Pon my life, I feel very queer at the contemplation of such an idea, I'll follow her.   280

  Meddle comes down,° L

Oh! perhaps this booby can inform me something about her. (*Meddle makes signs at him*) What the devil is he at?

MEDDLE It won't do. No. Ah! Um. It's not to be done.

COURTLY What do you mean?   285

MEDDLE (*points after Grace*) Counsel retained, cause to come off.°

COURTLY Cause to come off!

MEDDLE Miss Grace is about to be married.

COURTLY Is it possible?

MEDDLE Certainly. If *I* have the drawing out of the deeds—   290

COURTLY To whom?

MEDDLE Oh, I dare say! Ha! Hem! Oh yes! I dare say. Information being scarce in the market, I hope to make mine valuable.

COURTLY Married! Married! I've a great mind. (*Pacing the stage*)

MEDDLE Now I shall have another chance.   295

COURTLY I'll run and ascertain the truth of this from Dazzle.

  Exit Charles Courtly, LUE

MEDDLE It's of no use. He either dare not kick me, or he can't afford it. In either case, he is beneath my notice. Ah! Who comes here? Can it be Sir Harcourt Courtly himself? It can be no other.

  Enter Cool, L1E

Sir, I have the honour to bid you welcome to Oak Hall and the 300
village of Oldborough.°

COOL (*aside*) Excessively polite. (*Aloud*) Sir, thank you.

MEDDLE The township contains two thousand inhabitants.

COOL Does it! I am delighted to hear it. (*Crosses R*)

MEDDLE (*aside*) I can charge him for that. Ahem. Six and eightpence 305
is not much, but it is a beginning. (*Aloud*) If you will permit me, I
can inform you of the different commodities for which it is famous.

COOL Much obliged, but here comes Sir Harcourt Courtly, my
master, and Mr Harkaway. Any other time, I shall feel delighted.

MEDDLE Oh. (*Aside*) Mistook the man for the master. 310

    Meddle retires up.° Enter Max Harkaway and Sir Harcourt
    Courtly LIE

MAX Here we are at last. Now give ye welcome° to Oak Hall, Sir
Harcourt, heartily.

SIR HARCOURT (*languidly*) Cool, assist me.

    Cool, L, takes off his furred cloak, gloves; gives him white gloves
    and a white handkerchief, then places a flower in his coat

MAX Why, you require unpacking as carefully as my best bin of port.
Well, now you are decanted, tell me: what did you think of my park 315
as we came along?

SIR HARCOURT That it would never come to an end. You said it was
only a stone's throw from your infernal lodge to the house. Why,
it's ten miles at least.

MAX I'll do it in ten minutes any day. 320

SIR HARCOURT Yes, in a steam carriage.° [*To Cool*] Cool, perfume my
handkerchief.

MAX Don't do it. Don't! Perfume in the country! Why, it's high treason in the very face of Nature. 'Tis introducing the robbed to the
robber. Here are the sweets from which your fulsome essences° are 325
pilfered and libelled with their names. Don't insult them too.

SIR HARCOURT Oh! (*To Meddle who is by a rose bush*, LC; [*Sir
Harcourt*] *goes up R*) Cull me a bouquet, my man.

MAX (*turning*) Ah, Meddle! How are you? (*To Sir Harcourt Courtly*)
This is Lawyer Meddle. (*Goes up R*) 330

SIR HARCOURT Oh! I took him for one of your people.

MEDDLE Ah! Naturally. Um. Sir Harcourt Courtly, I have the honour
to congratulate. Happy occasion approaches. Ahem! I have no
hesitation in saying this *very* happy occasion approaches.

SIR HARCOURT (*LC*) Cool, is the conversation addressed towards me? 335

COOL (*L*) I believe so, Sir Harcourt.

MEDDLE (c) Oh, certainly! I was complimenting you.

SIR HARCOURT Sir, you are very good. The honour is undeserved, but I am only in the habit of receiving compliments from the fair sex. Men's admiration is so damnably insipid. (*Crosses to Max, who is seated on a bench, R*) If the future Lady Courtly be visible at so unfashionable an hour as this, I shall beg to be introduced.

MAX Visible! Ever since six this morning. I'll warrant ye. Two to one she is at dinner.

SIR HARCOURT Dinner! Is it possible! Lady Courtly dine at half past one p.m.!°

MEDDLE (*down L*) I rather prefer that hour to peck a little my—

SIR HARCOURT Dear me! Who was addressing you?

MEDDLE Oh! I beg pardon.

MAX (*calling*) Here, James!

    Enter James from room, LUE

Tell Miss Grace to come here directly.

    Exit James into house, LUE

Now prepare, Courtly, for, though I say it, she *is*—with the exception of my bay mare Kitty—the handsomest thing in the county. Considering she is a biped, she is a wonder! Full of blood,° sound wind and limb, plenty of bone, sweet coat, in fine condition, with a thoroughbred step, as dainty as a pet greyhound.

SIR HARCOURT Don't compare her to a horse.

MAX Well, I wouldn't, but she's almost as fine a creature; close similarities.

MEDDLE Oh, very fine creature! Close similarity amounting to identity.

SIR HARCOURT Good gracious, sir! What can a lawyer know about woman?

MEDDLE Everything. The consistorial court° is a fine study of the character, and I have no hesitation in saying that I have examined more women than Jenks or—

SIR HARCOURT Oh, damn Jenks!

MEDDLE Sir, thank you. Damn him again, sir, damn him again.

    Enter Grace Harkaway, from house, LUE

GRACE (*runs to him*) My dear uncle!

MAX Ah Grace! You little jade,° come here.

SIR HARCOURT (*eyeing her through his glass*) Oh dear!° She is a rural Venus! I'm astonished and delighted.

MAX Won't you kiss your old uncle? (*He kisses her*)

SIR HARCOURT (*draws an agonising face*) Oh! Ah. Um! *N'importe!*° My privilege in embryo. Hem! It's very tantalising, though.

MAX You are not glad to see me, you are not. (*Kissing her*)   375

SIR HARCOURT (*aside*) Oh, no, no. That is too much. I shall do something horrible presently, if this goes on. (*Aloud*) I should be sorry to
curtail any little ebullition of affection; but—Ahem! May I be
permitted?°

MAX Of course you may. There, Grace, is Sir Harcourt, your husband   380
that-will-be. Go to him, girl.

       Grace curtseys

SIR HARCOURT Permit me to do homage to the charms, the presence
of which has placed me in sight of paradise.

       Sir Harcourt Courtly and Grace Harkaway retire, LC. Enter
       Dazzle, from house LUE

DAZZLE (*R*) Ah! Old fellow, how are you? (*Crosses to him*)

MAX (*RC*) I'm glad to see you! Are you comfortably quartered yet, eh?   385

DAZZLE Splendidly quartered! What a place you've got here. Why, it's
a palace. Here, Hamilton.

       Enter Charles Courtley from house down R, Cool sees him and
       looks astonished

Permit me to introduce my friend Augustus Hamilton. (*Aside to Max*)
Capital fellow! Drinks like a sieve and rides like a thunderstorm.

MAX (*crosses to RC*) Sir, I'm devilish glad to see you. Here, Sir Harcourt,   390
permit me° to introduce to you—(*Goes up stage to Sir Harcourt*)

COURTLY (*R*) The devil!

DAZZLE (*aside, RC*) What's the matter?

COURTLY (*aside*) Why, that is my governor, by Jupiter!

DAZZLE (*aside*) What, old whiskers! You don't say that!   395

COURTLY (*aside*) It is! What's to be done now?

DAZZLE Oh, I don't know.

MAX (*advancing C*) Mr Hamilton, Sir Harcourt Courtly; Sir Harcourt
Courtly, Mr Hamilton.

SIR HARCOURT Hamilton! Good gracious! God bless me. Why,   400
Charles, is it possible. Why, Max, that's my son!

MAX Your son!

GRACE (*C*) Your son, Sir Harcourt! Have you a son as old as that
gentleman?

SIR HARCOURT No; that is—a—yes, not by twenty years—a—   405
Charles, why don't you answer me, sir?

COURTLY (*aside to Dazzle*) What shall I say?

DAZZLE (*aside*) Deny your identity.

COURTLY (*aside*) Capital! (*Pause—they look at each other—aloud*)
What's the matter, sir?   410

SIR HARCOURT How came you down here, sir?

COURTLY By one of Newman's best fours,° in twelve hours and a
quarter.

SIR HARCOURT Isn't your name Charles Courtly?

COURTLY Not to my knowledge.   415

SIR HARCOURT Do you mean to say you are usually called Augustus
Hamilton?

COURTLY Lamentable fact, and quite correct.

DAZZLE How very odd!

SIR HARCOURT Well, I never. Cool, is that my son?   420

COOL (L) No, sir, that is not Mr Charles, but is *very* like him.

MAX I cannot understand all this.

GRACE (*aside*) I think I can.

Max and Grace go up a little

DAZZLE (*aside to Courtly*) Give him a touch of the indignant.

COURTLY (*crosses RC*) Allow me to say, what, Sir What-d'ye-call'em,   425
Carthorse Hartly?

DAZZLE Sir Walker Cartly.

SIR HARCOURT Hartly, sir? Courtly, sir. Courtly!

COURTLY Well, Hartly or Courtheart, or whatever your name may be,
I say your conduct is—a—a—, and were it not for the presence of   430
this lady, I should feel inclined—to—to—

SIR HARCOURT No, no, that can't be my son. He never would address
me in that way. Sir, your likeness to my son Charles is so astonish-
ing, that it for a moment—the equilibrium of my etiquette—'pon
my life I—permit me to request your pardon.   435

MEDDLE (L) Sir Harcourt, don't apologise, don't. Bring an action.°
I'm witness.

SIR HARCOURT Someone take this man away.

Meddle goes up the stage with Cool. Enter James

JAMES Luncheon is on the table, sir.

Exit James

SIR HARCOURT Miss Harkaway, I never swore before a lady, in my life, 440
except when I promised to love and cherish° the late Lady Courtly,
which I took care to preface with an apology. I was compelled to the
ceremony and consequently not answerable for the language; but to
that gentleman's identity I would have pledged—my hair.

GRACE (*aside*) If that security were called for, I suspect the answer   445
would be 'no effects'!°

*Exeunt Sir Harcourt Courtly and Grace Harkaway into
house, LUE*

MEDDLE (*to Max*) I have something very particular to communicate.

MAX Can't listen at present.

> *Exit Max Harkaway, LUE into house*

MEDDLE (*to Dazzle and Courtly*) I can afford you information which
I—   450

DAZZLE Oh, don't bother!

COURTLY Go to the devil!

> *Exeunt Dazzle and Courtly into house*

MEDDLE Now I have no hesitation in saying that is the height of
ingratitude. Oh, Mr Cool, can you oblige me. (*Presents his account*)

COOL (*R*) Why, what is all this?   455

MEDDLE Small account *versus* you; to giving information concerning
the last census° of the population of Oldborough and vicinity, six
and eightpence.

COOL Oh, you mean to make me pay this, do you?

MEDDLE Unconditionally.   460

COOL Well, I have no objection; the charge is fair. But remember, I am
a servant on board wages;° will you throw in a little advice gratis, if
I give you the money?

MEDDLE Ahem! I will.

COOL A fellow has insulted me. I want to abuse him. What terms are   465
actionable?°

MEDDLE You may call him anything you please, providing there are
no witnesses.

COOL Oh, may I? (*Looks round*) Then, you rascally, pettifogging
scoundrel!   470

MEDDLE Hallo! (*Retreats to R*)

COOL (*following him*) You mean, dirty disgrace to your profession.

MEDDLE Libel! Slander!

COOL Ay, (*going up L, turns*) but where are your witnesses?

MEDDLE Give me the costs; six and eightpence.   475

COOL I deny that you gave me information at all.

MEDDLE You do!

COOL Yes, where are your witnesses?

> *Exit Cool into house, LUE*

MEDDLE Ah. Damme! I'm done at last!

> *Exit Mark Meddle, L°*

[*Curtain*]

3.

*A morning-room in Oak Hall, French windows opening to the
lawn, handsome pier-glasses, ottomans etc. round the stage; the
windows, R; fire-place C; door of entrance LUE*

*Max Harkaway and Sir Harcourt Courtly seated together, LC;
Dazzle R; Grace and Charles Courtly are playing at chess at
back, C. All dressed for dinner*

MAX (*aside to Sir Harcourt*) What can I do?

SIR HARCOURT Get rid of them civilly.

MAX What, turn them out, after I particularly invited them to stay a
month or two?

SIR HARCOURT Why, they are disreputable characters. As for that   5
young fellow, in whom my lady Courtly appears so particularly
absorbed, I am bewildered. I have written to town for° my Charles,
my boy. It certainly is the most extraordinary likeness.

DAZZLE (*R*) Sir Harcourt, I have an idea.

SIR HARCOURT Sir, I am delighted to hear it. (*Aside to Max*) That   10
fellow is a swindler.

MAX (*to Sir Harcourt*) I met him at your house.

SIR HARCOURT (*to Max*) Never saw him before in all my life.

DAZZLE (*crosses to Sir Harcourt*) I will bet you five to one that I can
beat you three out of four games at billiards with one hand.   15

SIR HARCOURT No, sir.

DAZZLE I don't mind giving you ten points in fifty.

SIR HARCOURT Sir, I never gamble.

DAZZLE You don't! Well, I'll teach you. Easiest thing in life. You have
every requisite; good temper—   20

SIR HARCOURT I have not, sir.

DAZZLE A long-headed° knowing old buck.

SIR HARCOURT Sir.

Sir Harcourt converses with Max

GRACE Really, Mr Hamilton, you improve. A young man pays us a
visit, as you half intimate, to escape inconvenient friends. That is   25
complimentary to us, his hosts.

COURTLY Nay, that is too severe.

GRACE After an acquaintanceship of two days, you sit down to teach
me chess and domestic economy° at the same time. Might I ask

106

where you graduated in that science, where you learned all that   30
store of matrimonial advice which you have obliged me with?

COURTLY I imbibed it, madam, from the moment I beheld you, and
having studied my subject *con amore*,° took my degrees from your
eyes.

GRACE Oh, I see you are a Master of Arts already.   35

COURTLY Unfortunately, no. I shall remain a bachelor,° till you can
assist me to that honour.

     Sir Harcourt rises

DAZZLE (*R, aside to Courtly*) How do you get on?

COURTLY (*aside to Dazzle*) Splendidly! Keep the old boy away.

SIR HARCOURT (*going to them*) Is the conversation strictly confiden-   40
tial, or might I join?

DAZZLE (*crosses to him*) Oh, not in the least, my dear sir, we were
remarking that rifle shooting was an excellent diversion during the
summer months.°

SIR HARCOURT (*L, drawing himself up*) Sir! I was addressing—   45

DAZZLE And I was saying, what a pity it was I couldn't find anyone
reasonable enough to back his opinion with long odds. Come out on
the lawn and pitch up your hat, and I will hold you ten to one I put
a bullet in it every time, at forty paces.

SIR HARCOURT No, sir. I consider you—   50

MAX (*at window, RUE*) Here, all of you, look here is Lady Gay
Spanker, coming across the lawn at a hand gallop!°

SIR HARCOURT (*running to the window, R*) Bless me, the horse is
running away!

MAX Look how she takes that fence! There's a seat.°   55

SIR HARCOURT (*comes down, LC*) Lady Gay Spanker. Who may she be?

GRACE (*down C*) Gay Spanker, Sir Harcourt? My cousin and dearest
friend. You *must* like her.

SIR HARCOURT It will be my *devoir*, since it is your wish, though it
will be a hard task in your presence.   60

GRACE I am sure she will like *you*.

SIR HARCOURT Ha! ha! I flatter myself.

COURTLY Who and what is she?

GRACE Glee, glee made a living thing. Nature in some frolic mood
shut up a merry devil in her eye and, spiting art, stole joy's bright-   65
est harmony to thrill her laugh° which peals out sorrow's knell. Her
cry rings loudest in the field;° the very echo loves it best, and as
each hill attempts to ape her voice, earth seems to laugh that it
made a thing so glad.

[handwritten margin note: use of asides etc evokes the style of Shakespearean comedies coupled with deception]

MAX Ay, the merriest minx I ever kissed.   70
    Lady Gay laughs offstage, L
LADY GAY (*offstage*) Max!
MAX Come in, you mischievous puss.
    Enter James, L
JAMES Mr Adolphus and Lady Gay Spanker.°
    Exit James. Enter Lady Gay Spanker, fully equipped in
    riding habit, etc., LUE
LADY GAY Ha! ha! Well, governor, how are ye? I have been down five
    times, climbing up your stairs° in my long clothes.° How are you,   75
    Grace, dear? (*Kisses her*) There, don't fidget, Max, and there (*kisses*
    him RC), there's one for you.
SIR HARCOURT (*L*) Ahem!
LADY GAY (*C*) Oh, gracious! I didn't see you had visitors.
MAX (*R*) Permit me to introduce, (*crosses C*) Sir Harcourt Courtly,   80
    Lady Gay Spanker. Mr Dazzle, Mr Hamilton, Lady Gay Spanker.
SIR HARCOURT (*aside*) A devilish fine woman!
DAZZLE (*aside to Sir Harcourt*) She's a devilish fine woman.
LADY GAY You mustn't think anything of the liberties I take with my
    old Papa here. Bless him! (*Kisses him again*)   85
SIR HARCOURT Oh no! (*Aside*) I only thought I should like to be in his
    place.
LADY GAY I am so glad you have come, Sir Harcourt. Now we shall be
    able to make a decent figure at the heels of a hunt.
SIR HARCOURT Does your Ladyship hunt?   90
LADY GAY Ha! I say, governor, does my ladyship hunt? I rather flatter
    myself that I do hunt! Why, Sir Harcourt, one might as well live
    without laughing as without hunting; it's indigenous to humanity.
    Man was formed expressly to fit a horse. Are not the hedges and
    ditches created for leaps? Of course. And I look upon foxes to be   95
    the most blessed dispensation of a benign providence.
SIR HARCOURT Yes, it is all very well in the abstract. I tried it
    once.
LADY GAY Once! Only once?
SIR HARCOURT Once, only once. And then the animal ran away with   100
    me.
    All laugh
LADY GAY Why, you would not have him walk.
SIR HARCOURT Finding my society disagreeable, he instituted a series
    of kicks, with a view to removing the annoyance; but, aided by the
    united stays° of the mane and tail, I frustrated his intentions. His   105

[handwritten margin note near lines 91–96: deftly suited to Harcourt, given their comic agency]

[handwritten margin note near lines 103–105: pace & folk humour]

next resource, however, was more effectual, for he succeeded in
rubbing me off against a tree.

DAZZLE Ha! ha! ha! How absurd you must have looked with your legs
and arms in the air, like a shipwrecked tea-table.

SIR HARCOURT I never looked absurd in my life. Ah, it may be very   110
amusing in relation, I dare say, but very unpleasant in effect.

LADY GAY I pity you, Sir Harcourt. It was criminal in your parents to
neglect your education so shamefully.

SIR HARCOURT Possibly; but be assured I shall never break my neck
awkwardly from a horse, when it might be accomplished with less   115
trouble from a bedroom window.

COURTLY (*aside R*) My dad will be caught by this she Bucephalus-
tamer.°

MAX (*to Sir Harcourt*) You must leave your town habits in the smoke
of London; here we rise with the lark.   120

SIR HARCOURT Haven't the remotest conception when that period is.

GRACE (*c*) The man that misses sunrise loses the sweetest part of his
existence.

SIR HARCOURT Oh, pardon me. I have seen sunrise frequently after a
ball, or from the window of my travelling carriage, and I always   125
considered it excessively disagreeable.

GRACE I love to watch the first tear that glistens in the opening eye of
morning, the silent song the flowers breathe, the thrilly° choir of
the woodland minstrels, to which the modest brook trickles
applause; these, swelling out the sweetest chord of sweet creation's   130
matins, seem to pour some soft and merry tale into the daylight's
ear, as if the waking world had dreamed a happy thing and now
smiled o'er the telling of it.

SIR HARCOURT The effect of a rustic education! Who could ever
discover music in a damp foggy morning, except those confounded   135
waits° who never play in tune, and a miserable wretch who makes a
point of crying 'Coffee' under my window just as I am persuading
myself to sleep. In fact, I never heard any music worth listening to,
except in Italy.

LADY GAY No? Then you never heard a well-trained English pack,   140
full cry.

SIR HARCOURT Full cry!

LADY GAY Ay! There is harmony, if you will. Give me the trumpet
neigh, the spotted pack just catching scent. What a chorus in their
yelp! The view-halloo,° blent with a peal of free and fearless mirth!   145
That's our old English music; match it where you can.

SIR HARCOURT (*LC, aside*) I must see about Lady Gay Spanker.

DAZZLE (*L, aside to Sir Harcourt*) Ah, would you—

MAX Ah! Sir Harcourt, had you been here a month ago, you would
have witnessed the most glorious run that ever swept over merry   150
England's green cheek; a steeplechase, sir, which I intended to
win, but my horse broke down the day before. I had a chance,°
notwithstanding, and but for Gay here I should have won. How I
regretted my absence from it! How did my filly behave herself,
Gay?   155

LADY GAY Gloriously, Max, gloriously! There were sixteen horses in
the field, all mettle to the bone. The start was a picture. Away we
went in a cloud, pell-mell, helter-skelter. The fools first as usual,
using themselves up. We soon passed them, first your Kitty, then
my Blueskin and Craven's colt last. Then came the tug.° Kitty   160
skimmed the walls, Blueskin flew o'er the fences, the colt neck and
neck and half a mile to run. At last, the colt baulked a leap and
went wild. Kitty and I had it all to ourselves. She was three lengths
ahead as we breasted the last wall, six feet, if an inch, and a ditch
on the other side. Now, for the first time, I gave Blueskin his head.   165
Ha! ha! Away he flew like a thunderbolt. Over went the filly, I over
the same spot, leaving Kitty in the ditch. Walked the steeple,°
eight miles in thirty minutes, and scarcely turned a hair. (*Crosses R
and LC*)

ALL Bravo! Bravo!   170

LADY GAY (*LC*) Do you hunt?

DAZZLE (*L*) Hunt! I belong to a hunting family. I was born on horse-
back and cradled in a kennel! Ay, and I hope I may die with a
whoo-whoop!°

LADY GAY Time then appears as young as love and plumes as swift a   175
wing. Away we go! The earth flies back to aid our course! Horse,
man, hound, earth, heaven! All, all, one piece of glowing ecstasy!
Then I love the world, myself and every living thing. My jocund
soul cries out for very glee, as it could wish that all creation had but
one mouth that I might kiss it. (*Goes up, C*)   180

SIR HARCOURT (*aside*) I wish I was the mouth.

MAX Why, we will regenerate you, baronet.

DAZZLE (*slapping his shoulder*) Aye, we'll regenerate you!
     Sir Harcourt angrily goes up and gets round to R

MAX But, Gay, where is your husband? Where is Adolphus?

LADY GAY (*coming down*) Bless me, where is my Dolly?   185

SIR HARCOURT You are married, then?

mocking of marriage relations.

LADY GAY I have a husband somewhere, though I can't find him just now. (*Calls*) Dolly, dear! (*Aside to Max*) Governor, at home I always whistle when I want him.

> Enter Mr Spanker, LUE. Grace Harkaway and Max meet him and shake hands

SPANKER Here I am. Did you call me, Gay?

effeminate man   190

SIR HARCOURT (*eyeing him*) Is that your husband?

LADY GAY (*aside*) Yes, bless his stupid face. That's my Dolly.

MAX (*to Spanker*) Permit me to introduce you to Sir Harcourt Courtly.

SPANKER How d'ye do? I—Ah. Um! (*Appears frightened*)   195

LADY GAY (*gets behind him, LC*) Delighted to have the honour of making the acquaintance of a gentleman so highly celebrated in the world of fashion.

SPANKER Oh, yes, delighted, I'm sure, quite, very, so delighted; delighted! (*Gets quite confused*)   200

LADY GAY Where have you been, Dolly? → *roles reversed — she is the more masculine one in the relationship.*

SPANKER Oh, ah, I was just outside.

MAX Why did you not come in?

SPANKER I'm sure I didn't. I don't exactly know; but I thought, as—perhaps—I can't remember.   205

DAZZLE Shall we have the pleasure of your company to dinner?

SPANKER I always dine—° usually—that is, unless Gay remains.

LADY GAY Stay dinner, of course. We came on purpose to stop three or four days with you.

GRACE Will you excuse my absence, Gay?   210

MAX What! What! Where are you going? What takes you away?

GRACE We must postpone the dinner till Gay is dressed.

MAX Oh, never mind. Stay where you are.

GRACE No, I must go.

MAX I say you shan't! I will be king in my own house.   215

GRACE Do, my dear uncle. (*Crosses*) You shall be king, and I'll be your prime minister. That is, I will rule and you shall have the honour of taking the consequences.

> Exit Grace Harkaway, L

LADY GAY Well said, Grace. Have your own way. It is the only thing we women ought to be allowed. *comment upon their position in society* 220

MAX Come, Gay, dress for dinner.

SIR HARCOURT (*R*) Permit me, Lady Gay Spanker.

LADY GAY (*C*) With pleasure. What do you want?

SIR HARCOURT To escort you.

LADY GAY Oh, never mind, I can escort myself, thank you, and Dolly   225
    too. Come, dear!

    Exit Lady Gay Spanker, R I E

SIR HARCOURT *Au revoir.*

SPANKER Ah, thank you!

    Spanker trips after her, R I E [and exits]

SIR HARCOURT What an ill-assorted pair.

MAX Not a bit! She married him for freedom, and she has it. He   230
    married her for protection, and he has it.

SIR HARCOURT How he ever summoned courage to propose to her, I
    can't guess.

MAX (*takes his arm*) Bless you, he never did. She proposed to him.
    She says he would, if he could; but as he couldn't, she did for   235
    him.

    Exeunt Max Harkaway and Sir Harcourt Courtly laughing,
    through lawn window, R. Enter Cool with a letter, L

COOL (*L*) Mr Charles, I have been watching to find you alone. Sir
    Harcourt has written to town for you.

COURTLY (*R*) The devil he has.

COOL He expects you down tomorrow evening.   240

DAZZLE (*C*) Oh, he'll be punctual. A thought strikes me!

COURTLY Pooh! Confound your thoughts! I can think of nothing but
    the idea of leaving Grace, at the very moment when I had estab-
    lished the most—

DAZZLE What if I can prevent her marriage with your governor?   245

COURTLY Impossible!

DAZZLE He's pluming himself for the conquest of Lady Gay Spanker.
    It will not be difficult to make him believe she accedes to his suit.
    And if she would but join in the plan.

COURTLY I see it all. And do you think she would?   250

DAZZLE I mistake my game if she would not.

COOL Here comes Sir Harcourt!

DAZZLE I'll begin with him. Retire and watch how I'll open the
    campaign for you.

    Charles Courtly and Cool retire through window RUE. Enter
    Sir Harcourt Courtly, by window, R

SIR HARCOURT [*aside*] Here is that cursed fellow again.   255

DAZZLE Ah, my dear *old* friend!

SIR HARCOURT Mr Dazzle.

DAZZLE I have a secret of importance to disclose to you. Are you a
    man of honour? Hush! Don't speak. You are. It is with the greatest

pain I am compelled to request you, as a gentleman, that you will   260
shun studiously the society of Lady Gay Spanker!

SIR HARCOURT   Good gracious! By what right do you make such a
demand?

DAZZLE   Why, I am distantly related to the Spankers.

SIR HARCOURT   Why, hang it, sir, if you don't appear to be related to   265
every family in Great Britain! *Dramatic irony*

DAZZLE   A good many of the nobility claim me as a connection. But, to
return, she is much struck with your address.° Evidently she laid
herself out for display.°

SIR HARCOURT   Ha! You surprise me!   270

DAZZLE   To entangle you.

SIR HARCOURT   Ha! ha! Why, it did appear like it.

DAZZLE   You will spare her for my sake. Give her no encouragement.
If disgrace come upon my relatives, the Spankers, I should never
hold up my head again.   275

SIR HARCOURT   (*aside*) I shall achieve an easy conquest, and a glorious.
Ha! ha! I never remarked it before, but this is a gentleman.

DAZZLE   May I rely on your generosity?

SIR HARCOURT   Faithfully. (*Shakes his hand*) Sir, I honour and esteem
you. But might I ask how you came to meet our friend Max Hark-   280
away in my house in Belgrave Square!

   Enter Charles Courtly from window, R. He sits on sofa at back

DAZZLE   Certainly. I had an acceptance° of your son's for one hundred
pounds.

SIR HARCOURT   (*astonished*) Of my son's? Impossible!

DAZZLE   Ah, sir, fact! He paid a debt for a poor, unfortunate man;   285
fifteen children, half a dozen wives, the devil knows what all.

SIR HARCOURT   Simple boy!

DAZZLE   Innocent youth, I have no doubt; when you have the hundred
convenient, I shall feel delighted.   → *playing to Harcourt's ideals*

SIR HARCOURT   Oh, follow me to my room, and if you have the docu-   290
ment it will be happiness to me to pay it. Poor Charles! Good heart!   *of his son*

DAZZLE   Oh, a splendid heart, I dare say!

   Exit Sir Harcourt Courtly, LUE

(*To Courtly*) Come here; bring your splendid heart here, write me
the bill.

COURTLY   (*R of table*) What for?   295

DAZZLE   What for? Why, to release the unfortunate man and his
family, to be sure, from jail.

COURTLY   Who is he?

DAZZLE Yourself.

COURTLY But I haven't fifteen children!   300

DAZZLE Will you take your oath of that?

COURTLY Nor four wives.

DAZZLE More shame for you, with all that family. Come, don't be
obstinate. Write, and date it back.°

COURTLY Ay, but where is the stamp?   305

DAZZLE Here they are, of all patterns. (*Pulls out a pocket-book*) I
keep them ready drawn in case of necessity, all but the date and
acceptance. Now, if you are in an autographic humour, you can
try how your signature will look across half a dozen of them.
There, write. Exactly, you know the place—across—good; and   310
thank your lucky stars that you have found a friend at last that
gives you money and advice. I'll give the old gentleman this,
and then you can relieve the necessities of your fifteen little
unfortunates.

    Exit Dazzle, LUE

COURTLY Things are approaching to a climax. I must appear *in pro-*   315
pria persona, and immediately; but I must first ascertain what are
the real sentiments of this riddle of a woman. Does she love me? I
flatter myself.—And even if she does, ought I to pursue this affair
further? My father's rival! As a dutiful son, I should feel concerned
for his happiness;—so I am; for I feel assured if Grace Harkaway   320
becomes his bride, he will forever be miserable. It is therefore my
duty as a loving son, clearly, to save my father. Yes, I'll be a sacrifice
and marry her myself. By Jove, here she comes! I shall never have
such an opportunity again. (*Retires up,* R)

    Enter Grace Harkaway, LUE

GRACE [*aside*] I wish I had never seen Mr Hamilton. Why do I shud-   325
der at the contemplation of this marriage, which till now was to me
a subject of indifference? (*Crosses* R) Am I in love? In love! If I am,
my past life has been the work of raising up a pedestal to place my
own folly on. I, the infidel, the railer!

COURTLY (*advancing,* L) Meditating upon matrimony, madam?   330

GRACE (*aside*) He little thinks he was the subject of my meditations.
(*Aloud*) No, Mr Hamilton, I—

COURTLY (*aside*) I must unmask my battery now.

GRACE (*aside*) How foolish I am. He will perceive that I tremble. I
must appear at ease.   335

    A pause

COURTLY Eh—ah—um!

GRACE Ah! (*They sink into silence again.* [*Then*] *aside*) How very awkward!

COURTLY (*aside*) It is a very difficult subject to begin. (*Aloud*) Madam—ahem—there was—is—I mean—I was about to remark —that I was about to observe—a—(*Aside*) Hang me if it is not a very slippery subject! I must brush up my faculties; attack her in her own way. Sing, O muse! Why, I have made love before to a hundred women! *Both unsure of how to deal with the attack as their pragmatic natures have both been lost*

GRACE (*aside*) I wish I had something to do, for I have nothing to say.

COURTLY Madam, there is a subject so fraught with fate to my future life that you must pardon my lack of delicacy, should a too hasty expression mar the fervent courtesy of its intent. (*Pause*) To you, I feel aware, I must appear in the light of a comparative stranger.

GRACE (*aside*) I know what's coming. *wrong knowledge of people*

COURTLY Of you, I know perhaps too much for my own peace.

GRACE (*aside*) He *is* in love.

COURTLY I forget all that befell before I saw your beauteous self: I seem born into another world; my nature changed. The beams of that bright face falling on my soul have from its chaos warmed into life the flowrets of affection, whose maiden odours now float towards the sun, pouring forth on their pure tongue a mite of adoration midst the voices of a universe. (*Aside*) That's something in her own style.

GRACE Mr Hamilton!

COURTLY You cannot feel surprised—

GRACE I am more than surprised. (*Aside*) I am delighted.

COURTLY Do not speak so coldly.

GRACE You have offended me deeply.

COURTLY No, madam. No woman, whatever her state, can be offended by the adoration even of the meanest. It is myself whom I have offended and deceived, but still I ask your pardon.

Asides once more put the audience in a position of power allowing them to laugh at the scenes inward nature

GRACE (*aside*) Oh! He thinks I'm refusing him. (*Aloud*) I am not exactly offended, but—

COURTLY Consider my position; a few days, and an insurmountable barrier would have placed you beyond my wildest hopes. You would have been my mother.

GRACE I should have been your mother!

    He starts up, annoyed at having betrayed himself
    (*Aside*) I thought so.

COURTLY (*aside*) Now I've done it! [*Aloud*] No, that is, I meant Sir Harcourt Courtly's bride.

GRACE (*with great emphasis*) Never!

COURTLY How! Never? May I then hope—? (*She turns away*) You turn away. You would not lacerate me by a refusal?

GRACE (*aside*) How stupid he is!   380

COURTLY Still silent! I thank you, Miss Grace. I ought to have expected this, fool that I have been. One course alone remains. Farewell!

GRACE (*aside*) Why, he doesn't expect me to make love to him. Now he's going.   385

COURTLY Farewell forever! (*Sits in armchair,* RC) Will you not speak one word? I shall leave this house immediately. I shall not see you again.

GRACE Unhand me, sir, I insist.

COURTLY (*aside*) Oh! What an ass I've been! (*Rushes up to her and*   390 *seizes her hand*) Release this hand? Never! Never! (*Kissing it*) Never will I quit this hand! It shall be my companion in misery, in solitude, when you are far away.

GRACE Oh! Should anyone come! (*Drops her handkerchief; he stoops to pick it up*) For heaven's sake, do not kneel.   395

COURTLY (*kneels*) Forever thus prostrate before my soul's saint, I will lead a pious life of eternal adoration!

GRACE Should we be discovered thus! Pray, Mr Hamilton, pray, pray.

COURTLY Pray! I am praying; what more can I do?

GRACE Your conduct is shameful.   400

COURTLY It is. (*Rises*)

GRACE And if I do not scream, it is not for your sake—but it might alarm the family.

COURTLY It might—it would. Say, am I wholly indifferent° to you? I entreat one word; I implore. You do not withdraw your hand—(*she*   405 *snatches it away; he puts his arm round her waist*) you smile.

GRACE Leave me, dear Mr Hamilton!

COURTLY Dear! Then I am dear to you. That word once more. Say, say you love me!

GRACE Is this fair?   410

    He catches her in his arms and kisses her. Enter Lady Gay
    Spanker, R

LADY GAY Ha! Oh!

GRACE Gay! Oh!

    Grace runs off through window R°

COURTLY (L) Fizgig!° The devil!

LADY GAY Don't mind me. Pray don't let me be any interruption!

COURTLY I was just—   415

LADY GAY Yes, I see you were.

COURTLY Oh, madam, how could you mar my bliss, in the very
ecstasy of its fulfillment?

LADY GAY I always like to be in at the death.° Never drop your ears.°
Bless you, she is only a little fresh.° Give her her head and she will   420
outrun herself.°

COURTLY Possibly; but what am I to do?

LADY GAY Keep your seat.

COURTLY But in a few days she will take a leap that must throw me.
She marries Sir Harcourt Courtly.   425

LADY GAY Why, that is awkward, certainly; but you can challenge him
and shoot him.

COURTLY Unfortunately that is out of the question.

LADY GAY How so?

COURTLY You will not betray a secret if I inform you?   430

LADY GAY All right. What is it?

COURTLY I am his son.

LADY GAY What, his son! But does he not know you?

COURTLY No, not he. I met him here by chance and faced it out: I
never saw him before in my life.   435

LADY GAY Beautiful! I see it all. You're in love with your mother that-
should-be—your wife that-will-be.

COURTLY Now, I think I could distance° the old gentleman, if you
will but lend us your assistance.

LADY GAY I will, in anything.   440

COURTLY You must know, then, that my father, Sir Harcourt, has
fallen desperately in love with you.

LADY GAY With me! (*Utters a scream of delight*) This is delicious!

COURTLY Now, if you only could—

LADY GAY Could! I will. Ha! ha! I see my cue. I'll cross his scent; I'll   445
draw him after me. Ho! ho! Won't I make love to him? Ha!

COURTLY The only objection might be Mr Spanker, who might—

LADY GAY No, he mightn't. He's no objection. Bless him, he's an
inestimable little character. You don't know him as well as I do, I
dare say. Ha! ha! (*Dinner bell rings*) Here they come to dinner. I'll   450
commence my operations on your governor immediately. Ha! ha!
How I shall enjoy it!

COURTLY Be guarded!

  Enter Max Harkaway, R; Sir Harcourt Courtly, L; Dazzle, R;
  Grace Harkaway, R; and Mr Spanker, R

MAX Now, gentlemen, Sir Harcourt, do you lead Grace.

LADY GAY I believe Sir Harcourt is engaged to me. (*Takes his arm*)   455

MAX Well, please yourselves.

> *They file out, LUE; Max Harkaway first, Charles Courtly and Grace Harkaway, Sir Harcourt Courtly coquetting with Lady Gay, leaving Dazzle, who offers his arm to Spanker and walks on; Spanker runs after him, trying to take it°*

[*Curtain*]

4.

A handsome drawing-room in Oak Hall, folding door, R and L,
chandelier, tables with books, drawings, etc.

Grace Harkaway and Lady Gay Spanker discovered,
drinking coffee

GRACE (*on ottoman, C*) If there be one habit more abominable than
another, it is that of the gentlemen sitting over their wine. It is a
selfish, unfeeling fashion and a gross insult to our sex.

LADY GAY (*R*) We are turned out just when the fun begins. How
happy the poor wretches look at the contemplation° of being rid of   5
us.

GRACE The conventional signal for the ladies to withdraw, is
anxiously and deliberately waited for.

LADY GAY Then I begin to wish I were a man.

GRACE The instant the door is closed upon us, there rises a roar.   10

LADY GAY In celebration of their short-lived liberty, my love;
rejoicing over their emancipation.

GRACE I think it very insulting, whatever it may be.

LADY GAY Ah, my dear, philosophers say that man is the creature of
an hour;—it is the dinner hour, I suppose.   15

DAZZLE (*offstage*) A song, a song.

> *Voice, as if in approval of a proposition, knocking on table etc.,*
> *'Bravo!' at back. Enter Servant with salver, R, to take coffee cups*
> *from Lady Gay and Grace Harkaway*

GRACE I am afraid they are getting too pleasant° to be agreeable.

LADY GAY I hope the squire will restrict himself. After his third bottle
he becomes rather voluminous.

DAZZLE AND MAX (*offstage*) Silence!   20

LADY GAY Someone is going to sing. (*Jumps up*) Let us hear.

> *Spanker is heard to sing 'A southerly wind and a cloudy sky'.°*
> *After verse, chorus, [all the offstage men joining in]*

GRACE Oh no, Gay, for heaven's sake!

LADY GAY Oho! ha! ha! Why, that is my Dolly. (*At the conclusion of the*
verse) Well, I never heard my Dolly sing before! Happy wretches,
how I envy them!   25

> *Enter James, L, with a note*

JAMES Mr Hamilton has just left the house for London.

119

GRACE Impossible! That is, without seeing—that is—

LADY GAY Ha! ha!

GRACE He never—Speak, sir!

JAMES He left, Miss Grace, in a desperate hurry, and this note, I   30
believe, for you. (*Presenting a note on a salver*)

GRACE For me!

> *Grace is about to snatch it, but restraining herself, takes it coolly.*
> *Exit James, L*

Excuse me, Gay?

LADY GAY Certainly.

GRACE (*reads* [*aside*]) 'Your manner during dinner has left me no   35
alternative but instant departure. My absence will release you from
the oppression which my society must necessarily inflict on your
sensitive mind. It may tend also to smother, though it can never
extinguish, that indomitable passion of which I am the passive victim. Dare I supplicate pardon and oblivion for the past. It is the last   40
request of the self-deceived, but still loving—Augustus Hamilton.'

> *Grace puts her hand to her forehead and appears giddy*

LADY GAY Hallo, Grace! Pull up.° What's the matter?

GRACE (*recovering herself*) Nothing—the heat of the room—so very
warm.

LADY GAY Oh! What excuse does he make? Particular unforeseen   45
business, I suppose?

GRACE Why, yes, a mere formula—a—a—You may put it in the fire.
(*She puts it in her bosom*)

LADY GAY (*aside*) It is near enough to the fire where it is.

GRACE (*c*) I am glad he's gone.

LADY GAY (*R*) So am I.   50

GRACE He was a disagreeable, ignorant person.

LADY GAY Yes; and so vulgar.

GRACE No; he was not at all vulgar.

LADY GAY I mean in appearance.

GRACE Oh! How can you say so. He was excessively *distingué*!°   55

LADY GAY Well, I might have been mistaken, but I took him for a
forward, intrusive—

GRACE Good gracious, Gay! He was very retiring—even shy.

LADY GAY (*aside*) It's all right. She is in love. Blows hot and cold in
the same breath.   60

GRACE How can you be a competent judge? Why, you have not known
him more than a few hours, while I—I—

LADY GAY Have known him two days and a quarter. I yield. I confess,

I never was, or will be, so intimate with him as you appeared to be! 65
Ha! ha!

> *Loud noise of argument—the folding doors, L, are thrown open.*
> *Enter the whole party of Gentlemen, apparently engaged in*
> *warm discussion; they assemble in knots, while the Servants*
> *hand coffee, etc.; Max Harkaway, Sir Harcourt Courtly,*
> *Dazzle and Mr Spanker together*

DAZZLE (*L*) But, my dear sir, consider the state of the two countries under such a constitution.°

SIR HARCOURT (*LC*) The two countries! What have they to do with the subject?

MAX (*LC*) Everything. Look at their two legislative bodies. 70

SPANKER (*L*) Ay, look at their two legislative bodies.

SIR HARCOURT Why, it would inevitably establish universal anarchy and confusion.

GRACE (*RC*) I think they are pretty well established already.

SPANKER Well, suppose it did, what has anarchy and confusion to do 75
with the subject?

LADY GAY (*RC*) Do look at my Dolly. He is arguing, talking politics;
'pon my life he is. (*Calling*) Mr Spanker, my dear!

SPANKER Excuse me, love, I am discussing a point of importance.

LADY GAY Oh, that is delicious. He must discuss that to me.° 80

> *Lady Gay goes up and leads him down, he appears to have*
> *shaken off his gaucherie,° she shakes her head*

Dolly! Dolly!

SPANKER Pardon me, Lady Gay Spanker, I conceive your mutilation of my sponsorial appellation° highly derogatory to my *amour propre*.°

LADY GAY Your what? Ho! ho! 85

SPANKER And I particularly request that, for the future, I may not be treated with that cavalier spirit which does not become your sex, nor your station, your ladyship.

LADY GAY You have been indulging till you have lost the little wit nature dribbled into your unfortunate little head. Your brains want 90
the whipper-in.° You are not yourself.

SPANKER Madam, I am doubly myself; and permit me to inform you that, unless you voluntarily pay obedience to my commands, I shall enforce them.

LADY GAY Your commands! 95

SPANKER Yes, madam. I mean to put a full stop to your hunting.

LADY GAY You do! Ah! (*Aside*) I can scarcely speak from delight.

(*Aloud*) Who put such an idea into your head, for I'm sure it is not an original emanation of your genius?

SPANKER Sir Harcourt Courtly, my friend. And now mark me! I request, for your own sake, that I may not be compelled to assert my a—my authority as your husband. I shall say no more than this: if you persist in this absurd rebellion—

LADY GAY Well?

SPANKER Contemplate a separation. (*He looks at her haughtily and retires, C*)

LADY GAY Now I'm happy. My own little darling, inestimable Dolly, has tumbled into a spirit, somehow. Sir Harcourt too! Ha! ha! He's trying to make him ill-treat me, so that his own suit may thrive.

SIR HARCOURT (*L, advances*) Lady Gay.

LADY GAY (*aside*) Now for it. (*They sit on ottoman, C*)

SIR HARCOURT What hours of misery were those I passed when, by your secession, the room suffered a total eclipse!

LADY GAY Ah, you flatter.

SIR HARCOURT No, pardon me, that were impossible. No, believe me, I tried to join in the boisterous mirth, but my thoughts would desert to the drawing-room. Ah! How I envied the careless levity and cool indifference with which Mr Spanker enjoyed your absence.

DAZZLE (*who is lounging in a chair, R*) Max, that madeira is worth its weight in gold. I hope you have more of it.

MAX (*R, talking with Grace and Spanker*) A pipe,° I think.

DAZZLE I consider a magnum° of that nectar and a meerschaum° of Canaster° to consummate the ultimatum° of all mundane bliss. To drown myself in liquid ecstasy and then blow a cloud on which the enfranchised soul could soar above Olympus.° Oh!

  Enter James, L

JAMES Mr Charles Courtly.

  Exit James

SIR HARCOURT Ah, now Max, you must see a living apology for my conduct.

  Enter Charles Courtly, dressed very plainly, L

Well, Charles, how are you? Don't be afraid. There, Max, what do you say now?

MAX (*RC*) Well, this is the most extraordinary likeness.

GRACE (*R, aside*) Yes, considering it is the original. I am not so easily deceived!

MAX (*crosses, LC, shaking hands*) Sir, I am delighted to see you.

COURTLY Thank you, sir.

DAZZLE (*R*) Will you be kind enough to introduce me, Sir Harcourt?

SIR HARCOURT This is Mr Dazzle, Charles.

COURTLY Which? (*Looking from Spanker, RC, to Dazzle, R, who crosses to RC [and] nearly tumbles over Spanker, who goes up; Courtly winks at Dazzle*) 140

SIR HARCOURT (*to Lady Gay*) Is not that refreshing? Miss Harkaway—Charles, this is your mother, or rather will be.

COURTLY Madam, I shall love, honour and obey° you punctually. (*He takes out a book, sighs and goes up reading*) 145

Enter James, L

SIR HARCOURT You perceive. Quite unused to society; perfectly ignorant of every conventional rule of life.

JAMES The doctor and the young ladies have arrived.

Exit James [and Servants]°

MAX The young ladies! Now we must to the hall. I make it a rule always to commence the festivities with a good old country dance, a 150
rattling Sir Roger de Coverly.° Come, Sir Harcourt.

SIR HARCOURT Does this antiquity require a whoo-whoop° in it?

MAX (*C*) Nothing but a nimble foot and a light heart.

SIR HARCOURT Very antediluvian indispensables. [*To Lady Gay*] Lady Gay Spanker, will you honour me by becoming my preceptor? 155

LADY GAY Why, I'm engaged; but (*aloud*) on such a plea as Sir Harcourt's, I must waive all obstacles. (*Gives her hand*)

MAX Now, Grace, girl, give your hand to Mr Courtly.

GRACE (*sitting, C*) Pray excuse me, uncle. I have a headache.

SIR HARCOURT (*aside, LC, leading Lady Gay*) Jealousy, by the gods! 160
Jealous of my devotions at another's fane! (*Aloud*) Charles, my boy! Amuse Miss Grace during our absence.

Exit Sir Harcourt Courtly, with Lady Gay Spanker, L

MAX (*C*) But don't you dance, Mr Courtly?

COURTLY (*R*) Dance, sir! I never dance.° I can procure exercise in a much more rational manner, and music disturbs my meditations. 165

MAX Well, do the gallant.°

Exit Max Harkaway, with Mr Spanker and Dazzle, L

COURTLY I never studied that art; but I have a prize essay on a hydro-static subject,° which would delight her, for it enchanted the Reverend Doctor Pump, of Corpus Christi.°

GRACE (*aside*) What on earth could have induced him to disfigure 170
himself in that frightful way? I rather suspect some plot to entrap me into a confession.

COURTLY (*aside*) Dare I confess this trick to her? No, not until I have
    proved° her affection indisputably. Let me see; I must concoct.°
    (*He goes to her, looking over his book; aloud*) Madam, I have been   175
    desired to amuse you.

GRACE Thank you.

COURTLY 'The labour we delight in physics pain.'° I will draw you a
    moral. Ahem! Subject: the effects of inebriety, which according to
    Ben Jonson° means perplexion° of the intellects,° caused by imbib-   180
    ing spirituous° liquors. About an hour before my arrival, I passed
    an appalling evidence° of the effects of this state. A carriage was
    overthrown; horses killed; gentleman in a hopeless state, with his
    neck broken—all occasioned by the intoxication of the post-boy.

GRACE That is very amusing.   185

COURTLY I found it edifying, nutritious food for reflection. The
    expiring man desired his best compliments to you.

GRACE To me! (*She rises*)

COURTLY Yes.

GRACE His name was—   190

COURTLY Mr Augustus Hamilton.

GRACE Augustus—oh! (*Affects to faint—sinking on the ottoman*)

COURTLY (*aside*) Huzza! She loves me.

GRACE But where, sir, did this happen?

COURTLY About four miles down the road.   195

GRACE He must be conveyed here.

    Enter James, L

JAMES Mr Meddle, madam.

    Exit James. Enter Mark Meddle, L

MEDDLE On very particular business.

GRACE The very person. My dear sir!

MEDDLE (*L*) My dear madam!   200

GRACE (*C*) You must execute a very particular commission for me
    immediately. Mr Hamilton has met with a frightful accident on the
    London road and is in a dying state.

MEDDLE Well! I have no hesitation in saying he takes it uncommonly
    easy. He looks as if he was used to it.   205

GRACE You mistake. That is not Mr Hamilton, but Mr Courtly, who
    will explain everything and conduct you to the spot.

COURTLY (*aside*) Oh! I must put a stop to all this or I shall be found
    out! (*Aloud*) Madam, that were useless; for I omitted to mention a
    small fact which occurred before I left Mr Hamilton. He died.   210

GRACE Dear me! Oh! Then we needn't trouble you, Mr Meddle.

(*Waltz music heard offstage, L*) —Hark! I hear they are commencing a waltz. If you will ask me, a turn or two in the dance may tend to dispel the dreadful sensation you have aroused.

COURTLY (*aside*) If I can understand her, hang me! Hears of my 215
death, screams out and then asks me to waltz. I am bewildered. Can she suspect me? I wonder which she likes best, me or my double. Confound this disguise, I must retain it. I have gone too far with my dad to pull up now. (*Aloud*) At your service, madam. (*He crosses behind to L and offers his hand*) 220

GRACE (*aside*) I will pay him well for this trick! [*Aloud*] Ah, poor Augustus Hamilton! *met his match - provides comedy in*

COURTLY Ah, madam! *the way they dance around the*

Exeunt Charles Courtly and Grace Harkaway, L *issue.*

MEDDLE Well, if that is not Mr Hamilton, scratch me out with a big blade, for I am a blot, a mistake upon the rolls.° There is an error in 225
the pleadings° somewhere, and I will discover it. I would swear to his identity before the most discriminating jury. By the by, this accident will form a capital excuse for my presence here. I just stepped in to see how matters worked° and—Stay! Here comes the bridegroom elect and, oh, in his very arms, Lady Gay Spanker! 230
(*Looks round*) Where are my witnesses? Oh, that someone else were here. However, I can retire and get some information, eh—Spanker versus Courtly—damages—witness. (*Gets into an armchair, R, which he turns round, the back to the audience*) *always switched on to the law*

Enter Sir Harcourt Courtly, supporting Lady Gay Spanker, L

SIR HARCOURT This cool room will recover you. 235

LADY GAY Excuse my trusting to you for support.

SIR HARCOURT I am transported. Allow me thus ever to support this lovely burden, and I shall conceive that paradise is regained.° (*They sit*)

LADY GAY Oh! Sir Harcourt, I feel very faint. 240

SIR HARCOURT The waltz made you giddy.

LADY GAY And I have left my salts in the other room.

SIR HARCOURT I always carry a *flacon* for the express accommodation° of the fair sex. (*Producing a smelling-bottle and sits, R of her*)

LADY GAY Thank you. Ah! (*She sighs*) 245

SIR HARCOURT What a sigh was there!°

LADY GAY The vapour of consuming grief.

SIR HARCOURT Grief! Is it possible, have *you* a grief? Are *you* unhappy? Dear me!

LADY GAY Am I not married? 250

marriage not seen as enjoyable rather a necessity

SIR HARCOURT What a horrible state of existence!

LADY GAY I am never contradicted, so there are none of those enliven-
ing interested° little differences, which so pleasingly diversify the
monotony of conjugal life, like spots of verdure.° No quarrels, like
oases in the desert of matrimony; no rows.   255

SIR HARCOURT How vulgar! What a brute!

LADY GAY I never have anything but my own way; and he won't
permit me to spend more than I like.

SIR HARCOURT Mean-spirited wretch!

LADY GAY How can I help being miserable?   260

SIR HARCOURT Miserable! I wonder you are not in a lunatic asylum,
with such unheard-of barbarism!

LADY GAY But worse than all that!

SIR HARCOURT Can it be out-Heroded?°

LADY GAY Yes, I could forgive that. I do; it is my duty. But only   265
imagine; picture to yourself, my dear Sir Harcourt, though I, the
third daughter of an earl, married him out of pity for his destitute
and helpless situation as a bachelor, with ten thousand a year—
conceive if you can—he actually permits me, with the most placid
indifference, to flirt with any old fool I may meet.   270

SIR HARCOURT Good gracious! Miserable idiot!

LADY GAY I fear there is an incompatibility of temper which renders a
separation inevitable.

SIR HARCOURT Indispensable, my dear madam. Ah! Had I been the
happy possessor of such a realm of bliss, what a beatific eternity   275
unfolds itself to my extending imagination. Had another man but
looked at you, I should have annihilated him at once; and if he had
the temerity to speak, his life alone could have expiated his crime.

LADY GAY Oh, an existence of such a nature is too bright for the eye
of thought, too sweet to bear reflection!   280

SIR HARCOURT My devotion, eternal, deep—

LADY GAY Oh, Sir Harcourt!

SIR HARCOURT (more fervently) Your every thought should be a
separate study, each wish forestalled by the quick apprehension
of a kindred soul.   285

LADY GAY Alas! How can I avoid my fate?

SIR HARCOURT If a life, a heart, were offered to your astonished view,
by one who is considered the index of fashion, the vane of the *beau
monde*; if you saw him at your feet, begging, beseeching your
acceptance of all, and more than this, what would be your answer—   290

LADY GAY Ah! I know of none so devoted.

SIR HARCOURT You do. (*Throwing himself upon his knees*) Behold Sir
   Harcourt Courtly!

> *Meddle jumps up in the chair and writes in his
> memorandum-book*

LADY GAY (*aside*) Ha, ha! Yoicks! Pug° has broken cover.

> *Meddle sits again*

SIR HARCOURT Speak, adored, dearest Lady Gay! Speak. Will you fly   295
   from the tyranny, the wretched misery of such a monster's roof,
   and accept the soul which lives but in your presence?

LADY GAY Do not press me. Oh spare a weak, yielding woman! Be
   contented to know that you are—alas!—too dear to me. But the
   world, the world would say— *society is always a concern*   300

SIR HARCOURT Let us be a precedent to open a more extended and
   liberal view of matrimonial advantages to society.

LADY GAY How irresistible is your argument! Oh, pause! (*They place
   their chairs back*)

SIR HARCOURT I have ascertained for a fact every tradesman of mine   305
   lives with his wife, and thus you see it has become a vulgar and
   plebeian custom.

LADY GAY Leave me. I feel I cannot withstand your powers of persua-
   sion. Swear that you will never forsake me. → *putting on female airs*

SIR HARCOURT Dictate the oath. May I grow wrinkled, may two   310
   inches be added to the circumference of my waist, may I lose the
   fall° in my back, may I be old and ugly the instant I forego one tithe
   of adoration!

LADY GAY I must believe you.

SIR HARCOURT Shall we leave this detestable spot, this horrible   315
   vicinity?

LADY GAY The sooner the better. Tomorrow evening let it be. Now let
   me return; my absence will be remarked. (*He kisses her hand*) Do I
   appear confused? Has my agitation rendered me unfit to enter the
   room?   320

SIR HARCOURT More angelic by a lovely tinge of heightened colour.

LADY GAY Tomorrow, in this room, which opens on the lawn.

SIR HARCOURT At eleven o'clock.

LADY GAY The rest of the family will be at supper; I'll plead indis-
   position; have your carriage in waiting, and four horses. Remember,   325
   please, be particular to have four. Don't let the affair come off
   shabbily. Adieu, dear Sir Harcourt.

> *Exit Lady Gay Spanker, R*

SIR HARCOURT (*marches pompously across the stage*) *Veni, vidi, vici!*°

127

*discourse of battle
courtship the battle of the
sexes in the play.*

Hannibal, Caesar, Napoleon, Alexander never completed so fair a
conquest in so short a time. She dropped fascinated. This is an   330
unprecedented example of the irresistible force of personal appearance combined with polished address. Poor creature! How she loves
me! I pity so prostrating a passion and ought to return it. I will. It is
a duty I owe to society and fashion.

    Exit Sir Harcourt Courtly, L

MEDDLE (*turns the chair round*) 'There is a tide in the affairs of men,   335
which taken at the flood, leads on to fortune.'° This is my tide. I am
the only witness. 'Virtue is sure to find its own reward.'° But I've
no time to contemplate what it shall be—something huge. Let me
see. Spanker versus Courtly, crim. con., damages placed at a hundred and fifty thousand pounds at least, for juries always decimate   340
your hopes.°

    Enter Mr Spanker, L

SPANKER I cannot find Gay anywhere.

MEDDLE (*aside*) The plaintiff himself! I must commence the action.°
(*Aloud*) Mr Spanker, as I have information of deep, vital importance to impart, will you take a seat? (*They sit solemnly—Meddle*   345
takes out a note-book and pencil) Ahem! You have a wife!

    Enter Lady Gay Spanker, R. She crosses behind to L and listens

SPANKER (*LC*) Yes, I believe I—

MEDDLE (*RC*) Will you be kind enough, without any prevarication, to
answer my questions? You have a wife?

SPANKER You alarm—I—   350

MEDDLE Compose yourself and reserve your feelings. Take time to
consider. You have a wife?

SPANKER Yes—

MEDDLE He has a wife; good. (*Writes*) A *bona fide*° wife, bound morally and legally to be your wife, and nobody else's in effect, except   355
on your written permission—

SPANKER But what has this—

MEDDLE Hush! Allow me, my dear sir, to congratulate you. (*Shakes*
his hand)

SPANKER What for?   360

MEDDLE Lady Gay Spanker is about to dishonour the bond of
wedlock, by eloping from you.

SPANKER (*starting*) What!

MEDDLE (*pushing him down again*) I thought you would be overjoyed.
Will you place the affair in my hands and I will venture to promise   365
the largest damages on record?

SPANKER (*start up*) Damn the damages! I want my wife. Oh, I'll go
and ask her not to run away. She may run away with me;° she may
hunt; she may ride; anything she likes. Oh, sir, let us put a stop to
this affair. 370

MEDDLE (*who has put the chairs back*) Put a stop to it! Do not alarm
me, sir. Sir, you will spoil the most exquisite brief that was ever
penned. It must proceed, it shall proceed. It is illegal to prevent it,
and I will bring an action against you for wilful intent to injure the
profession. 375

SPANKER Oh, what an ass I am! Oh, I have driven her to this. It was
all that damned brandy punch on the top of burgundy. What a fool
I was!

MEDDLE It was the happiest moment of your life.

SPANKER So I thought at the time; but we live to grow wiser. Tell me, 380
who is the vile seducer?

MEDDLE Sir Harcourt Courtly.

SPANKER Ha! He is my best friend.

MEDDLE I should think he is. If you will accompany me? Here is a
verbatim copy of the whole transaction in shorthand, sworn to by 385
me.

SPANKER Only let me have Gay back again.

MEDDLE Even that may be arranged. This way.

SPANKER That ever I should live to see my wife run away. Oh, I will
do anything; keep two packs of hounds; buy up every horse and ass 390
in England, myself included. Oh!
Exit Mr Spanker with Mark Meddle, R

LADY GAY Ha, ha, ha! Poor Dolly, I'm sorry I must continue to
deceive him. If he would but kindle up a little. So that fellow
overheard all. Well, so much the better.
Enter Charles Courtly, L

COURTLY My dear madam, how fares the plot. Does my governor 395
nibble?

LADY GAY Nibble! He is caught and in the basket. I have just left him
with the hook in his gills, panting for very lack of element.° But
how goes on your encounter?

COURTLY Bravely. By a simple ruse I have discovered that she loves 400
me. I see but one chance against the best termination I could hope.

LADY GAY What is it?

COURTLY My father has told me that I return to town again
tomorrow afternoon.

LADY GAY Well, I insist you stop and dine. Keep out of the way. 405

COURTLY   Oh, but what excuse can I offer for disobedience? What can I say when he sees me before dinner?

LADY GAY   Say—say Grace.°

> *Enter Grace Harkaway, L, who gets behind the window curtains, C*

COURTLY   Ha, ha!

LADY GAY   I have arranged to elope with Sir Harcourt myself tomorrow night.   410

COURTLY   The deuce you have!

LADY GAY   Now if you could persuade Grace to follow that example. His carriage will be in waiting at the Park. Be there a little before eleven, and it will just prevent° our escape. Can you make her agree to that?   415

COURTLY   Oh, without the slightest difficulty, if Mr Augustus Hamilton supplicates.

LADY GAY   Success attend you. (*Going, R*)

COURTLY   I will bend the haughty Grace. (*Going, L*)   420

LADY GAY   Do.

> *Exeunt all but Grace Harkaway severally°*

GRACE   (*at back*) Will you?   doesn't want to succomb

> *Exit Grace Harkaway*   to that role?

Act drop quickly°

5.

Scene as 4

Enter Cool, L

COOL This is the most serious affair° Sir Harcourt has ever been engaged in. I took the liberty of considering him a fool when he told me he was going to marry, but voluntarily to incur another man's encumbrance° is very little short of madness. If he continues to conduct himself in this absurd manner, I shall be compelled to   5
dismiss him.

Enter Sir Harcourt Courtly, equipped for travelling, R

SIR HARCOURT Cool!

COOL Sir Harcourt.

SIR HARCOURT Is my chariot in waiting?

COOL For the last half-hour at the park wicket.° But, pardon the   10
insinuation, sir, would it not be more advisable to hesitate a little for a short reflection, before you undertake the heavy responsibility of a woman?

SIR HARCOURT No, hesitation destroys the romance of a *faux pas*°
and reduces it to the level of a mere mercantile calculation.   15

COOL What is to be done with Mr Charles?

SIR HARCOURT Ay, much against my will, Lady Gay prevailed on me to permit him to remain. You, Cool, must return him to college. Pass through London and deliver these papers. Here is a small notice of the coming elopement for the *Morning Post*; this, by an   20
eyewitness, for the *Herald*; this, with all the particulars, for the *Chronicle*;° and the full and circumstantial account for the evening journals; after which, meet us at Boulogne.°

COOL Very good, Sir Harcourt. (*Going, L*)

SIR HARCOURT Lose no time. Remember: Hôtel Anglais, Boulogne-   25
sur-Mer. And, Cool, bring a few copies with you and don't forget to distribute some amongst my very particular friends.

COOL It shall be done.

Exit Cool, L

SIR HARCOURT With what indifference does a man of the world view the approach of the most perilous catastrophe! How many roses   30
will fade upon the cheek of beauty when the defalcation° of Sir Harcourt Courtly is whispered, then hinted, at last confirmed and

bruited.° I think I see them. Then, on my return, they will not dare to eject me. I am their sovereign. Whoever attempts to think of treason, I'll banish him from the West End. I'll cut him, I'll put him out of fashion!   35

Enter Lady Gay Spanker, R

LADY GAY Sir Harcourt!

SIR HARCOURT At your feet.

LADY GAY I had hoped you would have repented.

SIR HARCOURT Repented!   40

LADY GAY Have you not come to say it was a jest? Say you have!

SIR HARCOURT Love is too sacred a subject to be trifled with. Come, let us fly! See, I have procured disguises.°

LADY GAY My courage begins to fail me. Let me return.

SIR HARCOURT Impossible!   45

LADY GAY Where do you intend to take me?

SIR HARCOURT You shall be my guide. The carriage waits.

LADY GAY You will never desert me?

SIR HARCOURT Desert! Oh, heavens! Nay, do not hesitate. Flight, now, alone is left to your desperate situation! Come, every moment   50
is laden with danger. (*They are going, C*)

LADY GAY Oh, gracious!

SIR HARCOURT Hush! What is it?

LADY GAY I have forgotten—I must return.

SIR HARCOURT Impossible!   55

LADY GAY I must! I must! I have left Max, a pet staghound, in his basket, without whom life would be unendurable; I could not exist!

SIR HARCOURT No, no. Let him be sent after us in a hamper.

LADY GAY In a hamper! Remorseless man! Go, you love me not. How would you like to be sent after me—in a hamper? Let me fetch him.   60
Hark! I hear him squeal! Oh! Max, Max!

SIR HARCOURT Hush! For heaven's sake. They'll imagine you're calling the Squire. I hear footsteps. Where can I retire?

Sir Harcourt pulls the C blind up and goes off at the window.
Enter Mark Meddle, Mr Spanker, Dazzle and Max
Harkaway, L. Lady Gay screams

MEDDLE Spanker *versus* Courtly! I subpoena° every one of you, as witnesses! I have 'em ready—here they are, a shilling apiece.°   65
(*Giving them round*)

LADY GAY Where is Sir Harcourt?

MEDDLE There! Bear witness! Calling on the vile delinquent for protection!

132

SPANKER Oh, his protection! 70

LADY GAY What? Ha!

MEDDLE I'll swear I overheard the whole elopement planned, before any jury! Where's the book!°

SPANKER (*to Lady Gay*) Do you hear, you profligate!

LADY GAY Ha! ha! ha! ha! 75

DAZZLE But where is the wretched Lothario?°

MEDDLE Ay, where is the defendant?

SPANKER Where lies the hoary villain?

LADY GAY What villain?

SPANKER That will not serve you! I'll not be blinded that way! 80

MEDDLE We won't be blinded any way!

MAX I must seek Sir Harcourt and demand an explanation! Such a thing never occurred in Oak Hall before! It must be cleared up!

    Exit Max Harkaway, R

MEDDLE (*aside to Spanker*) Now, take my advice, remember your gender. Mind the notes I have given you! 85

SPANKER (*LC, aside*) All right! Here they are! (*To Lady Gay*) Now, madam, I have procured the highest legal opinion on the point—

MEDDLE (*L*) Hear, hear!

SPANKER And the question resolves itself into a—into—What's this? (*Looks at notes*) 90

MEDDLE A nutshell!

SPANKER Yes, we are in a nutshell. Will you, in every respect, subscribe to my requests, desires, commands—(*Looks at notes*) orders, imperative, indicative, injunctive° or otherwise.

LADY GAY (*aside, C*) 'Pon my life, he's actually going to assume the ribbons° and take the box-seat.° I must put a stop to this. [*Aloud*] I will! Mr Spanker, I've been insulted by Sir Harcourt Courtly. He tried to elope with me. I place myself under your protection. Challenge him. 95

DAZZLE (*R*) Oh! I smell powder! 100

LADY GAY [*aside*] I know it will all end in smoke.° Sir Harcourt would rather run than fight.

DAZZLE Command my services. My dear madam, can I be of any use?

SPANKER Oh! Challenge! I must consult my legal adviser!

MEDDLE No, impossible! (*Crosses RC*) 105

DAZZLE Pooh! The easiest thing in life! Leave it to me. What has an attorney to do with affairs of honour? They are out of his element!

MEDDLE Compromise the question!° Pull his nose! We have no objection to that.

DAZZLE (*turning to Lady Gay*) Well, we have no objection either, have   110
we?

LADY GAY No! Pull his nose; that will be something.

DAZZLE Yes, pull his nose.

SPANKER Yes, but who is to do it?

MEDDLE And, moreover, it is not exactly actionable!   115

DAZZLE Isn't it! Thank you. I'll note down that piece of information;
it may be useful.

MEDDLE How! Cheated out of my legal knowledge. (*Crosses to Dazzle,
who signifies he will pull his nose—he hastily gets back to L*)

LADY GAY (*crosses LC*) Mr Spanker, I am determined! I insist upon a   120
challenge being sent to Sir Harcourt Courtly! And, mark me, if you
refuse to fight him, I will.

MEDDLE Don't. Take my advice. You'll incapacit—

LADY GAY Look you, Mr Meddle, (*crosses to LC*) unless you wish me to
horsewhip you, hold your tongue.   125

MEDDLE What a she-tiger! I shall retire and collect my costs.

      Exit Mark Meddle, L

LADY GAY Mr Spanker, oblige me by writing as I dictate.

SPANKER [*calling after Meddle*] Don't go! [*Aside*] He's gone, and now I
am defenceless! Is this the fate of husbands? A duel! Is this the
result of becoming master of my own family?   130

LADY GAY Come, Dolly!

SPANKER I won't be dollied! (*Sits RC. Dazzle wheels him round to R
table and sits on arm of the chair*)

LADY GAY 'Sir, the situation in which you were discovered with my
wife admits neither of explanation nor apology.'   135

SPANKER Oh yes! But it does. I don't believe you really intended to
run quite away.

LADY GAY You do not, but I know better. I say I did; and if it had not
been for your unfortunate interruption, I do not know where I
might have been by this time. Go on.   140

SPANKER 'Nor apology.' I'm writing my own death warrant, committing suicide on compulsion.

LADY GAY 'The bearer'—

SPANKER That will be you.

DAZZLE I'm the bearer.   145

LADY GAY 'Will arrange all preliminary matters, for another day
must see this sacrilege expiated by your life, or that of'—the
bearer?

DAZZLE No, no.

able to manipulate the movements of society

LADY GAY 'Yours sincerely' (*looking at Dazzle*)—Very sincerely? 150
    Lady Gay and Dazzle repeat 'very sincerely' *which Spanker*
    repeats in astonishment
DAZZLE 'Dolly Spanker.'
LADY GAY Dolly? No, no!
SPANKER Oh! 'Adolphus Spanker.'
LADY GAY Now, Mr Dazzle. (*Gives the letter over Spanker's head*)
DAZZLE The document is as sacred as if it were a hundred pound bill. 155
LADY GAY We trust to your discretion.
SPANKER His discretion! Oh, put your head in the tiger's mouth and
    trust to his discretion.
DAZZLE My dear Lady Gay, matters of this kind are indigenous to my
    nature, independently of their pervading fascination to all human- 160
    ity. But this is more especially delightful, as you may perceive I
    shall be the intimate and bosom friend of both parties. (*Seals letter
    etc. with Spanker's seal,° pulling him up*)
LADY GAY Is it not the only alternative in such a case?
DAZZLE It is a beautiful panacea in any, in every case. (*Going. Returns*) 165
    By the way, where would you like this party of pleasure to come
    off?° Open air shooting is pleasant enough, but if I might venture
    to advise, we could order half a dozen of that madeira and a box of
    cigars into the billiard-room, so make a night of it, eh, Mr Spanker?
SPANKER I don't smoke. 170
DAZZLE Take up the irons° every now and then, string° for first shot
    and blaze away at one another in an amicable and gentlemanlike
    way; so conclude the matter before the potency of the liquor could
    disturb the individuality of the object,° or the smoke of the cigars
    render its outline dubious. Does such an arrangement coincide 175
    with your views?
LADY GAY Perfectly.
DAZZLE I trust to be shortly the harbinger of happy tidings.
    Exit Dazzle, L
SPANKER (*crosses* L) Lady Gay Spanker, are you ambitious of becom-
    ing a widow? 180
LADY GAY Why, Dolly, woman is at best but weak, and weeds°
    become me.
SPANKER Female, am I to be immolated on the altar of your vanity!
LADY GAY If you become pathetic, I shall laugh.
SPANKER Shall laugh? You *are* laughing. Farewell, base, heartless, 185
    unfeeling woman!
    Exit Mr Spanker, L

comical element

bad view of women as manipulative projected.

LADY GAY Ha! Well, so I am. I am heartless, for he is a dear good little
fellow, and I ought not to play upon his feelings; but 'pon my life he
sounds so well up at concert pitch that I feel disinclined to untune
him. Poor Dolly, I didn't think he cared so much about me. I will   190
put him out of pain.

>*Exit Lady Gay Spanker, L. Sir Harcourt Courtly comes down,
from C window*

SIR HARCOURT I have been a fool, a dupe of my own vanity. I shall be
pointed at as a ridiculous old coxcomb, and so I am. The hour of
conviction is *arrived*. Have I deceived myself? Have I turned all my
senses inwards, looking towards self, always self? And has the world   195
been ever laughing at me? Well, if they have, I will revert the joke.°
They may say I am an old ass; but I will prove that I am neither too
old to repent my folly, nor such an ass as to flinch from confessing
it. A blow half met is but half felt.

>*Enter Dazzle, L*

DAZZLE Sir Harcourt, may I be permitted the honour of a few   200
minutes' conversation with you?

SIR HARCOURT With pleasure.

DAZZLE Have the kindness to throw your eye over that. (*Gives the
letter*)

SIR HARCOURT (*reads*) 'Situation—my wife—apology—expiate—my   205
life.' Why, this is intended for a challenge.

DAZZLE Why, indeed I am perfectly aware that it is not quite *en règle*°
in the couching,° for with that I had nothing to do; but I trust that
the irregularity of the composition will be confounded in the
beauty of the subject.   210

SIR HARCOURT Mr Dazzle, are you in earnest?

DAZZLE Sir Harcourt Courtly, upon my honour I am, and I hope that
no previous engagement will interfere with an immediate reply *in
propria persona*. We have fixed upon the billiard-room as the scene
of action, which I have just seen properly illuminated in honour of   215
the occasion; and by the by, if your implements are not handy, I can
oblige you with a pair of the sweetest things you ever handled—
hair-triggered°—saw grip;° heirlooms in my family. I regard them
almost in the light of relations.

SIR HARCOURT Sir, I shall avail myself of one of your relatives. (*Aside*)   220
One of the hereditaments° of my folly. I must accept it. (*Aloud*) Sir,
I shall be happy to meet Mr Spanker at any time or place he may
appoint.

DAZZLE The sooner the better, sir. Allow me to *offer* you my arm. I

see you understand these matters. My friend Spanker is woefully   225
ignorant, miserably uneducated.

> *Exeunt Dazzle and Sir Harcourt, L. Enter Max Harkaway,*
> *with Grace Harkaway, R*

MAX (L) Give ye joy, girl, give ye joy. Sir Harcourt Courtly must
consent to waive all title to your hand in favour of his son Charles.

GRACE (R) Oh, indeed! Is that the pith of your congratulation?
Humph! The exchange of an old fool for a young one; so then, my   230
fate is reduced to this, to sacrifice my fortune or unite myself with a
worm-eaten edition of the classics.

MAX Why, he certainly is not such a fellow as I could have chosen for
my little Grace; but consider, to retain fifteen thousand a year. Now
tell me honestly—but why should I say honestly?—speak, girl,   235
would you rather not have the lad?

GRACE Why do you ask me?

MAX Why, look ye, I'm an old fellow; another hunting season or two,
and I shall be in at my own death. I can't leave you this house and
land, because they are entailed.° Nor can I say I'm sorry for it, for it   240
is a good law. But I have a little box with my Grace's name upon it,
where since your father's death and miserly will, I have yearly
placed a certain sum to be yours, should you refuse to fulfill the
conditions prescribed.

GRACE My own dear uncle! (*Clasping him round the neck*)   245

MAX Pooh, pooh! What's to do now?° Why, it was only a trifle. Why,
you little rogue, what are you crying about?

GRACE Nothing, but—

MAX But what? Come, out with it. Will you have Courtly?

> *Enter Lady Gay Spanker, L*

LADY GAY Oh! Max, Max!   250

MAX Why, what's amiss with you?

LADY GAY I'm a wicked woman,—

MAX What have you done?

LADY GAY Everything! Oh, I thought Sir Harcourt was a coward, but
now I find a man may be a coxcomb without being a poltroon. Just   255
to show my husband how inconvenient it is to hold the ribbons
sometimes, I made him send a challenge to the old fellow and he, to
my surprise, accepted it and is going to blow my Dolly's brains out
in the billiard-room.

MAX The devil!   260

LADY GAY Just when I imagined I had got my whip hand of him
again, out comes my linch-pin° and over I go. Oh!

MAX I will soon put a stop to that. A duel under my roof! Murder in
    Oak Hall! I'll shoot them both!

> *Exit Max Harkaway, L*

GRACE Are you really in earnest?   265

LADY GAY Do you think it like a joke! Oh, Dolly, if you allow yourself
    to be shot, I will never forgive you, never! Ah! He is a great fool,
    Grace; but I can't tell why, but I would sooner lose my bridle hand
    than he should be hurt on my account.

> *[Two shots heard.°] Enter Sir Harcourt Courtly, L*

Tell me, tell me, have you shot him; is he dead? My dear Sir Harcourt,   270
    you horrid old brute, have you killed him? I shall never forgive
    myself!

> *Exit Lady Gay Spanker, L*

GRACE (*R*) Oh! Sir Harcourt, what has happened?

SIR HARCOURT (*L*) Don't be alarmed, I beg. Your uncle interrupted
    us, discharged the weapons, locked the challenger up in the   275
    billiard-room, to cool his rage.

GRACE Thank heaven!

SIR HARCOURT Miss Grace, to apologise for my conduct were useless,
    more especially as I am confident that no feelings of indignation or
    sorrow for my late acts are cherished by you; but still, reparation is 280
    in my power, and I not only waive all title, right or claim to your
    person or your fortune, but freely admit your power to bestow them
    on a more worthy object.

GRACE This generosity, Sir Harcourt, is most unexpected.

SIR HARCOURT No, not generosity, but simply justice; justice!   285

GRACE May I still beg a favour?

SIR HARCOURT Claim anything that is mine to grant.

GRACE You have been duped by Lady Gay Spanker. I have also been
    cheated and played upon by her° and Mr Hamilton. May I beg that
    the contract between us may to all appearances be still held good?   290

SIR HARCOURT Certainly; although I confess I cannot see the point of
    your purpose.

> *Enter Max Harkaway with Charles Courtly, L*

MAX Now, Grace, I have brought the lad.

GRACE Thank you, uncle, but the trouble was quite unnecessary. Sir
    Harcourt holds to his original contract.   295

MAX The deuce he does!

GRACE And I am willing, nay, eager, to become Lady Courtly.

COURTLY (*aside*) The deuce you are!

MAX But, Sir Harcourt—

SIR HARCOURT One word, Max, for an instant.   300
    Sir Harcourt and Max retire off, at R

COURTLY (*aside*) What can this mean? Can it be possible that I have
been mistaken; that she is not in love with Augustus Hamilton?

GRACE (*aside*) Now we shall find how he intends to bend the haughty
Grace.

COURTLY Madam, are you really in earnest? Are you in love with my   305
father?

GRACE No, indeed I am not.

COURTLY Are you in love with anyone else?

GRACE No, or I should not marry him.

COURTLY Then you actually accept him as your husband?   310

GRACE In the common acceptation° of the word.

COURTLY (*aside*) Hang me if I have not been a pretty fool! (*Aloud*)
Why do you marry him, if you don't care about him?

GRACE To save my fortune.

COURTLY (*aside*) Mercenary, cold-hearted girl! (*Aloud*) Were you   315
never in love?

GRACE Never.

COURTLY (*aside*) Oh, what an ass I've been! (*Aloud*) I heard Lady Gay
mention something about a Mr Hamilton.

GRACE Ah, yes, a person who, after the acquaintanceship of two days,   320
had the assurance to make love to me, and I—

COURTLY Yes, you—Well?

GRACE I pretended to receive his attentions.

COURTLY (*aside*) It was the best pretence I ever saw! (*Aloud*) Yet you
seemed rather concerned about the news of his death?   325

GRACE (*aside*) What can I say? (*Aloud*) Ah, but my maid Pert's brother
is the post-boy, and I thought he might have sustained an injury,
poor boy.

COURTLY (*aside*) Curse the post-boy! (*Aloud*) Madam, if the retention
of your fortune be the plea on which you are about to bestow your   330
hand on one you do not love, and whose very actions speak his
carelessness for that inestimable jewel he is incapable of appreciating, know that I am devotedly, madly, attached to you.

GRACE You, sir? Impossible!

COURTLY Not at all, but inevitable. I have been so for a long time.   335

GRACE Why, you never saw me until last night.

COURTLY I have seen you in imagination. You are the ideal I have
worshipped.

GRACE Since you press me into a confession, which nothing but this

could bring me to speak, know I did love poor Augustus Hamilton,   340
  Max Harkaway and Sir Harcourt Courtly enter R
but he—he is—no more! Pray, spare me, sir.
COURTLY (*aside*) She loves me! And oh, what a situation I am in. If I
  own I am the man, he will overhear, and ruin me; if I do not, she'll
  marry him. What is to be done?
  Enter Lady Gay Spanker, L
LADY GAY Where have you put my Dolly? I have been racing all   345
  round the house. Tell me, is he quite dead?
MAX I'll have him brought in.
  Exit Max Harkaway, L
SIR HARCOURT (*R*) My dear madam, you must perceive this un-
  fortunate occurence was no fault of mine. I was compelled to act as
  I have done. I was willing to offer any apology, but that resource   350
  was excluded as unacceptable.
LADY GAY I know, I know. 'Twas I made him write that letter. There
  was no apology required. 'Twas I that apparently seduced you from
  the paths of propriety; 'twas all a joke, and here is the end of it.
  Enter Max Harkaway, Mr Spanker and Dazzle
Oh, if he had but lived to say 'I forgive you, Gay!'   355
SPANKER So I do!
LADY GAY (*seeing Spanker*) Ah! He is alive!
SPANKER Of course, I am.
LADY GAY Ha! ha! ha! (*Embraces him*) I will never hunt again, unless
  you wish it. Sell your stable—   360
SPANKER No, no. Do what you like, say what you like, for the future! I
  find the head of a family has less ease and more responsibility than
  I, as a member, could have anticipated. I abdicate!
  *Spanker and Lady Gay Spanker go up, his arm round her
  waist, hers on his shoulder. Enter Cool, L*
SIR HARCOURT Ah! Cool, here! (*Aside [to Cool]*) You may destroy
  those papers. I have altered my mind and I do not intend to elope at   365
  present. Where are they?
COOL As you seemed particular,° Sir Harcourt, I sent them off by the
  mail to London.
SIR HARCOURT Why, then, a full description of the whole affair will
  be published tomorrow.   370
COOL Most irretrievably!
SIR HARCOURT You must post to town immediately and stop the press.
COOL Beg pardon, but they would see me hanged first, Sir Harcourt.
  They don't frequently meet with such a profitable lie.

JAMES (*offstage, L*) No, sir! No, sir!   375
        Enter James
    Sir, there is a gentleman, who is calling himself Mr Solomon Isaacs,
    insists upon following me up.
        Exit James. Enter Mr Solomon Isaacs, L
ISAACS Mr Courtly, you will excuse my performance of a most dis-
    agreeable duty at any time, but more especially in such a manner. I
    must beg the honour of your company to town.   380
SIR HARCOURT What! How! What for?
ISAACS (*LC*) For debt, Sir Harcourt.
SIR HARCOURT (*C*) Arrested! Impossible! Here must be some mistake.
ISAACS Not the slightest, sir. Judgment has been given in five cases,
    for the last three months; but Mr Courtly is an eel rather too   385
    nimble for my men. We have been on his track and traced him
    down to this village with Mr Dazzle.
DAZZLE (*R*) Ah! Isaacs! How are you?
ISAACS Thank you, sir. (*Speaks to Sir Harcourt*)
MAX (*L*) Do you know him?   390
DAZZLE Oh, intimately. Distantly related to his family; same arms on
    our escutcheon; empty purse falling through a hole in a pocket;
    motto: 'Requiescat in pace',° which means, 'Let virtue be its own
    reward.'
SIR HARCOURT (*to Isaacs*) Oh! I thought there was a mistake! Know,   395
    to your misfortune, that Mr Hamilton was the person you dogged
    to Oak Hall, between whom and my son a most remarkable likeness
    exists.
ISAACS Ha! ha! Know to your misfortune, Sir Harcourt, that Mr
    Hamilton and Mr Courtly are one and the same person!   400
SIR HARCOURT Charles!
COURTLY (*up C*) Concealment is in vain. I am Augustus Hamilton.
SIR HARCOURT Hang me, if I didn't think it all along! Oh, you
    infernal, cozening° dog!
ISAACS Now then, Mr Courtly—   405
GRACE (*C*) Stay, sir, Mr Charles Courtly is under age.° Ask his father.
SIR HARCOURT Ahem! I won't. I won't pay a shilling of the rascal's
    debts; not a sixpence!
GRACE (*C*) Then I will. [*To Solomon Isaacs*] You may retire.
        Exit Isaacs, L
COURTLY I can now perceive the generous point of your conduct   410
    towards me and, believe me, I appreciate and will endeavour to
    deserve it.

MAX (*crosses*) Ha! ha! Come, Sir Harcourt, you have been fairly beaten. You must forgive him; say you will.

SIR HARCOURT So, sir, it appears you have been leading covertly an infernal town life.   415

COURTLY (*C*) Yes, please, father. (*Imitating Master Charles*)

SIR HARCOURT None of your humbug, sir! (*Aside*) He is my own son. How could I expect him to keep out of the fire? (*Aloud*) And you, Mr Cool, have you been deceiving me?   420

COOL (*R*) Oh! Sir Harcourt, if your perception was played upon, how could I be expected to see?

      Pause. Cool goes up and off, L

SIR HARCOURT Well, it would be useless to withhold my hand. There, boy!

      Sir Harcourt Courtly gives his hand to Courtly, L. *Grace*
      comes down on the R *side and offers her hand; he takes it*

What is all this? What do you want?   425

COURTLY Your blessing, father.

GRACE If you please, father.

SIR HARCOURT Oho! The mystery is being solved! So, so, you young scoundrel, you have been making love under the rose.°

LADY GAY (*LC*) He learnt that from you, Sir Harcourt.   430

SIR HARCOURT Ahem! What would you do now, if I were to withold my consent?

GRACE *Do* without it.

MAX The will says, if Grace marries anyone but you, her property reverts to your heir apparent; and here he stands.   435

LADY GAY Make a virtue of necessity.

SPANKER I married from inclination; and see how happy I am. And if ever I have a son—

LADY GAY Hush! Dolly, dear.

SIR HARCOURT Well! Take her, boy, although you are too young to   440 marry. (*They retire with Max*)

LADY GAY Am I forgiven, Sir Harcourt?

SIR HARCOURT Ahem! Why—a—(*Aside to Lady Gay Spanker*) Have you really deceived me?

LADY GAY Can you not see through this?   445

SIR HARCOURT And you still love me?

LADY GAY As much as ever I did.

SIR HARCOURT (*is about to kiss her hand, when Spanker interposes between them*) A very handsome ring indeed.

SPANKER Very. (*Puts her hand in his and they go up to Dazzle*)   450

SIR HARCOURT Poor little Spanker.

MAX (*coming down, L, aside to Sir Harcourt*) One point I wish to have
settled. Who is Mr Dazzle? → *tying up final loose ends.*

SIR HARCOURT (*c*) A relative of the Spankers, he told me.

MAX Oh no, a near connection of yours.   455

SIR HARCOURT Never saw him before I came here in all my life. (*To
Courtly*) Charles! Who is Mr Dazzle?

COURTLY Who? I don't know. [*To Dazzle*] Dazzle, Dazzle, (*Dazzle
comes, R*) will you excuse an impertinent question?

DAZZLE (*R*) Certainly.   460

COURTLY Who the deuce are you?

DAZZLE I have not the remotest idea! → *providing final
comic moments.*

ALL How, sir!

DAZZLE Simple question as you may think it, it would puzzle half the
world to answer. One thing I can vouch: Nature made me a gentle-   465
man, that is, I live on the best that can be procured for credit. I
never spend my own money when I can oblige° a friend. I'm always
thick on° the winning horse. I'm an epidemic on the trade of tailor.
For further particulars enquire of any sitting magistrate.

SIR HARCOURT And these are the deeds which attest your title° to the   470
name of gentleman? I perceive that you have caught the infection of
the present age. Charles, permit me, as your father, and you, sir, as
his friend, to correct you on one point. Barefaced assurance is the
vulgar substitute for gentlemanly ease; and there are many, who by
aping the *vices* of the great, imagine that they elevate themselves to   475
the rank of those whose faults alone they copy. No, sir. The title of
gentleman is the only one *out* of any monarch's gift, yet within the
reach of every peasant. It should be engrossed° by *Truth*, stamped
with *Honour*, sealed with *good feeling*, signed *Man* and enrolled in
every true young English heart.   480

Mr Spanker   Dazzle   Charles Courtly   Max Harkaway
Lady Gay Spanker   Sir Harcourt Courtly   Grace Harkaway

R   *L*°

[*Curtain*]

*social class is restored as a divine
property → noone can simply fake it*

ENGAGED

W. S. GILBERT

CHARACTERS OF THE PLAY

Cheviot Hill, a young man of property — Mr George Honey
Belvawney, his friend — Mr Harold Kyrle
Mr Symperson — Mr Howe
Angus Macalister, a Lowland peasant lad — Mr Dewar
Major MacGillicuddy — Mr Weathersby
Belinda Treherne — Miss Marion Terry
Minnie, Symperson's daughter — Miss Lucy Buckstone
Mrs Macfarlane, a Lowland widow — Miss Emily Thorne
Maggie, her daughter, a Lowland lassie — Miss Julia Stewart
Parker, Minnie's maid — Miss Julia Roselle

*Act 1: Garden of a cottage near Gretna, on the border between
England and Scotland.
Acts 2 and 3: Drawing-room in Symperson's house in London.*

*Three months' interval is supposed to elapse between Acts 1 and 2.
Three days' interval is supposed to elapse between Acts 2 and 3.*

Note: it is absolutely essential to the success of this piece that it should
be played with the most perfect earnestness and gravity throughout.
There should be no exaggeration in costume, make-up, or demeanour;
and the characters, one and all, should appear to believe, throughout,
in the perfect sincerity of their words and actions.°

W. S. GILBERT

24, The Boltons,°
12th October, 1877

1.

*Garden of a humble but picturesque cottage, near Gretna, on the
border between England and Scotland. The cottage, R, is covered
with creepers, and the garden filled with flowers. The door faces
audience. A wooden bridge leads off LUE. The whole scene is
suggestive of rustic prosperity and content.*

*Maggie Macfarlane, a pretty country girl, is discovered spinning
at a wheel, L, and singing as she spins. A rustic stool R. Angus
Macalister, a good-looking peasant lad, appears at back, crosses
to R, and creeps softly down to Maggie as she sings and spins, and
places his hands over her eyes*

ANGUS (R) Wha° is it?

MAGGIE (L) Oh, Angus, ye frightened me sae! (*He releases her*) And
see there, the flax is a' knotted and scribbled°, and I'll do naething
wi' it!

ANGUS Meg! My Meg! My ain bonnie Meg!   5

MAGGIE Angus, why, lad, what's wrang wi' 'ee? Thou hast tear drops
in thy bonnie blue een.

ANGUS Dinna heed them, Meg. It comes fra glowerin'° at thy bright
beauty. Glowerin' at thee is like glowerin' at the noon-day sun!

MAGGIE Angus, thou'rt talking fulishly. I'm but a puir brown hill-side 10
lassie. I dinna like to hear sic things from a straight honest lad like
thee. It's the way the dandy town-folk speak to me, and it does na
come rightly from the lips of a simple man.

ANGUS Forgive me, Meg, for I speak honestly to ye. Angus Macalister
is not the man to deal in squeaming compliments. Meg, I love thee 15
dearly, as thou well knowest. I'm but a poor lad, and I've little but
twa braw arms and a straight hairt to live by, but I've saved a wee bit
siller; I've a braw housie and a scrappie of gude garden-land; and
it's a' for thee, lassie, if thou'll gie me thy true and tender little
hairt!   20

MAGGIE Angus, I'll be fair and straight wi' 'ee. Thou askest me for my
hairt. Why, Angus, thou'rt tall, and fair, and brave. Thou'st a gude,
honest face, and a gude, honest hairt, which is mair precious than a'
the gold on earth! No man has a word to say against Angus Macalister; no, nor any woman neither.° Thou hast strong arms to work 25
wi', and a strong hairt to help thee work. And wha am I that I

should say that a' these blessings are not enough for me? If thou, gude, brave, honest man, will be troubled wi' sic a puir, little, humble mousie as Maggie Macfarlane, why, she'll just be the proudest and happiest lassie in a' Dumfries!   30

ANGUS My ain darling!

> *Maggie Macfarlane and Angus Macalister embrace. Enter*
> *Mrs Macfarlane, from cottage door, R*

MRS MACFARLANE Why, Angus, Maggie, what's a' this!

ANGUS Mistress Macfarlane, dinna be fasht wi' me; dinna think worse o' me than I deserve. I've loved your lass honestly these fifteen years, but I never plucked up the hairt to tell her so until now; and   35 when she answered fairly, it was not in human nature to do aught else but hold her to my hairt and place one kiss on her bonnie cheek.

MRS MACFARLANE (*R*) Angus, say nae mair. My hairt is sair at losing my only bairn; but I'm nae fasht wi' 'ee. Thou'rt a gude lad, and it's   40 been the hope of my widowed auld heart to see you twain one. Thou'lt treat her kindly, I ken that weel. Thou'rt a prosperous, kirk-going man, and my Mag should be a happy lass indeed. Bless thee, Angus; bless thee!

ANGUS (*C, wiping his eyes*) Dinna heed the water in my ee. It will come   45 when I'm ower glad. Yes, I'm a fairly prosperous man. What wi' farmin' a bit land, and gillieing odd times, and a bit o' poachin' now and again; and what wi' my illicit whusky still;° and throwin' trains off the line that the poor distracted° passengers may come to my cot,° I've mair ways than one of making an honest living and I'll   50 work them a' nicht and day for my bonnie Meg!

MRS MACFARLANE (*seated R*) D'ye ken, Angus, I sometimes think that thou'rt losing some o' thine auld skill at upsetting railway trains. Thou hast not done sic a thing these sax weeks and the cottage stands sairly in need of sic chance custom as the poor delayed   55 passengers may bring.

MAGGIE Nay, mither, thou wrangest him. Even noo, this very day, has he not placed twa bonnie braw sleepers across the up-line, ready for the express from Glaisgie, which is due in twa minutes or so. (*Crosses to L*)   60

MRS MACFARLANE Gude lad. Gude thoughtfu' lad! But I hope the unfortunate passengers will na' be much hurt, puir unconscious bodies!

ANGUS (*C*) Fear nought, mither. Lang experience has taught me to do my work deftly. The train will run off the line, and the traffic will   65

just be blocked for half-a-day, but I'll warrant ye that, wi' a' this,
nae mon, woman, or child amang them will get sae much as a
bruised head or a broken nose.

MAGGIE My ain tender-hearted Angus! He wadna hurt sae much as a
blatherin', buzzin' bluebottle flee!

Railway whistle heard, L

ANGUS Nae, Meg, not if takin' care and thought could help the poor
dumb thing! (*Wiping his eyes*) There, see, lass, (*looking off*) the
train's at a standstill and there's nae harm done. I'll just go and tell
the puir distraught passengers that they may rest them here, in thy
cot, gin they will, till the line is cleared again. Mither, get thy rooms
ready and put brose i' the pot, for mebbe they'll be hungry, poor
souls. Farewell, Meg; I'll be back ere lang, and if I don't bring 'ee a
full half-dozen o' well-paying passengers, thou may'st just wed the
red-headed exciseman!°

Exit Angus Macalister, L over bridge

MAGGIE Oh, mither, mither, I'm ower happy! I've nae deserved sic a
good fortune as to be the wife o' yon brave and honest lad!

MRS MACFARLANE Meg, thine auld mither's hairt is sair at the
thought o' losin' ye, for hitherto she's just been a' the world to 'ee;
but now thou'lt cleave to thine Angus, and thou'lt learn to love him
better than thy puir auld mither! But it mun be, it mun be!

MAGGIE Nay, mither, say not that. A gude girl loves her husband wi'
one love and her mither wi' anither. They are not alike, but neither
is greater nor less than the ither, and they dwell together in peace
and unity. That is how a gude girl loves.

MRS MACFARLANE And thou art a gude girl, Meg?

MAGGIE I am a varra gude girl indeed, mither, a varra, varra gude girl!

MRS MACFARLANE I'm richt sure o' that. Well, the puir belated passengers will be here directly, and it is our duty to provide for them
sic puir hospitality as our humble roof will afford. It shall never be
said o' Janie Macfarlane that she ever turned the weary traveller
fainting from her door.

MAGGIE My ain gentle-hearted mither!

Exeunt Maggie and Mrs Macfarlane together into cottage, R.
Enter Angus Macalister with Belvawney and Miss Treherne
over bridge, L. She is in travelling costume, and both are much
agitated and alarmed

ANGUS (*down R*) Step in, sir, step in, and sit ye doun for a wee. I'll just
send Mistress Macfarlane to ye. She's a gude auld bodie, and will
see to your comforts as if she was your ain mither.

70

75

80

85

90

95

100

BELVAWNEY Thank you, my worthy lad, for your kindness at this trying moment. I assure you we shall not forget it. (*Miss Treherne sits L*)

ANGUS Ah, sir, wadna any mon do as muckle? A dry shelter, a bannock and a pan o' parritch is a' we can offer ye, but sic as it is ye're   105
hairtily welcome.

BELVAWNEY (*L*) It is well. We thank you.

ANGUS (*foot on stool R*) For wha wadna help the unfortunate?

BELVAWNEY (*occupied with Miss Treherne, LC*) Exactly; every one would.   110

ANGUS Or feed the hungry?

BELVAWNEY No doubt.

ANGUS It just brings the tear drop to my ee to think—

BELVAWNEY (*leading him off*) My friend, we would be alone, this maiden and I. Farewell.   115

    Exit Angus Macalister, R, into cottage

Belinda, my own, my life! Compose yourself. It was in truth a weird and gruesome accident. The line is blocked, your parasol is broken and your butterscotch trampled in the dust, but no serious harm is done. Come, be cheerful. We are safe, quite safe.

MISS TREHERNE Safe! Ah, Belvawney, my own, own Belvawney.   120
There is, I fear, no safety for us so long as we are liable to be overtaken by that fearful major to whom I was to have been married this morning!

BELVAWNEY Major McGillicuddy? I confess I do not feel comfortable when I think of Major McGillicuddy.   125

MISS TREHERNE You know his barbaric nature and how madly jealous he is. If he should find that I have eloped with you, he will most surely shoot us both!

BELVAWNEY It is an uneasy prospect. (*Crosses to R. Suddenly*) Belinda, do you love me?   130

MISS TREHERNE (*advancing to him*) With an impetuous passion that I shall carry with me to the tomb!

BELVAWNEY Then be mine tomorrow! We are not far from Gretna, and the thing can be done without delay.° Once married, the arm of the law will protect us from this fearful man, and we can defy   135
him to do his worst.

MISS TREHERNE Belvawney, all this is quite true. I love you madly, passionately; I care to live but in your heart, I breathe but for your love; yet, before I actually consent to take the irrevocable step that will place me on the pinnacle of my fondest hopes, you must give   140

me some definite idea of your pecuniary position. I am not mercenary, heaven knows; but business is business, and I confess I should
like a little definite information about the settlements.

BELVAWNEY I often think that it is deeply to be deplored that these
grovelling questions of money should alloy the tenderest and most   145
hallowed sentiments that inspire our imperfect natures.

MISS TREHERNE It is unfortunate, no doubt, but at the same time it is
absolutely necessary.

BELVAWNEY Belinda, I will be frank with you. My income is £1000
a year, which I hold on certain conditions. You know my friend   150
Cheviot Hill, who is travelling to London in the same train with
us, but in the third class?

MISS TREHERNE (L) I believe I know the man you mean.

BELVAWNEY (C) Cheviot, who is a young man of large property, but
extremely close-fisted, is cursed with a strangely amatory dis-   155
position, as you will admit when I tell you that he has contracted a
habit of proposing marriage, as a matter of course, to every woman
he meets. His haughty father, who comes of a very old family—the
Cheviot Hills° had settled in this part of the world centuries before
the Conquest°—is compelled by his health to reside in Madeira.   160
Knowing that I exercise an all but supernatural influence over his
son, and fearing that his affectionate disposition would lead him to
contract an undesirable marriage, the old gentleman allows me
£1000 a year so long as Cheviot shall live single, but at his death or
marriage the money goes over to Cheviot's uncle Symperson, who   165
is now travelling to town with him.

MISS TREHERNE Then so long as your influence over him lasts, so
long only will you retain your income?

BELVAWNEY (crosses to L) That is, I am sorry to say, the state of the
case.   170

MISS TREHERNE (C, after a pause) Belvawney, I love you with an
imperishable ardour which mocks the power of words. If I were to
begin to tell you now of the force of my indomitable passion for
you, the tomb would close over me before I could exhaust the
entrancing subject. But, as I said before, business is business, and   175
unless I can see some distinct probability that your income will be
permanent, I shall have no alternative but to weep my heart out in
all the anguish of maiden solitude, uncared for, unloved, and alone!

Exit Miss Treherne, R, into cottage—quickly

BELVAWNEY (L) There goes a noble-hearted girl indeed! Oh for the
gift of Cheviot's airy badinage, oh for his skill in weaving a net   180

about the hearts of women! If I could but induce her to marry me at once before the dreadful major learns our flight! Why not? We are in Scotland. Methinks I've heard two loving hearts can wed, in this strange country, by merely making declaration to that effect. I will think out some cunning scheme to lure her into marriage unawares.   185

    Enter Maggie, R, from cottage

MAGGIE (*R*) Will ye walk in and rest a wee, Maister Belvawney? There's a room ready for ye, kind sir, and ye're heartily welcome to it.

BELVAWNEY (*L*) It is well. (*Maggie going*) Stop! Come hither, maiden.   190

MAGGIE (*RC*) Oh, sir! You do not mean any harm towards a puir, innocent, unprotected cottage lassie?

BELVAWNEY Harm! No; of course, I don't. What do you mean?

MAGGIE I'm but a puir, humble mountain girl; but let me tell you, sir, that my character's just as dear to me as the richest and proudest   195
lady's in the land. Before I consent to approach ye, swear to me that you mean me no harm.

BELVAWNEY Harm? Of course, I don't. Don't be a little fool! Come here.

MAGGIE (*aside*) There is something in his manner that reassures me.   200
It is not that of the airy trifler with innocent hairts. (*Aloud*)—What wad ye wi' puir, harmless Maggie Macfarlane, gude sir? (*Advancing to him*)

BELVAWNEY Can you tell me what constitutes a Scotch marriage?

MAGGIE Oh, sir, it's nae use asking me that; for my hairt is not my ain   205
to give. I'm betrothed to the best and noblest lad in a' the bonnie borderland. Oh, sir, I canna be your bride!

BELVAWNEY My girl, you mistake. I do not want you for my bride. Can't you answer a simple question? What constitutes a Scotch marriage?   210

MAGGIE Ye've just to say before twa witnesses, 'Maggie Macfarlane is my wife'; and I've just to say, 'Maister Belvawney is my husband', and nae mon can set us asunder. But, sir, I canna be your bride; for I am betrothed to the best and noblest—

BELVAWNEY I congratulate you. You can go.   215

MAGGIE Yes, sir.

    Exit Maggie, R, into cottage

BELVAWNEY It is a simple process; simple, but yet how beautiful! One thing is certain; Cheviot may marry any day, despite my precautions, and then I shall be penniless. He may die, and equally I shall

be penniless. Belinda has £500 a year. It is not much, but it would,   220
at least, save me from starvation.

Exit Belvawney, R2E. Enter Mr Symperson and Cheviot Hill
over bridge, L. They both show signs of damage. Their hats are
beaten in and their clothes disordered through the accident

SYMPERSON Well, here we are at last.

CHEVIOT Yes. Here we are at last, and a pretty state I'm in, to be sure.

SYMPERSON My dear nephew, you would travel third class and this is
the consequence. After all, there's not much harm done.   225

CHEVIOT Not much harm? What d'ye call that? (*Showing his hat*) Ten
and ninepence at one operation! My gloves split, one and four! My
coat ruined, eighteen and six! It's a coarse and brutal nature that
recognises no harm that don't involve loss of blood. I'm reduced by
this accident from a thinking, feeling, reflecting human being, to a   230
moral pulp, a mash, a poultice. Damme, sir, that's what I am! I'm a
poultice!

SYMPERSON Cheviot, my dear boy, at the moment of the accident you
were speaking to me on a very interesting subject.

CHEVIOT Was I? I forget what it was. The accident has knocked it   235
clean out of my head.

SYMPERSON You were saying that you were a man of good position
and fortune; that you derived £2000 a year from your bank; that
you thought it was time you settled. You then reminded me that I
should come into Belvawney's £1000 a year on your marriage, and   240
I'm not sure, but I rather think you mentioned, casually, that my
daughter Minnie is an Angel of Light.

CHEVIOT True, and just then we went off the line. To resume: Uncle
Symperson, your daughter Minnie is an Angel of Light, a perfect
being, as innocent as a new-laid egg.   245

SYMPERSON Minnie is, indeed, all that you have described her.

CHEVIOT Uncle, I'm a man of few words. I feel and I speak. I love that
girl, madly, passionately, irresistibly. She is my whole life, my whole
soul and body, my Past, my Present, and my To Come. I have
thought for none but her; she fills my mind, sleeping and waking;   250
she is the essence of every hope, the tree upon which the fruit of
my heart is growing; my own To Come!

SYMPERSON (*who has sunk overpowered onto stool, R, during this speech*)
Cheviot, my dear boy, excuse a father's tears. I won't beat about the
bush. You have anticipated my devoutest wish. Cheviot, my dear   255
boy, take her, she is yours!

CHEVIOT I have often heard of rapture, but I never knew what it was

till now. Uncle Symperson, bearing in mind the fact that your
income will date from the day of the wedding, when may this be?

SYMPERSON My boy, the sooner the better! Delicacy would prompt   260
me to give Belvawney a reasonable notice of the impending loss of
his income, but should I, for such a mere selfish reason as that, rob
my child of one hour of the happiness that you are about to confer
upon her? No! Duty to my child is paramount!

CHEVIOT On one condition, however, I must insist. This must be kept   265
from Belvawney's knowledge. You know the strange, mysterious
influence that his dreadful eyes exercise over me.

SYMPERSON I have remarked it with astonishment.

CHEVIOT They are much inflamed just now, and he has to wear green
spectacles. While this lasts, I am a free agent, but under treatment   270
they may recover. In that case, if he knew that I contemplated
matrimony, he would use them to prevent my doing so, and I cannot resist them; I cannot resist them! Therefore, I say, until I am
safely and securely tied up, Belvawney must know nothing about it.

SYMPERSON Trust me, Cheviot, he shall know nothing about it from   275
me. (*Aside*) A thousand a year! I have endeavoured, but in vain, to
woo Fortune for fifty-six years, but she smiles upon me at last! She
smiles upon me at last!

    Exit Mr Symperson, R, into cottage

CHEVIOT At length my hopes are to be crowned! Oh, my own, my
own, the hope of my heart; my love, my life!   280

    Enter Belvawney, R2E, who has overheard these words

BELVAWNEY Cheviot! Whom are you apostrophising in those terms?
You've been at it again, I see!

CHEVIOT (*C*) Belvawney, that apostrophe was private. I decline to
admit you to my confidence.

BELVAWNEY Cheviot, what is the reason of this strange tone of   285
defiance? A week ago I had but to express a wish to have it obeyed
as a matter of course.

CHEVIOT Belvawney, it may not be denied that there was a time when,
owing to the remarkable influence exercised over me by your extraordinary eyes, you could do with me as you would. It would be   290
affectation to deny it, your eyes withered my will; they paralysed
my volition. They were strange and lurid eyes, and I bowed to
them. Those eyes were my Fate, my Destiny, my unerring Must,
my inevitable Shall. That time has gone forever!

BELVAWNEY (*sits R*) Alas for the days that are past and the good that   295
came and went with them!

CHEVIOT Weep for them if you will. I cannot weep with you, for I loved them not. But, as you say, they are past. The light that lit up those eyes is extinct; their fire has died out; their soul has fled. They are no longer eyes, they are poached eggs. I have not yet sunk   300
so low as to be the slave of two poached eggs.

BELVAWNEY (*rises*) Have mercy. If any girl has succeeded in enslaving you—and I know how easily you are enslaved—dismiss her from your thoughts; have no more to say to her; and I will, yes, I will bless you with my latest breath!   305

CHEVIOT Whether a blessing conferred with one's latest breath is a superior article to one conferred in robust health we need not stop to inquire. I decline, as I said before, to admit you to my confidence on any terms whatever. (*Crosses to R*) Begone!

  Exit Belvawney, L2E

Dismiss from my thoughts the only woman I ever loved! Have no   310
more to say to the tree upon which the fruit of my heart is growing!
No, Belvawney, I cannot cut off my tree as if it were gas or water. I
do not treat women like that. Some men do, but I don't. I am not
that sort of man. I respect women; I love women. They are good;
they are pure; they are beautiful; at least many of them are.   315

  Enter Maggie from cottage R; he is much fascinated

This one, for example, is very beautiful indeed!

MAGGIE If ye'll just walk in, sir, ye'll find a bannock and a pan o' parritch waitin' for ye on the table.

CHEVIOT (*fascinated*) This is one of the loveliest women I ever met in the whole course of my life!   320

MAGGIE (*aside*) What's he glowerin' at? (*Aloud*) Oh sir, ye mean no harm to a poor Lowland lassie? (*Advancing to C*)

CHEVIOT Pardon me, it's very foolish. I can't account for it, but I am arrested, fascinated.

MAGGIE Oh gude sir, what's fascinated ye?   325

CHEVIOT I don't know. There is something about you that exercises a most remarkable influence over me. It seems to weave a kind of enchantment around me. I can't think what it is. You are a good girl, I am sure. None but a good girl could so powerfully affect me.
You *are* a good girl, are you not?   330

MAGGIE (*C*) I am a varra gude girl indeed, sir.

CHEVIOT I was quite sure of it. (*Gets his arm round her waist*)

MAGGIE I am a much better girl than nineteen out of twenty in these pairts. And they are all gude girls, too.

CHEVIOT (*LC*) My darling! (*Kisses her*)   335

MAGGIE Oh, kind sir, what's that for?

CHEVIOT It is your reward for being a good girl.

MAGGIE Oh, sir, I did na look for sic a recompense. You are varra, varra kind to puir little Maggie Macfarlane.

CHEVIOT I cannot think what it is about you that fascinates me so remarkably.   340

MAGGIE Maybe it's my beauty.

CHEVIOT Maybe it is. It is quite possible that it may be, as you say, your beauty.

MAGGIE I am remarkably pretty and I've a varra neat figure.   345

CHEVIOT There is a natural modesty in this guileless appreciation of your own perfection that is, to me, infinitely more charming than the affected ignorance of an artificial town-bred beauty.

MAGGIE Oh, sir, can I close my een to the picture that my looking-glass holds up to me twenty times a day? We see the rose on the   350 tree, and we say that it is fair;° we see the silver moon sailing in the braw blue heavens, and we say that she is bright; we see the brawling stream purling over the smooth stanes i' the burn, and we say that it is beautiful; and shall we close our een to the fairest of nature's works, a pure and beautiful woman? Why, sir, it wad just   355 be base ingratitude! No, it's best to tell the truth about a' things; I am a varra, varra beautiful girl!

CHEVIOT Maggie Macfarlane, I'm a plain, blunt, straightforward man, and I come quickly to the point. I see more to love in you than I ever saw in any woman in all my life before. I have a large income,   360 which I do not spend recklessly. I love you passionately; you are the essence of every hope; you are the tree upon which the fruit of my heart is growing, my Past, my Present, my Future; you are my own To Come. Tell me, will you be mine? Will you join your life with mine?   365

Enter Angus Macalister, R, who listens

MAGGIE Ah, kind sir, I'm sairly grieved to wound sae true and tender a love as yours, but ye're ower late, my love is nae my ain to give ye, it's given ower to the best and bravest lad in a' the bonnie Borderland!

CHEVIOT Give me his address that I may go and curse him!   370

MAGGIE (*kneels to Cheviot, LC*) Ah, ye must not curse him! Oh spare him, spare him, for he is good and brave, and he loves me, oh sae dearly, and I love him, oh sae dearly too. Oh sir, kind sir, have mercy on him, and do not, do not curse him, or I shall die! (*Throwing herself at his feet*)   375

CHEVIOT Will you, or will you not, oblige me by telling me where he is, that I may at once go and curse him?

ANGUS (*coming forward*) He is here, sir, but dinna waste your curses on me. Maggie, my bairn, (*raising her*) I heard the answer ye gave to this man, my true and gentle lassie! Ye spake well and bravely, Meg, well and bravely! Dinna heed the water in my ee; it's a tear of joy and gratitude, Meg, a tear of joy and gratitude! (*Passes Maggie to R*)

CHEVIOT (*touched*) Poor fellow! I will *not* curse him! (*Aloud*) Young man, I respect your honest emotion. I don't want to distress you, but I cannot help loving this most charming girl. Come, is it reasonable to quarrel with a man because he's of the same way of thinking as yourself?

ANGUS Nay, sir, I'm nae fasht, but it just seems to drive a' the bluid back into my hairt when I think that my Meg is loved by anither! Oh, sir, she's a fair and winsome lassie, and I micht as justly be angry wi' ye for loving the blue heavens! She's just as far above us as they are! (*Wiping his eyes and kissing her*)

CHEVIOT (*with decision*) Pardon me, I cannot allow that.

ANGUS Eh?

CHEVIOT I love that girl madly, passionately, and I cannot possibly allow you to do that; not before my eyes, I beg. You simply torture me.

MAGGIE (*to Angus*) Leave off, dear, till the puir gentleman's gone, and then ye can begin again.

CHEVIOT Angus, listen to me. You love this girl?

ANGUS I love her, sir, a'most as weel as I love mysel'!

CHEVIOT Then reflect how you are standing in the way of her prosperity. I am a rich man. I have money, position, and education. I am a much more intellectual and generally agreeable companion for her than you can ever hope to be. I am full of anecdote, and all my anecdotes are in the best possible taste. I will tell you some of them some of these days, and you can judge for yourself. Maggie, if she married me, would live in a nice house in a good square. She would have wine—occasionally. She would be kept beautifully clean. Now, if you really love this girl almost as well as you love yourself, are you doing wisely or kindly in standing in the way of her getting all these good things? As to compensation—why, I've had heavy expenses of late, but if—yes, if thirty shillings°—

ANGUS (*hotly*) Sir, I'm puir in pocket, but I've a rich hairt. It is rich in a pure and overflowing love, and he that hath love hath all. You canna ken what true love is, or you wadna dare to insult a puir but honest lad by offering to buy his treasure for money.

Cheviot retires up

MAGGIE (c) My ain true darling!

Angus Macalister and Maggie Macfarlane embrace

CHEVIOT Now, I'll not have it! Understand me, I'll not have it. It's simple agony to me.

Angus passes Maggie over L

Angus, I respect your indignation, but you are too hasty. I do not offer to buy your treasure for money. You love her. It will naturally cause you pain to part with her, and I prescribe thirty shillings, not as a cure, but as a temporary solace. If thirty shillings is not enough, why, I don't mind making it two pounds.

ANGUS Nae, sir, it's useless, and we ken it weel, do we not, my brave lassie? Our hearts are one as our bodies will be some day; and the man is na' born, and the gold is na' coined that can set us twain asunder!

MAGGIE (R) Angus, dear, I'm varra proud o' sae staunch and true a love. It's like your ain true self, an' I can say nae more for it than that. But dinna act wi'out prudence and forethought, dear. In these hard times twa pound is twa pound, and I'm nae sure that ye're acting richtly in refusing sae large a sum. I love you varra dearly— ye ken that right weel—an' if ye'll be troubled wi' sic a poor little mousie I'll mak' ye a true an' loving wife, but I doubt whether, wi' a' my love, I'll ever be worth as much to ye as twa pound. Dinna act in haste, dear; tak' time to think before ye refuse this kind gentleman's offer.

ANGUS Oh, sir, is not this rare modesty? Could ye match it amang your toun-bred fine ladies? I think not! Meg, it shall be as you say. I'll tak' the siller, but it'll be wi' a sair and broken hairt! (*Cheviot gives Angus money*) Fare thee weel, my love, my childhood's, boyhood's, manhood's love! Ye're ganging fra my hairt to anither, who'll gie thee mair o' the gude things o' this world than I could ever gie 'ee, except love, an' o' that my hairt is full indeed! But it's a' for the best; ye'll be happier wi' him—and twa pound is twa pound. Meg, mak' him a gude wife, be true to him, and love him as ye loved me. Oh, Meg, my poor bruised hairt is well nigh like to break!

Exit Angus Macalister, R, into cottage in great agony

MAGGIE (*looking wistfully after him*) Puir laddie, puir laddie! Oh, I did na ken till noo how weel he loved me!

CHEVIOT Maggie, I'm almost sorry I—poor lad, poor fellow! He has a generous heart. I am glad I did not curse him. (*Aside*) This is weakness! (*Aloud*) Maggie, my own, ever and for always my own, we will be very happy, will we not? 455

MAGGIE Oh, sir, I dinna ken, but in truth I hope so. Oh, sir, my happiness is in your hands noo; be kind to the puir cottage lassie who loves ye sae weel. My hairt is a' your ain, and if ye forsake me my lot will be a sair one indeed! 460

Exit Maggie Macfarlane, weeping, into cottage

CHEVIOT Poor little Lowland lassie! That's my idea of a wife. No ridiculous extravagance; no expensive tastes. Knows how to dress like a lady on £5 a year; ah, and does it too! No pretence there of being blind to her own beauties. She knows that she is beauti- 465 ful and scorns to lie about it. In that respect she resembles Symperson's dear daughter Minnie. My darling Minnie. (*Looks at miniature, sits L*) My own darling Minnie. Minnie is fair, Maggie is dark. Maggie loves me! That excellent and perfect country crea- ture loves me! She is to be the light of my life, my own To Come! 470 In some respects she is even prettier than Minnie—my darling Minnie, Symperson's dear daughter, the tree upon which the fruit of my heart is growing; my Past, my Present, and my Future, my own To Come! But this tendency to reverie is growing on me. I must shake it off. 475

Cheviot Hill rises, crosses to R. Enter Miss Treherne RC at back

Heaven and earth, what a singularly lovely girl!

MISS TREHERNE (*LC*) A stranger! Pardon me, I will withdraw! (*Going*)

CHEVIOT A stranger indeed, in one sense, inasmuch as he never had the happiness of meeting you before, but, in that he has a heart that can sympathise with another's misfortune, he trusts he may claim 480 to be regarded almost as a friend.

MISS TREHERNE May I ask, sir, to what misfortunes you allude?

CHEVIOT I—a—do not know their precise nature, but that perception would indeed be dull, and that heart would be indeed flinty, that did not at once perceive that you are very, very unhappy. Accept, 485 madam, my deepest and most respectful sympathy.

MISS TREHERNE (*L*) You have guessed rightly, sir. I am indeed a most unhappy woman.

CHEVIOT I am delighted to hear it—a—I mean I feel a pleasure, a melancholy and chastened pleasure, in reflecting that, if your dis- 490 tress is not of a pecuniary nature, it may perchance lie in my power to alleviate your sorrow.

MISS TREHERNE (*L*) Impossible, sir, though I thank you for your respectful sympathy.

CHEVIOT (*c*) How many women would forego twenty years of their 495 lives to be as beautiful as yourself, little dreaming that extraordinary loveliness can co-exist with the most poignant anguish of mind! But so too often we find it, do we not, dear lady?

MISS TREHERNE Sir! This tone of address, from a complete stranger.

CHEVIOT (*c*) Nay, be not unreasonably severe upon an impassionable 500 and impulsive man, whose tongue is but the too faithful herald of his heart. We see the rose on the tree and we say that it is fair; we see the bonnie brooks purling over the smooth stanes—I should say stones—in the burn, and we say that it is beautiful, and shall we close our eyes to the fairest of nature's works, a pure and beautiful 505 woman? Why, it would be base ingratitude indeed!

MISS TREHERNE I cannot deny that there is much truth in the sentiments you so beautifully express, but I am, unhappily, too well aware that, whatever advantages I may possess, personal beauty is not among their number. (*Sits L*) 510

CHEVIOT How exquisitely modest is this chaste insensibility to your own singular loveliness! How infinitely more winning than the bold-faced self-appreciation of under-bred country girls!

MISS TREHERNE I am glad, sir, that you are pleased with my modesty. It has often been admired. 515

CHEVIOT Pleased! I am more than pleased; that's a very weak word. I am enchanted. Madam, I am a man of quick impulse and energetic action. I feel and I speak. I cannot help it. Madam, be not surprised when I tell you that I cannot resist the conviction that you are the light of my future life, the essence of every hope, the 520 tree upon which the fruit of my heart is growing; my Past, my Present, my Future, my own To Come! (*Miss Treherne rises*) Do not extinguish that light, do not disperse that essence, do not blight that tree! I am well off; I'm a bachelor; I'm thirty-two; and I love you, madam, humbly, truly, trustfully, patiently. Paralysed 525 with admiration, I wait anxiously, and yet hopefully, for your reply.

MISS TREHERNE (*L*) Sir, that heart would indeed be cold that did not feel grateful for so much earnest, single-hearted devotion. I am deeply grieved to have to say one word to cause pain to one who 530 expresses himself in such well-chosen terms of respectful esteem, but, alas, I have already yielded up my heart to one who, if I mistake not, is a dear personal friend of your own.

CHEVIOT (*c*) Am I to understand that you are the young lady of property whom Belvawney hopes to marry?   535

MISS TREHERNE I am, indeed, that unhappy woman!

CHEVIOT And is it possible that you love him?

MISS TREHERNE With a rapture that thrills every fibre of my heart, with a devotion that enthralls my very soul! But there's some difficulty about his settlements.   540

CHEVIOT A difficulty! I should think there was. Why, on my marrying, his entire income goes over to Symperson! I could reduce him to penury tomorrow. As it happens, I *am* engaged, I recollect, to Symperson's daughter; and if Belvawney dares to interpose between you and me, by George, I'll do it! (*Crosses to* L)   545

MISS TREHERNE Oh, spare him, sir! (*Falls on knees*) You say that you love me? Then, for my sake, remain single forever. It is all I ask; it is not much. Promise me that you will never, never marry, and we will both bless you with our latest breath! (*Rises*)

CHEVIOT There seems to be a special importance attached to a bless-   550 ing conferred with one's latest breath that I entirely fail to grasp. It seems to me to convey no definite advantage of any kind whatever.

MISS TREHERNE Cruel, cruel man! (*Weeping. Crosses to* R)

    Enter Belvawney, in great alarm, over bridge L, *down to* C

BELVAWNEY We are lost! We are lost!

MISS TREHERNE What do you mean?   555

CHEVIOT Who has lost you?

BELVAWNEY Major McGillicuddy discovered your flight and followed in the next train. The line is blocked through our accident and his train has pulled up within a few yards of our own. He is now making his way to this very cottage! What do you say to   560 that?

MISS TREHERNE (*R*) I agree with you, we are lost!

CHEVIOT (*c*) I disagree with you; I should say you are found.

BELVAWNEY (*RC*) This man is a reckless fire-eater;° he is jealous of me. He will assuredly shoot us both if he sees us here together. I am   565 no coward, but I confess I am uneasy. (*Turns up*)

MISS TREHERNE Oh, sir, (*crosses to* C, *brings Cheviot forward*) you have a ready wit. Help us out of this difficulty and we will both bless you—

BELVAWNEY (*L*) With our latest breath!   570

CHEVIOT That decides me. Madam, remain here with me. Belvawney, withdraw. (*Belvawney retires* R) I will deal with this maniac alone. All I ask is, that if I find it necessary to make a statement that is not

consistent with strict truth, you, madam, will unhesitatingly
endorse it?   575

MISS TREHERNE I will stake my very existence on its veracity,
whatever it may be.

CHEVIOT Good. He is at hand. Belvawney, go.

    Belvawney retires to back, R, and exit [RC at back]

Now, madam, repose upon my shoulders, place your arms around
me so. Is that comfortable?   580

MISS TREHERNE It is luxurious.

CHEVIOT Good.

MISS TREHERNE You are sure it does not inconvenience you?

CHEVIOT Not at all. Go back, I like it. Now we are ready for him.

    Enter, LE, over bridge down to RC, Major McGillicuddy, with
    two Friends dressed as for a wedding, with white favours,° who
    remain on the bridge. McGillicuddy has pistols. All greatly
    excited

MCGILLICUDDY Where is the villain? I'll swear he is concealed   585
somewhere. Search every tree, every bush, every geranium. (*Sees*
Cheviot and Miss Treherne) Ha! They are here. Perjured woman!
I've found you at last.

MISS TREHERNE (*to Cheviot*) Save me!

    Belvawney appears at back, listening

MCGILLICUDDY Who is the unsightly scoundrel with whom you have   590
flown; the unpleasant-looking scamp whom you have dared to prefer to me? Uncurl yourself from around the plain villain at once,
unless you would share his fate.

    Maggie and Angus Macalister appear from cottage, R

MISS TREHERNE Major, spare him! (*Crosses to RC*)

CHEVIOT (*C*) Now, sir, perhaps you will be so good as to explain who   595
the deuce you are and what you want with this lady?

MCGILLICUDDY I don't know who you may be, but I'm McGillicuddy. I am betrothed to this lady. We were to have been married
this morning. I waited for her at the Church from ten till four, then
I began to get impatient.   600

CHEVIOT I really think you must be labouring under some delusion.

MCGILLICUDDY Delusion! Ha! ha!

    Two friends produce large wedding cake

Here's the cake!

CHEVIOT Still I think there's a mistake somewhere. This lady is my
wife.   605

MCGILLICUDDY What! Belinda! Oh, Belinda! Tell me that this

unattractive man lies; tell me that you are mine and only mine, now and forever!

MISS TREHERNE I cannot say that. This gentleman is my husband!

>*McGillicuddy falls sobbing on seat; Belvawney tears his hair in despair; Maggie sobs on Angus's shoulder, R*

Act Drop Quick

2.

Double drawing-room in Mr Symperson's House, door RC at back, open. Another door, LI E. Chair and stool RC. Piano R. Sofa LC. Indications that a wedding is about to take place. A plate of tarts and a bottle of wine on table, R against flat°

Enter Minnie Symperson, in wedding dress, followed by Parker, her maid, holding her train, RC

MINNIE (*c*) Take care, Parker. That's right. There! How do I look?

PARKER Beautiful, miss, quite beautiful.

MINNIE (*earnestly*) Oh, Parker, am I really beautiful? Really, *really* beautiful, you know?

PARKER Oh, miss, there's no question about it. Oh, I do so hope you and Mr Cheviot Hill will be happy. 5

MINNIE Oh, I'm sure we shall, Parker. He has often told me that I am the tree upon which the fruit of his heart is growing; and one couldn't wish to be more than *that*. And he tells me that his greatest happiness is to see me happy. So it will be my duty—my *duty*, Parker—to devote my life, my whole life, to making myself as happy as I possibly can. 10

Enter Mr Symperson, dressed for wedding, door in flat, R

SYMPERSON So, my little lamb is ready for the sacrifice. You can go, Parker.

Exit Parker, R

And I am to lose my pet at last; my little dickey-bird is to be married today! Well, well, it's for her good. I must try and bear it, I must try and bear it. 15

MINNIE And as my dear old Papa comes into £1000 a year by it, I hope he won't allow it to distress him too much. He must try and bear up. He mustn't fret. 20

SYMPERSON My child, I will not deny that £1000 a year is a consolation. (*Sits R*) It's quite a fortune. I hardly know what I shall do with it.

MINNIE I think, dear Papa, you will spend a good deal of it on brandy, and a good deal more on billiards, and a good deal more on betting.

SYMPERSON It may be so; I don't say it won't. We shall see, Minnie, we shall see. These simple pleasures would certainly tend to soothe your poor old father's declining years. And my darling has not done badly either, has she? 25

MINNIE No, dear Papa, only fancy! Cheviot has £2000 a year, from
shares in the Royal Indestructible Bank.   30

SYMPERSON (R) And don't spend £200. By the by I'm sorry that my
little bird has not contrived to induce him to settle anything on her.
That, I think, was remiss in my tom-tit.

MINNIE (RC, kneels) Dear Papa, Cheviot is the very soul of honour;
he's a fine, noble, manly, spirited fellow, but if he *has* a fault, it is   35
that he is very, oh very, *very* stingy. He would rather lose his heart's
blood than part with a shilling unnecessarily. He's a noble fellow,
but he's like that.

SYMPERSON Still I can't help feeling that if my robin had worked him
judiciously—   40

MINNIE Papa, dear, Cheviot is an all but perfect character, the very
type of knightly chivalry; but he *has* faults, and among other things
he's one of the worst tempered men I ever met in all my little life.
Poor, simple, little Minnie thought the matter over very carefully in
her silly childish way and she came to the conclusion, in her foolish   45
little noddle, that, on the whole, perhaps she could work it better
after marriage than before.

SYMPERSON Well, well, perhaps my wren is right. (*Rises*)

MINNIE (L) Don't laugh at my silly little thoughts, dear Papa, when I
say I'm sure she is.   50

SYMPERSON Minnie, my dear daughter, take a father's advice, the last
he will ever be entitled to give you. If you would be truly happy in
the married state, be sure you have your own way in everything.
Brook no contradictions. Never yield to outside pressure. Give in to
no argument. Admit no appeal. However wrong you may be, main-   55
tain a firm, resolute and determined front. These were your angel
mother's principles through life and she was a happy woman
indeed. I neglected those principles and, while she lived, I was a
miserable wretch.

MINNIE Papa, dear, I have thought over the matter very carefully in   60
my little baby-noddle, and I have come to the conclusion—don't
laugh at me, dear Papa—that it is my duty—my *duty*—to fall in
with Cheviot's views in everything *before* marriage, and Cheviot's
duty to fall into my views in everything *after* marriage. I think that
is only fair, don't you?   65

SYMPERSON Yes, I dare say it will come to that.

MINNIE Don't think me a very silly little goose when I say I'm sure it
will. Quite, quite sure, dear Papa. Quite.

   Exit Minnie, L

SYMPERSON (L) Dear child, dear child! I sometimes fancy I can see traces of her angel mother's disposition in her. Yes, I think, I *think* she will be happy. But, poor Cheviot! Oh lor, poor Cheviot! Dear me, it won't bear thinking of! 70

> *Enter Miss Treherne, R I E, unobserved. She is dressed in*
> *stately and funereal black*

MISS TREHERNE (RC) Come here, manservant. Approach. I'm not going to bite you. Can I see the fair young thing they call Minnie Symperson? 75

SYMPERSON Well really, I can hardly say. There's nothing wrong I hope?

MISS TREHERNE Nothing wrong? Oh thoughtless, frivolous, light-hearted creature! Oh reckless old butterfly! Nothing wrong? You've eyes in your head, a nose on your face, ears on each side of it, a brain of some sort in your skull, haven't you, butler? 80

SYMPERSON Undoubtedly, but I beg to observe I'm not the—

MISS TREHERNE Have you or have you not the gift of simple apprehension? Can you or can you not draw conclusions? (*Crosses to R*) Go to, go to, you offend me. 85

SYMPERSON (*aside, C*) There *is* something wrong, and it's *here.* (*Touching his forehead*) I'll tell her you're here. Whom shall I say?

MISS TREHERNE Say that one on whose devoted° head the black sorrows of a long lifetime have fallen, even as a funeral pall, craves a minute's interview with a dear old friend. Do you think you can recollect that message, butler? 90

SYMPERSON I'll try, but I beg, I *beg* to observe, I'm not the butler. (*Aside*) This is a most surprising young person!

> *Exit Mr Symperson, L I E*

MISS TREHERNE At last I'm in my darling's home, the home of the bright blithe carolling thing that lit, as with a ray of heaven's sunlight, the murky gloom of my miserable school-days. But what do I see? Tarts? Ginger wine? There are rejoicings of some kind afoot. Alas, I am out of place here. What have I in common with tarts?° Oh, I am ill-attuned to scenes of revelry! 95 100

> *Miss Traherne takes a tart and eats it. Enter Minnie*

MINNIE (LC) Belinda!

> *Minnie and Miss Treherne rush to each other's arms*

MISS TREHERNE (R) Minnie! My own long-lost lamb! This is the first gleam of joy that has lighted my darksome° course this many and many a day! And in spite of the change that time and misery have

brought upon me, you knew me at once! (*Eating the tart all this* 105
time)

MINNIE Oh, I felt sure it was you, from the message.

MISS TREHERNE How wondrously fair you have grown! And this
dress! Why, it is surely a bridal dress! Those tarts, that wine! Surely
this is not your wedding-day? 110

MINNIE Yes, dear, I shall be married in half an hour.

MISS TREHERNE Oh, strange chance! Oh, unheard-of coincidence!
Married! And to whom?

MINNIE Oh, to the dearest love, my cousin, Mr Cheviot Hill. Perhaps
you know the name? 115

MISS TREHERNE I have heard of the Cheviot Hills, somewhere.
Happy, strangely happy girl! You, at least, know your husband's
name. (*Sits on sofa L*)

MINNIE (*sits on sofa L*) Oh yes, it's on all his pocket-handkerchiefs.

MISS TREHERNE It is much to know. I do not know mine. 120

MINNIE Have you forgotten it?

MISS TREHERNE No, I never knew it. It is a dark mystery. It may not
be fathomed. It is buried in the fathomless gulf of the eternal past.
There let it lie.

MINNIE Oh, tell me all about it, dear. 125

MISS TREHERNE It is a lurid tale. Three months since I fled from a
hated one who was to have married me. He pursued me. I confided
my distress to a young and wealthy stranger. Acting on his advice, I
declared myself to be his wife; he declared himself to be my husband. We were parted immediately afterwards and we have never 130
met since. But this took place in Scotland; and by the law of that
remarkable country we are man and wife, though I didn't know it at
the time.

MINNIE (*rises*) What fun!

MISS TREHERNE (*c*) Fun! Say, rather, horror, distraction, chaos! I am 135
rent with conflicting doubts! Perhaps he was already married; in
that case, I am a bigamist. Maybe he is dead; in that case, I am a
widow. Maybe he is alive; in that case, I am a wife. What am I? Am I
single? Am I married? Am I a widow? Can I marry? Have I married? May I marry? Who am I? Where am I? What am I? What is 140
my name? What is my condition in life? If I am married, to whom
am I married? If I am a widow, how came I to be a widow, and
whose widow came I to be? Why am I his widow? What did he die
of? Did he leave me anything? If anything, how much, and is it
saddled with conditions? Can I marry again without forfeiting it? 145

Have I a mother-in-law? Have I a family of step-children, and if so, how many, and what are their ages, sexes, sizes, names and dispositions? These are questions that rack me night and day, and until they are settled, peace and I are not on terms! (*Crosses to* R)

MINNIE Poor dear thing!   150

MISS TREHERNE (C) But enough of my selfish sorrows. (*Goes up to table* C, *and takes a tart. Minnie is annoyed at this*) Tell me about the noble boy who is about to make you his. Has he any dross?°

MINNIE (L) I don't know. (*Secretly removes tarts to another table* L, *close to door*) I never thought of asking. I'm such a goose. But Papa knows.   155

MISS TREHERNE Have those base and servile things called settlements been satisfactorily adjusted? (*Eating*)

MINNIE I don't know. It never occurred to me to inquire. But Papa can tell you.

MISS TREHERNE The same artless little soul!   160

MINNIE (*standing so as to conceal tarts from Belinda*) Yes, I am quite artless; quite, quite artless. But now that you *are* here you will stay and see me married.

MISS TREHERNE I would willingly be a witness to my darling's joy, but this attire is, perhaps, scarcely in harmony with a scene of   165
revelry.

MINNIE Well, dear, you're not a cheerful object and that's the truth.

MISS TREHERNE And yet these charnel-house rags may serve to remind the thoughtless banqueters that they are but mortal.

MINNIE I don't think it will be necessary to do that, dear. Papa's   170
sherry will make *that* quite clear to them.

MISS TREHERNE Then I will hie me home, and array me in garments of less sombre hue.

MINNIE I think it would be better, dear. Those are the very things for a funeral, but this is a wedding.   175

MISS TREHERNE I see very little difference between them. But it shall be as you wish, (*crosses to* L) though I have worn nothing but black since my miserable marriage. Farewell, dearest Minnie. There is breakfast, I suppose?

MINNIE Yes, at dear Cheviot's house.   180

MISS TREHERNE That is well. I shall return in time for it. Thank heaven I can still eat!

> *Miss Treherne takes a tart from table, at door* L, *and exit* [L IE], *followed by Minnie, who expresses annoyance at Belinda's greediness. Enter Cheviot Hill,* RC *at back. He is dressed as for a wedding*

CHEVIOT Here I am at last, quite flurried and hot after the usual row
with the cabman, just when I wanted to be particularly calm and
self-contained. I got the best of it though. Dear me, this is a great   185
day for me, a great day. Where's Minnie, I wonder? Arraying herself for the sacrifice, no doubt. Pouf! (*Sits R*) This is a very nervous
occasion. I wonder if I'm taking a prudent step. Marriage is a very
risky thing. It's like chancery; once in it, you can't get out of it and
the costs are enormous.° There you are, fixed. Fifty years hence, if   190
we're both alive, there we shall both be, fixed. That's the devil of it.
It's an unreasonably long time to be responsible for another person's expenses. I don't see the use of making it for as long as that. It
seems greedy to take up half a century of another person's attention. Besides, one never knows, one might come across somebody   195
else one liked better; that uncommonly nice girl I met in Scotland,
for instance. No, no, I shall be true to my Minnie (*rises and crosses to
L*), quite true. I am quite determined that nothing shall shake my
constancy to Minnie.
   Enter Parker, RC at back
What a devilish pretty girl!   200
PARKER (*aside*) He's a mean young man, but he ought to be good for
half-a-crown today.
CHEVIOT Come here, my dear. A—how do I look?
PARKER (*R*) Very nice indeed, sir.
CHEVIOT (*C*) What, really?   205
PARKER Really.
CHEVIOT What, tempting, eh?
PARKER Very tempting indeed.
CHEVIOT Hah! The married state is an enviable state, Parker.
PARKER *Is* it, sir? I hope it may be. It depends.   210
CHEVIOT What do you mean by 'it depends'? You're a member of
the Church of England, I trust? Then don't you know that in
saying 'it depends' you are flying in the face of the marriage
service? Don't go and throw cold water on the married state,
Parker. I know what you're going to say; it's expensive. So it is, at   215
first, very expensive, but with economy you soon retrench that. By
a beautiful provision of nature, what's enough for one is enough
for two. This phenomenon points directly to the married state as
our natural state.
PARKER (*R*) Oh, for that matter, sir, a tigress would get on with you.   220
You're so liberal, so gentle, so—there's only one word for it—dove-
like.

CHEVIOT (*c*) What, you've remarked that, eh? Ha! ha! But, dove-like
as I am, Parker, in some respects, yet (*getting his arm round her*) in
other respects—(*aside*) deuced pretty girl!—(*aloud*) in other   225
respects I am a man, Parker, of a strangely impetuous and head-
strong nature. I don't beat about the bush. I come quickly to the
point. Shall I tell you a secret? There's something about you, I
don't know what it is, that—in other words, you are the tree upon
which—[*Aside*] No, no, damn it, Cheviot. Not today, not today.   230

PARKER What a way you have with you, sir!

CHEVIOT What, you've noticed that, have you? Ha! ha! Yes, I have a
way, no doubt. It's been remarked before. Whenever I see a pretty
girl—and you are a very pretty girl—I can't help putting my arm
like that. (*Putting it round her waist*) Now, pleasant as this sort of   235
thing is, and you find it pleasant, don't you? (*Parker nods*) Yes, you
find it pleasant. Pleasant as it is, it is decidedly wrong.

PARKER It is decidedly wrong in a married man.

CHEVIOT It is decidedly wrong in a married man. In a married man
it's abominable, and I shall be a married man in half-an-hour.   240
So, Parker, it will become necessary to conquer this tendency, to
struggle with it, and subdue it, in half-an-hour. (*Getting more affectionate*) Not that there's any real harm in putting your arm round
a girl's waist. Highly respectable people do it when they waltz.

PARKER Yes, sir, but then a band's playing.   245

CHEVIOT True, and when a band's playing it don't matter, but when a
band is *not* playing, why it's dangerous, you see. You begin with this
and you go on from one thing to another, getting more and more
affectionate, until you reach *this* stage. (*Kissing her*) Not that there's
any real harm in kissing, either; for you see fathers and mothers,   250
who ought to set a good example, kissing their children every day.

PARKER Lor, sir, kissing's nothing. Everybody does that.

CHEVIOT That is your experience, is it? It tallies with my own. Take it
that I am your father, you are my daughter—or take it even that I
am merely your husband and you my wife, and it would be   255
expected of me. (*Kissing her*)

PARKER But I'm not your wife, sir.

CHEVIOT No, not yet, that's very true, and, of course, makes a difference. That's why I say I must subdue this tendency; I must struggle
with it; I must conquer it, in half-an-hour.   260

MINNIE (*offstage*) Parker, where's Mr Cheviot?

CHEVIOT There is your mistress, my dear. She's coming. Will you
excuse me? (*Releasing her*) Thank you. Good day, Parker.

PARKER (*disgusted*) Not so much as a shilling and that man's worth thousands! 265

> *Exit Parker. Enter Minnie,* LIE

CHEVIOT My darling Minnie, my own, own To Come! (*Kissing her*)

MINNIE Oh, you mustn't crush me, Cheviot, you'll spoil my dress. How do you like it?

CHEVIOT It's lovely. It's a beautiful material.

MINNIE (L) Yes; dear Papa's been going it.° 270

CHEVIOT Oh, but you're indebted to me for that beautiful dress.

MINNIE To you! Oh, thank you, thank you!

CHEVIOT Yes. I said to your Papa: 'Now do for once let the girl have a nice dress; be liberal; buy the very best that money will procure, you'll never miss it.' So, thanks to me, he bought you a beauty. 275 Seventeen and six a yard if it's a penny. Dear me! To think that in half-an-hour this magnificent dress will be *my* property!

MINNIE Yes. Dear Papa said that as you had offered to give the break-fast at your house, he would give me the best dress that money could procure. 280

CHEVIOT Yes, I *did* offer to provide the breakfast in a reckless moment; that's so like me. It was a rash offer, but I've made it, and I've stuck to it.° Oh, then there's the cake.

MINNIE Oh, tell me all about the cake. (*Cheviot and Minnie sit on sofa L*) 285

CHEVIOT It's a very pretty cake. Very little cake is eaten at a wedding breakfast, so I've ordered what's known in the trade as the three-quarter article.

MINNIE I see; three-quarters cake and the rest wood.

CHEVIOT No; three-quarters wood, the rest cake. Be sure, my dear, 290 you don't cut into the wood, for it has to be returned to the pastry-cook to be filled up with cake for another occasion. I thought at first of ordering a seven-eighths article; but one isn't married every day, it's only once a year—I mean it's only now and then. So I said: 'Hang the expense; let's do the thing well.' And so it's a three- 295 quarters.

MINNIE How good you are to me! We shall be very happy, shall we not?

CHEVIOT I—I hope so, yes. I *hope* so. Playfully happy, like two little kittens. 300

MINNIE That will be delightful.

CHEVIOT Economically happy, like two sensible people.

MINNIE Oh, we must be very economical.

CHEVIOT No vulgar display. No pandering to a jaded appetite. A refined and economical elegance; that is what we must aim at. A simple mutton chop, nicely broiled, for you; and *two* simple mutton chops, *very* nicely broiled, for me.   305

MINNIE And some floury° potatoes—

CHEVIOT A loaf of nice household bread—

MINNIE A stick of celery—   310

CHEVIOT And a bit of cheese, and you've a dinner fit for a monarch.

MINNIE Then how shall we spend our evenings?

CHEVIOT We'll have pleasant little fireside games. Are you fond of fireside games?

MINNIE Oh, they're great fun.   315

CHEVIOT Then we'll play at tailoring.

MINNIE Tailoring? I don't think I know that game.

CHEVIOT It's a very good game. You shall be the clever little jobbing tailor, and I'll be the particular° customer who brings his own materials to be made up. You shall take my measure, cut out the cloth (real cloth, you know), stitch it together and try it on; and then I'll find fault like a real customer, and you shall alter it until it fits, and when it fits beautifully that counts one to you.   320

MINNIE Delightful!

CHEVIOT Then there's another little fireside game which is great fun. We each take a bit of paper and a pencil and try who can jot down the nicest dinner for ninepence, and the next day we have it.   325

MINNIE Oh, Cheviot, what a paradise you hold open to me! (*Rises*)

CHEVIOT Yes. How's Papa?

MINNIE He's very well and very happy. He's going to increase his establishment on the strength of the £1000 a year and keep a man-servant.   330

CHEVIOT I know. I've been looking after° some servants for him; they'll be here in the course of the morning. A cook, a housemaid, and a footman. I found them through an advertisement. They're country people and will come very cheap.   335

MINNIE How kind and thoughtful you are! Oh, Cheviot, I'm a very lucky girl!

Exit Minnie, LIE

CHEVIOT Yes, I think so too, if I can only repress my tendency to think of that tall girl I met in Scotland! Cheviot, my boy, you must make an effort. You are going to be married and the tall girl is nothing to you!   340

Enter Parker

PARKER Please, sir, here's a gentleman to see you.

CHEVIOT Oh, my solicitor, no doubt. Show him up.

PARKER And please, some persons have called to see you about an 345
advertisement.

CHEVIOT Oh, Symperson's servants. To be sure. Show up the
gentleman, and tell the others to wait.

> *Exit Parker, RC at back. Enter Belvawney. He looks very*
> *miserable, RC at back*

CHEVIOT Belvawney! This is unexpected. (*Much confused*)

BELVAWNEY Yes, Cheviot. At last we meet. Don't, oh don't frown 350
upon a heartbroken wretch.

CHEVIOT (*C*) Belvawney, I don't want to hurt your feelings, but I will
not disguise from you that, not having seen you for three months, I
was in hopes that I had got rid of you forever.

BELVAWNEY Oh, Cheviot, don't say that. I am so unhappy. And you 355
have it in your power to make me comfortable. Do this, and I will
bless you with my latest breath!

CHEVIOT It is a tempting offer. I am not proof against it. We all have
our price, and that is mine. Proceed.

BELVAWNEY Miss Treherne, Belinda, whom I love so dearly, won't 360
have anything to say to me.

CHEVIOT It does her credit. She's a very superior girl.

BELVAWNEY It's all through you, Cheviot. She declares that the
mutual declaration you made to protect her from McGillicuddy
amounts to a Scotch marriage. 365

CHEVIOT What!!!

BELVAWNEY She declares she is your wife. She professes to love me as
fondly as ever; but a stern sense of duty to you forbids her to hold
any communication with me.

CHEVIOT Oh, but this is absurd, you know! 370

BELVAWNEY Of course it is; but what's to be done? You left with
Symperson immediately after making the declaration. As soon as
she found you were gone she implored me to tell her your name and
address. Of course I refused, and she quitted me telling me that she
would devote her life to finding you out. 375

CHEVIOT (*aside, L*) But this is simple madness. I can't have it! This
day, too, of all others! If she'd claimed me last week, or even yesterday, I wouldn't have minded, for she's a devilish fine woman; but if
she were to turn up now! (*Aloud*) Belvawney, my dear friend, tell
me what to do. I'll do anything. 380

BELVAWNEY (*C*) It seems that there's some doubt whether this cottage, which is just on the border, is in England or Scotland. If it is in England, she has no case; if it is in Scotland, I'm afraid she has. I've written to the owner of the property to ascertain, and if, in the meantime, she claims you, you must absolutely decline to recognise this marriage for a moment. 385

CHEVIOT Not for one moment!

BELVAWNEY It was a mere artifice to enable her to escape from McGillicuddy.

CHEVIOT Nothing more! 390

BELVAWNEY It's monstrous, perfectly monstrous, that that should constitute a marriage. It's disgraceful, it's abominable. Damme, Cheviot, it's immoral.

CHEVIOT So it is; it's immoral. That settles it in *my* mind. It's immoral. 395

BELVAWNEY You're quite sure you'll be resolute, Cheviot?

CHEVIOT Resolute? I should think so! Why, hang it all, man, I'm going to be married in twenty minutes to Minnie Symperson!

BELVAWNEY What!

CHEVIOT (*confused at having let this out*) Didn't I tell you? I believe 400 you're right; I did *not* tell you. It escaped me. Oh yes, this is my wedding-day.

BELVAWNEY (*R*) Cheviot, you're joking, you don't mean this! Why, I shall lose £1000 a year by it, every penny I have in the world! Oh, it can't be. It's nonsense! 405

CHEVIOT What do you mean by nonsense? The married state is an honourable estate, I believe? A man is not looked upon as utterly lost to all sense of decency because he's got married, I'm given to understand? People have been married before this, and have not been irretrievably tabooed in consequence, unless I'm grossly 410 misinformed? Then what the dickens do you mean by saying 'nonsense' when I tell you that I'm going to be married?

BELVAWNEY Cheviot, be careful how you take this step. Beware how you involve an innocent and helpless girl in social destruction.

CHEVIOT What do you mean, sir? 415

BELVAWNEY You cannot marry. You are a married man.

CHEVIOT Come, come, Belvawney, this is trifling.

BELVAWNEY You are married to Miss Treherne. I was present and can depose to the fact.

CHEVIOT Oh, you're not serious. 420

BELVAWNEY Never more serious in my life.

CHEVIOT But, as you very properly said just now, it was a mere arti-

fice. We didn't mean anything. It would be monstrous to regard
that as a marriage. Damme, Belvawney, it would be immoral!

BELVAWNEY I may deplore the state of the law, but I cannot stand   425
tamely by and see it deliberately violated before my eyes.

CHEVIOT (*wildly*) But, Belvawney, my dear friend, reflect; everything
is prepared for my marriage, at a great expense. I love Minnie
deeply, devotedly. She is the actual tree upon which the fruit of my
heart is growing. There's no mistake about it. She is my own To   430
Come. I love her madly, rapturously. (*Going on his knees to Belvawney*) I have prepared a wedding breakfast at a great expense to
do her honour. I have ordered four flys° for the wedding party. I
have taken two second-class Cook's tourists' tickets° for Ilfracombe,° Devon, Exeter, Cornwall, Westward Ho!° and Bideford   435
Bay.° The whole thing has cost me some twenty or twenty-five
pounds, and all this will be wasted, utterly wasted, if you interfere.
Oh, Belvawney, dear Belvawney, let the recollection of our long and
dear friendship operate to prevent your shipwrecking my future
life. (*Sobbing hysterically*)   440

BELVAWNEY I have a duty to do. I must do it. (*Going R*)

CHEVIOT But reflect, dear Belvawney; if I am married to Miss
Treherne, you lose your income as much as if I married Minnie
Symperson. (*Falls on sofa, L*)

BELVAWNEY (*at sofa*) No doubt, if you could prove your marriage to   445
Miss Treherne. But you can't—(*With melodramatic intensity*)

CHEVIOT Those eyes!

BELVAWNEY You don't know where she is—(*With fiendish exultation*)

CHEVIOT Oh, those eyes!

BELVAWNEY The cottage has been pulled down and the cottagers   450
have emigrated to Patagonia°—

CHEVIOT Oh, those eyes!

BELVAWNEY I'm the only witness left. *I* can prove your marriage,
if I like; but you can't. Ha! ha! ha! ha! (*With Satanic laugh*) It's
a most painful and unfortunate situation for you; and, believe   455
me, dear Cheviot, you have my deepest and most respectful
sympathy.

    Exit Belvawney, RC at back

CHEVIOT This is appalling; simply appalling! The cup of happiness
dashed from my lips just as I was about to drink a life-long draught.
The ladder kicked from under my feet just as I was about to pick   460
the fruit of my heart from the tree upon which it has been growing
so long. I'm a married man! More than that, my honeymoon's past

and I never knew it! Stop a moment, though. The bride can't be found; the cottage is pulled down, and the cottagers have emigrated. What proof is there that such a marriage ever took place? There's only Belvawney, and Belvawney isn't a proof. Corroborated by the three cottagers, his word might be worth something; uncorroborated, it is worthless. I'll risk it. He can do nothing; the bride is nowhere; the cottagers are in Patagonia, and— 465

> *At this moment Mrs Macfarlane, Maggie, and Angus Macalister appear RC at back. They stand bobbing and curtseying in rustic fashion to Cheviot, whom they do not recognise. He stares aghast at them for a moment, then staggers back to sofa*

CHEVIOT The man, the woman, and the girl, by all that's infernal! 470

MRS MACFARLANE (*R*) Gude day, sir. We've just ca'd to see ye about the advertisement. (*Producing paper*)

CHEVIOT I don't know you, I don't know you. Go away.

> *Cheviot buries his head in a newspaper, and pretends to read, on sofa*

MAGGIE (*L*) Ah, sir, ye said that we were to ca' on ye this day at eleven o'clock, and sae we've coom a' the way fra Dumfries to see ye. 475

CHEVIOT I tell you I don't know you. Go away. I'm not at all well. I'm very ill and it's infectious.

ANGUS (*C, wiping his eye*) We fear no illness, sir. This is Mistress Macfarlane, the gude auld mither, who'll cook the brose and boil the parritch, and sit wi' ye and nurse ye through your illness till the sad day ye dee! 480

> *Cheviot pokes a hole with his finger through newspaper, and reconnoitres unobserved*

MRS MACFARLANE And this is Meg, my ain lass, Meg!

CHEVIOT (*aside*) Attractive girl, very. I remember her perfectly.

MRS MACFARLANE And this is Angus Macalister, who's going to marry her and who'll be mair than a son to me! 485

ANGUS Oh, mither, mither, dinna say it, for ye bring the teardrop to my ee, an' it's no canny for a strong man to be blithering and soughing like a poor weak lassie! (*Wiping his eye*)

> *Angus and Mrs Macfarlane sit. Maggie advances to hole in newspaper and peeps through*

MAGGIE Oh, mither, mither! (*Staggers back into Angus's arms, R*)

MRS MACFARLANE What is it, Meg? 490

ANGUS (*R*) Meg, my weel lo'ed Meg, my wee wifie that is to be, tell me what's wrang wi' 'ee.

MAGGIE Oh, mither, it's him; the noble gentleman I plighted my troth

to° three weary months agone! The gallant Englishman who gave   495
Angus twa golden pound to give me up!

ANGUS It's the coward Sassenach who well nigh broke our Meg's
heart!

MRS MACFARLANE (*RC*) My lass, my lass, dinna greet, maybe he'll
marry ye yet.

CHEVIOT (*desperately*) Here's another! Does anybody else want to   500
marry me? Don't be shy. You, ma'am, (*to Mrs Macfarlane, crosses to
C*) you're a fine woman; perhaps *you* would like to try your luck?

MAGGIE (*C*) Ah, sir! I dinna ken your name, but your bonnie face has
lived in my twa een, sleeping and waking, three weary, weary
months! Oh, sir, ye should na' ha' deceived a trusting, simple Low-   505
land lassie. 'Twas na' weel done, 'twas na' weel done! (*Weeping on
his shoulder; he puts his arm round her waist, C*)

CHEVIOT (*softening, LC*) My good girl, what do you wish me to do? I
remember you now perfectly. I *did* admire you very much; in fact, I
do still. You're a very charming girl. Let us talk this over, calmly   510
and quietly. (*Maggie moves away*) No, you needn't go. You can stop
there if you like. There, there, my dear! Don't fret. (*Aside*) She *is* a
very charming girl, I almost wish I—I really begin to think I—No,
no, damn it, Cheviot, not today!

MAGGIE Oh, mither, he told me he loved me!   515

CHEVIOT So I did. The fact is, when I fell in love with you—don't go
my pretty bird—I quite forgot that I was engaged. There, there! I
thought at the time that you were the tree upon which the fruit of
my heart was growing; but I was mistaken. Don't go; you needn't
go on that account. It was another tree—   520

MAGGIE (*L*) Oh, mither, it was anither tree! (*Weeping on Cheviot's
shoulder*)

MRS MACFARLANE (*R*) Angus, it was anither tree! (*Weeping on Angus's
shoulder*)

ANGUS Dinna, mither, dinna; I canna bear it! (*Weeps*)   525

CHEVIOT Yes, it was another tree—you can remain there for the
present—in point of fact, it was growing on both trees. I don't
know how it is, but it seems to grow on a great many trees—a
perfect orchard—and you are one of them, my dear. Come, come,
don't fret, you are one of them!   530

    Enter Minnie and Mr Symperson

MINNIE Cheviot!

SYMPERSON What is all this?

CHEVIOT (*rapidly referring to piece of paper given to him by Mrs*

Macfarlane, as if going over a washerwoman's bill) 'Twenty-four pairs socks, two shirts, thirty-seven collars, one sheet, forty-   535
four nightshirts, twenty-two flannel waistcoats, one white tie.' Ridiculous, quite ridiculous. I won't pay it.

MINNIE Cheviot, who is this person who was found hanging on your neck? Say she is somebody; for instance, your sister or your aunt. Oh, Cheviot, say she is your aunt, I implore you!   540

The three cottagers curtsey and bow to Minnie

SYMPERSON Cheviot, say she is your aunt, I command you!

CHEVIOT (*C*) Oh, I beg your pardon. I didn't see you. These ladies are—are my washerwomen. Allow me to introduce them. They have come—they have come for their small account.

Maggie, who has been sobbing through this, throws herself hysterically on to Cheviot's bosom, C

There's a discrepancy in the items—twenty-two flannel waistcoats   545
are ridiculous, and, in short, some washerwomen are like this when they're contradicted—they can't help it—it's something in the suds: it undermines their constitution.

SYMPERSON (*sternly*) Cheviot, I should like to believe you, but it seems scarcely credible.   550

MAGGIE (*crosses to LC*) Oh, sir, he's no telling ye truly. I'm the puir Lowland lassie that he stole the hairt out of, three months ago, and promised to marry; and I love him sae weel—sae weel, and now he's married to anither.

CHEVIOT Nothing of the kind. I—   555

SYMPERSON You are mistaken and so is your mith-mother. He is not yet married to anith-nother.

MAGGIE Why, sir, it took place before my very ain eyes, before us a', to a beautiful lady, three months since. (*Retires, C*)

MINNIE Cheviot, say that this is not true. Say that the beautiful lady   560
was somebody; for instance, your aunt. Oh, say she was your aunt, I implore you!

SYMPERSON (*sternly*) Cheviot, say she was your aunt, I command you!

CHEVIOT Minnie, Symperson, don't believe them. It was no mar-riage. I don't even know the lady's name. I never saw her before;   565
I've never seen her since. It's ridiculous. I couldn't have married her without knowing it. It's out of the question!

SYMPERSON Cheviot, let's know exactly where we are. I don't much care whom you marry, so that you marry someone. That's enough for me. But please be explicit, for this is business and mustn't be   570
trifled with. Tell me all about it. (*Sits in chair, R*)

CHEVIOT (*in despair*) I cannot!

    Enter Belvawney, RIE

BELVAWNEY I can.

SYMPERSON Belvawney!

BELVAWNEY I was present when Cheviot and a certain lady declared   575
themselves to be man and wife. This took place in a cottage on the
Border, in the presence of these worthy people.

SYMPERSON (*L*) That's enough for me. It's a Scotch marriage!
Minnie, my child, we must find you someone else.

    Minnie crosses to L

Cheviot's married. Belvawney, I am sorry to say, I deprive you of your   580
income.

BELVAWNEY I beg your pardon, not yet.

SYMPERSON Why not?

BELVAWNEY In the first place, it's not certain whether the cottage was
in England or in Scotland; in the second place, the bride can't be   585
found.

SYMPERSON But she *shall* be found. What is her name?

BELVAWNEY That I decline to state.

SYMPERSON But you shall be made to state. I insist upon knowing the
young lady's name.   590

    Enter Miss Treherne, in a light and cheerful dress, RIE.

BELVAWNEY (*amazed*) Belinda Treherne!

MISS TREHERNE (*rushing to Minnie, LC*) Minnie, my own old friend!

CHEVIOT (*RC*) 'Tis she!

MISS TREHERNE (*turns and recognises Cheviot*) My husband!

CHEVIOT My wife!   595

    Miss Treherne throws herself at Cheviot's feet, kissing his hands
    rapturously. Belvawney staggers back. Minnie faints in her
    father's arms, L. Maggie sobs on Angus's breast, R. Picture

[*Curtain*]

3.

*Same as 2. Belvawney discovered with Miss Treherne and
Minnie. He is singing to them. Miss Treherne is leaning
romantically on R of piano. Minnie is seated, picturesquely, on a
stool on his L*

BELVAWNEY (*sings*)
    Says the old Obadiah to the young Obadiah,
      I am drier, Obadiah, I am drier.
CHORUS   *I am drier.*
BELVAWNEY *Says the young Obadiah to the old Obadiah,*
    I'm on fire, Obadiah, I'm on fire. 5
CHORUS   *I'm on fire.*°
MINNIE Oh, thank you, Mr Belvawney. How sweetly pretty that is.
Where can I get it?

MISS TREHERNE (*R*) How marvellous is the power of melody over the
soul that is fretted and harassed by anxiety and doubt. I can under- 10
stand how valuable must have been the troubadours of old, in the
troublous times of anarchy. Your song has soothed me, sir.
BELVAWNEY (*C*) I am indeed glad to think that I have comforted you a
little, dear ladies. (*Rises*)
MINNIE (*rises*) Dear Mr Belvawney, I don't know what we should have 15
done without you. What with your sweet songs, your amusing riddles and your clever conjuring tricks, the weary days of waiting
have passed like a delightful dream.
MISS TREHERNE (*R*) It is impossible to be dull in the society of one
who can charm the soul with plaintive ballads one moment, and the 20
next roll a rabbit and a guinea-pig into one.
BELVAWNEY (*C*) You make me indeed happy, dear ladies. But my joy
will be of brief duration, for Cheviot may return at any moment
with the news that the fatal cottage was in Scotland, and then, oh,
Belinda, what is to become of me? 25
MISS TREHERNE How many issues depend on that momentous question? Has Belvawney a thousand a year or is he ruined? Has your
father that convenient addition to his income or has he not? May
Maggie marry Angus or will her claim on Cheviot be satisfied? Are
you to be his cherished bride or are you destined to a life of solitary 30
maidenhood? Am I Cheviot's honoured wife or am I but a broken-

hearted and desolate spinster? Who can tell! Who can tell! (*Crosses to Minnie*, L)

BELVAWNEY (*goes to window in second drawing-room,* C) Here is a cab with luggage. It is Cheviot! He has returned with the news! (*Comes down to* RC) Ladies, one word before I go. One of you will be claimed by Cheviot, that is very clear. To that one, whichever it may be, I do not address myself. But to the other, whichever it may be, I say, I love you, whichever you are, with a fervour which I cannot describe in words. If you, whichever you are, will consent to cast your lot with mine, I will devote my life to proving that I love you and you only, whichever it may be, with a single-hearted and devoted passion, which precludes the possibility of my ever entertaining the slightest regard for any other woman in the whole world. I thought I would just mention it. Good morning!

    Exit Belvawney, R

MISS TREHERNE How beautifully he expresses himself. He is indeed a rare and radiant being.

MINNIE (*nervously*) Oh, Belinda, the terrible moment is at hand.

MISS TREHERNE Minnie, if dear Cheviot should prove to be my husband, swear to me that that will not prevent your coming to stop with us, with dear Cheviot and me, whenever you can.

MINNIE Indeed I will. And if it should turn out that dear Cheviot is at liberty to marry me, promise me that that will not prevent you looking on our house, on dear Cheviot's and mine, as your home.

MISS TREHERNE I swear it. We will be like dear, dear sisters.

    Enter Cheviot Hill, as from journey, RIE, *with bag and rug*

MISS TREHERNE Cheviot, tell me at once, are you my own—husband?

MINNIE Cheviot, speak, is poor, little, simple Minnie to be your bride?

CHEVIOT (*sits on chair,* R) Minnie, the hope of my heart, my pet fruit tree! Belinda, my Past, my Present, and my To Come! I have sorry news, sorry news.

MISS TREHERNE (*aside*) Sorry news! Then I am *not* his wife.

MINNIE (*aside*) Sorry news! Then she *is* his wife.

CHEVIOT My dear girls, my very dear girls, my journey has been fruitless. I have no information!

MISS TREHERNE *and* MINNIE No information!

CHEVIOT None. The McQuibbigaskie has gone abroad! (*Sits on sofa*)

    Both ladies fall weeping into chairs

MISS TREHERNE More weary waiting; more weary waiting!

MINNIE Oh, my breaking heart; oh, my poor bruised and breaking   70
heart! (*Sits on stool, R*)

CHEVIOT We must be patient, dear Belinda. Minnie, my own, we
must be patient. After all, is the situation so very terrible? Each of
you has an even chance of becoming my wife, and in the meantime I
look upon myself as engaged to both of you. I shall make no distinc-   75
tion. I shall love you both, fondly, and you shall both love me. My
affection shall be divided equally between you and we will be as
happy as three little birds.

MISS TREHERNE (*L, wiping her eyes*) You are very kind and thoughtful, dear Cheviot.   80

MINNIE I believe, in my simple little way, that you are the very best
man in the whole world.

CHEVIOT (*deprecatingly*) No, no.

MINNIE Ah, but do let me think so. It makes me so happy to think so!

CHEVIOT Does it? Well, well, be it so. Perhaps I am! And now tell me,   85
how has the time passed since I left? Have my darlings been dull?

MISS TREHERNE We should have been dull indeed but for the airy
Belvawney. The sprightly creature has done his best to make the
lagging hours fly. He is an entertaining rattlesnake—I should say,
rattletrap.°   90

CHEVIOT (*jealous*) Oh, *is* he so? Belvawney has been making the hours
fly, has he? I'll make *him* fly, when I catch him!
   Miss Treherne sits on sofa, LC

MINNIE His conjuring tricks are wonderful.

CHEVIOT Confound his conjuring tricks!

MINNIE Have you seen him bring a live hen, two hair brushes, and a   95
pound and a half of fresh butter out of his pocket-handkerchief!

CHEVIOT No, I have not had that advantage!

MISS TREHERNE It is a thrilling sight.

CHEVIOT So I should be disposed to imagine. Pretty goings on in my
absence! You seem to forget that you two girls are engaged to be   100
married to *me*!

MISS TREHERNE (*rises*) Ah, Cheviot, do not judge us harshly. We love
you with a reckless fervour that thrills us to the very marrow, don't
we, darling? But the hours crept heavily without you and when, to
lighten the gloom in which we were plunged, the kindly creature   105
swallowed a live rabbit and brought it out, smothered in onions,
from his left boot, we could not choose but smile. The good soul
has promised to teach *me* the trick. (*Crosses to L*)

CHEVIOT Has he? That's his confounded impudence. Now, once for

all, I'll have nothing of this kind. One of you will be my wife and   110
until I know which, I will permit no Belvawneying of any kind
whatever, or anything approaching thereto. When that is settled,
the other may Belvawney until she is black in the face.

MISS TREHERNE And how long have we to wait before we shall know
which of us may begin Belvawneying?   115

CHEVIOT I can't say. It may be some time. The McQuibbigaskie has
gone to Central Africa. No post can reach him and he will not
return for six years.

MISS TREHERNE Six years! Oh, I cannot wait six years! Why, in six
years I shall be eight-and-twenty.   120

MINNIE Six years! Why, in six years the Statute of Limitations° will
come in and he can renounce us both.

MISS TREHERNE True, you are quite right. (*To Cheviot*) Cheviot, I
have loved you madly, desperately, as other woman never loved
other man. This poor inexperienced child, who clings to me as the   125
ivy clings to the oak, also loves you as woman never loved before.
Even that poor cottage maiden, whose rustic heart you so recklessly
enslaved, worships you with a devotion that has no parallel in the
annals of the heart. In return for all this unalloyed affection, all we
ask of you is that you will recommend us to a respectable solicitor.   130

CHEVIOT (*RC*) But, my dear children, reflect; I can't marry all three. I
am most willing to consider myself engaged to all three and that's
as much as the law will allow. You see I do all I can.° I'd marry all
three of you, with pleasure, if I might; but, as our laws stand at
present, I'm sorry to say, I'm very sorry to say, it's out of the   135
question.

    Exit Cheviot Hill, RIE

MISS TREHERNE Poor fellow. He has my tenderest sympathy; but we
have no alternative but to place ourselves under the protecting aegis
of a jury of our countrymen!

    Enter Mr Symperson, L, with two letters

SYMPERSON Minnie, Miss Treherne, the post has just brought me   140
two letters. One of them bears a Marseilles postmark and is, I doubt
not, from the McQuibbigaskie! He must have written just before
starting for Central Africa.

MINNIE From the McQuibbigaskie? Oh, read, read!

MISS TREHERNE (*R*) Oh, sir! How can you torture us by this delay?   145
Have you no curiosity?

SYMPERSON (*L*) Well, my dear, very little on this point. You see
it don't much matter to me whom Cheviot marries. So that he

marries someone, that's enough for me. But however, *your* anxiety
is natural, and I will gratify it. (*Opens letter and reads*) 'Sir, in reply   150
to your letter, I have to inform you that Evan Cottage is certainly in
England. The deeds relating to the property place this beyond all
question.'

MINNIE In England!

MISS TREHERNE (*sinking into chair, RC*) This blow is indeed a crusher.   155
Against such a blow I cannot stand up! (*Faints*)

MINNIE (*on her knees, R of Belinda*) My poor Belinda, my darling
sister, love, oh forgive me, oh forgive me! Don't look like that!
Speak to me, dearest, oh speak to me, speak to me.

MISS TREHERNE (*suddenly springing up, R*) Speak to you? Yes, I'll   160
speak to you! All is *not* yet lost! True, he is not married to me, but
why should he not be? I am as young as you! I am as beautiful as
you! I have more money than you! I will try, oh how hard I will try!

MINNIE Do, darling; and I wish, oh how I wish you may get him!

MISS TREHERNE (*at door, spitefully*) Minnie, if you were not the   165
dearest little friend I have in the world I could pinch you!

Exit Miss Treherne, RIE

SYMPERSON (*who has been reading the other letter, LC*) Dear me, how
terrible!

MINNIE (*RC*) What is terrible, dear Papa?

SYMPERSON Belvawney writes to tell me the Indestructible Bank   170
stopped payment yesterday and Cheviot's shares are waste paper.

MINNIE Well, upon my word. There's an end of *him*!

SYMPERSON An end of him. What do you mean? You are not going to
throw him over?

MINNIE Dear Papa, I am sorry to disappoint you, but unless your   175
tom-tit is very much mistaken, the Indestructible was not registered under the Joint Stock Companies Act of '62°, and in that case
the shareholders are jointly and severally liable to the whole extent
of their available capital. Poor little Minnie don't pretend to have a
business head; but she's not *quite* such a donkey as *that*, dear Papa.   180

SYMPERSON You decline to marry him? Do I hear rightly?

MINNIE I don't know, Papa, whether your hearing is as good as it was,
but from your excited manner I should say you heard me perfectly.

Exit Minnie, RIE

SYMPERSON (*C*) This is a pretty business! Done out of a thousand a
year, and by my own daughter! What a terrible thing is this inces-   185
sant craving after money! Upon my word, some people seem to
think that they're sent into the world for no other purpose but

to acquire wealth; and, by Jove, they'll sacrifice their nearest and dearest relations to get it. It's most humiliating, most humiliating!

Enter Cheviot Hill, in low spirits, RIE

CHEVIOT (*throwing himself into a chair. Sobs aloud*) Oh! Uncle 190 Symperson, have you heard the news?

SYMPERSON (*angrily*) Yes, I *have* heard the news; and a pretty man of business *you* are to invest all your property in an unregistered company!

CHEVIOT Uncle, don't *you* turn against me! Belinda is not my wife! 195 I'm a ruined man; and my darlings, my three darlings, whom I love with a fidelity which, in these easy-going days, is simply Quixotic, will have nothing to say to me. Minnie, your daughter, declines to accompany me to the altar. Belinda, I feel sure, will revert to Belvawney and Maggie is at this present moment hanging round that 200 Scotch idiot's neck, although she knows that in doing so she simply tortures me. Symperson, I never loved three girls as I loved those three—never! never!—and now they'll all three slip through my fingers, I'm sure they will!

SYMPERSON Pooh, pooh, sir. Do you think nobody loses but you? 205 Why, I'm done out of a thousand a year by it.

CHEVIOT (*moodily*) For that matter, Symperson, I've a very vivid idea that you won't have to wait long for the money.

SYMPERSON What d'you mean? Oh, of course, I understand.

CHEVIOT Eh? 210

SYMPERSON Mrs Macfarlane! I have thought of her myself. A very fine woman for her years; a majestic ruin, beautiful in decay. My dear boy, my very dear boy, I congratulate you.

CHEVIOT Don't be absurd. I'm not going to marry anybody.

SYMPERSON Eh? Why, then how—? I don't think I quite follow you. 215

CHEVIOT (*R*) There is another contingency on which you come into the money. My death.

SYMPERSON To be sure! I never thought of that! And, as you say, a man can die but once.

CHEVIOT I beg your pardon. I didn't say anything of the kind; *you* 220 said it; but it's true, for all that.

SYMPERSON I'm very sorry; but, of course, if you have made up your mind to it—

CHEVIOT Why, when a man's lost everything, what has he to live for?

SYMPERSON True, true. Nothing whatever. Still— 225

CHEVIOT His money gone, his credit gone, the three girls he's engaged to gone.

SYMPERSON I cannot deny it. It is a hopeless situation. Hopeless, quite hopeless.

CHEVIOT His happiness wrecked, his hopes blighted; the three trees upon which the fruit of his heart was growing, all cut down. What is left but suicide?   230

SYMPERSON True, true! You're quite right. Farewell. (*Going*)

CHEVIOT Symperson, you seem to think I *want* to kill myself. I don't want to do anything of the kind. I'd much rather live, upon my soul I would, if I could think of any reason for living. Symperson, can't you think of *something* to check the heroic impulse which is at this moment urging me to a tremendous act of self-destruction?   235

SYMPERSON Something! Of course I can! Say that you throw yourself into the Serpentine—which is handy. Well, it's an easy way of going out of the world, I'm told; rather pleasant than otherwise, I believe; quite an agreeable sensation, I'm given to understand. But you—you get wet through; and your—your clothes are absolutely ruined.   240

CHEVIOT (*mournfully*) For that matter, I could take off my clothes before I went in.   245

SYMPERSON True, so you could. I never thought of that. You could take them off before you go in. There's no reason why you shouldn't, if you do it in the dark—and *that* objection falls to the ground. Cheviot, my lion-hearted boy, it's impossible to resist your arguments, they are absolutely convincing.   250

Mr Symperson shakes Cheviot's hand and exit, LIE

CHEVIOT Good fellow, Symperson. I like a man who's open to conviction! But it's no use. All my attractions are gone and I can*not* live unless I feel I'm fascinating. Still, there's one chance left—Belinda! I haven't tried her. Perhaps, after all, she loved me for myself alone! It isn't likely, but it's barely possible.   255

Enter Belvawney, RIE, *who has overheard these words*

BELVAWNEY Out of the question; you are too late! I represented to her that you are never likely to induce any one to marry you now that you are penniless. She felt that my income was secure and she gave me her hand and her heart.   260

CHEVIOT Then all is lost. My last chance is gone and the irrevocable die is cast! Be happy with her, Belvawney; be happy with her!

BELVAWNEY (*R*) Happy! You shall dine with us after our honeymoon and judge for yourself.

CHEVIOT (*sits on sofa,* L) No, I shall not do that. Long before you return I shall be beyond the reach of dinners.   265

BELVAWNEY I understand. You are going abroad. Well, I don't think you could do better than try another country.

CHEVIOT (*tragically*) Belvawney, I'm going to try another world! (*Drawing a pistol from his pocket*)

BELVAWNEY (*alarmed*) What do you mean?

CHEVIOT In two minutes I die!

BELVAWNEY You're joking, of course?

CHEVIOT Do I look like a man who jokes? Is my frame of mind one in which a man indulges in trivialities?

BELVAWNEY (*in great terror*) But my dear Cheviot, reflect—

CHEVIOT Why should it concern you? You will be happy with Belinda. You will not be well off, but Symperson will, and I dare say he will give you a meal now and then. It will not be a nice meal, but still it will be a meal.

BELVAWNEY (*C*) Cheviot, you mustn't do this. Pray reflect; there are interests of magnitude depending on your existence.

CHEVIOT (*C*) My mind is made up. (*Rising and cocking the pistol*)

BELVAWNEY (*wildly*) But I shall be ruined!

CHEVIOT There is Belinda's fortune.

BELVAWNEY She won't have me if I'm ruined! Dear Cheviot, don't do it. It's culpable. It's wrong!

CHEVIOT Life is valueless to me without Belinda. (*Pointing the pistol to his head*)

BELVAWNEY (*desperately*) You shall have Belinda. She is much, very much to me, but she is not everything. Your life is very dear to me; and when I think of our old friendship —! Cheviot, you shall have anything you like, if you'll only consent to live!

CHEVIOT If I thought you were in earnest; but no, no. (*Putting pistol to head*)

BELVAWNEY In earnest? Of course I'm in earnest! Why, what's the use of Belinda to me if I'm ruined? Why, she wouldn't look at me.

CHEVIOT But perhaps if I'm ruined, she wouldn't look at *me*.

BELVAWNEY Cheviot, I'll confess all, if you'll only live. You,—you are *not* ruined!

CHEVIOT Not ruined?

BELVAWNEY Not ruined. I—I invented the statement.

CHEVIOT (*in great delight*) You invented the statement? My dear friend! My very dear friend! I'm very much obliged to you! Oh, thank you, thank you a thousand times! Oh, Belvawney, you have made me very, very happy! (*Sobbing on his shoulder, then suddenly springing up*) But what the devil did you mean by circulating

270

275

280

285

290

295

300

305

such a report about me? How dare you do it, sir? Answer me that, sir.

BELVAWNEY I did it to gain Belinda's love. I knew that the unselfish 310
creature loved you for your wealth alone.

CHEVIOT It was a liberty, sir; it was a liberty. To put it mildly, it was a liberty.

BELVAWNEY It was. You're quite right—that's the word for it—it was a liberty. But I'll go and undeceive her at once. 315

> *Exit Belvawney, RIE*

CHEVIOT Well, as I've recovered my fortune and with it my tree, I'm about the happiest fellow in the world. My money, my mistress, and my mistress's money, all my own. I believe I could go mad with joy!

> *Enter Mr Symperson, L, in deep black; he walks pensively,*
> *with a white handkerchief to his mouth, crosses to R, sits*

CHEVIOT What's the matter?

SYMPERSON (R) Hallo! You're still alive? (*Disappointed*) 320

CHEVIOT Alive? Yes. Why, (*noticing his dress*) is anything wrong?

SYMPERSON No, no, my dear young friend, these clothes are symbolical. They represent my state of mind. After your terrible threat, which I cannot doubt you intend to put at once into execution—

CHEVIOT My dear uncle, this is very touching. This unmans me. But, 325
cheer up, dear old friend, I have good news for you.

SYMPERSON (*alarmed*) Good news? What do you mean?

CHEVIOT I am about to remove the weight of sorrow which hangs so heavily at your heart. Resume your fancy check trousers, I have consented to live. 330

SYMPERSON Consented to live? Why, sir, this is confounded trifling. I don't understand this line of conduct at all. You threaten to commit suicide; your friends are dreadfully shocked at first, but eventually their minds become reconciled to the prospect of losing you. They become resigned, even cheerful; and when they have brought them- 335
selves to this Christian state of mind, you coolly inform them that you have changed your mind and mean to live. It's not business, sir, it's not business. (*Crosses to L*)

CHEVIOT But, my dear uncle, I've nothing to commit suicide for. I'm a rich man and Belinda will, no doubt, accept me with joy and 340
gratitude.

SYMPERSON Belinda will do nothing of the kind. She has just left the house with Belvawney, in a cab, and under the most affectionate circumstances.

CHEVIOT (*alarmed*) Left with Belvawney? Where have they gone? 345

SYMPERSON I don't know. Very likely to get married.

CHEVIOT (*aghast*) Married?

SYMPERSON Yes, before the registrar.

CHEVIOT (*excitedly*) I've been sold! I see that now! Belvawney has
done me! But I'm not the kind of man who stands such treatment   350
quietly. Belvawney has found his match. Symperson, they may get
married, but they shall not be happy. I'll be revenged on them both
before they're twenty-four hours older. She marries him because
she thinks his income is secure. I'll show her she's wrong. I won't
blow out my brains; I'll do worse.   355

SYMPERSON What?

CHEVIOT I'll marry.

SYMPERSON Marry?

CHEVIOT Anybody. I don't care who it is.

SYMPERSON Will Minnie do?   360

CHEVIOT Minnie will do. Send her here.

SYMPERSON In one moment, my dear boy, in one moment!

    Exit Mr Symperson hurriedly, RIE

CHEVIOT Belinda alone in a cab with Belvawney! It's maddening to
think of it! He's got his arm round her waist at this moment, if I
know anything of human nature! I can't stand it. I cannot and I will   365
not stand it! I'll write at once to the registrar and tell him she's
married. (*Sits at writing table, L, and prepares to write*) Oh, why am
I constant by disposition? Why is it that when I love a girl I can
think of no other girl but that girl, whereas, when a girl loves me
she seems to entertain the same degree of affection for mankind at   370
large? I'll never be constant again. Henceforth I fascinate but to
deceive!

    Enter Minnie, RIE, crosses to L

MINNIE Mr Cheviot Hill, Papa tells me that you wish to speak to me.

CHEVIOT (*hurriedly, writing at table*) I do. Miss Symperson, I have no
time to beat about the bush; I must come to the point at once. You   375
rejected me a short time since. I will not pretend that I am pleased
with you for rejecting me; on the contrary, I think it was in the
worst taste. However, let bygones be bygones. Unforeseen circumstances render it necessary that I should marry at once, and you'll
do. An early answer will be esteemed, as this is business. (*Resumes*   380
his writing)

MINNIE Mr Hill, dear Papa assures me that the report about the loss
of your money is incorrect. I hope this may be the case, but I cannot
forget that the information comes from dear Papa. Now dear Papa

is the best and dearest Papa in the whole world, but he has a lively   385
imagination, and when he wants to accomplish his purpose, he does
not hesitate to invent, I am not quite sure of the word, but I think it
is 'bouncers'.°

CHEVIOT (*writing*) You are quite right, the word is bouncers.
Bouncers or bangers;° either will do.   390

MINNIE Then forgive my little silly fancies, Mr Hill; but, before I
listen to your suggestion, I must have the very clearest proof that
your position is, in every way, fully assured. (*Retires up c*)

CHEVIOT (*rises*) Mercenary little donkey! I will not condescend to
proof. I renounce her altogether. (*Strikes gong bell*)   395
       Enter Maggie with Angus Macalister and Mrs Macfarlane,
       RIE. *Angus has his arm round Maggie's waist*

CHEVIOT (*suddenly seeing her*) Maggie, come here. Angus, do take
your arm from round that girl's waist. Stand back and don't you
listen. (*Excitedly*) Maggie, three months ago I told you that I loved
you passionately. Today I tell you that I love you as passionately as
ever. I may add that I am still a rich man. Can you oblige me with a   400
postage stamp? (*Maggie gives him a stamp from her pocket—he sticks
it on to his letter*) What do you say? I must trouble you for an
immediate answer, as this is not pleasure; it's business.

MAGGIE (*c*) Oh, sir, ye're ower late. Oh, Maister Cheviot, if I'd only
ken'd it before! Oh, sir, I love ye right weel. The bluid o' my hairt is   405
nae sae dear to me as thou. (*Sobbing on his shoulder*) Oh Cheviot, my
ain auld love! My ain auld love!

ANGUS (*aside*) Puir lassie, it just dra's the water from my ee to hear
her. Oh, mither, mither! My hairt is just breaking. (*Sobs on Mrs
Macfarlane's shoulder*)   410

CHEVIOT (*c*) But why is it too late? You say that you love me. I offer to
marry you. My station in life is at least equal to your own. What is
to prevent our union?

MAGGIE (*wiping her eyes*) Oh, sir, ye're unco guid to puir little Maggie, but ye're too late; for she's placed the matter in her solicitor's   415
hands and he tells her that an action for breach° will just bring
damages to the tune of a thousand pound. There's a laddie waiting
outside noo, to serve the bonnie writ on ye! (*Turns affectionately to
Angus, retires up c*)

CHEVIOT (*falling sobbing on to sofa*) No one will marry me. There is a   420
curse upon me, a curse upon me. No one will marry me; no, not
one!

MRS MACFARLANE (*c*) Dinna say that, sir. There's mony a woman, nae

young, soft, foolish lassie, neither, but grown women o' sober age
who'd be mair a mither than a wife to ye; and that's what ye want,   425
puir laddie, for ye're no equal to takin' care o' yersel'. (*Crosses to L*)

CHEVIOT Mrs Macfarlane, you are right. I am a man of quick
impulse. I see, I feel, I speak. I—you are the tree upon which—that
is to say—no, no, damn it, I can't, I can't! One must draw the line
somewhere. (*Turning from her with disgust*)   430

MRS MACFARLANE But ye need not draw the line at me! (*Retires up*)
> *Enter Miss Treherne and Belvawney. They are followed by
> Mr Symperson and Minnie*

CHEVIOT Belinda! Can I believe my eyes? You have returned to me.
You have not gone off with Belvawney after all? Thank heaven,
thank heaven! (*Getting hysterical*)

MISS TREHERNE I thought that, as I came in, I heard you say some-   435
thing about a tree.

CHEVIOT You are right. As you entered I was remarking that I am a
man of quick impulse. I see, I feel, I speak. I have two thousand a
year and I love you passionately. I lay my hand, my heart, and my
income, all together, in one lot, at your feet!   440

MISS TREHERNE Cheviot, I love you with an irresistible fervour that
seems to parch my very existence. I love you as I never loved man
before and as I can never hope to love man again. But, in the belief
that you were ruined, I went with my own adored Belvawney before
the registrar and that registrar has just made us one! (*Turns   445
affectionately to Belvawney*)

BELVAWNEY (*R, embraces Belinda*) Bless him for it, bless him for it!

CHEVIOT (*deadly calm*) One word. I have not yet seen the letter that
blights my earthly hopes. For form's sake, I trust I may be permitted
to cast my eye over that document? As a matter of business, that's all.   450

BELVAWNEY Certainly. Here it is. You will find the situation of the cottage described in unmistakable terms. (*Hands the letter to Cheviot*)

CHEVIOT (*reads*) 'In reply to your letter I have to inform you that
Evan Cottage is certainly in England. The deeds relating to the
property place this beyond all question.' Thank you; I am satisfied.   455
(*Takes out pistol*)
> *During this Belinda has placed her arm over Cheviot's
> shoulder, to read the letter with him*

BELVAWNEY (*RC*) Now, sir, perhaps you will kindly release that young
lady. She is my wife!
> *Cheviot's arm has crept mechanically round Miss Treherne's
> waist*

MISS TREHERNE (*c*) Oh, Cheviot! Kindly release me, I am his wife!

CHEVIOT (*releasing her*) Crushed! Crushed! Crushed! (*Sinks on sofa, L*)   460

SYMPERSON (*looking over his shoulder at letter, reads*) 'Turn over.'

CHEVIOT (*despairingly*) Why should I? What good would it do? Oh, I see. I beg your pardon. (*Turns over the page*) Hallo! (*Rises*)

ALL What?   465

CHEVIOT (*reads*) 'P.S.—I may add that the border line runs through the property. The cottage is undoubtedly in England, though the garden is in Scotland.'

MISS TREHERNE And we were married in the garden!

CHEVIOT (*amorously*) Belinda, we were married in the garden!   470

> *Belinda leaves Belvawney, and turns affectionately to Cheviot, who embraces her*

BELVAWNEY Belinda, stop a bit! Don't leave me like this!

MISS TREHERNE Belvawney, I love you with an intensity of devotion that I firmly believe will last while I live. But dear Cheviot is my husband now. He has a claim upon me which it would be impossible, nay, criminal to resist. Farewell, Belvawney. Minnie may yet   475
be yours!

> *Belvawney turns sobbing to Minnie, who comforts him; Miss Treherne crosses back to Cheviot*

Cheviot, my husband, my own old love. If the devotion of a lifetime can atone for the misery of the last few days, it is yours, with every wifely sentiment of pride, gratitude, admiration, and love.

CHEVIOT (*embracing her*) My own! My own! Tender blossom of my   480
budding hopes! Star of my life! Essence of happiness! Tree upon which the fruit of my heart is growing! My Past, my Present, my To Come!

> *Picture. Cheviot is embracing Miss Treherne, c. Belvawney is being comforted by Minnie, c, up stage. Angus is solacing Maggie, R, and Mrs Macfarlane is reposing on Symperson's bosom, LC*

Curtain

ADDITIONAL PASSAGES

A. At 1.282, passage (reprinted from LC) to follow 'I've stuck to it'.

It's a nice breakfast.

MINNIE From Gunter's°?

CHEVIOT No, it's not from Gunter's. The fact is a railway refreshment-room keeper owed me some money, which I had to take out in stock, so I had the materials by me, otherwise I should have gone to Gunter's. It will be a nice breakfast. Six pounds of picnic biscuits, three dozen Abernethys,° a tin of small captains,° a centre dish of barley sugar and butterscotch, garnished with picnic biscuits, and a delicious trifle made of small captains steeped in milk. Did you ever taste a small captain steeped in milk, beaten up with half-a-pot of currant jelly? It's delicious. Then for substantials there are pork pies in quarters, some delicate sausage rolls (which I can guarantee), some Banbury cakes and a dish of peculiarly rich sandwiches, under a glass case. Then for tipple, we've a number of nice travelling flasks of sherry, rum, and brandy dotted about the table, some claret at elevenpence-halfpenny; a very generous wine.° It must be generous, or it wouldn't let itself go so cheap. Then there'll be no end of soda water grouped on a magnificent silver sideboard, a bottle of soda water by each plate and a trophy of soda water grouped on a magnificent silver epergne°, decorated with boxes of butterscotch, chocolate cream, barley sugar, Banbury cakes and peppermint lozenges. It's a beautiful object and would make a good photograph. It's quite my own idea. It's not like a regular conventional wedding breakfast.

MINNIE Not a bit. What a clever head my darling has.

CHEVIOT Yes, it's a nice head.

B. At 3.133, passage (reprinted from LC) to follow 'You see I do all I can'.

Let me review the situation. Belinda asserts that she is married to me. Very good. I shall always be most happy, at any time, to consider myself married to Belinda. She is a most delightful girl and would suit me in every way; but other interests are involved and we

must make it a matter of proof. Minnie, a most agreeable young 5
person whom I was on the point of marrying when Belinda turned
up, claims me as her promised husband. Now, I want Minnie to
understand that nothing would give me greater pleasure than to
marry her. She is a most interesting girl and I should like it amaz-
ingly; but, if I'm already married to Belinda, how can I? Maggie, to 10
whom on the spur of the moment I thoughtlessly engaged myself,
also calls on me to fulfil my promise. Now, it would give me considerable satisfaction to marry Maggie. She is an agreeable girl—
for her station in life particularly so. But if I'm already married to
one lady and absolutely committed to another, how can she expect 15
me to complicate matters still further by marrying a third?

THE HIGH BID

HENRY JAMES

CHARACTERS OF THE PLAY

(cast of the London performance, His Majesty's Theatre,
18 February 1909)

Captain Clement Yule	Alexander Forbes-Robertson
Mr Prodmore	Edward Sass
Chivers	Ian Robertson
Mrs Gracedew	Gertrude Elliott
Cora Prodmore	Miss Esme Hubbard
Young Man°	Alexander Cassy
English Tourists	Messrs S. T. Pearce, Pilling, Tyndall, Stewart, Gaze, Boag
	Misses Lily Price, Mabel Gill, Roberts, Juliet Hardinge
American Tourists	Messrs W. Ringham, Wilmot, C. B. Vaughan
	Misses Maud Buchanan, Sylvia Buckley, Whitaker.°

1.

The central hall, high and square, brown and grey, flagged°
beneath and timbered above, of an old English countryhouse;
originally very fine and still very interesting, but much worn
and not a little decayed, though retaining its principal
features and properties: the old oak panelling, reaching high
on the walls with faded tapestry above it in some places and
dark old portraits in others; and with, besides the great
chimney-piece, four important points for entrance and exit.
One of these is the fine old stone or oak staircase, descending,
in full view of the audience, as from a gallery, above, which
connects it with the upper parts of the house; the next, quite
at the back and to the right, the door of the vestibule or
anteroom forming part of the main approach to the hall
from offstage. Further down, also to the right, so that it is, by
the width of the stage, opposite the high old chimney-place,
which is to the left, the door to other apartments on the same
level. At the back, or wherever it can conveniently and
suitably come, to the left, the door to the old garden°, which
opens and which stands open at the rising of the curtain, to a
quarter visibly different from that of the main entrance,
spoken of hereafter as the ingress and egress from and to the
park. The air of a long and beautiful summer afternoon
comes in from some high old window or two, where glazed
escutcheons and quartering of family arms make a faded
colour, and from the glimpse, if possible, of the old garden in
the open doorway.

Enter Chivers, the old whitehaired Servant of the house,
dilapidated, much darned and repaired, but scrupulously neat
and with a little aged, conciliatory stoop, a perfect manner and
tone and a universal gentleness and sadness, comes in from
apartments to right and goes restlessly and nervously towards the
issue to the park as if expectant of somebody or something. While
he shuffles across, is pulled up by the high gay voice that comes
down from above.

THE VOICE (*clear and bright, but as from far off*) I hope you don't mind
the awful time I take!

CHIVERS (*immediately, as alertly as possible, at foot of stairs and anxiously listening up*) Oh, it's all right, mum,° you can please yourself. There ain't nobody *come* yet!   5

THE VOICE I'm roaming round as I *told* you. I like to poke round alone!

CHIVERS (*assenting, encouraging, cheerful*) Oh, mum, I gave you the whole free range!

THE VOICE (*with a happy laugh*) Well, I'm *taking* it, anyway, but don't   10
you fear I'll be lost!

CHIVERS (*reassuring, cordial*) Oh, I quite *trust* you, mum!

THE VOICE (*as if liking to keep up the talk*) I guess I know my way round!

CHIVERS (*quaintly amused*) Ah, I'll be *bound* you do!   15

THE VOICE (*as enchanted with everything*) I *must* tell someone. I never saw anything so sweet.

CHIVERS (*accommodating, gratified*) It do indeed, mum, be mainly thought grand! (*Then warning, conscientious*) Only *please*, mum, mind the low doors!   20

THE VOICE (*confident, gay, ringing out*) Oh, I ain't too *tall*! I'll mind low doors all right! And the lovely little ups and downs, ever so deliciously many!

CHIVERS (*in position*) Many, many, as you *say*, mum! (*With a little quavering old expressive sigh*) As many as in a poor man's life!   25

THE VOICE (*continuing to rave*) And the dear little crooked steps, all over the place!

CHIVERS Ah, *mind* the little crooked steps! (*Kindly, fatherly, quavering out his joke*) We mustn't ever take too many of *them*, mum, eh?
(*Listening still, but losing the answer to this, he catches something else*   30
instead, which he repeats) 'Not coming up too?' (*Apologetic, conciliating*) Not if you'll kindly *indulge* me, mum. I must be where I can watch the bell! (*After which, as, while he has waited an instant, no further sound comes, he turns away with the resigned explanatory sigh for himself*) It takes watching as well as hearing! Poor dear old bell,   35
broken down old bell. (*Then as he seems to have his eye up to where it may tinkle in its dusky corner, the old bell hoarsely but limply sounds, and he starts for the door to the park as if he has been sleeping at his post*) Mercy, if I didn't watch!

> Chivers opens the house-door and Cora Prodmore appears,
> breathless and anxious, lest she should be too late. She comes in
> with this fear

CORA (*two-and-twenty, high-coloured, unsuccessfully over-dressed,*   40

*uncontrollably embarrassed, flurried and frightened, but a
well-meaning creature and a good 'sort'*)° My father? Has he
come?

CHIVERS Mr Prodmore? Not yet, Miss, but I've had his orders.

CORA (*panting a little*) So have I and I'm glad I'm not late. He's to *find*
me here. I'll wait.

CHIVERS Certainly, Miss, at your *ease;* and if there's anything I can *do*
for you—

CORA Nothing at all, thanks; I'll just stay here.

CHIVERS (*moving to the tea-room; encouraging, accommodating*) Then I
shall be close at hand.

> Exit Chivers, R. [Enter Young Man, whom Cora does not see
> immediately]

CORA (*left alone, has a look about, but only to start, in an instant, at sight
of Young Man, who meets her eyes of a sudden, at left in the open
doorway to garden and from whom she almost recoils. When Chivers has
gone; all sudden alarm and dismay on seeing 'Young Man' left*) Goodness gracious! You've got *here*? (*With intense reproach; as if he's
utterly in the wrong*) My dear—My dear—How *could* you?

YOUNG MAN (*coming in with every precaution; and breathless with his
whole situation*) After we parted I felt I couldn't *stand* it; couldn't
either wait there *alone* or leave you to your *fate;* and as a fellow at
work in the park told me your father hadn't yet passed—in *state!*—
I came on and got round quicker, by the shortest cut and three sunk
fences,° reaching the garden, I'm sure, *unseen.*

CORA (*all wonder, horror and despair at his perversity*) And what good
does such folly *do* you?

YOUNG MAN (*ardent, insistent*) The good of letting me stay with you,
after all, rather than hang *about*, like a *sneak*, a mile *off*! (*Pressing it
upon her; pleading, sincere*) The good, Cora, won't you please *see*, of
our meeting him *together*!

CORA (*with undiminished dismay and protest*) How can you be so *mad*?
When we've had all that *out*? As if, on his great occasions, his field-
days, as they call them at home, I can do *anything* but grovel!

YOUNG MAN (*impatient, contradictious, rebellious*) You talk, you know,
without a notion of what this occasion *is*!

CORA (*holding her ground*) I never know till I *see* him. I have to *come* to
find out. He wires me an order when I'm away, as he presses a
button for a clerk. Whatever it may be I've first to *take* it. So do as
we *agreed* or I shall be ruined by having consented!

YOUNG MAN (*breaking in with spirit*) What you consented to was my

keeping you in view, so long as we might be noticed, at a respectful   80
distance; and I couldn't even do *that*, when we got to the train at
Bellborough,° with you and that chattering woman in a first-class
carriage and *me* in a beastly third that was as crowded as a cattle-
truck!

CORA (*insisting on her policy and more and more anxious*) I *gave* you at   85
the cost of much danger and delay, the walk to the old grotto by
that wild footpath—

YOUNG MAN (*taking her up in his impatience*) And it's to that damp
hole I've got to go *back*?

CORA (*in reprehension and derision of his tone about it*) You didn't think   90
it so damp when you kept me there so long. (*Then as the house-bell
rings; with sharpest anxiety*) There he *is*; for heaven's sake *go*!

YOUNG MAN (*at garden door, but still unwilling and uncertain*) And let
you face him *alone*?

CORA (*casting about her in her apprehension and agitation, as if helpless*   95
where to turn) You've upset me so that I can't yet face him! (*Suppli-*
cating with intensity; all this for both of them, rapid and breathless) Go
away, go, go!

YOUNG MAN (*in doorway; as for a new understanding*) Where, and
what then, *now*?   100

CORA (*panting, deciding*) I'll *tell* you there. (*As she points to the garden*)
But *quick*!

> *On which the Young Man vanishes before Chivers's re-entrance.*
> *Enter Chivers from tea-room.*

CORA (*just barring his way with a flurried, intense appeal, which makes*
her grab his arm) If it's my father, I'm not *here*!

CHIVERS (*bewildered*) Then *where*, Miss?   105

CORA (*feverish*) Not here, not here, not here! *Understand*?

CHIVERS (*all at sea, but as accommodating as ever, while the bell sounds*
afresh and Cora has gained the door to garden) You *leave*?

CORA (*at door*) I come *back*, but I've not *arrived*!

> *With which she disappears while Chivers goes up to admit Mr*
> *Prodmore, with a dazed word to himself as he does so.*

CHIVERS What *does* come over them?°   110

> *Enter Mr Prodmore and comes down, followed in all humility by*
> *Chivers after the latter has closed the entrance almost in the*
> *manner, or with the gravity, of a warden dropping the*
> *drawbridge of an old castle.*

PRODMORE (*a massive, important, vulgar man, dressed as for an occasion*
of weight and with an air of expecting on all occasions every possible

attention. He looks at nothing, but, as having encountered from the very threshold a disappointment, speaks with surprise and disgust) No one here even yet? 115

CHIVERS *(still in all humility)* I'm sorry to say no one has come sir; but I've had a telegram from Captain Yule.

PRODMORE *(sternly deprecating, as if it would be the old man's fault)* Not to say he ain't coming?

CHIVERS *(reassuringly)* He was to take the 2.20 from Paddington. He 120 certainly *should* be here!

PRODMORE *(absolute)* He should have been here this hour or more. And so should my fly-away *daughter!*

CHIVERS *(respectfully taking the liberty to wonder)* Would they be a-coming—a—*together*, sir? 125

PRODMORE 'Together'? For what do you take Miss Prodmore? *(Then after the other has deprecated with protesting hands any imputation, he condescendingly explains)* It *is* in a sense true that their 'coming together', as you call it, is exactly what I've made my *plans* for today; my calculation was that we should all punctually converge 130 on this spot. Attended by her trusty maid, Miss Prodmore, who happens to be on a week's visit to her grandmother at Bellborough, was to take the 1.40 from that place. I was to drive over, ten miles, from the most convenient of my seats.° *(Speaking as if he had twenty)* Captain Yule *(this with a climax of complacency)* was finally 135 to shake off for a few hours the peculiar occupations that engage him.

CHIVERS *(who has listened all deferentially, but a little blankly; rising to this last vivid image)* They *must* be peculiar, sir, when a gentleman comes into a property like this and goes three months without so 140 much as a nat'ral curiosity—! *(Hastening to be clear)* I don't speak of anything but what *is* nat'ral, sir; but there have *been* people here—

PRODMORE *(taking him up as with the pride of positive proprietorship; his head much in the air)* There have repeatedly been people here!

CHIVERS *(abounding in his sense)* As you *say*, sir—to be shown over. 145 *(Then as it so sadly comes over him)* With the master himself *never* shown!

PRODMORE *(with high decision)* He *shall* be—so that nobody shall miss him.

CHIVERS *(making good his own sense of it all)* It will be a mercy indeed 150 to look on him; but I meant that he has not been taken round.

PRODMORE *(as if requiring no light; least of all from such a source)* That's what I meant too. *I'll* take him round and round and round:

I'll take him till he spins; it's exactly what I've come for! (*With the vision of this intended proceeding he looks with a sweep over the place; concluding with a confidence that fairly makes him sociable*) He can't fail to be affected, though he *has* been up to his neck in such a different class of thing.   155

CHIVERS (*as wondering what class of thing it can be, expresses a timid loyal hope*) In nothing, I daresay, but what's *right*, sir—?   160

PRODMORE (*distinct, assured, resonant*) In everything that's abomin-ably *wrong*! (*Then as the doorbell again sounds in the same manner as before*) But here he *is*!

> Chivers, as under the surprise and shock of this last revelation,
> has been but the more agitatedly launched upon his duty of
> quickly answering the bell. He reaches the door from the park
> while Mr Prodmore, his large white waistcoat fairly expanding
> with his increase of presence, continues to pervade the foreground.
> He is thus important and expectant there a little when the sounds
> from the back suddenly cause the collapse of his tension. Enter
> Cora Prodmore. She has appeared at the door opened to her
> and, while her father's back is presented to her view, has eagerly,
> yet as if always a little in fear, surrendered her parasol and
> extra wrap to the old man. Her father meanwhile, adjusting
> his consciousness to what has happened, proceeds.

PRODMORE Only Cora? (*But then rectifying his thought as she comes down*) Well, whatever he resists, he shan't at any rate resist *her*! (*He receives the girl, however, as with the habit and on the principle of strict discipline*) I've *waited*. What do you *mean*?   165

CORA Waited, Papa? Oh I'm too *sorry*!

PRODMORE (*as with the habit of snubbing and confounding her even when she more or less grovels*) Would you then, if I had *not* had patience for you, have wished not to *find* me? (*Following it up as from enjoyment of the effect of this*) Would you have preferred me to have cleared *out*? (*Then as she but gasps her protest*) Why the dickens are you so *late*?   170

CORA (*with imperfect presence of mind*) I'll *tell* you, Papa! (*But as he waits for her definite statement it fails her, almost as for the terror of him; so that, looking about her as for vague help in her trouble, all she can do is to close her eyes to her danger. She catches at her one possible relief from it*) I feel rather *faint*. Could I have some *tea*?   175

PRODMORE (*after considering both the idea and his daughter's substantial shape*) Well, as I shall expect you to put forth *all* your power—*yes*! (*To Chivers, who, after admitting the girl, has been vaguely occupied,*   180

*up, with his general domestic anxieties, and has again, unnoticed by the
others, stopped at the foot of the stairs with an interest in some sound of
movements above; after which, his ear catching Cora's appeal, he has*   185
come down) Some tea.

CHIVERS (*all responsive and as to be very agreeable to the young lady*) I
did think it might be required! (*Then when he has gained the door of
the other apartments*) I'll lay it out here.

    Exit Chivers

CORA (*recovering enough to rise from the chair into which she has sunk on*   190
professing faintness) It was my train, Papa, so very awfully behind. I
walked up, you know, too, from the station. There's such a lovely
footpath across the *park*.

PRODMORE (*as with the habit of examining almost any statement made
him*) You've been roaming the country then alone?   195

CORA (*precipitate*) Oh dear, no, not *alone*! (*She speaks as if she has never
heard of such a thing and has really had a train of attendants; yet is able
to fill it out only by saying*) There were *ever* so many people about.

PRODMORE (*speaking from the point of view as of his personal convenience; and even from that of a new exclusiveness*) Nothing is more   200
possible, everywhere, than to find *too* many! But where, among
them all, is your trusty *maid*?

CORA (*making up in a wild promptitude what she lacks in real assurance*) I
didn't *bring* her. (*She looks about at the old portraits as if to appeal to
them to help her to remember why: but then as they give no sign, has a*   205
separate inspiration) She was so extremely *unwell*.

PRODMORE (*shocked*) Wasn't she to understand from the first that we
don't *permit*—

CORA (*quickly meeting it*) Anything of that sort? Oh yes, Papa, I
thought she understood.   210

PRODMORE But she *doesn't*? (*He presses the point, but she's too much at
a loss; so he becomes more peremptory*) What on earth's the *matter*
with her?

CORA (*who has rolled her frightened eyes vainly over the place*) I really
don't know, but I think that at Granny's she *eats* too much.   215

PRODMORE (*with instant decision*) I'll soon put an end to *that*! (*Then
seeing the girl's situation in the light of this failure of her companion*)
You expect then to pursue your adventures quite into the night; to
return to Bellborough as you *came*?

CORA (*finding her feet a little more*) Exactly as I came, Papa dear, under   220
the protection of a new friend I've just made, a lady who was in my
railway carriage and who is also going back by the 6.19. She was,

like myself, on her way to this place, and I expected to *find* her here.°

PRODMORE (*chilling on the spot any such expectations*) What does she   225
want at this place?

CORA (*clearly stronger for her new friend than for herself*) She wants to
see it.

PRODMORE (*reflecting on this complication*) Today? (*Then as if it's practically presumptuous on the new friend's part*) Today won't *do*.   230

CORA So I suggested. (*Then lighting° as with the recall of it*) But do you
know what she *said*?

PRODMORE (*as if he neither knows nor wants to*) How should I know
what a vagrant *nobody* says?

CORA (*as with an accession of new strength, so that she can almost contra-*   235
dict him) She isn't a *nobody* and is a vagrant only in the sense of
being an *American*.

PRODMORE (*as visited after an instant by a flash of calculation*) An
American?

CORA Yes, and she's *wild*—   240

PRODMORE (*who knows all about that*) Americans mostly *are*!

CORA Eager, I mean, to see this house. 'Wild' was what she herself
called it, and I think she also said she was 'just mad'.

PRODMORE (*reviewing the affair*) She gives a fine account of herself,
but (*quite dismissing the affair*) she won't *do*.°   245

CORA (*with courage for the odd lady and as seeing how little she will
accept such a sentence*) Well, when I told her that this particular *day*
perhaps wouldn't, she said it would just *have* to.

PRODMORE (*amused at such fatuity*) For *what*, then, with such grand
airs?   250

CORA (*ready*) Why, I suppose, for what Americans want.

PRODMORE (*who has measured that quantity*) They want *everything*!

CORA (*taking it from him, wishing for her friend*) Then I wonder she
hasn't arrived.

PRODMORE (*prepared for this formidable person*) When she does I'll   255
tackle her; and I shall thank you, in future, not to take up, in trains,
with loud—and possibly loose!—women of whom you know
nothing.

CORA (*glad to controvert this*) Oh, I did know something, for I saw her
yesterday at Bellborough.   260

PRODMORE (*as if resenting for her even this experience*) And what was
she doing at Bellborough?

CORA Staying at the Blue Dragon, to see the old Abbey. She says she just *loves* old abbeys. (*To which the girl adds with rising intelligence*) It seems to be the same feeling that brought her over today to see this old house.

PRODMORE (*derisive and superior*) She 'just loves' old houses? Then why the deuce didn't she accompany you properly, since she *is* so pushing, to the door?

CORA Because she went off in a fly to see first the old hospital. (*Sympathetically*) She just loves old hospitals. She asked me if this isn't a show-house.° I told her (*with a look at her father and then as uncertain and anxious to disclaim responsibility*) that I hadn't, really, the least idea.

PRODMORE (*almost with ferocity*) It *is*, if there ever *was* one! (*And then as she stands snubbed*) I wonder, on such a speech, what she thought of *you*.

CORA (*candidly and humbly confessing*) I know. She *told* me.

PRODMORE (*considering his offspring*) That you're really a hopeless frump?

CORA (*appearing, oddly enough, almost to court this description*) That I'm not, as she rather funnily called it, a *show-girl*.

PRODMORE (*ruffled*) To think of your having to be *reminded*, by the very strangers you pick up, of what my daughter should pre-eminently be! (*Then, however, as making the best of this humiliation*) Your friend, at any rate, is evidently at high pitch!

CORA (*with confidence*) Well, when she comes, you'll hear her distinctly enough! (*Then warming to her plea*) But don't judge her, Papa, till you do. She's tremendously clever. There seems to be nothing she doesn't know.

PRODMORE (*prompt*) And there seems to be nothing you *do*. You're not tremendously clever, Miss Prodmore; so you'll permit me to demand of you a slight effort of intelligence. Make one as you've *never* made it. (*Then as, having impressed and even alarmed her, he holds her gaping attention a little and sounds the high note*) I'm expecting Captain Yule.

CORA (*taking it rather blinkingly in*) The owner of this property?

PRODMORE (*with reservations*) That's what it depends on you to *make* him.

CORA (*gaping and wondering*) On *me*?

PRODMORE (*facing the need of lucidly instructing her*) He came into it three months ago by the death of his great-uncle, who had lived to ninety-three, but who, having quarrelled mortally with his father, had always refused to receive either sire or son.

CORA (*vague, scantily enlightened*) But *now* at least doesn't he live here? 305

PRODMORE So little that he comes here today for the very first time. I've some business to discuss with him that can best be discussed on this spot; and it's a vital part of that business that you also should take pains to make him welcome.

CORA (*struck with the oddity*) Welcome to his own house? 310

PRODMORE (*emphatic*) That it's *not* his own house is just the point I seek to make! The way I look at it is that it's my house. The way I look at it even, my dear, (*and in his demonstration of his ways of looking he quite genially expands*) is that it's *our* house. The whole thing is mortgaged, as it stands, for every inch of its value; and I 315 enjoy the high advantage. Do you follow me? (*He fairly trumpets it*)

CORA (*fairly bounding, on her side, to a full perception*) Of holding the mortgages?

PRODMORE (*surprised and even gratified at her unprecedented quickness*) You keep up with me better than I *hoped*. I have Captain Yule in my 320 hands. I hold every scrap of paper, and it's a precious collection.

CORA (*making out more in this and looking, for the first time, with attention, over the impressive place itself*) Do you mean that you can come down on him?°

PRODMORE (*triumphant*) I don't need to 'come', my dear; I *am* 325 'down'. *This* is 'down'! (*He raps, jubilantly, with his stick, the hard pavement of the hall*) I 'came' many weeks ago, commercially and financially speaking, and haven't since budged from the place.

CORA (*moving a little about under the impression of this, when turning, with a spasm of courage*) Are you going to be very *hard*? 330

PRODMORE (*as if willing, in his strength, to play a little with her fear*) With you?

CORA (*very straight now*) No, that doesn't matter. Hard with the Captain.

PRODMORE (*slightly impatient*) 'Hard' is a stupid shuffling° term. 335 (*Almost snappishly*) What do you *mean* by it?°

CORA Well, I don't understand business; but I think I understand *you*, Papa, enough to gather that you've got, indeed, as usual, a striking advantage.

PRODMORE (*complacent, but consciously reasonable*) As usual, I *have* 340 scored; but my advantage won't be 'striking' perhaps till I've sent the blow home. (*More blandly, but still firmly*) What I, as a father, appeal to you at present to do is, well, to nerve my arm! I look to you, Cora, to see me through.

CORA (*attentive, cautious*) Through what, then? 345

PRODMORE Through this most *important* transaction. Through the
    speculation of which you've been the barely dissimulated subject.
    (*Letting her have it practically all*) I've brought you here to receive
    an impression and I've brought you, even more, to *make* one.

CORA (*pretending by a quick instinct to more vagueness than she feels*) But   350
    on *whom*?

PRODMORE On *me*, to begin with, by being neither a minx nor a
    milksop! And then, Miss, on *him*.

CORA (*alarmed as she really takes it in*) On Captain Yule?

PRODMORE By bringing him to the point.   355

CORA But, father, (*quavering in anguish*) to *what*?

PRODMORE (*lucid*) The point where a gentleman *has* to.

CORA (*wondering and faltering*) Go down on his knees?

PRODMORE (*after debate and demur*) No, they don't *do* that.

CORA (*with all her apprehension*) What *do* they do?   360

PRODMORE (*declining responsibility for details*) He will know himself.

CORA (*distressed and impetuous*) Oh no indeed he won't! (*Natural*)
    They don't ever.

PRODMORE (*peremptory*) Then the sooner they learn, whoever
    teaches 'em, the *better*; the better I mean in particular (*with an*   365
    intention perceptibly vicious) for the master of this house. (*As to make*
    her easy about it) I'll guarantee that he shall *understand that*, for I
    shall do my proper part.

CORA (*more aghast the more she thinks of it*) But how on earth, sir, can I
    ever do *mine*? (*Earnestly impressing it on him*) To begin with, you   370
    know, I've never *seen* him.

PRODMORE (*who has taken out his watch and then, having consulted it,*
    puts it back with a gesture that seems to dispose at the same time and in
    the same manner of the objection) You'll see him *now*, and *plenty* of
    him, from one moment to the other. He's remarkably handsome,   375
    remarkably ambitious, remarkably clever, and—to be so many other
    such remarkable things—remarkably young.° He has one of the
    best and oldest names in this part of the country; a name that, far
    and wide here, one could do so much with that I'm simply indig-
    nant to see him do so little. I propose, my dear, to do with it all he   380
    hasn't done, and I further propose, to that end, first to get *hold* of it.
    (*Then, as presenting her almost graciously with his whole thought*) It's
    you, Miss Prodmore, who shall take it, with your fair fingers, out of
    the fire. . . .

CORA (*gaping still at the terrible figures he employs*) The fire?   385

PRODMORE Out of the *mud*, then, if you prefer! You must pick it up, with a graceful movement, do you see? My plan is, in short (*with the full bright, cheering demonstration*) that when we've brushed it off and rubbed it down a bit, blown away the dust and touched up the rust, as we've all *facility* for doing, my daughter shall worthily *bear* it.   390

CORA (*grave, with the dawn of a deeper resistance*) You speak of *your* plan, Papa. But does it happen also to be Captain Yule's?

PRODMORE (*looking at her hard, as if to warn her off the ground of irony*) His plans have not yet quite matured. But nothing is more   395
natural than that (*with high significance*) they shall do so on the sunny south wall of Miss Prodmore's best manner.

CORA (*with a nervous laugh*) You talk of them, Papa, as if they were sour little plums! (*With a rising spirit*) You exaggerate, I think, the warmth of Miss Prodmore's nature. It has always been thought   400
remarkably cold.

PRODMORE (*very absolute; all to the point*) Then you'll be so good, my dear, as to *confound*—it mightn't be amiss even to scandalise—that opinion. (*Then both as father and man of business*)° I've spent twenty years in giving you what your poor mother used to call first-rate   405
advantages and they've cost me hundreds and hundreds of pounds. What *I* call an advantage you know is a thing that shall be an advantage to *me.* It's now time, therefore, that both as a parent and as a man accustomed to do business, I should have some news of my investment. (*Treating the subject luminously*) I couldn't help   410
your temper°—*that* I recognise; nor your taste, nor even your unmistakable resemblance to the estimable but far from orna-mental woman who brought you forth; but if I laid your education on so thick it was just that you should have, damn you, what we *want* of you today. (*Formidable*) Do you mean to tell me you haven't   415
got it?

CORA (*distressed, at a loss*) Doesn't it depend on what you *do* want?

PRODMORE (*highly definite*) I want what *Captain Clement Yule* will naturally want!

CORA (*immensely wondering*) And Captain Yule—?   420

PRODMORE Will want *charm*! Do you mean to say you haven't got *any*?

CORA (*modest, infinitely embarrassed*) How can I *tell*, Papa? He may not *think*!

PRODMORE (*winding up sharp*) Do your duty, Miss, and never mind   425
what he 'thinks'! (*Supremely impatient*) Don't look at him like a sick cow, and he'll be sure to think *right*!

CORA (*wounded, but resisting, clinging to some line of defence*) I remember
   your saying once, some time ago, that this was just what he'd be sure
   not to do; I mean when he began to go in for his dreadful ideas—   430

PRODMORE (*taking her again boldly up*) About the 'radical programme', the 'social revolution',° the spoliation of everyone and
   the destruction of everything? (*Amused at her simplicity*) Why, you
   stupid thing, I've worked round to a complete agreement with him.
   The taking from those who have by those who haven't, what is it   435
   but just to *receive*, from consenting hands, the principal treasure of
   the rich? *That's* quite the style of opinion I *want* him to have. (*Then
   while she hangs attentive*) I regard my daughter—let it flatter her to
   know—as my largest property and I freely hand her *over*. I shall, in
   other words, forgive his low opinions if he renounces them for *you*.   440

CORA (*as with a glimpse, then, of salvation*) He *won't* renounce them!
   (*With brave resolution*) He *shan't*!

PRODMORE (*still glowing, to the point of good-humour, with conscious
   felicity of statement*) If you suggest that you're in political sympathy
   with him, you mean then that you'll take him as he *is*?   445

CORA (*her head very high and quite ringing out*) I won't take him at *all*!
   (*But then, agitated, by the sound of wheels in the park° and with her
   dignity dropping straight*) A fly?° (*She turns right and left for a retreat
   or an escape, but her father has already caught her by the wrist; which
   causes her pitifully to pant*) Surely you don't want me to pounce on   450
   him *thus*?

PRODMORE (*holding her off by the arm as to judge of the force of this
   deprecation of her appearance*) Your fine frock won't *do*—with what
   it *cost* me?

CORA (*her decent dignity coming back; pleading*) It's not my frock, Papa,   455
   it's his thinking I've come here for him to *look* at me!

PRODMORE (*who, as if rather struck by this, and even a little touched,
   has released her*) He doesn't think it, and I'll see that he shan't, in
   any manner to *shock* him, be *aware* of it!

CORA (*who has reached, for retreat, to R the door of the apartments and   460
   speaks distressfully*) But he's aware you want me to *hook* him!

PRODMORE (*whom the apparent approach of his visitor has already
   thrown back upon his 'manner'*) The way to 'hook' him will be not to
   be hopelessly *vulgar*. (*Then sharply definite*) He doesn't know that
   you know anything.   465

   *The house-bell has clinked as he speaks and the old butler comes
   back from preparing tea. Enter Chivers from R, leaving door
   open.° Prodmore waves the girl off to the apartments*

Await us there with tea and mind you have Charm!

> *Exit Cora Prodmore throwing up her arms as to disclaim*
> *everything; while Chivers has shuffled straight up to back to*
> *answer the bell, opening the house-door and admitting the visitor.*
> *Enter Captain Clement Yule, whom Chivers straightway*
> *precedes down the stage as for the eager joy of proclaiming him.*
> *Prodmore, who was° under the impression for an instant of his*
> *daughter's final air, for better or for worse, has at once become,*
> *none the less, all 'attitude' for the reception of Yule.*

CHIVERS (*announcing*) Captain Yule!

> *Exit Chivers, R*

PRODMORE (*who has during the previous scene either kept on his hat or put it on at a given moment for emphasis, now removing it*) Delighted at last to *see* you here!   470

YULE (*of distinguished and refined, but in a high degree manly appearance, dressed in a darkish tweed suit and with a red necktie in a sailor's knot; has, on entering, taken off, instinctively, as in sudden homage to all the ghosts of all his ancestors, a soft brown hat. He has clearly felt himself at once struck with their collective presence and with the whole* 475 *place; but he puts out his hand with responsive simplicity, though also a shade of friendly amusement*) If I've not come before, Mr Prodmore, it was, very frankly speaking, from the dread of seeing *you*!

PRODMORE (*highly genial, rejoicing in the promise of his aspect*) Ah, but my presence, sir, is not without its honourable motive!   480

YULE (*with a sad, intelligent smile*) It's just its honourable motive that makes me wince at it! (*Frank, resigned, good-humoured*) Certainly I've no illusions about the ground of our meeting; though indeed I may not know quite so well what I'm about, in my poor way, as *you* know what *you* are. Your thorough knowledge of what you're about   485 has at any rate placed me at your mercy. You hold me in the hollow of your hand.

PRODMORE (*not afraid of any tribute, even if slightly ironic, to his financial subtlety*) Well, Captain Yule, if an honest man or two, in this old country of ours, didn't take care to know what he's about, where   490 should we *any* of us be? (*After an instant, while he has shone with the force of this homely question; recognising the reality of things*) I don't deny that when, in general, I go in deep I don't go in for *nothing*. (*Smiling shrewdly*) I make my plunge pay double!

YULE (*quietly amused*) You make it pay so well—'double' surely   495 doesn't do you justice!—that, if I've understood you, you can do quite as you like with this preposterous, this (*as he looks about him*) prodigious place. Haven't you brought me down just to treat me to the *sight* of your doing it?

PRODMORE (*diplomatic*) I've decidedly brought you down to make you open your *eyes*! (*Then as if more specifically to business*) Of course, you know, you can always *clear* the property. You can pay off the—a—rather heavy encumbrances.

YULE (*always a trifle ironic and as if taking in constantly, no matter how much in spite of himself, the fine old elements of the place*) 'Pay off', Mr Prodmore? What can I pay off with?

PRODMORE (*deep, yet easy*) You can always raise money.

YULE (*vague to positive blankness*) What can I raise it on?

PRODMORE (*massively gay*) On your great political future!

YULE (*with a movement which disposes of the idea*) Oh, I've not taken, for the short run at least, the lucrative line; and I know what you think of *that*.

PRODMORE (*granting then, indulgently, that he does; but as desiring none the less to help his friend through; all benevolently*) I hold that you keep, in public, very dangerous company; but I also hold that you're extravagant mainly because you've nothing at stake. (*Developing with pleasant confidence*) A man has the right opinions as soon as he finds he has something to *lose* by having the wrong. Haven't I already hinted to you how to set your political house in order? You're reduced to the lower regions because you keep the best rooms empty. *These* are the best rooms, sir, (*indicating the whole place*) even of your *political* house. (*Then, as having let him take in, attentive and wondering a little, this pregnant image*) You're a firebrand, in other words, my dear Captain, simply because you're the most wasted of charming *men* and the most unnatural of *bachelors*. *That* ailment's one of the early complaints we all pass through, but it's soon over and the treatment quite simple. I have your *remedy*.

YULE (*detached and 'off',° perfunctory and sceptical, as through the more important effect on him of the interesting place, though all still in spite of himself*) One of those sad remedies that are worse than the disease?

PRODMORE (*prompt and positive*) There's nothing worse, that I've ever heard of, than your particular fix. (*With assurance*) Least of all a heap of gold!

YULE (*as he lets the bright image dangle, but still detached*) A heap of gold?

PRODMORE (*with a flourish*) In the lap of a fine, fresh lass! (*With energy*) Give pledges to fortune, as somebody says, *then* we'll talk. You want money; that's what you want. Well, *marry* it!   540

YULE (*never stirring, save that his eyes, which can't close themselves to the place, vaguely stray. He speaks with his rather indifferent smile*) Of course I could do that in a moment!

PRODMORE It's even just my own *danger* from you. I perfectly recognise that *any* woman would now jump—   545

YULE (*breaking in a bit dryly*) I don't like jumping women, Mr Prodmore; though that perhaps is a detail. It's more to the point that I've yet to see the woman whom by an advance of my *own*—

PRODMORE (*interrupting in turn*) You'd care to keep in the really   550 attractive position?

YULE (*prompt and decided*) Which can never of course be anything but *waiting*, very quietly!

PRODMORE (*abounding in that sense*) Never, never *anything*! Very, *very* quietly! (*He banishes all other thoughts*)° But I haven't *asked* you, you   555 know, to make a marked advance.

YULE (*with his detachment*) You've only asked me to *receive* one?

PRODMORE (*just faltering*) Well, I've asked you—I asked you a month ago—to think it all over.

YULE (*without hesitation*) I *have* thought it all over, and the strange   560 effect seems to be that my eyes have got accustomed to my darkness. I seem to make out, in the gloom of my meditations, that, at the worst, I can let the whole thing slide.

PRODMORE (*with a scandalised start*) This great property?

YULE Isn't it this great property that positively throws me up? If I can   565 afford neither to live on it, to work it, nor to free it, I can at least let it save its own *bacon* and pay its own *debts*. I can say to you simply: 'Take it, my dear sir, and the devil take *you*!'

PRODMORE (*still more shocked, but persuasively smiling it off*) You wouldn't be so recklessly *rude*!   570

YULE (*generally and particularly amused at him*) Why *not*, if I'm a firebrand and a keeper of low company and a general nuisance? Sacrifice for sacrifice that might very well be the *least*!

PRODMORE (*arrested but an instant; still acute and plausible*) How do you *know*, if you haven't compared them? It's just to *make* the   575 comparison in all the right condition, that you're here at this hour. (*He takes, with a large, though vague, exhibitory gesture, a turn or two about*) Now that you stretch yourself, for an hour's relaxation and rocked, as it were, by my friendly *hand*, in the ancient cradle of

your race, can you seriously entertain the idea of *parting* with such a   580
venerable family relic?

YULE (*affected a little by this appeal, turns away, moves up, his hands in
his pockets, looks about; then stands a moment, his back presented, his
face not seen, in a brief concentration of thought. Then as with a certain
impatience he faces about*) The cradle of my race bears, for me, Mr   585
Prodmore, a striking resemblance to its *tomb*. (*A trifle perversely and
profanely*) Oh dear, dear, dear—(*It ends in a small ambiguous,
inscrutable wail, not without tenderness. But he has adopted the profane
view*) Mercy *on* us, how melancholy!

PRODMORE (*his lips pursed out, deprecates from a business point of view*   590
this depreciation) Melancholy? More, you think, than is favourable?

YULE (*who has taken in certain decayed details*) No, not more than is
favourable—to ghosts, to rats, perhaps to other parasites and certainly to bad *dreams*! (*He repeats the refrain*) Melancholy, musty,
mouldy (*then with a poke either of his toe or of his stick, from the table*   595
*on which he has laid it, at a gap in the old stuff, with which a low seat
has been re-covered*)—mangy! Is this the character *throughout*?

PRODMORE (*his practical eyes on the tell-tale tatter, but his assured gesture making light of it*) You must judge for yourself; you must go
over the house. (*Disconcerted but for an instant, he sees his right line*) It   600
does look a bit run down, but I'll *tell* you what I'll do. I'll do it *up* for
you, neatly. I'll throw *that* in!

YULE (*consistently amused*) Will you put us on the telephone, or install
the electric light?

PRODMORE (*a little perplexed at this irony, but holding his course*) Well,   605
damn it, if you'll meet me half*way*! (*He explains, expatiates*) We're
dealing here, if you take me, with *fancy-values*.° Don't you feel, as
you embrace the scene, a sort of something-or-other down your
back?

YULE (*who again and again loses himself and then abruptly reverts*) If I   610
should begin to tell you what I 'feel', I think I should have to name
first a strange stiffening of the spine, as if from the sense of my
having instinctively swallowed, on the spot, the whole ramrod of
reaction.

PRODMORE Reaction?   615

YULE Reaction, I mean, against *these* pretensions. (*Candidly, sincerely*)
The whole face of things is too queer; too cold; too cruel.

PRODMORE (*quite failing to follow; yet in virtuous protest*) 'Cruel'?

YULE (*completing his thought as he moves about*) Like the face of some
stuck-up distant relation who won't speak first. I see in the stare of   620

the old dragon, I smell in the damp of his very breath, all the
helpless mortality he has tucked away!

PRODMORE (*really at a loss*) Lord, Captain, you *have* fancies!°

YULE (*half interested, half irritated, as his fancies multiply*) I don't
know what's the matter, but there *is* more here than meets the eye.   625
(*He tries, as might be, to puzzle it out*) I miss all the presences. I feel
all the absences. I touch old hands. I hear old voices, I see the old
ghosts.

PRODMORE (*his commercial shrewdness reviving*) The old ghosts, Captain Yule, are worth so much a dozen, and with no reduction, I   630
must remind you, with the rate indeed rather *raised*, for the quantity taken! (*Then as feeling the air cleared by this sally; cheering,
patronisingly*) Look about you, at your ease, a little *more*. Make
yourself quite at *home*.

YULE (*after having looked at him rather hard an instant*) Thank you   635
very much, Mr Prodmore. May I light a cigarette?

PRODMORE (*bland for the question*) In your own house, Captain?

YULE That's just the question: it seems so much less my own house
than before I had come into it! (*He offers his friend a cigarette, which
that gentleman accepts, also taking a light from him, then he lights his   640
own and begins to smoke*) As I understand you, you *lump* your two
conditions? I mean I must accept both or neither?

PRODMORE (*as if this is indeed what he wants to talk about*) You will
accept *both*, for, by doing so, you'll clear the property at a stroke.
The way I put it is this, see, that if you'll stand for Gossage you'll   645
get returned for Gossage.

YULE (*taking it in*) And if I get returned for Gossage I shall marry
your daughter. Accordingly, (*lucid and definite*) if I marry your
daughter—

PRODMORE (*prompt, loyal*) I'll burn up before your eyes every scratch   650
of your pen, I'll make such a bonfire of your obligations as the
whole country will flock to see. There won't be a penny to *pay*,
there'll only be a position to take. You'll take it with peculiar *grace*.

YULE (*appearing to consider, but keeping most of his thoughts to himself*)
Peculiar, Mr Prodmore, *very*!   655

PRODMORE (*completing the picture without heeding his tone*) You'll settle down here in comfort and honour.

YULE (*irritated, but turning away as to turn it off*) Are you very sure of
the 'honour', if I turn my political coat?

PRODMORE (*making nothing of this*) You'll only be turning it back   660
again to the way it was *always* worn! (*Persuasive, convincing*)

Gossage will receive you with open arms and press you to a heaving Tory bosom. That bosom (*he follows himself up*) has never heaved but to sound conservative principles. The cradle, as I've called it— or at least the rich warm *coverlet*—of your race, Gossage was the 665 political property, so to speak, of generations of your family. Stand therefore in the good old interest, and you'll stand like a lion.

YULE (*amused*) Ah, I'm afraid you mean that I must first *roar* like one.

PRODMORE Oh, I'll do the roaring! (*It's as if he shakes his mane*) Leave that to *me*. 670

YULE Then why in the name of political good manners don't you stand yourself?

PRODMORE (*ready*) Because, you see, my good manners aren't *all* political. My *best* ones, Captain Yule, are just those I'm showing you now and here. I don't stand myself because I'm not a remark- 675 ably handsome young man with the grand old home and the right old name, because I'm a different sort of matter altogether. But if I haven't these advantages, you'll do justice to my natural desire that my *daughter* at least shall have them.

YULE (*after watching himself smoke a moment*) Doing justice to natural 680 desires is exactly what, of late, I've tried to make a study of, and what, let me remind you, I've been loaded, in some quarters, with abuse for!° But I confess I don't quite grasp the deep attraction you appear to discover in so large a surrender of your interests.

PRODMORE (*all at his ease*) My surrenders are my own affair; and, as 685 for my interests, since I never, on principle, give anything for noth-ing, I daresay I may be trusted to know 'em when I see 'em. You come high;° I don't for a moment deny it; but when I look at you, in this pleasant intimate way, my dear boy, if you'll allow me so to describe things, I recognise one of those cases, unmistakable when 690 really met, in which one must put down one's money. There's not an article in the whole shop, if you don't mind the comparison, that strikes me as better value. (*With a frank bold burst*) I intend you shall be, Captain, the true comfort of my life!

YULE (*motionless, smoking*) May I inquire if Miss Prodmore's ideas of 695 comfort are as well defined—and in *her* case, I may add, as touch-ingly *modest*—as her father's? Is she a responsible party to this ingenious arrangement?

PRODMORE (*embarrassed, yet after an instant*) I appreciate the high character of your scruple. (*Then as after hesitating how best to* 700 *describe the young lady*) Miss Prodmore, sir, may perhaps best be described as a large smooth sheet of blank, though gilt-edged paper.

No image of any tie but the pure and perfect *filial* has yet, I can answer for it, formed itself on the considerable expanse. But for that image to be projected—   705

YULE (*as trying really to face this possibility; though putting it jocosely*) I've only in *person* to appear?

PRODMORE (*full of sympathetic assent*) And naturally, in person, do yourself, as well as the young lady, credit, by which I mean justice! Do you remember what you said when I first, in London, laid the   710 matter before you?

YULE (*recalling*) I think I said it struck me I should first take a look at—what do you call it—the *corpus delicti*.°

PRODMORE You should first see for yourself what you had really come into? I was not only eager for that, but I'm willing to go   715 further. (*Hanging fire an instant, but hopeful*) I'm quite ready to hear you say you think you should also first see the young *lady*!

YULE (*doing justice to this precaution*) There *is* something in that then, since you mention it!

PRODMORE I think you'll find that there's everything! (*Looking again*   720 *at his watch*) Which will you take first?

YULE (*a bit vague*) 'First'?

PRODMORE The young lady or the house?

YULE (*astonished*) You don't mean to say your daughter's *here*?

PRODMORE (*taking all the responsibility*) In the morning-room.   725

YULE (*in consternation*) *Waiting* for me?

PRODMORE (*reassuring*) Ah, as long, you know, as you *like*!

YULE (*really dismayed at his push*) Oh, longer than *this*, please! (*Then as it comes over him*) Do you mean she *knows*?

PRODMORE That she's here on *view*? (*Faltering but an instant; equal to*   730 *the occasion*) She knows nothing *whatever*. She's as unconscious as the rose on its stem!

YULE (*visibly relieved*) That's *right* then; please, let her *remain* so! (*Looking also at his watch*) I'll first take the house.

PRODMORE (*all ready to oblige*) Shall I go round *with* you?   735

YULE (*more gravely now than by his tone hitherto and after briefest reflection*) Thank you; I'd rather, on the whole, go round alone.

    Enter Chivers from right. He looks from under a bent brow, all
    uncertain and anxious and with much limpid earnestness, as
    feeling his own fate at stake, from one of the men to the other,
    and then with an appeal for sympathy seems to cast himself
    upon Yule

CHIVERS (*with gentle, but extreme encouragement, as he passes round the young man*) There's *tea* on, sir! (*With which he waits, putting some object straight, or otherwise busying himself, as if, quite yearningly, either to remain with Yule or to accompany him*)   740

PRODMORE (*as with discretion and decision*) Then I'll join my daughter. (*Then as he has gained door on right, with an appropriate smile and a gathering-in of his fingers as to present a flower*) The *rose*, Captain, on its *stem*!   745

>   *Exit Mr Prodmore to apartments*

YULE (*left thinking, with his eyes rather absently at first on Chivers, whom he then seems to focus*) I say, my friend, what *colour* is the 'rose'?

CHIVERS (*at a loss, but ready to meet him on anything; staring through a dimness that presently glimmers*) The rose, sir? (*He turns to the open door of the old garden and the shining day; they suggest to him the application of the question*) Rather a kind of brilliant—   750

YULE (*interested, struck*) Oh, a 'brilliant'—°

CHIVERS (*innocent, earnest*) Old-fashioned *red*, just tending a little to purple. (*Smiles as with the pride of thus being able to testify: though his smile the next instant drops*) It's the only one *left*, on the old west wall.   755

YULE (*much amused, but in all kindness*) My dear man, I'm not alluding to the sole ornament of the garden, but to the young lady at present in the morning-room. Do you happen to have noticed if she's *pretty*?

CHIVERS (*who stands queerly rueful*) Laws, sir! It's a matter I mostly *do* notice. (*Then deeply, mildly discreet*) But wouldn't it rather be, sir, on such an occasion as this, sir, a matter—like—of *taste*?   760

YULE (*just a little wondering; but with sympathy*) You regard the occasion as—extraordinary?

CHIVERS (*with his highest emphasis*) A great one for *me*, all round, sir. (*Longingly*) If there's anything I can *do* for you, sir—   765

YULE (*as if pleased with him*) You can advise me in the sense I mention: as to your impression of the value—I speak only of the *value*!—of the entertainment about to be offered me.

CHIVERS (*staring again, bewildered*) Oh, I've laid it all out, quite regular!   770

YULE (*freshly amused*) I'm not speaking of your tea-table, which I'm sure is charming!

CHIVERS (*catching on*) I see, of the young lady herself, sir. (*Then, as desirous to satisfy, but ruefully deliberating and even with the hint of scratching his old head*) Well, sir—   775

YULE (*taking pity on him and not really pressing him; yet so charmed with his touching old type that he likes to draw him out*) I know, as you

say, that young ladies are a matter of taste, but that's why I appeal
with such confidence to yours.   780

CHIVERS (*facing then, with all his gentleness, his responsibility*) Well, sir,
mine was always a sort of fancy for something more merry-like.

YULE She isn't merry-like then, poor Miss Prodmore? Ah, if you
come to that, neither am I! (*He throws up the subject, however, without further pressure; he drops for the present Miss Prodmore*) But it   785
doesn't signify. (*He's really more interested in Chivers himself*) What
are *you*, my dear man?

CHIVERS (*as if he really has to think a bit*) Well, sir, I'm not quite *that*.
(*Appealing to his friend's indulgence*) Whatever in the world has there
been to *make* me?   790

YULE (*washing his hands of it*) I mean to whom do you beautifully
belong?

CHIVERS (*who has really to think it over*) If you could only just *tell* me,
sir! I seem quite to waste *away* —for someone to take an *order* of.

YULE (*looking at him in compassion*) Who pays your *wages*?   795

CHIVERS (*very simply*) No one at all, sir.

YULE (*taking from his waistcoat pocket a gold coin, which he places with a
little sharp click on a table near at hand*) Then there's a *sovereign*.
(*Then having turned resignedly away*) And I haven't *many*!

CHIVERS (*leaving the money on the table and only watching his friend*)   800
Ah then, shouldn't it stay in the *family*?

YULE (*wheeling round, struck by the figure he makes in this offer; visibly
touched and bridging a long transition with a single tone*) I think it *does*,
old boy.

CHIVERS (*all his appreciative eyes on him now*) I've served your house,   805
sir.

YULE How long?

CHIVERS All my *life*.

YULE (*after they have stood a bit face to face; the younger man making
things out*) Then I won't give *you* up!   810

CHIVERS Indeed, sir, I hope you won't give up *anything*!

YULE (*taking up his hat*) It remains to be *seen*. (*He looks over the place
again; his eyes wander to the open door*) Is that the *garden*?

CHIVERS It *was*! (*With a sigh like the creak of the wheel of time*) Shall I
show you how it *used* to be?   815

YULE (*taking an instant for what he sees of it from where he stands*) It's
just as it *is*, alas, that I happen to require it! (*Then at garden door*)
Don't *come*. I want to *think*.

    Exit Captain Clement Yule to garden

CHIVERS (*left alone, takes up the coin that has remained on the table and, after a look sufficient fully to identify and appreciate it, puts it in his pocket*) What does he want, poor dear, to 'think' about? 820
> *His speculation, however, is checked by the high, clear vocal sound that heralds the appearance at the top of the stairs of the wonderful figure of the visiting lady; who, having taken possession of the place above, prepares, with the high pitch of her interest, gaily to descend. Enter Mrs Gracedew from the gallery, speaking as she comes down*

MRS GRACEDEW (*on the stairs*) Housekeeper! Butler! Old family servant!

CHIVERS (*in quick remembrance, half dismayed, half dazzled, of a duty neglected*) Oh, I should have told him of *her*! 825

MRS GRACEDEW (*with beautiful laughter and rustling garments; as if approaching amid an escort and with music*) Did you think I had got snapped down in an old box like that poor girl—what's-her-name? the one who was poking round *too*—in the celebrated poem?° (*Her manner to him all on the basis of a relation, the frankest and easiest,* 830 *already formed by what has happened between them before he gave her the range*)° You dear, delightful man, why didn't you *tell* me?

CHIVERS (*under the charm again, but vague*) 'Tell' you, mum—

MRS GRACEDEW (*prompt, happy*) That you're so perfectly—perfect! (*As if she had almost been swindled*) You're ever so much better than 835 anyone has ever said. Why, in the name of all that's lovely has nobody ever said *anything*—as nobody for that matter, with all the fun there is, *does* seem ever to say anything! (*Then, as to tell him all about the place he seems, poor dear, really to understand so little*) You're everything in the world you *ought* to be and not the shade of 840 anything you *oughtn't*!

CHIVERS (*fluttered, flattered, bewildered*) Well, mum, I try!

MRS GRACEDEW (*downright*) Oh no you don't, that's *just* your *charm*. (*She explains with her free benevolence*) *I* try—I have to; but you do *nothing*. Here you simply *are*. You can't help it. 845

CHIVERS (*overwhelmed*) Me, mum?

MRS GRACEDEW (*who has been speaking of the house itself, applies her delight to his image as well*) Yes, you too, you positive old *picture*. (*Perfectly familiar in her appreciation*) I've seen the old masters, but you're the old master! 'The good and faithful *servant*'—Rembrandt 850 van *Rhyn*'.° With three Baedeker° stars. *That's* what you are. (*His humility doesn't check her*) The house is a vision of beauty and *you're* just worthy of the house, I can't say *more* for you!

CHIVERS (*candidly helpless*) I find it a bit of a strain, mum, to keep up, fairly to call it, with what you *do* say.   855

MRS GRACEDEW (*quite happily understanding*) That's quite what everyone *finds* it! Yet I haven't come here to suffer in *silence*, you know, to suffer, I mean, from envy, or rage, or despair. (*Full of movement and of sincerity of interest, observing, almost measuring, everything in the place, she takes notes, while she gossips, jots down signs* 860 *for her own use in a small book of memoranda that she carries*) You almost kill me; however, I take some killing! (*Then again, to explain herself to his perpetual amaze*) I mean you're so fatally *right* and so deadly *complete*, that if I wasn't an angel I could scarcely *bear* it; with every fascinating feature I had already heard of and thought I 865 was *prepared* for, and ever so many others that, strange to say, I *hadn't* and *wasn't*, and that you just spring right *at* me like a series of things going off; a sort of what-do-you-call-it, eh? A royal *salute*, a hundred *guns*!°

CHIVERS (*with a dim vision of what she means*) I saw as soon as you 870 arrived, mum, that you were looking for more things than ever *I* heerd tell of!

MRS GRACEDEW Oh, I had got you by *heart*, from books, prints, photographs; I had you in my pocket when I came; so, you see, as soon as you were so good as to give me my head and let me loose, I 875 knew my way *about*. You're all here, every inch of you, and now at last (*with decision*) I can do what I *want*!

CHIVERS (*in dim apprehension*) And pray, mum, what might *that* be?

MRS GRACEDEW Why, take you right *back* with me, to Missoura Top. 880

CHIVERS (*trying, heroically to focus this fate*) Do I understand, mum, that you require to take *me*?

MRS GRACEDEW (*leaping, delighted at the idea*) Do you mean to say you'd *come*, as the old family servant? Then *do*, you nice real thing; it's just what I'm dying for; an old family servant! You're somebody 885 else's, yes, but everything over here is somebody else's, and I want, too, a second-hand one, in good order; all ready *made*, as *you* are, but not too much done up. You're the best I've struck yet, and I wish I could have you *packed*—put up in paper and *bran*°—as I shall have my old *pot* there. (*She whisks about, remembering, recover-* 890 *ing, eager*) Don't let me *forget* my precious pot! (*Excited, with quick transitions, she appeals all sociably to the old man, who shuffles up sympathetically to where, out of harm, the valuable piece she has ori-ginally brought in with her as a trophy, has been placed, to await her*

departure, on a table) Don't you just love old *crockery*? That's   895
awfully sweet old *Chelsea.*°

CHIVERS (*who has taken the pot up with tenderness, though, in his agitated state, not with all the caution usually at his command and, struck
with something, turns the precious piece round*) Where is it I've known
this *very* bit, though not to say, as *you* do, by name? (*Then as it*   900
suddenly comes to him) In the pew-opener's° front *parlour*!

MRS GRACEDEW No, in the pew-opener's best *bedroom*: on the old
chest of drawers, you know, with those ducks of brass *handles*. I've
got the handles too; I mean the whole *thing*; and the brass fender (*as
she looks at her notes*) and the fire-irons and the sweet blue pig off   905
the chimney and the chair her grand-mother *died* in. (*Then as with
real regret*) Not in the *fly*; it's such a bore they have to be *sent*!

CHIVERS (*with the pot still in his hands, gaping at the list of acquisitions,
but approving her prudence as well*) You did right to take this out,
mum, when the fly went round to the stables. Them flymen do be   910
cruel rash with anything that's *delicate*. (*About to return the vessel to
its safe niche, he himself has, however, betrayed by his trembling zeal, a
dreadful little disaster; the matter of a few seconds, a false movement, a
stumble, a knock, a gasp, a shriek, then an utter little crash. He almost
shouts with despair*) Mercy *on* us, mum. I've brought shame on my   915
old grey *hairs*!

MRS GRACEDEW (*who has simultaneously shrieked, but has quickly
recovered herself, struck more than with anything else by the beauty of
Chivers's compunction*) The way you *take* it it's too sweet, you're too
quaint really to *live*! (*She keeps it up to cheer him*) The way you *said*   920
that, now; it's just the very *type*!° That's all I *want* of you now; to *be*
the very type. It's what you *are*, you poor dear thing, for you can't
help it; and it's what everything and everyone *else* are, over here: so
that you had just better all make up your minds to it and not try to
shirk it. There was a type in the *train* with me, the 'awfully nice girl'   925
of all the English novels, the 'simple maiden in her flower'° of—
who is it? your great *poet*. *She* couldn't help it either; in fact I
wouldn't have *let* her! (*With which, starting, she remembers*) By the
way, she was coming right *here*. Has she come?

CHIVERS (*who has picked up in dire silence the fragments of the pot, to*   930
*place them carefully elsewhere, makes no answer till he has returned
from these dumb rites of burial*) Miss Prodmore is here, mum. She's
having her tea.

MRS GRACEDEW (*amused, recognising*) Yes, that's exactly *it*; they're
always having their tea!   935

CHIVERS With Mr Prodmore, in the morning-room. (*Then to be exact*)
Captain Yule has not yet joined them.

MRS GRACEDEW (*vague*) Captain Yule?

CHIVERS The new master, who's in the garden. He's also just arrived.

MRS GRACEDEW (*still vague*) Oh? (*Then as if noting it, though not as if*   940
it much matters) She didn't tell me about *him*.

CHIVERS Well, mum, it's a strange sort of *thing* to tell. He had
never—like, mum—so much as *seen* the place.

MRS GRACEDEW (*interested, but not amazed*) Before today—*so*? His
very *own*? (*Then as for the oddity of it*) Well, I hope he *likes* it!   945

CHIVERS (*moved to boldness*) I haven't seen many, mum, that like it as
much as *you*.

MRS GRACEDEW Oh! (*She makes a motion of the head that means more
than she can say and throws up her arms half in a sort of embrace, half
in a sort of despair at privation*) I should like it still better if it were   950
my very own!

CHIVERS Well, mum, if it wasn't against my duty I could wish indeed
it *were*! (*Then conscientiously*) The *Captain*, mum, is the lawful heir.

MRS GRACEDEW (*struck, as if this charms her*) That's another of your
lovely old things; I adore your lawful heirs! (*Then as with growing*   955
interest) He has come to take possession?

CHIVERS (*with importance*) He's a-taking° of it now.

MRS GRACEDEW (*her interest immediately clinched*) What does he do
and how does he do it? Can't I *see*? (*Then as he looks blank*) There's
no grand fuss—?   960

CHIVERS (*a bit reproving*) I scarce think him, mum, the gentleman to
make any about *anything*!

MRS GRACEDEW (*thinking; a little disappointed, then resigned*) Well,
perhaps I like them better when they *don't*! (*Then always all familiar*) I daresay you think *I* fuss. For I, you see, (*as she turns about*   965
again and lovingly sighs) have also taken *possession*!

CHIVERS (*really rising to her with a smile*) It was you, mum, took it *first*!

MRS GRACEDEW (*sadly shaking her head*) Ah, but for a poor little *hour*!
He's for *life*.

CHIVERS (*discreetly granting that*) For *mine*, mum, I do at least *hope*!   970

MRS GRACEDEW (*who makes again the circuit of the hall and picks up
without interest, as a sign of the intention of going, some small object—
a rolled up pair of gloves, say—that she has deposited on her first
arrival in some place where the others won't have seen it; or even simply
resumes possession of the note-book she has within a few moments put   975
down, sticking the pencil back into its sheath; anything, in short, that*

will strike in a small way the note of departure) I shall *think* of you, you know, here *together*. (*She looks vaguely about as for anything else; then abruptly, with her eyes on him quite tenderly*) Do you suppose he'll be *kind* to you? 980

CHIVERS (*his hand in his trousers-pocket, turning over his sovereign*) He has *already* been, mum.

MRS GRACEDEW (*with emphasis*) Then be sure to be so to *him*! (*After which, as the house-bell sounds*) Is that his bell?

CHIVERS (*wondering*) I must see *whose*! 985

> *He hurries up to back. Exit Chivers, disappearing in the*
> *ante-room of the approach from the park*

MRS GRACEDEW (*alone a moment, with her air in which happy possession is so oddly and charmingly mixed with desperate surrender and with a last look round as for something she may possibly have missed; a look that carries her eyes straight to some small object—a plaque suspended on one of the walls, say—and on which she pounces with her cry of* 990 *recognition*) Why, bless me if it ain't *Limoges*!° (*She detaches it, to admire it; she has it in her hands a minute to take it in; then, with a tragi-comic sigh and a violent effort, she hooks it up again, dusting off her fingers as she turns away in renouncement*) I wish awfully I were a *bad* woman. (*Quite sincerely*) Then, if I were the right sort, I'd take 995 it and *run*! (*She stands an instant, thinking of it hard, she turns again for another look at it from where she is; then with a wail of protest*) What a place for *Limoges*! (*With the thought she goes straight back to it, unhooks it afresh and, looking at it with renewed intelligence, comes down with it in her hands. Startled, however, while she thus holds it, by* 1000 *a sound up at left, she whisks about to become aware of the gentleman who has appeared in the doorway from the garden and has been arrested there at sight of her. But she has all her familiar presence of mind; catches straight on, all gaily, to his identity*) Oh, Captain Yule, I'm delighted to meet you! It's such a comfort to ask you if I *may*! 1005

> *Enter Captain Clement Yule from the garden*

YULE (*to whom this has been said as with the whole compass of the stage between them; coming down, surprised, but taking her in and ready for anything in the way of vague courtesy*) If you 'may', madam—

MRS GRACEDEW Why, just *be* here, don't you know, and poke round. (*The plaque in her hands and not now embarrassed by it, she presents* 1010 *such a course as almost vulgarly natural*) Don't tell me I *can't* now, because I already *have*: I've been upstairs and downstairs and in my lady's chamber!°—I'm not even sure I haven't been in my *lord's*! I got round your lovely *servant*; if you don't look out I'll *grab* him!

223

(*Then as if fairly provoked to the last familiarity by some charm in the* 1015
very stare with which he meets her amazing serenity) If you don't look
out, you know, I'll grab everything! (*She gives fair notice, she plays
with his frank stupefaction*) That's what I came *over* for, (*she explains*)
just to lay your country *waste.* Your house (*she explains further*) is a
wild old dream; and besides, (*dropping, oddly and quaintly, into real* 1020
responsible judgment) you've got some quite good things. Oh yes, you
have; a number; don't coyly pretend you haven't! (*Her familiarity,
her equality, her everything take these flying leaps and alight before
him, as it were, without turning a hair*) Don't you *know* you have? Just
look at *that*! (*She thrusts her plaque before him, but he takes and holds* 1025
*it so blankly, with an attention so merely engaged and dazed by herself,
that she breaks out as in pity for his ignorance of his values*) Don't you
know *anything*? Why it's *Limoges*!

YULE (*who can only laugh out his mystification*) It seems *absurd*, but I'm
not in the least acquainted with my *house*; I've never happened to 1030
see it.

MRS GRACEDEW (*upon him like a flash, she seizes his arm*) Then do let
me *show* it to you!

YULE (*able to say nothing else*) I shall be *delighted*!
    *But he has spoken also as if really wanting nothing better; so that
    he has a change of tone on seeing Chivers return breathless from
    his answering of the bell at back. Enter Chivers from ante-room*
Who in the world's there? 1035

CHIVERS (*coming down, full of it*) A party!

YULE (*just disconcerted*) A 'party'?

CHIVERS (*confessing to the worst*) Over from Gossage, to see the
house.

MRS GRACEDEW (*for whom this 'worst' is quite good enough and who* 1040
blazes up as at a spark) Oh, let *me* show it! (*Then bethinking herself,
remembering kindly and ruefully for Chivers*) Dear me, I forgot; you
get the tips! (*Then with a better light*) But I'll get them too—see?—
and simply hand them *over*! (*And she appeals to Yule on it*) Perhaps
they'll be bigger, for *me*! 1045

YULE (*all amused and interested now*) I should think they'd be enormous, for *you*! (*Only, with more concentration*) But I *should* like—I
should like extremely, you know—to go over with you *alone*.

MRS GRACEDEW (*struck, smiling at him sweetly*) Just you and me?

YULE (*falling absolutely in*) Just you and me, as you *did*, you know, 1050
kindly propose.

MRS GRACEDEW (*standing reminded, but, as on second thoughts, revising,*

224

even pleading, a little, and having her first inconsequence) That must
be for *after* —

YULE (*urgent*) Ah, but not too *late*. (*He looks at his watch*) I go back   1055
tonight.

CHIVERS (*with a quaver of disappointment and protest*) Law-a-*mercy*,
sir!

MRS GRACEDEW (*struck by this note, touched by it and addressing herself
straight to the old man, while Yule, at sound of her question, turns*   1060
away) You want to *keep* him? (*But before Chivers can answer she takes
in something, as from Yule's motion and presented back, that determines
her*) Then I'll *help* you, for the more we go over the *better!*°

CHIVERS (*relieved, ravished and so far forgetting himself, while the Captain still doesn't see, as to put out his hand all gratefully, which Mrs*   1065
*Gracedew meets with a small quick amused shake of it that is equivalent
to a vow*) Shall I show them straight *in*, sir?

YULE (*responsively and gaily enough, but still a little off and without
looking at him*) By all means, if there's *money* in it!

    Exit Chivers to ante-room

MRS GRACEDEW (*who, left with Yule, has suddenly bethought herself*)   1070
Oh, and I promised to show it to Miss Prodmore! (*Apparently all
happy in this thought, she appeals on the spot to the young man*) Will
you kindly *call* her?

YULE (*instantly cold; blank*) 'Call' her? Dear Lady,° I don't *know* her!

MRS GRACEDEW (*smiling but decided*) You *must* then; she's wonderful!   1075
(*He answers with a sign of impatience, which, zealous for the girl, she
doesn't take up because aware the next instant of Cora's having
appeared in doorway to right*) See? She's charming!

    *Enter Cora Prodmore from the tea-room; pausing but for a glare
    of recognition, then hurrying across, under Yule's almost equally
    scared eyes, to seek her friend's protection. This protection Mrs
    Gracedew promptly and genially gives, at once addressing her*

Miss Prodmore, let me present Captain Yule. (*She bridges the great
gulf with her quick, free span*) Captain Yule, Miss Prodmore, Miss   1080
Prodmore, Captain Yule.

    Enter Mr Prodmore from tea-room

CORA (*at sight of her father, clutching at what seems her best resource and
emulating as by instant contagion Mrs Gracedew's form*) Papa, let me
'present' you to Mrs Gracedew, Mrs Gracedew, Mr Prodmore, Mr
Prodmore, Mrs Gracedew.   1085

MRS GRACEDEW (*with a free salute, taking in Mr Prodmore as she
has taken everything else, and distinctly repeating his name*) Mr

Prodmore. So happy to meet your daughter's *father*. Your daughter's so perfect a *specimen*.

PRODMORE (*who has come down, in his importance, and has been at first* 1090
left by this ceremony very much at sea, suddenly, like a practical man,
feels in it something to his interest) So perfect a specimen, *yes*! (*With*
which he radiates toward Yule as if to pass it on)

MRS GRACEDEW (*as unconscious of this manœuvre and only lost in*
appreciation of Cora, whom she covers with a gaze that practically 1095
keeps her there fixed and exposed, quite on exhibition) So fresh, so
quaint, so absolutely the real *thing*!

PRODMORE (*testifying in his degree also to her influence by the way he*
irresistibly takes it from her as to his advantage for an effect on Yule)
So fresh, so quaint, so absolutely the real *thing*! 1100

> *Its action on Yule is to throw him off to his distance, and the*
> *whole space of the stage is now between him and Mrs Gracedew,*
> *with what next takes place occupying the large interval. Enter*
> *Chivers from the ante-room, leading his train, accompanied and*
> *half surrounded, that is, by the party visiting the house; simple*
> *sight-seers of the half-holiday order, plain provincial folk who*
> *are, on the spot, at sight of the ladies and gentlemen, rather*
> *awestruck. The old man's effort, is to keep them well together,*
> *and as he gets his squad to centre Mrs Gracedew, all interest, all*
> *wonder for his discharge of his function, is nearest them*

CHIVERS (*mechanical, perfunctory, as with the habit of long years he*
shows the place off) This, ladies and gentlemen, is perhaps the most
important feature, the grand old 'istoric baronial '*all*. Being, from
all accounts, the most ancient portion of the *edifice*, it was erected in
the very earliest *ages*. Some do say (*detached, dispassionate*) in the 1105
course of the *fifteenth* century.

MRS GRACEDEW (*all sympathetic attention, but uncontrolledly breaking*
in) I say in the course of the *fourteenth*, my dear, you're robbing us
of a hundred years!

CHIVERS (*yielding without a struggle*) I do seem, in them dark old cen- 1110
turies, sometimes to *trip* a little. (*Rather pathetically put out, while his*
audience, pressing close, stand further expectant, though visibly more
interested in the beautiful lady than in anything else, and he yet
endeavors to address the group with a dignity undiminished) The Gothic
roof° is much *admired*, but the west gallery a modern *addition*. 1115

MRS GRACEDEW (*amused, horrified, protesting*) What in the name of
Methuselah° do you call 'modern'? (*Then irresistibly, with an*
immediate benignant authority, she can't help making it right) It was

here at the visit of James the *First*, in 1611,° and is supposed to
have served, in the charming detail of its ornament, as a pattern for   1120
several constructed in his reign. The great fireplace (*directing their
unanimous attention to it*) *is*, however, fourteenth century.°

CHIVERS (*all gratefully takes it from her;° though as after waiting for her
to proceed, not wishing to lay on her the whole of the burden. His
companions stand gaping at her while she genially smiles back; where-   1125
upon he again takes up his tale; their heads all moving toward each
thing he notes*) The tapestry on the left *Italian*, the elegant wood-
work *Flemish*.

MRS GRACEDEW (*who really can't conscientiously let it pass, but who
speaks with the sweetest charity*) Pardon me if I just put that *right*.   1130
The elegant *wood-work* Italian, the tapestry on the *left* Flemish.
(*She puts it to him before them all; the fun of it, of having her say
about the beautiful place, drives her on; she wants in fine° to relieve
Chivers*) Do you really mind if *I* just do it? Oh, I know *how*: I can do
quite beautifully the housekeeper at Castle Gaunt.° (*As if already   1135
intimate with each visitor, she treats them all as if it's a game they must
play with her; greeting the two or three nearest, breaking down their
awe*) How d'ye do? Happy to *meet* you. Ain't it thrilling? (*Then
really to do it and as if to take them everywhere, she imitates the grand
manner of the housekeepers in castles*) Keep well *together*, please,   1140
we're not doing puss-in-the-corner.° I've my duty to *all* parties; I
can't be partial to *one*!

A VISITOR (*spokesman for his group, making bold*) How many parties,
now, can you manage?

MRS GRACEDEW (*perfectly prompt*) Two. The party up, and the party   1145
down. (*Then while poor Chivers gasps no less at her presence of mind
than at the liberty just taken with her, she kisses her hand at him for
reassurance and proceeds, in the highest spirits, with her business, pointing to one of the escutcheons in the high hall window*) This stained
glass in the windows is the *record* of the race! Observe in that centre   1150
the style of the family *arms*. (*Then carrying all eyes to another quarter
and a tall black old picture of a long-limbed worthy in white trunk-
hose°*) And observe in that portrait the style of the family *legs*! (*She
leaps from point to point; shows her friends what is best for them*)
Observe the suit of armour worn at Tewkesbury. Observe the tat-   1155
tered banner carried at Blenheim.° (*Her auditors, hanging on her
words, bob their heads wherever she points, but Yule, Prodmore and
Cora, in their way equally held, visibly have eyes but for herself alone.
She observes this on Yule's part and smiles at him in all confidence. This*

pause, this exchange of a long look between them, seems to determine in 1160
her a sort of climax; which she utters really, with her eyes on him, as if
most of all for his benefit) Observe, above all, that you're in one of
the most interesting old houses, of its *type*, in *England*; for which
the ages have been tender and the generations *wise*: letting it change
so slowly that there's always more left than *taken*; living their lives 1165
in it, but (*with charming persuasive unction*) letting *it shape* their
lives!

PRODMORE (*rising to the miraculous effect of this wonderful stranger
who, dropped for him from the skies, seems so extraordinarily to play his
game*) A most striking and suitable tribute to a real historical 1170
monument! (*All approving and encouraging and, for that matter, not
backward in gallantry*) You do, madam, bring the whole thing *out*!

VISITOR (*the one who has already with such impunity ventured, has on this
a loud renewal of boldness, but for the benefit of a near neighbour,
whom he delightedly nudges*) Doesn't she indeed, Jane, bring it *out*? 1175

MRS GRACEDEW (*with a friendly laugh catching the words in their passage*) But who in the world wants to keep it *in*? It isn't a *secret*, the
beautiful *truth*! It isn't a frightened *cat* or a political party! (*The
housekeeper, with her excited sense of the place, drops from her; the sense
asserts itself as too personal for that, and she soars again at random to* 1180
the noble spring of the roof) Just look at those lovely *lines*! (*They all
bob back their heads, all but Captain Clement Yule, who, motionless in
his place, never takes his eyes from the speaker; while several of the
'party', subdued, overwhelmed, fascinated, elbow each other with
strange sounds. She finds wherever she turns a pretext for breaking out*) 1185
Just look at the tone of that *arras*! And at the gilding of that *leather*!
And at the cutting of that *oak*! And (*throwing up her hands and
dropping her arms again—it's so universal*) the dear old flags of the
very *floor*! (*It keeps rushing over her, and the sense of having to part
with it is, all despairingly, in the passion of the tribute she renders*) To 1190
look, in this place, is to (*very big*) LOVE!

A VOICE (*from some nudging member of the group; with an artless guffaw
and probably a private pinch for one of the ladies*) I *say*, so much as
that?

THE PINCHED LADY (*excited to loud pertness*) Won't it depend on who 1195
you *look* at?

PRODMORE (*responding in the highest spirits; making his profit of the
simple joke*) It certainly does depend, Miss! (*Delightedly expanding*)
Do you hear *that*, Captain? You must 'look', for the right *effect*, at
the right *person*! 1200

MRS GRACEDEW (*as if she at least has not been looking at the wrong; while she addresses Prodmore quite as if the party isn't there or doesn't in the least matter*) I don't think Captain Yule dares. He doesn't do justice!

YULE (*while, in spite of her gay face, she falters and he waits; speaking very gravely*) To what, madam? 1205

MRS GRACEDEW (*boldly, but blandly*) Well, to the value of your *house*.

YULE (*still watching her a moment*) I like at least to hear you *express* it.

MRS GRACEDEW (*fairly impatient; as if throwing it up*) I can't 'express' it! It's too inexpressible! 1210

PRODMORE (*whom this suits down to the ground; cheeringly, soothingly, always with his patronising note*) Do what you *can* for it, madam. It would bring it quite *home*!

MRS GRACEDEW (*communing with the genius of the place and taking another try*) Well, the value's a fancy-value! 1215

PRODMORE (*triumphant, exuberant, appealing to Yule*) Exactly what I *told* you!

MRS GRACEDEW (*developing, explaining, putting it in a nutshell*) When a thing's unique, it's unique!

PRODMORE (*taking it for every bit he requires; casting it upon the echoes*) It's unique! 1220

A VISITOR (*taking it up, as with intelligent decision, for the general benefit*) It's unique!

SEVERAL VOICES (*not to be left behind*) Unique, unique!

MRS GRACEDEW (*finding herself so sustained, but giving it essentially, and with all her authority, to the lawful heir*) It's worth anything you *like*! 1225

PRODMORE (*passing it on as the very truth he has contended for*) Anything you *like*!

A VISITOR (*again, as from the effect of the pleasant discussion and the general interest*) Twenty thousand now? 1230

MRS GRACEDEW (*down on him like a shot*) I wouldn't *look* at twenty thousand!

ANOTHER PERSON (*taking courage*) *Thirty* then, as it stands?

MRS GRACEDEW (*pausing but an instant*) It would be giving it *away*! 1235

PRODMORE (*enchanted; taking and diffusing her word for it*) It would be giving it *away*!

SOME VISITORS (*led on to positive sociability*) You'd hold out for *forty*?

MRS GRACEDEW (*requiring a minute to answer, while the whole place, in all the converging pairs of eyes attached to her, seems to hang on her words; which she addresses, however, specifically and responsibly to* 1240

Yule) Fifty thousand, Captain Yule, is what I *think* I should propose. (*And she accepts serenely the general impression made by this high
figure*)

PRODMORE AND THE PARTY (*collectively taking it up; all of course*   1245
with high relish and sympathy) Fifty thousand! Fifty thousand!

PRODMORE (*speaks alone; reacting, with bright, assured reference to
Yule, into a pledge, thus offered Mrs Gracedew, that no business transaction is dreamt of*) You talk of 'proposing', but he'll never part with
the dear old *home*!   1250

MRS GRACEDEW (*taking it from him as all she is in a position to want;
yet as if, alas, it also dreadfully sounds for her the note of final rupture,
which she still instinctively postpones*) Then I'll go over it again while
I've the *chance*. (*And to this end she immediately remembers again the
housekeeper at Castle Gaunt; marshalling, with a grand sweep, the*   1255
compact party) We now pass to the Grand Staircase.°

YULE (*whose concentrated motionless attention during all the preceding
finds a significant climax in the clear high tone in which he now for the
first time speaks*) Please let them pass *without* you.

MRS GRACEDEW (*wondering but interested and, since he asks it, immedi-*   1260
ately, after another look at him, throwing up her game) Let them pass,
let them pass!

YULE Many thanks. (*Then to Chivers, in nervous impatience and with a
free, comprehensive, imperative gesture*) For God's sake *remove* them!

CHIVERS (*at once fluttering forward and taking up Mrs Gracedew's*   1265
words) We now pass to the Grand Staircase.

> They all pass, the party led by Chivers. They huddle to the
> staircase, mounting it after him with their various signs and
> demonstrations, a general show of rising interest. Exeunt
> Chivers and party

YULE (*as soon as Chivers has complied, to Mrs Gracedew*) I should like
to *speak* to you.

MRS GRACEDEW Here?

YULE (*seeing movement of Cora; disconcerted, still more impatient*)   1270
Anywhere!

CORA (*who, visibly, anxiously, all through, has been watching her chance,
and with whose design Yule's proposal seems to interfere; getting round
to her friend with intensity*) Mrs Gracedew, *I* should like to speak to
you!   1275

PRODMORE (*watching and down on her straight while Yule, put off by
the girl's pounce, turns sharply away, goes up*) After Captain Yule, my
dear! (*He thus gives the measure of his naturally wanting only to*

promote those moments of conference for Yule with the wondrous lady which, through her enthusiasm for the place, may work to his own 1280 *advantage. He waves Cora on to the staircase as if her natural and very convenient place is in the tour of inspection under Chivers)* Avail yourself now of the chance to see the *house!*

CORA (*delaying, resisting in spite of him, and managing it through her failure to draw her friend at once from an interesting attention to the* 1285 *restless discomposed manner of Yule's retreat, his keeping his distance, as it were, till the field is cleared of the Prodmores. He reaches again the door of the garden, where Mrs Gracedew's eyes keep him company enough to leave the girl free for the instant to plead with her father unnoticed)* She'll *help* me, I think, Papa! 1290

PRODMORE (*with all cheerfulness, without roughness now; only as knowing better still than Cora what is good for them*) That's exactly what strikes me, love, but *I'll* help you too! (*He gives her, with gay resolution, towards the stairs, a push proportioned both to his authority and to her quantity; and she has to mount a little, climbing in the wake of* 1295 *the party, while he himself, Yule being, with his back always turned, more and more detached, gets now at Mrs Gracedew, making his point with her, in bright confidence, on the basis of her recent opinions*) Just pile it *on!*

MRS GRACEDEW (*her attention returning; though her eyes are still on* 1300 *Yule, whose attitude while he gazes from his doorway into the grey old court or whatever seems somehow to admonish her*) He isn't in *love?* (*Then as Prodmore, rather wincing, demurs*) I mean with the *house.*

PRODMORE (*clearer*) Not half *enough.* (*Urgent*) Bring him *round.*

MRS GRACEDEW (*her impression of the young man's worried air combining with this established fact to determine her*) Very well, I'll *bring* him. 1305

CORA (*from the stairs, renewing her appeal, sending across a loud, distressful quaver*) Mrs Gracedew, won't you *see* me?

MRS GRACEDEW (*all kind response now, but looking at her watch, while the note of the girl's voice, acting on Yule's condition, has made him,* 1310 *clapping his hand to the back of his head, in expressive despair, slip straight out of the doorway and pass from sight*) In ten minutes!

PRODMORE (*bland and assured, in fact quite gallant; consulting his own watch*) You could put him through in *five,* but I'll allow you twenty! (*Then with a flourish to Cora from where he stands*) There! 1315

> *Cora has but time to snatch from her friend a mute understanding, a compact Mrs Gracedew seals by blowing over at her a kiss of radiant but vague comfort; for her father is already upon her to sweep her to the region above. Exeunt*

*Cora Prodmore and Mr Prodmore by the staircase; after which
only Mrs Gracedew sees that Yule has vanished and that she is
alone. She has at this an uncertainty, looks after him° as with
a question. She stands hesitating as whether to follow him, then
moves as deciding to do so. But she thinks better of this and comes
down again; still, however, to meet afresh her doubt; all with
an effect charmingly droll. Quickly, at last, as he still doesn't
reappear, she goes straight toward garden, the Curtain falling
while she moves*

2.

*Still the old hall, a few moments later, with Captain Clement
Yule, at rise of the Curtain, standing again in doorway of
garden; but now looking down at Mrs Gracedew, who is seated to
right. Everything to conduce during these first minutes to the
effect of the extreme brevity of the little interval; and of its
having presumably, inferentially, happened that, before the
break, she has simply gone up to within view of the outer region,
the old grey court or garden, or whatever, and seen there that,
having taken his restless turn, with time for the Prodmores to get
off, he is on his way back; on which, again, with the instinct of
not appearing to pursue him, she has quickly come down again
and dropped into a chair, so that he shall find her there, and even
in a manner awaiting him. Already, however, with his rather
troubled, puzzled, drawn-out return, she has been there moments
enough to have lost herself on her own side, in sudden intense and
interesting thought; which is why they are thus before us, in
silence, long enough for us to take them well in: she, unconscious
for the minute and with her eyes fixed on a point in the floor, and
he watching her first from the doorway and then as he slowly
comes nearer*

YULE (*grave and with all courtesy, but as if he is really a good deal
puzzled*) How do you come to know so much about my house?

MRS GRACEDEW (*startled at first, but just smiling as her attention comes
back*) How do *you* come to know so little?

YULE (*very gently*) Of course it must strike you as strange. It's not my   5
fault, madam. (*Then as if really wondering quite how to put it*) A
particular complication of odd—and rather unhappy!—things has
kept me, till this hour, from coming *within a mile* of it.

MRS GRACEDEW (*showing by her charmed but always gay response that
this is exactly the note that takes her; while she tenderly glows at him,*   10
*across the space, as it were, for his being so prompt an embodiment of it,
and for his looking like such an interesting one*) Do you know I'm
really *glad* to hear you say that? It may sound 'sort of' selfish, but it
is so sweet to find 'complications'—things that are, as you call
them, odd and unhappy!   15

YULE (*a bit amused at this view of it and desiring to say no more, yet not less, than he means; with the general sense of all he does mean also rather rising before him*) All I mean is, well, that it *has* been strange.

MRS GRACEDEW Oh, don't *apologise*, whatever you do: I shouldn't forgive you if it *hadn't* been! (*Then ever so frankly and kindly*) I   20
like its being the first time. I mean of your coming. (*Then with curiosity*)° Haven't you ever *wanted* to come?

YULE (*still amused, for all his preoccupation*) It was no use my 'wanting'. I simply *couldn't*.

MRS GRACEDEW (*with a really quickened little yearning of interest*)   25
Why, you poor *thing*! (*Then after considering him a little in this melancholy light*) Well, now that you *have* come, I hope at least you'll *stay*. (*And as if struck with his not quite looking so*) Do, for goodness' sake, make yourself comfortable. Don't of all things in the world (*utterly repudiating the thought*) mind *me*!   30

YULE (*with a motion as for the oddity of it and the sadness going a little out of his smile*) That's exactly what I wanted to say to *you*! Don't mind *me*!

MRS GRACEDEW (*while something in the tone of this amuses her too*) Well, if you *had* been haughty I shouldn't have been quite *crushed*—should I?   35

YULE (*the last remnant of his gravity now, for the time, completely yielding*) Ah, I'm *never* 'haughty'. Never, never!

MRS GRACEDEW (*cheerfully*) Fortunately then, as I'm never crushed! (*Then as it strikes her while she gently studies him*) I guess I'm not   40
really so *crushable* as you.

YULE (*with a rather rueful, sceptical shrug*) Aren't we really all 'crushable'—by the right thing?

MRS GRACEDEW (*considering it a little*) Don't you mean rather by the wrong?   45

YULE (*while he begins to get a little more accustomed to her being so extraordinary*) Are you sure we in every case know them apart?

MRS GRACEDEW (*weighing the responsibility, as if the question might be interesting, yet easily concluding*) I always do. Don't you?   50

YULE (*serious*) Not quite every time!

MRS GRACEDEW (*prompt*) Oh, I don't think, thank goodness, we've positively 'every time' to distinguish!

YULE (*debating it*) Yet we must always *act*.

MRS GRACEDEW (*accepting it as far as it goes*) Whether we 'must' or   55
not, I fear I always *do*! (*Then more gravely and as in familiar apology*) You'll certainly think I've taken a line today!°

YULE Do you mean that of mistress of this house? (*Then prompt and not in the least attenuating*) Yes, you do seem in good possession.

MRS GRACEDEW (*with no pretence of denying it and only thinking of him*) *You* don't seem in *any*, good or *bad*! (*Then as to encourage him*) You don't comfortably *look* it, I mean. You don't look (*she develops it frankly, seriously*) as I *want* you to.

YULE (*as if it's when she's most serious that she's funniest; but also as if it's when she's funniest that she's most charming*) How do you 'want' me to look?

MRS GRACEDEW (*as, while he looks at her, trying to make up her mind yet not altogether succeeding*) When you look at *me* you're all *right*. (*Then candidly, but as if she regrets it*) But you can't always be looking at *me*. (*Casting about as to test him better*) Look at that chimney-piece.

YULE (*after doing his best for it*) Well?

MRS GRACEDEW (*surprised*) You mean to say it isn't *lovely*?

YULE (*returning to it without passion; then throwing up his arms as incompetent*) I'm sure I don't *know*. (*As more or less putting himself in her hands*) I don't mean to say *anything*! I'm a rank *outsider*.

MRS GRACEDEW (*quick and as if it's more than she could have hoped*) Then you must let me put you up!°

YULE (*amused, as drawing her*) Up to what?

MRS GRACEDEW (*absolute*) Up to everything! (*Then as noticing the first thing that comes to her to please him*) You were smoking when you first came in. Where's your cigarette?

YULE (*willingly producing another*) I thought perhaps I mightn't *here*.

MRS GRACEDEW (*absolute again*) You may everywhere.

YULE (*bending his head gratefully to the information*) Everywhere.

MRS GRACEDEW (*diverted at° his docility and at their relation generally*) It's a rule of the house!

YULE (*quite meeting her on it*) What delightful rules!

MRS GRACEDEW How could such a house have any others? (*Then as, for the house, all 'there' again*) I *may* go up just once more, mayn't I, to the long gallery?

YULE (*naturally vague*) The 'long gallery'?

MRS GRACEDEW (*taking herself up*) Ah, I forgot you've never *seen* it. Why, it's the principal thing *about* you! (*Then, full on the spot, of the pride of showing it*)° Come right *up*!

YULE (*whom it doesn't suit to move and who has already, in sign of this, half seated himself on the angle of a smooth old table, only looking at her a moment and smoking*) There's the party 'up'.

MRS GRACEDEW (*recognising*) So *we* must be the party down? (*Accommodating*) Well, you must give me a *chance*. That gallery's   100
the great thing about you and the principal one I came *over* for.

YULE (*as if she's strangest of all when she, in her astounding serenity, explains*) Where in the name of goodness did you come over from?

MRS GRACEDEW (*immediate*) Missoura Top, where I'm building— (*then with consummate serenity*) just in this style. (*Imperturbable*) I   105
came for plans and ideas. I felt I must look right *at* you.

YULE (*wondering*) But what did you know *about* us?

MRS GRACEDEW (*keeping it a moment with a smile as if it's too good to give him all at once*) Everything!

YULE (*his wonder increased*) At 'Missoura Top'?   110

MRS GRACEDEW Why not? It's a growing place; forty thousand the last census; with nineteen schools. So you see we know things.

YULE (*staring; between diversion and dismay*) Bless us, you've been to 'nineteen'?

MRS GRACEDEW (*promptly, but as if having quickly and candidly*   115
reckoned) Well, I guess I've been to nine. And I *teach* in six.

YULE (*his amused curiosity growing*) And what do you teach?

MRS GRACEDEW (*smiling, serene*) I teach Taste.

YULE (*wondering, echoing; as finding it a little vague for a course by itself*) As a 'subject'?   120

MRS GRACEDEW (*cheerfully, definite*) Yes, just Taste. (*Amused even a little at herself*) I'm 'death' on Taste! But of course before I taught it I had to *get* it. So it was I got your picture.

YULE (*again startled*) Mine?

MRS GRACEDEW (*signing with her head as to all the other aspects and*   125
always amused at the way he receives the information in which he appears so deficient) A water-colour I chanced on in Boston.

YULE (*with the same wonder*) In Boston?

MRS GRACEDEW (*as if he is really too droll*) Haven't you heard of Boston either?   130

YULE (*considering*) Yes, but what has Boston heard of *me*?

MRS GRACEDEW It wasn't 'you', unfortunately, it was your divine South Front. The drawing struck me so that I got you *up*°—in the books.

YULE (*as if still, however absurdly, but half making it out, and as if even just suspecting her absolute literal veracity*) Are we in the books?   135

MRS GRACEDEW (*who almost, for his blankness, gives him up*) Did you never happen to *hear* of it? (*Then, from the impression of his face, for the real interest of his blankness*) Where in the name of the 'simple life' have *you* come over from?

YULE (*very definitely and gently, but as if scarce expecting her to follow*)   140
The East End of London.°

MRS GRACEDEW (*as having followed perfectly, but as not quite satisfied*)
What were you *doing* there?

YULE (*a little over-consciously, but very simply*) Working, you see.
When I left the army, which was much too slow unless one was   145
personally a whirlwind of war, I began to make out that, for a
fighting man—

MRS GRACEDEW (*taking him straight up*) There's always somebody or
other to 'go for'.

YULE (*considering her while he smokes; interested in her interest, and as if*   150
she may after all understand) The enemy, yes, everywhere in force.
(*Without a particle of flourish, very quietly*) I went for *him*. Misery
and ignorance and vice. Injustice and privilege and wrong. Such as
you *see* me—

MRS GRACEDEW (*understanding quickly and beautifully*) You're a rabid   155
Reformer? (*Then with a certain dryness of yearning*) I wish we had
you at Missoura Top!

YULE (*as if regarding for an instant with a certain complacency his pos-*
sible use there, but then remembering other matters) I fear my work is
nearer home. I hope, since you're so good as to seem to *care*, to   160
perform part of that work in the next House of Commons. My
electors have wanted me—

MRS GRACEDEW (*in complete possession of it*) And you've wanted *them*,
and that has been why you couldn't come down.

YULE (*appreciating her easy grasp*) Yes, for all this later time. (*Then as*   165
if deciding, in spite of his habit of reserve, to tell her more) And before
that, from my rather dismal childhood up—

MRS GRACEDEW (*breaking in; gentle but eager*) Was your childhood
'dismal'?

YULE Absurdly. (*Then as if feeling with pleasure the sympathy and curi-*   170
osity in her face, but not wanting too much to let himself go) But I must
tell you about that—

MRS GRACEDEW (*quick*) Another time? Very good then, we must have
it *out*. (*Smiling at him*) I do *like* your dark pasts over here!

YULE (*a bit sadly amused*) Well, in *my* 'dark past' there was another   175
reason—for the ignorance I seem to find you here to *dispel*. (*Decid-*
ing to mention it) A family feud.

MRS GRACEDEW (*clutching at the interest of this*) Ah, how *right*! I *hoped*
I'd strike some sort of a feud! (*Expressing frankly her joy*) That
rounds it *off and* spices it *up*, and, for the heartbreak with which I   180

take *leave* of you, just makes the fracture *complete*! (*Then, as if her reference to her taking leave suddenly brings her back to time and space, proportion and propriety, the realities and relations of things, she turns about with her instinct of not leaving or forgetting anything she may have bought or may take. This in turn, however, makes the sight of the staircase remind her*) Must I really *wait*—to go *up*?   185

YULE (*who, watching her movement, has turned again to restlessness, shift-ing, coming round, tossing away unconsciously a cigarette but just begun and placing himself as if practically to bar her retreat; where he breaks out abruptly as if still so imperfectly satisfied*) Only till you tell me   190
this. If you absolutely meant a while ago there (*referring back to the scene with the party*) that this old thing is so precious?

MRS GRACEDEW (*pulled up; with amazement and quite with pity*) Do you literally need I should *say* it? Can you stand here and not *feel* it? (*Then, with all her conviction, a new rush of her impression*) It's a   195
place to adore! (*But casting about as for an expression intense enough*)

YULE (*so interested*) To adore, yes?

MRS GRACEDEW (*with cumulative effect*) Well, as you'd adore a per-son! (*Then as if she can add nothing to this, which says all; and while some sound of voices or movements, some recall of the lapse of the hour,   200
comes down from the 'party up' and makes her take a decision, she passes straight to the stairs*) Good-bye!

YULE (*who has let her reach the stairs and has got to his distance while she does so; and who speaks now with an intensity, a sharpness of meaning he has not yet used; quite as if the point she has just made has brought   205
them the more together*) I think I 'feel' it, you know; but it's simply *you*, your presence, as I may say, and the remarkable way you put things, that *make* me. (*Then as if it comes to him while she listens that it may help him a little to alarm her*) I'm afraid that in your *absence*— (*He strikes a match to smoke again*)   210

MRS GRACEDEW (*arrested, vague*) In my absence—

YULE (*while he lights his cigarette*) I may come *back*—(*Smoking*)

MRS GRACEDEW (*echoing it almost sharply*) 'Come back?' I should like to see you *not*!

YULE (*still having smoked*) I mean to my old idea—   215

MRS GRACEDEW (*wholly turning round on him now; as if he has created a vagueness*) What idea are you talking about?

YULE (*letting her have it*) Well, that one *could* give it up.

MRS GRACEDEW (*as if, after all she has done, aghast and bewildered*) Give up Covering? *How*, in the name of sinful waste, or *why*?   220

YULE (*very definite*) Because I can't afford to keep it.

MRS GRACEDEW (*prompt, practical, as if his mountain is a molehill*)
Can't you *let* it?

YULE (*smoking first*) Let it to *you*?

MRS GRACEDEW (*laughing out as in triumph at the thought and with her*   225
laugh bringing her nearer) I'd take it like a *shot*!

YULE (*after an instant; while, taking her statement bravely and respon-*
sibly, he looks down, rather fixedly, in thought) I shouldn't have the
face to charge you a rent that would make it worth one's while; and
(*then after a break, raising his eyes*) I think even you, dear lady,   230
wouldn't have the face to offer me one. (*He pauses, but with some-*
thing that checks her now in any impulse to rush in; speaking as if he
really can't but see the thing clear) My 'lovely' inheritance is Dead
Sea fruit.° It's mortgaged for all it's worth, and I haven't the means
to pay the *interest*. If by a miracle I could scrape the money together   235
it would leave me without a penny to *live* on. (*Puffs his cigarette*
profusely) So if I *find* the old home at last, I lose it by the same *luck*!°

MRS GRACEDEW (*who has hung upon his words till her hope goes; when*
she violently reacts) I never heard of anything so awful! Do you mean
to say you can't arrange—   240

YULE (*prompt and clear*) Oh yes. An 'arrangement', if that be the name
to give it, has been definitely *proposed* to me.

MRS GRACEDEW (*all relieved*) What's the matter then? For pity's sake,
you poor thing, definitely *accept* it!

YULE (*as if her sweet simplifications but make him wince*) I've made up   245
my mind in the last quarter of an hour that I can't. It's such a
peculiar case.

MRS GRACEDEW (*frankly wondering; her bias clearly sceptical*) How
peculiar?

YULE (*who finds the measure difficult to give*) Well, more peculiar than   250
most cases.

MRS GRACEDEW (*not satisfied*) More peculiar than mine?

YULE Than 'yours'? (*He looks at her, all candidly, as if he knows nothing*
about hers)

MRS GRACEDEW (*with a movement of her shoulders, as if it takes a*   255
Briton to 'know nothing' after one feels that one has practically told him
everything; yet indulgent, none the less, to this particular specimen, and
deciding to be rudimentary) I forgot. You don't know mine. (*Then*
bethinking herself) But no matter. What *is* yours?

YULE (*bringing himself to the point*) Well, the fact is, I'm asked to   260
change.

MRS GRACEDEW (*vague*) To change what?

YULE (*as wondering how he can put it, but at last simplifying*) My—
  attitude!

MRS GRACEDEW (*with an amused reaction from her blankness*) Is *that*   265
  all? Well, you're not a bronze monument.

YULE No, I'm not a bronze monument; but on the other hand, don't
  you see, I'm not a whirling windmill. (*Then as making his explanation complete*) The mortgages, I'm humiliated to confess, have all
  found their way, like gregarious silly sheep, into the hands of one   270
  person, a devouring wolf, a very rich, a very sharp, man of money.
  He has me, you see, in a cleft *stick*. He consents to make things what
  he calls 'easy' for me, but requires that, in return, I shall do something for *him* that, don't you know, rather sticks in my *crop*.

MRS GRACEDEW (*following close*) Do you mean something wrong?   275

YULE (*as if it's exactly what he feels*) Quite beastly brutally wrong.

MRS GRACEDEW (*turning it over like something of price*) Anything
  immoral?

YULE (*promptly*) Yes, I may certainly call it immoral.

MRS GRACEDEW (*after waiting for him to say more*) Too bad to *tell*?   280

YULE (*throwing up his arms with a fidget, as if it's for her to judge*) He
  wants me to give *up*—(*But he has a pause as if it* is *almost too bad to
  mention*)

MRS GRACEDEW (*as wondering what it can be that is scarce nameable;
  yet naturally the more curious; pressing*) To 'give up'—   285

YULE Well, my fundamental views.

MRS GRACEDEW (*as with a drop*) Oh-h! (*She has expected more*) Nothing but—*that* sort of thing?

YULE (*with surprise*) Surely 'that sort of thing' is enough when one has
  so very *much* of it! (*He develops for his justification*) The surrender   290
  of one's opinions when one has (*he rather ruefully smiles*) so very
  many—

MRS GRACEDEW (*down on him like a flash and with a laugh on the oddity
  of the plea*) Well, I guess I've about as 'many' as *anyone;* but I'd
  'swap', as they say out West, the whole precious collection! (*With   295
  which she casts about the hall for something of the equivalent price and
  then, as she catches it, points to the great cave of the fireplace*) I'd take
  that set!

YULE (*scarce taking it in*) The fire-irons?

MRS GRACEDEW (*emphatic*) For the whole 'fundamental' lot! (*Nearer   300
  to these objects, she fondly values them*) *They're* three hundred years
  old. Do you mean to tell me your wretched 'views'—

YULE (*amused, catching on*) Have anything like that *age*? No, thank

God; my views, 'wretched' as you please, are quite in their *prime*! They're a hungry little family that has got to be *fed*. They keep me awake at night! 305

MRS GRACEDEW (*appreciating that inconvenience*) Then you must make up your sleep! (*Her impatience growing with her interest*) Listen to *me*!

YULE (*admiringly ironic*) That would scarce be the *way*! (*Then more earnestly*) You must surely see that a fellow can't chuck his *politics*. 310

MRS GRACEDEW (*as demuring to the logic of the term he employs*) 'Chuck' them?

YULE Well, sacrifice them.°

MRS GRACEDEW (*with a gesture that seems to say 'Is that all?' while she reverts to the object she has just pointed out*) I'd sacrifice mine for that old fire-back° with your arms! (*Then while he scarce more than gapes at the fire-back; so that she's again impatient*) See how it has *stood*. 315

YULE (*while his spirit, at this, flares up*) See how I've 'stood'! I've glowed with a hotter fire than anything in any *chimney* and the warmth and light I diffuse have attracted no little attention. (*Remonstrant, appealing*) How can I consent to reduce them to the state of that desolate *hearth*? 320

MRS GRACEDEW (*over the chimney-place where, freshly struck with the fine details of the desolation, she lingers and observes an instant, lost in her deeper impression; and then turns away under the whole general effect*) It's magnificent! 325

YULE (*with the note of his docility under instruction*) The fire-back?

MRS GRACEDEW Everything, everywhere! I don't understand your haggling! 330

YULE (*after the briefest hesitation*) That's because you're ignorant. (*Then immediately guessing that he has applied to her the very word in the language she can least bear, he hastens to explain*) I mean what's *behind* my reserves.°

MRS GRACEDEW (*as after trying to read in his face what this queer quantity would naturally be*) What *is* behind them? 335

YULE Why, my whole political *history*! Everything I've said. Everything I've *done*. My scorching *addresses*, my scarifying letters, reproduced in all the *papers*. I needn't go into details, but, such as you see me here, dear lady, and harmless as I look, I'm a rabid, roaring, raving, radical. 340

MRS GRACEDEW (*making her question absolute and utter*) Well, what if you *are*?

YULE (*moved to mirth by her so characteristic coolness*) Simply *this*, that

I can't therefore, from one day to the other, pop up at Gossage in   345
the purple pomp of the opposite camp. There's a want of what I
may call *transition*; and, though I know that, in a general way, lovely
women see no more *use* for transition than the swallows atop of a
cathedral-tower see for the winding stair that takes the panting
tourist *up*, I should seem to need—as a mere wingless pedestrian,   350
madam—to be able to tell, at least, how I *came*. It may be timid to
fear being *asked*; it may be abject not to *like* having to *say*. (*With
decision*) But that's how *I* am!

MRS GRACEDEW (*as, pulled up a little at having to take him as he is,
since she doesn't quite know what to do about it, she thinks hard a*   355
*minute; meanwhile mechanically, with one hand, just pushing some
object on a table or elsewhere straight, or smoothing down with her foot
the corner of an old rug*) Have you thought very much *about* it?

YULE (*rendered vague again by merely having watched her*) About what?

MRS GRACEDEW About what Mr Prodmore wants you to do.   360

YULE (*disconcerted*) Oh then you know it's *he*?

MRS GRACEDEW (*so preoccupied, so brave, that she's a bit dry*) I'm not
of an intelligence absolutely *infantile*.

YULE (*granting it amusedly*) You're the sharpest Tory I've ever *met*! I
didn't mean to mention my friend's *name* but (*with a shrug, giving*   365
up his scruple) since *you've* done so—

MRS GRACEDEW (*already all there; pressing*) It's *he* who's the devouring wolf? It's *he* who holds your mortgages?

YULE (*as, rather decently, not to give Prodmore the least bit disloyally
away*) Well, he holds plenty of others too, I dare say, and (*as to make*   370
a little end of it) he treats me very handsomely.

MRS GRACEDEW (*her demur immediately*) You call *that* handsome,
such a condition?

YULE (*seeing her suddenly inconsequent*) Why, I thought it just the condition you professed you could *meet*!   375

MRS GRACEDEW (*measuring her inconsequence, but boldly making the
best of it and resorting to even rather sharp impatience for the purpose*)
We're not talking of what *I* can meet! (*With which then to be inconsequent all the way*)° Why doesn't he stand *himself*?

YULE Well, like other devouring wolves, he's not personally *adored*.   380

MRS GRACEDEW Not even when he offers such liberal terms?

YULE (*as forced to explain*) I dare say he doesn't offer them, to
everyone.°

MRS GRACEDEW (*eager at this*) Only *you*? *You're* personally adored?
You'll be still more if you *stand*? (*Then as if herself answering her*   385

questions, seeing it clear, triumphantly making it sure) *That's*, you poor
lamb, why he *wants* you!

YULE (*as if he can but honourably accept this account of the matter*) I'm
the bearer of my *name*, I'm the representative of my *family*, and to
my family and my name, since you've *led* me to it, this countryside   390
has been for generations indulgently attached.

MRS GRACEDEW (*taking up as with instant passion the cause of the
Lawful Heir; concluding from it for everything*) You do, of course,
what you *will* with this countryside.

YULE Yes, (*so far assenting*) if we do it as genuine Yules. I'm obliged of   395
course to grant you that your genuine Yule's a Tory of Tories. It's
Mr Prodmore's reasoned conviction that I should carry Gossage in
that character, but in that character *only*. They won't look at me in
any *other*.

MRS GRACEDEW (*with her view of that general question*) Don't be too   400
sure of people's not 'looking at' you!

YULE (*making the point gayly but modestly*) We must leave out my
personal beauty.

MRS GRACEDEW (*with decision*) We *can't*! Don't we take in Mr
Prodmore's?   405

YULE (*scarcely prepared*) You call Mr Prodmore 'beautiful'?

MRS GRACEDEW (*highly distinct*) Hideous. (*Then as if that at least is
settled forever*) What's the extraordinary interest he attaches—

YULE To the return of a Tory? Oh, (*seeing it clear*) his desire is born of
his *fear*, his terror on behalf of Property; which he sees, somehow,   410
with an intensely personal, with a quite prodigious capital P. He has
a great deal of *that* solid article, and very little of anything *else*.

MRS GRACEDEW (*interested, though with her reserves and bethinking
herself*) Do you call that nice daughter 'very little'?

YULE (*consciously vague*) Is she very *big*? I really didn't notice her, and   415
moreover she's just a part of the Property.° He thinks things are
going too *far*.

MRS GRACEDEW (*with immense decision; taking a line and sitting
straight down on it and on a hard chair*) Well, they *are*!

YULE (*discomposed, as he thus stands before her, at her appearing again to   420
fail him*) Aren't you then a lover of justice?

MRS GRACEDEW A passionate one! (*Sitting there as upright as if she
held the scales*) Where's the justice of your losing this house? (*Then
as with a high judicial decision*) To keep Covering you must carry
Gossage!   425

YULE (*bewildered, rueful*) As a renegade?

MRS GRACEDEW As a genuine Yule. What business have you to be
anything *else*? (*She is perfectly convinced*) You must *close* with° Mr
Prodmore, you must stand in the Tory interest. (*Then rising as she
makes it all out*) If you *will* I'll conduct your *canvass*.   430

YULE (*almost distractedly fascinated*) That puts the temptation *high*!

MRS GRACEDEW (*impatient as of his manner; waving away the mere personal tribute; moved to eloquence*) Ah, don't look at me as if *I* were the
'temptation'! Look at this sweet old human home and feel all its
gathered memories. (*Urgent*) Do you know what they *do* to me? (*Then   435
as she takes them all in again*) They speak to me for Mr Prodmore.

YULE (*as trying to do as she again instructs him; but as having also to take
account of other things*) Well, there are other voices and other
appeals than *these*, you know, things for which I've spoken, repeatedly and loudly, to others than *you*. (*Then as if almost with the very   440
accent and emphasis of those occasions*). One's 'human home' is all
very well, but the rest of one's humanity is better! (*She gives at this
a charming wail of protest; she turns impatiently away*) I see you're
disgusted with me and I'm sorry; but one must take oneself as
circumstances and experience have *made* one and it's not my fault,   445
don't you know, if they've made me a very modern man. I see
something else in the world than the beauty of old show-houses and
the glory of old show-families. There are thousands of people in
England who can show no houses *at all*, and (*with the emphasis of
sincerity*) I don't feel it utterly shameful to share their poor *fate*.   450

MRS GRACEDEW (*roused at this, but unwilling to lose ground and moved
to use, with a sad and beautiful headshake, an eloquence at least equal to
his own*) We share the poor fate of humanity whatever we do and we
do much to help and console when we've something precious to
show. (*Then warming, with all charm, to her work*) What on earth is   455
more precious than what the ages have slowly *wrought*? (*Specious,
ingenious*) They've trusted us—the brave centuries!—to *keep* it; to
do something, in our turn, for them. (*Then in earnest, tender, pleading possession of her idea*) It's such a virtue, in anything, to have
lasted; it's such an honour, for anything, to have lasted; it's such an   460
honour, for anything, to have been *spared*. (*After which, for the very
climax of her plea for charity*) To all strugglers from the wreck of
time hold out a pitying hand!

YULE (*moved, but with no retort to such dazzling sophistry quite ready at
once, so that he throws himself, just chaffingly,° on the first side-issue*)   465
What a plea for looking backward, dear lady, to come from
Missoura Top!

MRS GRACEDEW (*shedding his irony; holding up her head; speaking with the highest competence*) We're making a past at Missoura Top as fast as ever we *can*, and (*with a sharp smile and hand-gesture of warning*) I should like to see you lay your hand on an hour of the one we've made! (*Then with her always prompt and easy humour*) It's a tight fit, as yet, I *grant*, and (*all ingenious*) that's just why I like, in *yours*, to find room, don't you see, to turn round. (*Then as knowing and able to say just what she thus intensely and appreciatively means*) You're *in* it, over here, and you can't get *out*. (*Hence lucidly concluding*) So just make the *best* of that and treat it all as part of the fun!

YULE (*quite enjoying now the discussion*) The whole of the fun to me, madam, is in hearing you *defend* it! It's like your defending melancholy madness, or hereditary gout, or chronic rheumatism, the things I feel aching in every old bone of these old walls and groaning in every old *draught* that must for centuries have blown *through* them.

MRS GRACEDEW (*as feeling no woman to be shakeable who is so prepared to be just all round*) If there be aches—there *may* be—you're here to *soothe* them; and if there be draught—there indeed *must* be!—you're here to stop them up. (*Then intenser*) And do you know what I'm here for? If I've come so far and so straight I've almost wondered myself. I've felt with a kind of *passion*, but now I see *why* I've felt. (*Having moved about the hall with the excitement of this perception and separated from him at last by a distance across which he follows her discovery with a visible suspense, she brings out her vivid statement*) I'm here for an act of salvation. I'm here to avert a wrong.

YULE (*after they have stood a moment, while she glows, while she fairly shines, face to face across the distance*) You're here, I think, madam, to be a memory for all my *future*!

MRS GRACEDEW (*taking it then at the worst for that and coming nearer while she sociably and subtly argues*) You'll be one for *mine*, if I can see you by that *hearth*. Why do you make such a fuss about changing your politics? (*Then with a flare of gay emphasis*) If you'd come to Missoura Top too you'd change them quick enough! (*But seeing further still and striking harder, she rises again to bright eloquence with the force of her plea*) What do politics amount to compared with religions? Parties and programmes come and go, but a duty like this *abides*. (*Driving it home, pressing him closer, bringing it out*) There's nothing you can break with that would be like breaking *here*. The very words are ugly and cruel, as much sacrilege as if you had been trusted with the key of the temple. This *is* the temple! (*Very high*

470

475

480

485

490

495

500

505

and confident) Don't *profane* it! Keep up the old altar *kindly*, you can't raise a new one as *good*. (*Reasoning, explaining, with her fine, almost feverish plausibility*) You *must* have beauty in your life, don't you see, that's the only way to make sure of it for the lives of others. Keep leaving it to *them*, to all the poor others, and heaven only knows what will *become* of it! Does it take one of *us* to feel that, to preach you the *truth*? Then it's good, Captain Yule, we come right over; just to see, you know, what you may happen to be 'up to'. (*With her sense of proportion again, as always, playing into her sense of humour*) We know what we haven't *got*, worse luck, so that if you've happily got it you've got it also for *us*. You've got it in *trust*, you see, and oh we have an eye on you! You've had it so for *me*, all these dear days of my drinking it in, that, to be grateful, I've wanted regularly to do *something*. (*With the rich assumption, the high confidence, of having convinced him*) Tell me now I shall have *done* it, I shall have kept you at your *post*!

YULE (*who, all this strongly working on him and seeming to give him so much to decide so terribly and so quickly, fidgets away and, struggling with it, threshing it out, goes up to door of garden while, as spent with her eloquence and her intensity, she subsides again upon her hard, high-backed chair awaiting the light these movements of his may throw on the degree of her success. He looks out into his old garden a moment; then fidgets round to come down, speaking with a rather strained and convulsed smile*) You have a standpoint quite your own and a style of eloquence that the few scraps of parliamentary training I've picked up don't seem to fit me at all to *deal* with.° (*Highly reasonable*) Of course I don't pretend, you know, that I don't *care* for Covering.

MRS GRACEDEW (*as taking this for a gain, though finding his tone almost comically ingenuous; and coming back to the chance for her that she has already two or three times all but grasped*) You haven't even *seen* it yet! (*Then chaffingly, charmingly*) Aren't you a bit *afraid*?

YULE (*bethinking himself; then perfectly candid and amused also at having to say it*) Yes, tremendously. But if I *am*, (*more gravely*) it isn't only Covering that *makes* me.

MRS GRACEDEW What else is it?

YULE Everything. But it doesn't in the least matter. (*As if, really, with everything in his case so formidably mixed, nothing in the least matters*) You may be quite correct. When we talk of the house your voice comes to me somehow as the wind in its old chimneys.

MRS GRACEDEW (*for the drollery of this image*) I hope you don't mean I *roar*!

YULE (*attenuating this awkwardness; as light about it as possible*) No, nor   550
yet perhaps that you *whistle*! (*Then keeping this up*) I don't believe
the wind does *here*—either. It only whispers (*he seeks gracefully to
explain*) and more or less sobs and sighs—

MRS GRACEDEW (*breaking in*) And, when there are *very* funny
gentlemen round, I hope, more or less shrieks with laughter!   555

YULE (*arrested by this, stopping now rather gravely before her*) Do you
think I'm a 'very funny' gentleman?

MRS GRACEDEW (*taking it from him while she sits; touched by it as an
appeal more personal than any he has yet made; but hesitating*) I
think—I think—! (*Then going straight up and turning away*) I think   560
more things than I can *say*!

YULE (*watching her for the moment during which, as under the emotion
sounding in her words, she keeps her back turned; then with abrupt
emphasis and decision*) It's all right.

MRS GRACEDEW (*brought straight round*) Then you promise?   565

YULE To meet Mr Prodmore? (*With his strained smile again, as he
consciously thus disappoints her by delay*) Oh, dear no! Not yet.
(*Insistent*) I must *wait*. I must *think*.

MRS GRACEDEW (*who has at first one of her desperate drops of her arms
for the check represented by this; but then seems to control herself to   570
patience*) When have you to *answer* him?

YULE (*very quickly; as with the intention of reassurance, but the effect of
despair*) Oh, he gives me *time*!

MRS GRACEDEW (*his tone upsetting her again*) *I* wouldn't give you
time! (*Then with intensity*) I'd give you a *shaking*! (*She moves   575
about, as feeling the good minutes slip; then facing him again as if it's
more than she can stand*) For God's sake, at any rate, (*waving him
vehemently away*) go *upstairs*!

YULE (*at a distance from her; aghast, not budging*) And literally *find* the
dreadful man?   580

MRS GRACEDEW (*as her eyes catch sight of Cora, who reappears at top of
stairs, relieved, elated*) He's coming *down*!
     Enter Cora Prodmore by staircase

YULE (*while Cora's attention, as she descends, fixes only Mrs Gracedew,
on whom, thus cautiously prowling down, she rests an undeviating glare;
disconcerted, alarmed, ready for anything to escape the girl's range, and   585
as he moves round, to give her a wide berth, seeing his best course in the
direction from which she has come and, when the stairs are clear, eagerly
taking it*) I'll go *up*!
     Exit Captain Clement Yule by staircase

CORA (*who has crossed with him, yet with visible avoidance of seeing him; and changing the pace at which she has stolen away from above almost to a leap and a bound as soon as the coast is clear; rushing to her wonderful friend*) I've come *back* to you; I want to *speak* to you! (*Then in the pathos and the vehemence of her need*) May I *confide* in you? 590

MRS GRACEDEW (*wholly unprepared as yet for this, but immediately amused*) You *too*? (*Then with her gay reflection*) Why, it *is* good we came over! 595

CORA (*grateful, ingenuous*) It is *indeed*! You were so very *kind* to me and seemed to think me so *curious*.

MRS GRACEDEW (*responsive; liking her; believing in her honest type*) Well, I loved you for it and it was nothing moreover to what you thought *me*! 600

CORA (*a little embarrassed, but candid*) I loved *you*. (*Then generous; glowing*) But I'm the *worst*! And (*as if it so much explains her*) I'm solitary. 605

MRS GRACEDEW (*gay but positive*) Ah, so am *I*! (*Then with one of her quaint effects of familiar generalisation*) A *very* queer thing, I think, is mostly found alone. But, since we have that link, by all means 'confide'!

CORA Well, I was met here by tremendous *news*! (*Taking her plunge, producing it with a purple glow*) He wants me to *marry* him! 610

MRS GRACEDEW (*amiably receptive, but failing as yet to follow*) 'He' wants you?

CORA (*so clear to herself*) Papa, of course. He has settled it.

MRS GRACEDEW (*still blank*) Settled what? 615

CORA Why, the whole question. That I must *take* him.

MRS GRACEDEW (*just as much at sea*) But, my dear, take *whom*?

CORA (*as if surprised at this first lapse of her friend's universal intelligence*) Why, Captain Yule, who just went *up*.

MRS GRACEDEW (*with a large full stare*) Oh! (*Then with a sharper note, as the queer picture seems to break on her, looking straight away from Cora*) Oh! 620

CORA (*almost apologetically explaining*) I thought you'd probably *know*.

MRS GRACEDEW (*considering her now humanely enough, but still speaking with clear emphasis*) I *didn't* 'know'. I couldn't *possibly* 'know'. (*Then, in the light of this odd fact, looking the girl up and down, taking her in more and more and moved to wonder, decidedly, by the odd fact itself*) Has Captain Yule *asked* you? 625

CORA (*clear as a bell; not doubting of anything her father has settled with*

him) No—but he *will*. (*In complete possession of the subject now*) He'll   630
do it to keep the house. It's mortgaged to Papa, and Captain Yule
buys it *back*.

MRS GRACEDEW (*as with a quick lurid illumination*) By *marrying* you?

CORA (*instructed, to her cost; indoctrinated*) By giving me his name and
his position. (*Then with her lucidity even greater than her modesty*)   635
They're awfully great, and they're the *price*, don't you see? (*With
all the effect of her substantial presence*) *My* price. Papa's price. Papa
wants them.

MRS GRACEDEW (*hugely staggered and bewildered; piecing this together,
yet finding gaps*) But his name and his position, great as they may   640
be, are his dreadful *politics*.

CORA (*as helped, at once, by her being aware of them*) Ah! You *know*
about his Dreadful Politics? (*Still perfectly clear*) He's to change
them—to get *me*. And if he gets *me*—

MRS GRACEDEW (*like a shot; breathless*) He keeps the house?   645

CORA (*with lucid assent*) I go *with* it. He's to have us both. But only
(*she duly demonstrates*) if he *changes*. (*With all her competence*) The
question is, *will* he change?

MRS GRACEDEW (*for whom the question is indeed so weighty; appearing
profoundly to entertain it*) I see. (*Taking it all in*) *Will* he change?   650

CORA (*with further lucid reach*) *Has* he changed?

MRS GRACEDEW (*as if this possibility, so serenely uttered, is really a little
too much for her now startled nerves; so that she speaks with abrupt
impatience*) My dear child, how in the world should *I* know?

CORA (*unconsciously piling it up; detached and judicial merely; terribly   655
consistent*) The thing is that he hasn't seemed to *care* enough for the
house. *Does* he care?

MRS GRACEDEW (*who moves away, passing over to the fireplace, where
she stands a moment looking mechanically, without seeing them, at the
fine features she has lately admired; then facing about with quite a new   660
tone*) You had better *ask* him!

CORA (*before her across the interval; unconscious of any irony and of
the effect she produces; and almost as if entertaining Mrs Gracedew's
suggestion, conclusive, logical, fatal*) If he does care he'll *propose*.

MRS GRACEDEW (*catching sight of Yule at top of stairs, just as she had   665
shortly before, from opposite side of stage, caught sight of Cora; and
making out from this fact of his rapid return that her own ardour has
practically worked upon him, has taken such effect that he now comes
down to act; but passing swiftly across to let the girl have it, in a quick
whisper*) He *does* care! He'll *propose*.   670

Enter Captain Clement Yule by staircase

CORA (*whom Mrs Gracedew's rush at her only has made aware; determined now instantly, by the young man's approach, and still more by
her friend's so confident appreciation of it; and moving to left as he
appears to threaten an advance from the Stairs to right and towards
Mrs Gracedew, so that she makes for garden door as easiest escape*) Oh   675
dear, oh dear!

YULE (*coming down, rather awkward at result of his return*) I drive Miss
Prodmore away!

MRS GRACEDEW (*as with instant presence of mind and taking fifty things
in; smiling to ease them both off*) It's all *right*! (*Then beaming at Cora*   680
as with full intelligence) Do you *mind*, one moment? I've something
to say to Captain Yule.

CORA (*up at left, looking from one to the other*) Yes, but I've also something more to say to *you*.

YULE (*as if addressing her for the first time, he* must *be civil*) Do you   685
mean *now*?

CORA (*fluttered at his address and, as it were, receding from it*) No, but
before she *goes*.

MRS GRACEDEW (*all consideration*) Come back in a moment then, I'm
not going. (*With which she blows her afresh the same familiar kiss as on*   690
her last previous exit)

> Cora at her distance, but still facing them, waits just enough to
> show, with a wondering look, some sudden fear or suspicion, her
> alarm at the possibility of her friend's urging on Yule to 'make
> up' to her, to put himself on her father's side; after which she
> dashes out. Exit Cora Prodmore to garden; while Mrs Gracedew,
> affected by her manner, addresses Yule

MRS GRACEDEW What in the world's the *matter* with her?

YULE (*who waits a moment, watching her while she moves further from
him, before speaking*) I'm afraid I only know what's the matter with
me. (*Then gravely and coldly*) It will doubtless give you pleasure to   695
learn that I've closed with Mr Prodmore.

MRS GRACEDEW (*who, moving to left has reached the great chimney
again; where she stands, her back turned to him, gazing into the
fireplace during a marked pause*) I thought you said he gave you
time.   700

YULE Yes, but you produced just now so immense an effect on me
that I thought best not to *take* any. I came upon him there and I
burnt my ships.°

MRS GRACEDEW (*in the same posture*) You do what he *requires*?

YULE (*rather hard and grim*) I do what he requires. I felt the tremen- 705
dous force of all you *said* to me.

MRS GRACEDEW (*turning toward him sharp on this; speaking with an
odd quick curtness*) So did *I*, or I shouldn't have said it!

YULE (*with a laugh a little dry, as an effect of her tone*) You're perhaps
not aware that you wield an influence of which it's not too much to 710
say—

MRS GRACEDEW (*while he casts about as for how to put it strongly and
vividly enough; and still with her strange sharpness*) To say what?

YULE Well, that it's practically *irresistible*!

MRS GRACEDEW (*taking this in, having to accept it and its consequence,* 715
*as her own act; but not able to keep down a flare of feeling which
rings out ironic*) You've given me the most flattering proof of my
influence that I've ever enjoyed in my *life*!

YULE (*wondering at her; so mystified that he is moved to a defence, with
some spirit, of the act she appears now to regard so oddly*) This was 720
inevitable, dear madam, from the moment you had converted me—
and in about three *minutes* too—into the absolute echo of your
raptures.

MRS GRACEDEW (*with an extraordinary air of having forgotten all about
them*) My 'raptures'? 725

YULE (*amazed*) Why, about my old home.

MRS GRACEDEW (*quitting the fireplace, moving to right, then at last
recognising his allusion without the aid of looking at him*) Oh yes—
your old home. (*As coming back to it from far away*) It's a nice,
tattered, battered old thing! (*Looking round at it mechanically,* 730
coldly) It has defects of course; there would be many things to be
said. But (*dryly, letting it go*) there's no use mentioning them
now.

YULE (*who has crossed her, in his emotion, to left; really astounded at her
change of tone and not a little nettled*) I'm bound to say then that you 735
might have mentioned some of them *before*!

MRS GRACEDEW (*consciously and ruefully perverse, but covering her
want of logic, so far as she can, with a show of reason, though speaking
also with a certain indulgence*) If you had really gone over the
house—as I almost went on my *knees* to you to do!—you might 740
have discovered some of them yourself.

YULE (*with heat at her injustice*) How can you say *that* when I was
precisely in the very act of it? (*Perfectly clear, making good what he
has done*) It was just *because* I was, that the first person I met above
was Mr Prodmore; on which, feeling that I must come to it sooner 745

or later, I simply gave in to him on the spot; I yielded him, to have it well *over*, the whole of his *point*.

MRS GRACEDEW (*down to right, seeming to gaze from afar at some strange dim fact that she requires a minute to do justice to; though finally succeeding after a fashion in doing it*) Let me then congratulate   750
you on at last knowing what you *want*!

YULE (*still stupefied at the way she has gone back on him*) I only know so far *as you* know it! (*Explaining, keeping it before her*) I struck while the iron was *hot*, or at least while the *hammer* was!

MRS GRACEDEW (*now with more control over her discomposure; brighter*   755
and more conciliatory) Of course I recognise that it can rarely have been exposed to such a fire. I blazed up and (*very frankly and candidly*) I know that when I burn, well, (*as she casts about*) I do it as *Chicago* does.°

YULE (*amused, in spite of everything else, at her image*) Isn't that usually   760
down to the ground?

MRS GRACEDEW (*as if glad to laugh again; throwing up her light arms*) As high as the *sky*! (*Then, as if this has helped her to come back, though still with a certain detachment, quite a different tone from her previous, to the practical question*) I suppose you've still *formalities* to   765
go through.

YULE With Mr Prodmore? (*As if he'll suppose in the matter anything she likes; and speaking quickly, as if he has no idea and no care what such formalities may be*) Oh, endless tiresome ones, no doubt!

MRS GRACEDEW (*as if this view of them makes her wonder and has even*   770
possibly a new light) You mean they'll take so very, very long?

YULE (*as with this resolution at once determined in him*) Every hour, every month, that I can possibly make them *last*!

MRS GRACEDEW (*struck at his tone, but as wishing after all to be prudent for him; soothing him down*) You mustn't drag them out *too* much,   775
must you? Won't he think in that case you may want to *retract*?

YULE (*as with a light coming to himself from this possible fear of Mr Prodmore's*) Well, I shouldn't be so terribly upset by his mistake, you know, (*with a certain bravado*) even if he *did*!

MRS GRACEDEW (*shocked, as to nip any such inconsequence of his in the*   780
bud) Oh, it would never do to give him any colour at all for supposing you not to feel that you've, as one may say, fully pledged your *honour*.

YULE (*conceding this; feeling he must show, however ruefully, what he realises*) Of course, of course; when I *do* so awfully feel it!   785

MRS GRACEDEW (*as if it's on her conscience all the same, to keep him up to it*) How can you possibly *not*, anymore than you can't intensely feel how one's honour's everything in *life*?

YULE (*meeting the assured tone, the note, as it were, of restored sociability with which she speaks of him as at one with her on that point; giving her every assurance*) Oh yes, everything in *life*!   790

MRS GRACEDEW (*this manner from him really bringing back her brightness*) Wasn't it just of the question of the 'honour' of things that we talked a while ago, and of the difficulty of sometimes keeping our sense of it *clear*? There's no more to be said, therefore (*with just the faintest break or softest sigh, between a quaver and a wail*) except that I   795 leave you to your ancient glory, as I leave you to your straight duty. (*She speaks as with the picture of these things well before her; though as with having herself but to turn away from them*) I hope you'll do justice to dear old Covering in spite (*with a nervous laugh*) of its   800 weak *points*; and I hope above all you'll not be incommoded—

YULE (*as she really, under everything, breaks down a little*) 'Incommoded'—

MRS GRACEDEW (*casting about, very distressful*) Well, by such a *rage*—

YULE (*vague, while she rather emotionally hesitates, as to what she may   805 mean; yet with a particular apprehension of his own*) You suppose it will be a 'rage'?

MRS GRACEDEW (*not resisting amusement at the alarm of his look*) Are you afraid of the love that kills?

YULE (*still with his supposition; all serious*) Will it 'kill'—   810

MRS GRACEDEW (*held now by her mirth at his stare*) Great passions *have* killed, you know!

YULE (*wondering, minimising*) Should you call it a 'great' passion?

MRS GRACEDEW (*her emphasis now gay*) Surely, when so *many* feel it!

YULE (*his idea no longer serving him; with a fall to bewilderment*) But   815 *how* many?

MRS GRACEDEW Let's see. (*She makes as reckoning them up*) If you count them all—

YULE (*interrupting her by the gasp with which he throws himself back*) 'All'?   820

MRS GRACEDEW (*arrested in turn by his cry; slightly mystified*) I see. You knocked off *some*. About *half*?

YULE (*giving it up as black darkness*) Whom on earth are you talking about?

MRS GRACEDEW (*lucid*) Why, the electors—   825

YULE (*leaping at it*) Of Gossage? (*With immense relief*) Oh!

MRS GRACEDEW (*as if she couldn't possibly have meant anything else*) I got the whole thing up before I came. (*Definite, competent*) There are six thousand of them. Really a fine figure!

YULE (*who has sharply passed from her, to cover his mistake, and, as by   830 the awkwardness of it, has been carried half round the hall; where, rueful at his stupidity, yet with the air still not cleared for him of the image of his error, he catches her last words only to make of them again, confusedly, coming down, a wrong application*) Has she really a fine figure?   835

MRS GRACEDEW (*her own attention 'off' now; preoccupied at last wholly with her imminent farewell*) 'She'?

YULE (*embarrassed again at his self-betrayals, but as if really, in the conflict of his emotions, he doesn't know where he is*) Aren't we talking—   840

MRS GRACEDEW (*prompt*) Of Gossage? Oh yes, 'she' has every charm! (*Then with the same promptness; almost with curtness; absolute*)° Good-bye.

YULE (*throwing up his arms in real despair, in spite of her having done her work, while she moves*) You don't mean to say you're *going*!   845

MRS GRACEDEW (*as in disciplined despair and resignation; accepting it*) Why, I've got to go back *some* time!

YULE (*as with the wonder and the question irresistibly rising; though not even yet, even yet*° *quite understanding, himself, the full point of his desire for knowledge*) But what is it—a—you go back to?   850

MRS GRACEDEW (*as a matter of course*) Why, to my big beautiful home, such as it is.

YULE (*after an instant; ingenuously*) Is it *very* beautiful?

MRS GRACEDEW (*simply*) Very. But not to be compared to this. To begin with, it's a mile too big.   855

YULE (*as with a vain attempt to focus it; almost literal*) A 'mile'?

MRS GRACEDEW (*almost impatient—her house being so little in question*) Well, for one person.

YULE (*as suddenly struck*) Are you only—a—one person?

MRS GRACEDEW (*with a short laugh*) Why, do you think I look like   860 two? (*After an instant*) I'm a lone, lone woman—(*after another instant, simply*) since my husband died.

YULE (*with a movement and a repressed vibration*) Oh! (*Then again as if, for some difference it may make, his recognition is not repressible*) Oh!   865

MRS GRACEDEW Four years ago. (*Always simply*) I'm quite alone. (*As if there's nothing more to be said about it*) So there it is!

YULE (*immensely and intensely taking it in*) I see. There it is. (*Then as to

*conjure a certain awkwardness; to disguise the betrayal of too sharp an
emotion at this*) A great big empty house.   870

MRS GRACEDEW (*quietly prompt*) A great big empty life! (*Then simply
still, yet also just a little vaguely and sadly*) Which I try to fill; which
I try to fill!

YULE (*gently ironic*) Which you try to fill with 'taste'?

MRS GRACEDEW (*good-humoured, philosophic*) Well, with all I've *got*!   875

YULE (*grave*) You fill it with your goodness.

MRS GRACEDEW It will be filled for the rest of my days, I think, with
my success! (*Smiling*) That is with yours!

YULE (*as but vaguely and remotely conscious of his own*) Ah, 'mine'!

MRS GRACEDEW (*possessed only with her idea*) Why what do you want   880
of more? (*As he makes a sceptical impatient gesture*) If your house is
saved!

YULE (*his eyes on her as if intensely and excitedly thinking; then speaking
with quick decision*) I'll tell you if you'll *wait*! Don't go till I *see* you!
(*Having jerked out his watch*) I go back, under *promise*, to Prodmore.   885

MRS GRACEDEW Then don't let me for a moment more keep you
away from him. (*Then as if it's beautifully and terribly a matter of
course*) You must have such lots to talk comfortably over.

YULE (*who, though he assents in form, looking at his watch again, keeps
away from the stairs, gets further away, gets up to left and toward door*   890
of garden; where he remains as with an idea he's too paralysed to apply)
I certainly feel, you know, that I must see him again. (*His watch in
his hand, though not looking at it*) Yes, decidedly, I *must*!

MRS GRACEDEW (*with light detachment and indicating garden, a perceptible effect of irony*) Is he out *there*?   895

YULE (*coming straight away as at the possibility*) No, I left him in the
long gallery.

MRS GRACEDEW (*flashing again into eagerness at this*) You *saw* the long
gallery then? (*All sincere*) Isn't it divine?

YULE (*blank, incompetent*) I didn't notice it. (*Then oddly plaintive*)   900
How *could* I?

MRS GRACEDEW (*his face so rueful that she breaks into a laugh, though
with all her impatience for him*) How *couldn't* you? Notice it *now*
then! (*On which she turns away with a gesture of despair at him; but
after a moment, while he only stands planted, divided, tormented, look-*   905
*ing after her, she faces about, not hearing his step on the stair, and takes
another tone, half imperious, half droll, at still finding him there*)
Captain Yule, you've got to (*insistent, emphatic, characteristic*) assimi-
late that gallery!

YULE (*still looking at her with a fixed strained, strange smile, almost a*   910
grimace of pain) Will you *wait* for me then?

MRS GRACEDEW (*meeting his look an instant and then as if made uneasy,*
of a sudden, by something in it and in his tone, while she turns off and
speaks with a note of sharper and higher admonition, of greater impera-
tive curtness, than she has used at all) Ah, go up, sir!   915

> *It affects him so that, with a start, reaching the staircase, he*
> *mounts briskly several steps, gets in fact half-way; where again he*
> *has an arrest, an hesitation, and, while he looks down at her,*
> *descends again a step or two. She waits, motionless, for him to*
> *disappear; then, as aware of his pause, turns once more to make*
> *sure of him. A look seems to pass between them on this, which*
> *fairly settles him, so that with a gesture at once brave and*
> *desperate, he quickly decides and remounts. He does disappear.*
> *Exit Captain Clement Yule by the staircase.*
>
> *Satisfied of this after an instant, she addresses herself, with an*
> *immense, almost articulate sigh of relief that is at the same time*
> *almost a wail of sorrow, to her own affairs; the great affair, that*
> *is, already three or four times defeated, of her getting away, but*
> *this even a bit vaguely and helplessly now; and breaking down,*
> *with a pause again, as soon as she has begun to move. The pang of*
> *what she has been left there to think of prompts her to brief,*
> *intense selfcommunion*

Why didn't he tell me *all*? But (*throwing up her arms and letting them*
fall at her sides as in supreme renouncement) it was none of my business! (*Yet it continues to hold her*) What does he mean to do? (*Then*
as answering herself) What should he do but what he *has* done? And
(*following up this sense of it*) what *can* he do, when he's so deeply   920
committed, when he's practically engaged, when he's just the same
as married—and as *buried*? (*With which, concluding, as for immediate,*
however melancholy, action) The thing for *me* to 'do' is just to pull
up short and bundle out:° to remove from the scene they encumber
the numerous fragments (*as she looks about her*)—well, of *what*?   925

> *She has turned about, in her trouble, while she exhales these*
> *questions and has caught herself up on this last at sight of Cora*
> *Prodmore, who, returning from the garden, has reappeared in the*
> *doorway up at left. Enter Cora Prodmore from garden. Mrs*
> *Gracedew has at this moment by the same token, spied near her,*
> *on some table or chair where they have been placed after the*
> *accident, the pieces of the vase smashed by Chivers; of which,*
> *accordingly, with a happy thought, she avails herself to strike off*

> *a public solution of the appeal she has a moment before launched*
> *upon the air and which Cora may have caught*

Of my old Chelsea pot! (*She has, over the pathetic morsel, a gay, yet*
sad, headshake and lays it down again, as having spoken for Cora's
benefit its little funeral oration)

CORA (*who has come down, staring in simple dismay at the signs of the*
smash and referring it, as she refers everything, to her principal fear)   930
Has he been *breaking* —

MRS GRACEDEW (*laughingly tapping her heart*) Yes, we've had a scene!
He went up again to your father.

CORA (*with a motion of regret, sorry; as if she may possibly have to pay*
for Mr Prodmore's missing him) Papa's not there. He just came down   935
to me the other way.

MRS GRACEDEW (*with instant resignation*) Then he can *join* you here.
I'm going.

CORA (*pleading, made bold by her apprehensions*) Just when I've come
back to you at the risk of again interrupting—though I really hoped   940
he had *gone!*—your conversation with Captain Yule?

MRS GRACEDEW (*letting this ball quite drop; with dry detachment*) I've
nothing to say to Captain Yule.

CORA (*surprised, rather resentful*) You had a good deal to say ten
minutes *ago!*   945

MRS GRACEDEW (*not perturbed; clear*) Well, I've said it, and it's over.
(*Plain, definite, tranquil*) I've nothing more to say at *all!* (*Then, as*
quite relinquishing the subject, bethinking herself of a freer and brighter
interest) What has become of my delightful party?

CORA (*clear*) They've been dismissed through the court and garden.   950
But they've announced the probable arrival of a fresh lot.

MRS GRACEDEW (*as with a sudden envious joy at hearing of this*) Why,
what times you do *have!* (*Then as generously, as quite sincerely inter-*
ested for the girl) *You* must take the fresh lot, since the house is now
practically yours.   955

CORA (*blank, not in the least accepting it*) 'Mine'?

MRS GRACEDEW (*as surprised in turn at her stupidity*) Why, if you're to
marry Captain Yule.

CORA (*in a flash and almost with a jump*) I'm *not* to marry Captain
Yule!   960

MRS GRACEDEW (*wholly at sea*) Why the dickens then did you tell me
but ten minutes ago that you *were*?

CORA (*only bewildered at the charge and intensely rebutting it*) I told you
nothing of the *sort!* (*In the highest degree positive; referring lucidly to*

what she has said) I only told you that the alliance, as Papa calls it,   965
has been *ordered* me.

MRS GRACEDEW (*breaking out in humour as from the force of her relief*)
Like a dose of medicines or a course of *baths*?

CORA (*not moved to mirth; serious, as to justify her expression*) Well, as a
remedy—   970

MRS GRACEDEW (*quickly taking her up as she casts about; charming to
her, delighted with her*) Not, surely, for your being so nice and *charming*? (*Scouting everything*) We don't want you cured of *that*!

CORA (*with her just grievance*) Papa wants me 'cured' of everything.
(*With the highest decision*) But I won't *listen* to him!   975

MRS GRACEDEW (*risking it, for certainty, after an instant, even at cost of
seeming to urge*) Nor to Captain Yule himself?

CORA (*with all her firmness, all her air, now, of knowing where she is and
what she wants*) I won't *look* at him!

MRS GRACEDEW (*instantly, though as with a wail, almost a sharp shriek,*   980
for lost time) Ah, my dear, then why didn't you let me *know*?

CORA (*perfectly straightforward*) I was on the very point of it when he
came in and *frightened* me!

MRS GRACEDEW (*as struck with this; considering*) You think him
'frightening'?   985

CORA (*perfectly logical*) Why, when he wants to get *at* me!

MRS GRACEDEW (*considering her fondly*) And you absolutely don't
want him to get 'at' you?

CORA (*with a motion of her shoulders as if it's too unutterably a matter of
course*) Why, it's just to *tell* you, so I'm *here*!   990

MRS GRACEDEW (*as with supreme decision; taking it all on herself*)
Then, my dear, he shan't! (*Her emotion, over the difference made by
this, over the clearance of her mistake, shows for the moment as almost
too much for her; so that as if then suddenly conscious of the self-
betrayal involved in this and bethinking herself also of the little*   995
reparation she owes Cora, she explains, but almost pantingly) Pardon
me; I misunderstood. I somehow took for granted—

CORA (*as she drops, from the impossibility of saying all she has taken for
granted*) You took for granted I'd *jump* at him? (*So pleased she has
settled it*) Well, now you can take for granted, *I won't*!   1000

MRS GRACEDEW (*drawn to her, enchanted with her and, as for this reason
wanting to express a further interest in her*) You prefer not to be
'cured'?

CORA (*lucid*) Not by doctors who don't know what's the *matter* with
me!   1005

MRS GRACEDEW (*amused at this turn, adopting it*) Yet Doctor *Yule* seems remarkably clever!

CORA (*having turned this over and in consequence almost bouncing about*) Then why don't you marry him yourself?

MRS GRACEDEW (*as perfunctorily thoughtful; with a rise of her shoulders and a sort of happy philosophic sigh*) Well, I've got *fifty* reasons! (*After an instant*) I rather think one of them must be that he hasn't happened to *ask* me.   1010

CORA (*as doing justice to it, but more fully interested in her own*) Well, I haven't got fifty reasons, but I *have* got one.   1015

MRS GRACEDEW (*amused*) You mean your case is one of those in which safety is *not* in numbers? (*And then as Cora, in her simplicity, doesn't catch on*) It *is* when reasons are bad that one needs so many!

CORA (*her simplicity untroubled, though her purpose is visibly rising*) My reason's tremendously *good*.   1020

MRS GRACEDEW (*sympathetic*) I see. An older friend.

CORA (*as starting a little at her quick divination, but also a little as at some warning sound or some possible check from the quarter of the garden; then recovering herself and coming quickly back to let herself go, to pour out her tale, while the coast is yet clear*) I've been trying this hour, in my terrible need of advice, to *tell* you about him! (*Pantingly and with all intensity*) After we parted, you and I, at the station, he suddenly turned *up* there, my older friend; and I took a little quiet walk with him which gave you time to get here before me and of which Papa's in a state of ignorance that I don't really know whether to bless or to *dread*!   1025   1030

MRS GRACEDEW (*immensely interested, but assuming a high gravity and making immediately the practical application of her confidence*) You want me then to *inform* Mr Prodmore?

CORA (*thus directly challenged, can only, in her predicament, feel her uncertainty and her fears; so that she seems mainly to cast about*) I really don't know *what* I want! (*Unsupported, yearning, candid*) I think, Mrs Gracedew, I just want *kindness*.   1035

MRS GRACEDEW (*as if patient and tender with her, but necessarily definite*) And how do you *understand* 'kindness'?   1040

CORA (*clear about that; honest*) Well, I mean *help*!

MRS GRACEDEW (*as before*) And how do you understand 'help'?

CORA (*turning about in her embarrassment and her appeal; feeling it come down but to one thing*) I'm afraid I only understand that I *love* him.

MRS GRACEDEW (*still all serious and as if the information is valuable, but she has to think from step to step*) And does he love *you*?   1045

CORA (*after a sturdy, honest pause, very simply*) Ask him!

MRS GRACEDEW (*as weighing this practicability*) Where *is* he?

CORA (*as with a large confident look all over the place*) Waiting.

MRS GRACEDEW (*vague and as, for action, requiring more*) But *where?*   1050

CORA (*after an instant, as having just hesitated quite to bring out this detail of her duplicity*) In that funny old grotto.

MRS GRACEDEW (*for but a moment vague; quickly recalling it*) Half way from the park gate?

CORA (*assenting, but with the impulse of pleading for it*) It's ever so *nice!*   1055

MRS GRACEDEW (*as turning it over; business-like*) Oh, I know it!

CORA (*anxious*) Then will you *see* him?

MRS GRACEDEW (*inscrutable, for the minute; dry*) No.

CORA (*taken aback*) 'No'?

MRS GRACEDEW (*as before*) No. (*Then as amplifying*) If you want   1060
help—

CORA (*while she pauses as with the fullness of her thought*) Ah, God knows I do!

MRS GRACEDEW (*in full possession*) You want a great *deal!*

CORA (*responsive, throwing up her arms*) Oh so awfully much! (*With this   1065
immensity all before her*) I want all there *is!*

MRS GRACEDEW (*as having, with the highest responsibility, taken her line*) Well, you shall *have* it.

CORA (*delighted, convulsively holding her to it*) 'All there is'?

MRS GRACEDEW (*looking well at her before making the announcement;   1070
then sharply making it*) I'll see your father.

CORA (*immensely grateful; overjoyed*) You dear delicious lady! (*Then as for full assurance, Mrs Gracedew still looking thoughtful and grave*) He's intensely sympathetic!

MRS GRACEDEW (*surprised, sceptical*) Your father?   1075

CORA Ah, no, the other person. (*With candid enthusiasm*) I *do* so believe in him!

MRS GRACEDEW (*looking at her searchingly an instant; interested; then fully embracing her cause*) Then I do too, and I like him for believing in *you.*   1080

CORA (*encouraged, convinced*) Oh, he does *that,* does it far more than Captain Yule; I could see just at one glance that, though *he,* poor man, may be trying his best to, he hasn't made much headway *yet.*

MRS GRACEDEW (*interested now for herself*) Ah, you think he hasn't made much headway yet?   1085

CORA (*wondering; as if this may be, even now, a little disconcertingly, the note of dissent*) What do *you* think?

MRS GRACEDEW Oh, my dear, how should I know? (*Innocent and blank, but bright*) I'm so *out* of it all!

CORA (*denying this; not accepting such a tone; urgent and serious*) Why, 1090 ain't we just exactly bringing you in?

MRS GRACEDEW (*amused, then as deciding afresh*) Well, I'll come in for *you*!

CORA (*reassured again, appreciative and expressing it by a motion, after which, with further confidence, as for clearness*) And hasn't he also 1095 *complained* of me?

MRS GRACEDEW Captain Yule? (*Then, while she bethinks herself shocked, almost scandalised*) Do you suppose I'd for a moment have *let* him? (*After which, seriously, scrupulously; bethinking herself further*) He does know—I mean by *that*—what I think of you *myself*. 1100

CORA (*satisfied, triumphant*) Then you see how little it *affects* him!

MRS GRACEDEW (*as quite seeing, but making the logical reflection on it*) Yes, but that isn't so much against *you*—

CORA (*catching on*) As against *you*? (*But rejecting this; positive*) Ah, if he doesn't *mind* you— 1105

MRS GRACEDEW (*catching her up*) It's in that case against *him*? (*Inscrutable but good-humoured*) Well, we shall see how much he 'minds' me! (*Then getting back to the immediate and the practical*) But your° father *forbids* you his rival?

CORA (*only asking to tell and perfectly definite*) He *would*, of course, if 1110 he had more *fear*; but we've been so sure he'd hate it, we two, that we've managed to be awfully *careful*. He's the son of the richest man at Bellborough, he's granny's godson and he'll inherit his father's business, which is simply immense. Oh, from the point of view of things he's *in*,° (*hereditarily sharp and com-* 1115 *petent about this*) he's almost as good as Papa himself. (*Then keeping her story clear*) He has been away for three days, and if he met me just now at the station, where, on his way back, he had to change, it was by the merest chance in the world. (*After which, all conclusively*) I wouldn't have shown him I *care* for him if he 1120 hadn't been *nice*.

MRS GRACEDEW (*with a laugh*) A man's always 'nice' when you *do* show him you care for him!

CORA (*stimulated, more than meeting it*) He's nicer still when he shows you he cares for *you*! 1125

MRS GRACEDEW (*reasonably assenting*) Nicer of course than when he shows you he *doesn't*! But are you sure you can *trust* this gentleman?

CORA (*emphatic*) As sure as that I *can't* trust the other.

MRS GRACEDEW (*as for conscience sake*) Ah, but the other hasn't got *near* enough!   1130

CORA (*taking her up with the same spirit*) No, thank goodness, nor ever shall!

MRS GRACEDEW (*as with a last question for the last degree of possession of it; laying her ground*) You mean of course till too *late*.

CORA (*resolutely; as really having all hers*) *Ever* so much!   1135

MRS GRACEDEW (*who stands° a moment quite fixedly, yet at the same time absently, studying her, and then comes back abruptly to business almost as with an effect of sharp impatience*) Then what's the *matter* —with the gentleman in the grotto?

CORA (*now for the first time faltering*) The matter for *Papa* is his name. 1140

MRS GRACEDEW (*surprised*) Nothing but his name?

CORA (*whose eyes roll, in her embarrassment, from below to above and all over the place*) Yes, but—

MRS GRACEDEW (*amused, yet inviting*) But it's *enough*?

CORA (*fixing as in mild anguish a distant point*) *Not* enough. That's just 1145 the *trouble*.

MRS GRACEDEW (*as with a delicacy to surmount, but kindly curious*) What then *is* it?

CORA (*deciding to speak*) Pegg.

MRS GRACEDEW (*vague*) Nothing else?   1150

CORA (*serious, resigned*) Nothing to *speak* of. (*Distinctly but sadly*) Hall.

MRS GRACEDEW (*still wondering*) Nothing *before*?

CORA (*calmly desperate and throughout this always looking at distances*) Not a letter.

MRS GRACEDEW (*formulating it, turning it over*) Hall Pegg? (*Then as 1155 having winced at the sound, having recognised the inadequacy, but restraining indecent comment*) Oh!

CORA (*as having accepted the worst, but turning off with a renewed sense of what this is*) It sounds like a hat-rack!

MRS GRACEDEW (*who continues to study and sound it*) 'Hall Pegg'? 'Hall 1160 Pegg'? Oh. (*She seems to wonder what may be done about it, but also, seeing no issue, to drop her arms a little in despair. But it occurs to her to ask*) How many has Mr Prodmore?

CORA How many names? (*Considering, but only to see it makes it worse*) I believe he somehow makes out *five*.   1165

MRS GRACEDEW (*prompt, derisive*) Oh, that's *too* many!

CORA (*conscientious, to meet all sides of the question*) Papa unfortunately doesn't *think* so, when Captain Yule, I understand, has *six*.

MRS GRACEDEW (*taken; with immense interest; candid*) Six?

CORA (*clear*) Papa, at tea there, told me them *all*.   1170

MRS GRACEDEW (*frankly wondering*) And what *are* they?

CORA Oh, all sorts. (*She begins to recall*) 'Marmaduke Clement—'

MRS GRACEDEW (*cutting in; checking herself*) I see. 'Marmaduke Clement' will *do*. (*Consciously dropping° that interest; coming back, with decision, to the point*) But so will yours!   1175

CORA Mine? (*Rueful*) You mean *his*.

MRS GRACEDEW (*resolute*) The same thing. What you'll *be*.

CORA (*emulating her optimism; trying it; ringing it out*) 'Mrs Hall Pegg'?

MRS GRACEDEW (*with an inevitable shrug, as it falls flat in the noble* 1180 *space; but trying kindly to cover it up*) It won't make you a bit less *charming*.

CORA (*as if she has realised this, or at least hopes for it; making the best of it*) Only for Papa!

MRS GRACEDEW (*guaranteeing it*) Never for *me*!   1185

CORA (*in the highest degree appreciative; gratefully caressing*) You accept it *more* than gracefully. But if you could only make *him*—

MRS GRACEDEW (*all attention, yet also all wonder*) 'Him'? Mr Pegg?

CORA (*clear; resigned*) No, he naturally *has* to accept it. But Papa.

MRS GRACEDEW (*considering critically this large order; yet as if it* 1190 *belongs, after all, to what she has undertaken*) Well, it will be a *job*. But I *will*. (*Then on another spasm of Cora's gratitude; sustained, inspired*) And I'll make him *say* he does!

CORA (*yearning; as with the dream of it*) Oh if I could only *hear* him!

MRS GRACEDEW (*crystalline now; with a gesture of dismissal of that* 1195 *question decided*) It will be enough if *I* do.

CORA (*appreciating her tone, satisfied*) Yes then, I think it *will*. (*And as if now ready to go*) I'll give you *time*.

MRS GRACEDEW (*as with the sharpness of her complete scheme*) Thank you! But before you give me 'time', give me something *better*.   1200

CORA (*wondering, as if, having parted with her secret, she has parted with her all*) 'Better'?

MRS GRACEDEW (*luminous*) If I help you, you know, you must help *me*.

CORA (*ready but vague*) But *how*?   1205

MRS GRACEDEW (*sharp*) By a clear *assurance*. That if Captain Yule should propose to you you'll unconditionally *refuse* him.

CORA (*as with the relief of it being only that*) With my dying breath.

MRS GRACEDEW (*holding her, intensifying*) Will you give me even a *pledge*?   1210

CORA (*solid and sound; looking about her as for a paper*) Do you want me to *sign—*

MRS GRACEDEW (*immediate*) No, don't 'sign'!

CORA (*at a loss*) Then *what* shall I do?

MRS GRACEDEW (*turning off as under an emotion; but after a few vague* 1215 *steps facing her again*) Kiss me.

CORA (*responsive, in her arms; then as with all arranged*) We meet of course at the station.

MRS GRACEDEW (*while they hold each other*) If all goes *well*. But where shall you *be* meanwhile?   1220

CORA (*instant, surprised*) Can't you guess?

MRS GRACEDEW (*jumping to it*) At that funny old *grotto*? (*Then clasping her again with the flourish of an arm; holding her, keeping her; hurrying her up to back*) I'll *start* you to it!

> *With which, thus united, they quickly disappear into ante-room of main entrance, right, while curtain falls*

3.

*The hall again after the lapse of a few minutes; with Mr
Prodmore just appearing, at left, in doorway from garden. As he
comes down briskly, on same side, Mrs Gracedew who has at the
same moment entered, at right, from the ante-room where she has
been seeing Cora off through the park, comes down as with a
similar expression of no more time to lose; so that, though on his
own entrance, he has not seen her emerge, but simply finds her
there, a little fluttered, but carrying it off. They are confronted
over the width of the stage. She has in her whole air the sense of a
return now to the more immediate and sterner reality and of
having got, with all resolution, for this particular encounter, as
quickly as possible under arms*

PRODMORE (*as addressing the whole place, with his peremptory note, the
instant he has entered*) My daughter's not here?

MRS GRACEDEW (*a little blown,° as if panting from her recent rapid
transaction, and holding her hand lightly to her heart; but bracing
herself, bright, ready for him*) Your daughter's not here. But (*smiling   5
bravely*) it's a convenience to me, Mr Prodmore, that *you* are, for
I've something very particular to *ask* you.

PRODMORE (*who has crossed, on this, straight to right; at the door of the
lower rooms*) I shall be delighted to answer your question, but I must
first put my hand on Miss Prodmore. (*Then, however, as he pauses at   10
the sudden bright possibility*) Unless indeed she's occupied in there
with Captain Yule?

MRS GRACEDEW (*now at left; after keen consideration, with her eyes
dropped, but raising them to him, as she speaks, with all her courage and
with high distinctness*) I don't think she's occupied, anywhere, with   15
Captain Yule.

PRODMORE (*coming straight away from the door, his hands in his pockets;
with a flash of wonder*) Then where the deuce *is* Captain Yule?

MRS GRACEDEW (*highly diplomatic; guarding her manner; careful of
each of her steps*) His absence, for which I'm (*with a vague, nervous,   20
cheery laugh*) *responsible* is just what renders the enquiry I speak of
to you *possible*. (*Then as breaking ground, all debatingly, for the
'enquiry'*) What will you take? (*Hanging fire in spite of herself*) What
will you take?

PRODMORE (*feeling in it as yet only some odd, vague, but characteristic,* 25
general solicitude) 'Take'? (*Distinct and curt*) Nothing more, thank
you. I've just had a cup of tea. (*Then on a second thought; remember-*
ing manners) Won't *you* have one?

MRS GRACEDEW Yes, with pleasure; but not yet. (*Then casting about*
her with the sense of what must come before this; at close quarters 30
with her 'job' and, instinctively, anxiously, a little painfully, pressing
her light hand a moment to her eyes) Not *yet*.

PRODMORE (*as vaguely struck by this; making sure*) You wouldn't be
better for it immediately?

MRS GRACEDEW (*positive*) No. (*Distinct again*) No, I don't want to be 35
'better'. (*Then afresh with her nervous laugh*) I'm beautifully *well*!
(*On which, and on his motion of satisfied acceptance, though also as*
after a supreme roll of her eyes over the place, she comes back to her
attack) I want to know how you'd *value*—

PRODMORE (*instantly alert for that sweet word; putting himself as* 40
quickly in her place, that of a real connoisseur; so that he's already
genial about it) One of these charming old things that takes your
fancy?

MRS GRACEDEW (*looking at him, with one of her spasms of resolution,*
very straight now and quite hard) They *all* take my fancy. 45

PRODMORE (*enjoying it, with his noted geniality, as the joke of a rich*
person; the kind of joke he sometimes makes himself) 'All'?

MRS GRACEDEW (*as really and brilliantly meaning it*) Every single one!
(*Then as if this has already made a good basis; taking familiarly for*
granted the ground they have covered at a stride) Should you be 50
willing to *treat*,° Mr Prodmore, for your interest in the *whole* nice
thing?

PRODMORE (*throwing back his head; struck; yet wondering here at some*
missing links) Am I to take it from you then that you *know* about my
interest— 55

MRS GRACEDEW (*with a conscious strained smile, but raising light and*
airy hands which just dispose, by a flourish, of any of the difficulties
attending such a certainty) Everything.

PRODMORE (*accepting her knowledge then; but more reserved and as for*
an important rectification) Pardon me, madam! (*Explaining*) You 60
don't know 'everything' if you don't know that my interest, (*pom-*
pous) considerable as it might well have struck you, has just ceased
to—the least bit invidiously perhaps—*predominate*! I've given it up
(*with a confidential, an agreeable smile, as to soften the blow*) for a
handsome equivalent. 65

MRS GRACEDEW (*not at all staggered; all there to meet it*) You mean for a splendid son-in-law.

PRODMORE (*as perfectly possessed of what he means, but with his constant responsibility to 'form'*) It will be by some such description as the term you use that I shall doubtless, hereafter, in the common course, permit myself to allude to Captain Yule. (*Then as on a further genial vision*) Unless indeed I call him—(*But he drops the bolder thought*) It will depend on what he calls *me*.

MRS GRACEDEW (*after a moment, as with a still larger judgment of this*) Won't it depend a little on what your daughter herself calls him?

PRODMORE (*considering the question, then settling it, radiantly, in the sense of the highest delicacy*) No. *That* mystery of their united state will be between the happy pair!

MRS GRACEDEW (*still advancing into the subject as with the flicker of all her light*) Am I to take it from you then—I adopt your excellent phrase—that Miss Prodmore has already accepted him?

PRODMORE (*his head still in the air and his manner seeming to signify that he has put his Fact down on the table and that she can take it or not as she likes*) Her character, formed by my assiduous care, enables me to locate her, I may say even to *time* her, from moment to moment, (*massive, clear-faced, watch in hand*) with all but mathematical certainty! (*Then as he complacently surveys his watch*) It's my assured conviction that she's combining inclination with duty even while we sit here!

MRS GRACEDEW (*who, after having with a high, odd, but inarticulate sound, half an apprehensive groan and half a smothered joy, 'taken it from him' in all its fatuity and folly, gives way to her nervousness and moves up and round; invoking comfort and support, with all her eyes, from the whole picture, before speaking, abruptly, on an effective change of tone*) Dear Mr Prodmore, why are you so awfully rash as to make your daughter *afraid* of you? (*With increasing confidence, as she has broken this ice*) You should have taught her to confide in you. (*Advisingly, soothingly, serenely*) She has clearly *shown* me that she *can* confide.

PRODMORE (*with a frown; pulled up by this new note*) She 'confides' in *you*?

MRS GRACEDEW Well, (*facing him, smiling, laughing*) you may 'take it from me'! (*Then as if seeing her way now*) Let me suggest that, as fortune has thrown us together a minute, you follow her good example.

PRODMORE Oh!

MRS GRACEDEW° (*she puts out a hand to check him; she knows what she's about; she takes her further step*) Tell me for instance the ground of your objection to poor Mr Pegg.

PRODMORE Pegg?   110

MRS GRACEDEW° (*then as he starts at the name and remains blank, for excess of amazement, at her audacity; distinct, categorical and as already with the sense of success*) I mean Mr Pegg of Bellborough, Mr Hall Pegg, the godson of your daughter's grandmother and the associate of his father in their flourishing house: to whom—as *he* is,   115
dear young man, to *it* and to *her*°—Miss Prodmore is devotedly attached.

PRODMORE (*who has sunk in his dismay into the nearest chair, staring amazedly before him*) It has gone as far as *that*?

MRS GRACEDEW (*triumphant now; towering above him*) It has gone so   120
far that you must let it go the rest of the way!

PRODMORE (*physically prostrate, but the solid gasping pretension, the habit of massive dignity of him, asserting themselves through everything, with deep resentment at having been 'done'*) It's too monstrous
of you to have plotted with her to keep me in the dark!   125

MRS GRACEDEW (*without insolence, only all candid and explanatory*) Why, it's only when you're kept in the dark that your daughter's kept in the light! (*Clear, completing, explaining, almost accommodating; as in the interest of the merest common sense*) It's at her own earnest request that I plead to you for her liberty of choice. She's   130
an honest girl; perhaps even a peculiar girl. And she's not a baby. You overdo, I think, in your natural solicitude, the nursing! (*Then committing herself all the way*) She has a perfect right to her *preference*.

PRODMORE (*helpless, overwhelmed; appealing with vain majesty from   135
his chair*) And, pray, haven't I a perfect right to *mine*?

MRS GRACEDEW (*indulgent, kindly; but absolute, distinct, clear as a bell*) Not at her expense. (*Then as letting him know it fairly for his very own sake*) You expect her to give up too much.

PRODMORE (*immediate, vehement*) And what has she expected *me* to   140
give up? What but the desire of my *heart* and the dream of my *life*? (*As if he has never heard of anything so fantastic; and has moreover, against Mrs Gracedew's game of opposition, this crowning card to play*) Captain Yule announced to me but a few minutes since his uncontrollable *impatience* to get in his bid!   145

MRS GRACEDEW (*not at all upset by it, having her own reasons*) Well, if he does get it in, I think he'll simply find—

PRODMORE (*while she hangs fire as for effect and they look at each other hard*) Find *what*?

MRS GRACEDEW (*sharp, downright*) Why, that she won't do business.   150

PRODMORE (*whom it brings to his feet; erect, absolutely*) She *will*!

MRS GRACEDEW (*with a gay undaunted headshake; insistent*) She won't.

PRODMORE (*passionate, making for the staircase*) She *shall*!

MRS GRACEDEW (*getting there with a rush and a spring, before him; barring the way with her arms out; so that as a result of it they rise there confronted for the moment like real enemies*) She shan't! (*Her   155 movement, her attitude, her finer passion, check him and hold him thus as by their spell; during which she looks at him as a lady lion-tamer, at the circus, may look at one of the creatures she's accustomed to cow. After which, as having felt the spell work, she comes back, on one of her   160 sudden sharp changes of note, to their real question*) Now tell me how much!

PRODMORE (*giving way under it, yielding ground, turning off and coming down, where, on the opposite side from which he has gone up, he stands wiping his brow with a crimson silk pocket handkerchief and   165 already recognising in her question the light of a new and different, possibly even a bigger, chance; which glimpse of compensation he doesn't, however, at once confess to°*) How can I 'tell' you anything so preposterous?

MRS GRACEDEW (*perfectly ready to show him how*) Simply by comput-   170 ing the total amount to which, for your benefit, this poor old estate is burdened! (*Then as, after moving away from her with a toss of impatience, he has paused for attention, his back expressively presented*) If I've upset you by my proof, as I may call it, that your speculation is built on the sand, let me atone for that by my wish to take off   175 your hands an investment from which you draw so little profit.

PRODMORE (*in the same position; his attention still further held*) And pray what profit will you derive—

MRS GRACEDEW (*all cheerful, as with reasons, of a private nature, that suffice to her*) Ah, that's my own secret! (*Then as if this ought to   180 content him*) I just *want* the nice old thing!

PRODMORE (*moving further away; with high decision*) So do *I*, damn me! (*Stuffing into his breast-pocket, with a thrust of resolution, the crimson handkerchief taken out to mop his brow*) And that's why I've practically *paid* for it!   185

MRS GRACEDEW (*who waits a moment, all considerate, all perceptive, as taking in this; then brings out, as if her proposal is exactly and most reasonably, quite coaxingly, founded on all the facts of his case*) I'll

'practically pay' for it, Mr Prodmore—if you'll only tell me your
figure.   190

PRODMORE (*slowly turning round to this, but not yet looking at her*) My
figure?

MRS GRACEDEW (*sweet, serene*) Your figure.

PRODMORE (*looking at her now, across their interval, very hard for an
instant; then, his hands in his pockets, throwing back his head as for a* 195
gaze through space and speaking very dryly) My figure would be
quite my own!

MRS GRACEDEW (*her laugh nervous again, but all brave, all consciously
and expressly cheerful and hopeful*) Then it will match in that respect
this overture, which is quite *my* 'own'! (*As taking for granted thus* 200
every smoothness)° As soon as you let me know it I cable to Missoura
Top to have the money, (*with an artless assumption of every facility*)
well, sent right straight out to you.

PRODMORE (*highly superior; only dryly amused at this fine feminine
conception of business*) You imagine that having the money 'sent 205
right straight out to me' will make you owner of this place?

MRS GRACEDEW (*her head on one side, considering the question, while,
nervously, she draws with one hand the end of her scarf, draws her long
gloves, or something of that kind, through the grasp of the other; and
speaks as if it's rather a question for debate, for appreciation*) No, not 210
quite perhaps. But I'll settle the rest with Captain Yule.

PRODMORE (*planted there with his legs apart now, his hands behind his
coat-tails and with a superior sway of his upper person to and fro a
moment, so that he looks down first, over his large white waistcoat, at
his patent-leather laced boots, with their bright tan-coloured tops, then* 215
over the legs of his rather loud cross-barred° trousers and finally, set-
tling his head in his florid blue neck-tie, up, with sustained reserve at the
roof) Captain Yule has nothing to *sell*.

MRS GRACEDEW (*blank, though sharply ironic; infinitely surprised*)
Then what have you been trying to *buy*?   220

PRODMORE (*in whom this question, ringing out clear, determines a sudden
quick and startled apprehension*) Do you mean to say you're after
that? (*Then while her face meets his intensity of emphasis and the queer
knowing grimace with which it's accompanied; the effect of all of which
is to make her, under his eyes, turn away with a mute comment, in her* 225
*lightly raised and dropped, her repudiating, disclaiming arm, on his
perceptible vulgarity*) Is your proposal that I should transfer my
investment to you for the mere net amount your conception of a
fair bargain?

MRS GRACEDEW (*facing more about to him; weighing it; grave*) Pray   230
then what's yours?

PRODMORE (*ready; definite; hard*) Mine would be—quite evidently,
dear madam!—not that I should simply get my money back, but
that I should get the effective value of the house.

MRS GRACEDEW (*not at all disconcerted*) But isn't the 'effective value   235
of the house' just what your money expresses and what your
getting it back, in a beautiful lump, would *realise* to you?

PRODMORE (*with a sidelong shrewd contraction of the eye turned to her
while he faces front*) No, madam! It's just what *yours* does and what
your expenditure of it, in a 'beautiful lump', would realise to *you*.   240
(*Complacent for his happy advantage*)° You'll remember that you've
already *dealt* for us, a little, in beautiful lumps!°

MRS GRACEDEW (*as vague at first; then understanding, but all candid
about it*) With those good people, when I showed the place
off?   245

PRODMORE (*agreeably amused*) You seemed to be *taking* bids then.

MRS GRACEDEW (*shut up, for the moment, in her appearance of beautiful
blank vagueness*) 'Taking' them?

PRODMORE (*so diverted at the reminiscence*) So like an auctioneer!
(*With a fine free laugh*)° You ran it up high!   250

MRS GRACEDEW (*embarrassed, but always brave; fighting the ground,
attenuating*) I certainly did, if saying it's charming—

PRODMORE (*taking her up; derisive*) 'Charming'?° You said it's magnificent; you said it's supreme; you said it's unique. (*Triumphant*)
That was your striking expression; with which everyone agreed.   255
(*Following it up*) You called it the very model of its type. (*More than
accusatory; really crushing; jubilant*) Oh you got in *deep*.

MRS GRACEDEW (*as if it's indeed an indictment, a little pale, her smile
rather set; yet bearing up*) Possibly. (*She has seated herself and, while
she turns this over, follows with her eyes the point of her parasol, say;*   260
scratching the old floor of the hall) But taunting me with my absurd
high spirits and the dreadful liberties I took doesn't in the least tell
me how deep *you're* in!

PRODMORE (*all contentedly and easily responsive*) For *you*, Mrs
Gracedew? (*Then while he dandles and looks at his shoes and at the*   265
roof again, as if to give the effect of his answer time to accumulate) I'm
in to the tune of fifty thousand.

MRS GRACEDEW (*still seated in the same way; her eyes raised to his face a
moment, then again thoughtfully dropped; very quiet*) That's a great
deal of money, Mr Prodmore.   270

PRODMORE (*promptly, crudely, rejoicingly*) So I've often had occasion to *say* to myself!

MRS GRACEDEW (*quietly following up her thought and defining her position*) If it's a large sum for *you* then, it's a still larger one for *me*. (*She occupies there the position she so defines, but stating her case all reasonably*) We women, poor things that we are, have more modest ideas.

PRODMORE (*quite closed to any force in this*) Is it as a 'modest idea' that you describe your extraordinary intrusion? (*Expressing his climax only by his dandle*)

MRS GRACEDEW (*as if lost in the sense of her innocent community with her sex, no question and no climax reach her*) I mean I think we measure things often more *exactly*!

PRODMORE (*as quite thanking her for the words*) Then you measured *this* thing 'exactly' half an hour *ago*!°

MRS GRACEDEW (*as if the time he mentions is a long way to go back, yet as making the effort and the journey; from which she returns with an amused candid recall*) Was I *very* grotesque?

PRODMORE (*this word on the contrary not at all suiting him*) 'Grotesque'?

MRS GRACEDEW (*as really wanting to know*) I mean *did* I go on about it?

PRODMORE (*immediate, specific, vivid*) 'Go on'? You worked it up as, in the course of a considerable experience, I've never heard *any* auctioneer! You banged the desk. You raved and shrieked.

MRS GRACEDEW (*lost as in the happy but quite detached recognition*) We *do* shriek at Missoura Top. (*Musing, admitting*) Yes, and, when we *like* things, we 'rave'.

PRODMORE (*as proof not only against blandishments, but even now against symptoms of undue or premature sociability*) I don't know what you do at Missoura Top, but I know what you did at Covering End!

MRS GRACEDEW (*as having found, after a moment, her line, getting up*) So do *I* then! (*As if meaning that this is what she has done from the beginning*) I took you aback! You weren't prepared for my wild ways.

PRODMORE (*brisk and resolute*) No, and I'm not prepared *yet*.

MRS GRACEDEW (*as if she can quite do justice to it; like a doctor diagnosing his case*) Yes, you're too *astonished*.

PRODMORE (*curt; treating this as a blandishment; not facing her; looking over her head*) My astonishment's my own *affair*, not less so than my memory!

MRS GRACEDEW (*liberal, intelligent, beautifully mild and gay*) Oh, I *yield* to your memory, which, for all your great affairs, must have become today so wonderful! (*After which, quickly, before he can speak*) And I confess to my extravagance. (*Then imperturbably, as if he will quite understand*) But quite, you know, *as* extravagance.

PRODMORE (*clear of all connection with it; shaking it off*) I don't *at all* 'know'! Nor what you *call* extravagance.

MRS GRACEDEW (*gaily, perfectly knowing*) Why, 'working you up'. Banging the desk, raving and shrieking. (*In clearest explanation*) I worked you up just to *please* you!

PRODMORE (*after an instant; looking at her and her beauty up and down, on this testimony of how such wonderful things have been set in motion for him, and not, after all, without effect; though the conscious hardness with which he still resists may seem at first to contradict that*) So you 'just', as you call it, said what you didn't *believe*?°

MRS GRACEDEW (*with dignity, yet with radiant, with supreme candour*) Yes. For *you*.

PRODMORE (*suspicious, vague*) For 'me'?

MRS GRACEDEW (*casting about her, conscious under his eye; then finding as a matter of course her other reason*) And for those good people.

PRODMORE Oh! (*Sarcastic*) Should you like me to call them *back*?

MRS GRACEDEW (*gay*) No. (*Quite clear about it*) I did what house-keepers do.

PRODMORE (*not fitting this in*) 'Housekeepers'?

MRS GRACEDEW (*sweetly, lucidly*) I exaggerated.

PRODMORE (*as if scandalised*) You misrepresented?

MRS GRACEDEW (*charmingly*) Well°—I strained a point. 'For the good of the house'?

PRODMORE (*taking it in, but unappeased, as at a highly suspicious story*) Then if we ain't what you *say*, (*hanging fire here, holding her with the question very searchingly, all the more that while he has this pregnant pause she consciously looks away*) why the devil do you *want* us? Why the devil (*as she still says nothing and takes, as it were, no notice*) did you say you'd offer fifty thousand?°

MRS GRACEDEW (*brought round to him as by the odd faint recall of this from far, far back; a little wan*) Did I say that? (*With a little expressive shrug, as if she can't imagine why*) It was a figure of speech!

PRODMORE (*prompt, triumphant*) Then *that's* the kind of figure we're talking about!

> Then while she raises a vague, though rather consciously ineffective, hand of protest, he sees Chivers, who appears at the

door from garden and at sight of whom Mrs Gracedew makes
also a motion of relief and hope, getting further away from
Prodmore and letting the old man, whom her eyes fondly fix,
come down between them. Enter Chivers from garden. The effect
of this is that he draws to himself instantly Mr Prodmore's high
displeasure

Have you seen Miss Prodmore? If you *haven't*, find her at *once*.

MRS GRACEDEW (*at whom alone Chivers has looked, from the first, and*
from whom, even under Prodmore's challenge, he doesn't take his eyes;
speaking now as in full possession of all her wits; and as always to
Chivers, very kindly, quite caressingly) You won't, my dear man,   355
'find her at once'; you won't perhaps, very easily, *ever* find her
again. (*Then bracing herself as for the supreme truth to Prodmore and*
this time quite not flinching) Cora has gone with Mr Pegg.

PRODMORE (*astounded*) Pegg has *been* here?

MRS GRACEDEW (*letting him, with the same high spirit have it all*) He   360
walked with her from the station.

PRODMORE (*stupefied*) When she *arrived*? (*Piecing it together*) That's
why she was so *late*?

MRS GRACEDEW (*serene, even gay*) Why I got here *first*. (*Then with*
her conscious habit of success, the sense of how it always floats her,   365
and will in a manner float her now, into port, over no matter what
shallows and after no matter what bumps) I think I get *everywhere*
first.

PRODMORE (*aggravated, harsh, eyeing her as through menacing lids*)
Isn't the question, ma'am, rather where I shall expect to 'get', and   370
what? (*Then as she meets this, keeping up her brave face, but in smiling*
inscrutable silence; peremptory, rude) In which direction did they *go*?

MRS GRACEDEW (*taking her time thus to make up her mind*) I think I
must let you find *out*!

PRODMORE (*pulled up, as unable, in the conditions, to deal with her;*   375
addressing himself wrathfully to Chivers, who has but stood bewildered
and gaping) Call my carriage, you monster. (*Then, while Chivers,*
starting in obedience as if fairly to dodge a brick hurled at him, shuffles
up with all speed to the door to park, Prodmore letting himself go so far
as he dares at Mrs Gracedew) So you abetted and protected this   380
wicked, low intrigue.

Exit Chivers to park°

MRS GRACEDEW (*still taking her time; making some half-circle round*
and about, all thoughtfully and patiently, even a little pityingly, while
she trails her dress down; now indifferent, above all, to any violence)

You're too disappointed to see your real interest. Oughtn't I 385
therefore in common charity to point it *out* to you?

PRODMORE (*facing her question all icily, yet so far as to treat it as one*)
What do *you* know of my disappointment?

MRS GRACEDEW (*perfectly frank, courageous and kind*) I know
everything. 390

PRODMORE (*wrapped up in his wrong; as if not hearing her*) What do
you know of my real interest?

MRS GRACEDEW (*perfectly gentle, reasonable, ready; also perfectly clear*)
I know enough for my purpose, which is to offer you a handsome
condition. (*Putting it squarely before him*) I think it's not I who have 395
protected the happy understanding that you call by so ugly a name;
it's the happy understanding that has put *me*, (*with increased confidence and clearness*) well, in a position! (*Pursuing as she sees this
holds him*) *Do* drive after them, if you like, but catch up with them
only to *forgive* them. If you'll do *that*—(*But she waits, concentrated* 400
*and serious; as if, wound-up though she may be, it's still a good deal to
bring out*)

PRODMORE (*as with a stimulated nose now for her possibilities*) Well, if I
do exactly what it's odious to me to do—

MRS GRACEDEW (*bringing it, ringing it out*) Well, I'll do the same! 405

PRODMORE (*cold, utterly uncommitted*) And what do you call the
same?°

MRS GRACEDEW I'll pay your price.

PRODMORE (*with the same superiority*) What do you *call* my price?

MRS GRACEDEW (*as if it's too obvious*) Why, the sum you just 410
mentioned. Fifty thousand.

PRODMORE (*stupefied; derisive, as if she's joking, while he settles his head
in his florid neck-gear*) That's not my price, and never for a moment
was! Besides, (*his hands in his pockets, square and erect on his large
patent-leather feet*) my price is *up*! 415

MRS GRACEDEW (*disappointed, stricken; echoing it as with a long wail*)
'Up'?

PRODMORE (*fairly enjoying the sound of her*) Up, *up*, UP. Seventy
thousand.

MRS GRACEDEW (*as, called on for so high a stake, she turns away over-* 420
whelmed) Oh-h, deary *me*!

PRODMORE (*up at right, as to gain his carriage; immutable, absolute*) It's
to take or to *leave*!

MRS GRACEDEW (*who has at first seemed to look at it as out there before
them in the middle of the hall in all its monstrous exorbitance, and* 425

thereby as if only to 'leave'; changing, making, also at right, a quick restraining sign up to Prodmore at sight of Yule on the staircase; who, arrested for an instant half way by finding them together, then comes down with decision and at left, looks from one to the other; Mrs Gracedew meanwhile watching him arrive and drawing from him a supreme inspiration) Seventy thousand then!   430

    Enter Captain Clement Yule by staircase

PRODMORE *(having during Yule's entrance but glared at him from where he stands; and continuing to glare even while Mrs Gracedew, with her rapid, dissimulated nearer approach, right, has launched her desperate figure)* Seventy thousand. *Done!*   435

    Exit Mr Prodmore, with bang of door, to ante-room and park

YULE *(at left, astonished)* He's gone? I've been *looking* for him!

MRS GRACEDEW *(agitated, breathless, in fact quite heaving; but doing her best to dissemble, to keep herself together and spoil nothing now by a mistake, pantingly)* I don't think, you know, you *need* him—now.   440

YULE *(mystified)* 'Now'?

MRS GRACEDEW *(smiling, though a little blown; but trying to be plausible, more coherent)* I mean that, if you don't *mind,* *(with a vague awkward laugh)* you must treat with *me.* I've arranged with Mr Prodmore to take it over.   445

YULE *(perfectly blank, his hands in his pockets)* Take *what* over?

MRS GRACEDEW *(as wondering, in embarrassment, when it comes to the point, what she can call it; but casting about also as if she misses, or would like, a little more help from his imagination or his readiness)* Why, your big debt.   450

YULE *(only, however, the less helpful and the more bewildered)* Can you—without 'arranging' with *me?*

MRS GRACEDEW *(moving about, nervous, turning it over as if as much as possible to oblige him)* That's precisely what I *want* to do. *(Then more brightly and sociably, as she thinks further)* That is, I mean, I want you to arrange with *me.* *(Smiling at him, encouraging to his dimness)* Surely you will, won't you?   455

YULE *(his dimness persisting in spite of her brightness)* But if I arrange with anybody—*(Not able to see)*

MRS GRACEDEW *(while she waits, cheerfully and hopefully, as for this miracle of his vision)* Yes?   460

YULE *(in darkness)* ° How do I perform my engagement?

MRS GRACEDEW *(considering it as if he might have fifty)* The one to Mr Prodmore?

YULE (*assenting as if for her own assistance*) 'The one'. *The* one. *That's*   465
the worst.

MRS GRACEDEW Certainly. (*With an old happy laugh*) The worst!

YULE (*his gloom yielding a little to his always renewed amusement at her;
yet as moving, in his puzzlement, a little more out of her reach and
stating the case of her apparent perversity*) You speak as if it's being   470
the worst made it the best!

MRS GRACEDEW (*knowing what he means*) It does, for *me*. (*Then as
almost maternally cheering and instructive*) You don't *perform* any
engagement.°

YULE (*as requiring a moment to take it in; but then with the leap of a   475
light to his face*) He lets me *off*?

MRS GRACEDEW (*as delighted to give him the news*) He lets you off!

YULE (*taking it in further, making it out, staring before him; but then
wincing, pulling himself up, clouded again*) Oh I see; I lose my
house!   480

MRS GRACEDEW (*shocked at his simplifications*) *Dear* no,° that doesn't
follow! (*After an instant*) You simply arrange with *me* to keep it.

YULE (*sincerely wondering*) 'Simply'? (*Not making it out*) How do I
arrange?

MRS GRACEDEW (*as cheerfully, sociably preaching patience*) Well, we   485
must *think*. We must wait. (*As if it's a mere detail, only the principle
granted; fairly talking as if to a reasonable child*) We'll find some way
all right!

YULE (*quite willing to hope so, yet failing completely to see; and with an
awkward nervous laugh for it*) Yes, but what way *shall* we find? (*Then   490
as if he can think only of the impossible ways, the ways that don't fit
now*) With Prodmore, you see, (*with a still greater awkwardness for
his having even thus indirectly to refer to it*) it was, as you say, 'simple'
enough.

MRS GRACEDEW (*thinking, demurring, downright*) I never called *that*   495
simple!

YULE (*as wondering what, and how much, she knows; defining, however
ruefully, his relation to the Prodmore terms*) It was at any rate clear.
(*After an instant*) I could marry his daughter.

MRS GRACEDEW (*as in slow, conscious amazement, pointed irony, long-   500
drawn and fine*) *Could* you?

YULE (*breaking, under the effect of it, into a laugh of conscious, shame-
faced retraction, minimising, for his dignity, attenuating for his taste*)
Well, never perhaps quite wholly and *entirely* that, when it came, as
one may say, to the last scratch. But (*stating it, for his consistency, for*   505

his sincerity, with difficulty) there were points, you see, that I had at least to consider.

MRS GRACEDEW (*while she listens and he, as it were, flounders; natural and tender, as if it's more than she can bear*) Oh you poor dear!

YULE (*completing, under this note of sympathy, his explanation*)° He put it in such a way that I had to—a—(*then rapid, short*) pretend to think of it. (*Then as she takes this from him, in all its dreadfulness, as it were, only with the silence of her so feeling for him; sociably*) You didn't *suspect* that?

MRS GRACEDEW (*just impenetrable again*) That you were 'pretending'?

YULE (*his hands rubbing the back of his head; considering to give the best account of it*) Well, that I was *trying*.°

MRS GRACEDEW (*as if these personal appeals from him really touch her too much; breaking off from him as by the effect on her nerves of her positive excess of interest*) Don't ask me too many questions!

YULE (*looking after her now as if he wonders why*) But isn't this just the moment for questions? (*Not following her, but, by a movement, a turn, rather more quiet and effective than quick or sharp, meeting and arresting her where she comes down, or round; and speaking for the first time as if a care for the appearance and the impression he may have made finally concern him*) What *did* you suppose?

MRS GRACEDEW (*brushing, without indifference, past him, not stopping to say it, saying it as she goes*) Why, I supposed you were in *distress*.

YULE (*placed so that he now, at left or wherever, looks after her again while she moves right*) About his terms?

MRS GRACEDEW (*who has seated herself again right, while her last movement and manner have kept him, as it were, left with the stage between them*) About his terms, of course! (*Then as quietly amused*) Not about his religious opinions.

YULE (*his gratitude too great even for such mild gaiety as that; his perception and admiration all growing now for the sureness with which her instinct and her intelligence have guided her*) You really, in your beautiful sympathy, *guessed* my fix?

MRS GRACEDEW (*seated, serenely diverted, not viewing this as so very much a miracle*) Dear Captain Yule, it stuck too immensely *out of* you!

YULE (*his smile just a trifle sickly, while he wonders at the figure he may have cut*) You mean I gasped like a drowning man?

MRS GRACEDEW (*assenting then with decision to this interpretation*) Till *I* plunged in!

YULE (*considering her for a moment from where he stands; she meanwhile not looking at him, but either only straight before her, or as, occupied with her own thought at some slab of the old floor; then, however, turning away and keeping up left before he speaks*) You *saved* me!

MRS GRACEDEW (*as accepting it, but not insisting on it; only, in all happy lucidity and recognised responsibility concluding from it*) What a pity, now, *I* haven't a daughter!

YULE (*who has moved, in his meditation, as far up left, say, as door of garden, or perhaps only has hovered before the great chimney-place; arrested by this odd expression of hers; thinking of it a moment with his back still turned to her; then facing about, blank, challenging, for the question*) What on earth should I *do* with her?

MRS GRACEDEW (*frankly ironic, sympathetically amused at his expense; the space between them not diminished*) You'd *treat* her, I hope, better than you've treated Miss Prodmore.

YULE (*pulled up, distressed, not expecting this implication; as colouring with shame*) Then have I been *base*?

MRS GRACEDEW (*only looking at him at first, always across their interval, as in admiration of his incurable candour and in compassion for her own small joke; then impulsively, as for her similar ejaculations of a few moments before*) Oh you sweet simple man!

YULE (*from the same place; relieved then; his momentary fear carried off; though his modesty once more a little compromised by her so wonderful quaintness and directness*) Of course; I'm all *right*, and I feel but one regret, which, however, is immense. (*Putting it perfectly before her*) I've nothing, nothing whatever, not a scrap of service nor a thing you'd care for, to offer you in compensation.

MRS GRACEDEW (*slowly rising now; standing there a moment before she speaks; and even showing amusement for the highly definite way in which he has put it*) I'm not, as they say, 'on the make'. (*Then gravely and a bit proudly, though not the least pompously*) I didn't do it for payment!

YULE (*also after an instant, still where he was; but as if, by some idea of his own, he now 'has' her*) What then did you do it for?

MRS GRACEDEW (*who has not moved, either from her position directly before her chair, casting about, looking up and over the place as for some plausible account of her motive; then suddenly finding it*) I did it because I hated Mr Prodmore.

YULE (*wondering, sceptical*) So much as all that?

MRS GRACEDEW (*a little impatient; as from the inconvenience of this challenge; shifting, though not radically, her position*) Oh well, of course you know how much I like the house. (*Then with gained*

clearness, making it fit; explaining it) My hates and my likes can
never live happily together. I have always to get one of them *out*.
The one I had to get out this time—and it was very big and well-   590
developed—was that man.

YULE (*with a candour of participation; a sort of momentary peace*) Yes
you got him indeed—'out'! (*As recalling the vivid image of it that he
has caught on his re-entrance; as living over again his impression of it*)
Yes, I saw him *go*. (*Then while his inner vision seems for an instant to*   595
attend Mr Prodmore's retreat) How in the world did you *do* it?

MRS GRACEDEW (*vague, as if these strokes are difficult to reproduce*) Oh,
I don't know. Women—(*She smiles at him, while she tries to bethink
herself; as a representative of their ready helpful genius, and as if such
an account of the matter may suffice*)   600

YULE (*looking at her firmly; as if well aware*) Precisely; women. (*Then
after an instant, always at left and with a long, rapid, abrupt transition*) May I smoke again?

MRS GRACEDEW Certainly. (*Then re-seated and as amused while he
re-lights*) But I managed Mr Prodmore without cigarettes.   605

YULE (*frank; almost innocently confidential; while he puffs*) *I* couldn't
manage him, *with* or without!

MRS GRACEDEW (*explicit, but not derisive*) So I *saw*!

YULE (*completing his statement*) *I* couldn't 'get him out'.

MRS GRACEDEW (*gay*) So *he* saw!   610

YULE (*struck, just a bit rueful*) Yes—he *must*. (*Then losing himself in his
smoke; liking now, so much more at his ease, really to talk it over*)
Where has he *fled* to?

MRS GRACEDEW (*definite*) I haven't the least *idea*. (*Then prompt though
improvising, or at least bethinking herself*) But I *meet* him again, very   615
soon.

YULE (*after a significant pause now*) And when do you meet *me*?

MRS GRACEDEW (*very simply and kindly*) Why, whenever you come to
see me. (*On which, now at last really gathering herself, coming back to
the most immediate fact, she gets up again, looking about for her scarf or*   620
*shawl or cape or whatever and speaking as if her actual concern must be
all with the ebbing minute*) At present, you see, there *are* such things
as trains.

YULE (*so preoccupied and absorbed for his own larger question that he
renders her no help with her belongings, mechanically echoing*) 'Trains'?   625

MRS GRACEDEW Surely. I didn't *walk*!

YULE No, but even 'trains'! (*His attitude, his face, his voice, all deprecating her departure, all clinging to her stay;° dejectedly*) You really fly?

MRS GRACEDEW (*smiling, appropriating the image*) I *try* to. (*Then as if really to finish*) Good-bye. 630

YULE (*Who has already, with quiet concentration, and as absolutely having to, got between her and the door up right; where he stands as to ignore or postpone or defeat her farewell*) I said just now I had nothing to *offer* you. But of course I've the house *itself.*

MRS GRACEDEW (*down to left where she has come to pick up or recover* 635 *something; wondering, brightly staring*) The house? Why I've *got* it!

YULE (*with a motion as if this has no sense*) 'Got' it?

MRS GRACEDEW (*explaining*) All in my *head*, I mean. (*Confident, satisfied; making light of any other relation to it*) That's all I *want!*

YULE (*puzzled; studying her; mistrustful of this*) Why, I thought you 640 *loved* it so!

MRS GRACEDEW (*prompt, sincere*) I love it far too much to deprive *you* of it.

YULE (*unshaken*) How in the world would it be 'depriving'?

MRS GRACEDEW (*prompt again; definite*) It's enough that it would be 645 turning you *out.*

YULE (*with raised voice, in full contradiction and derision*) Why, dear lady, I've never been *in!*

MRS GRACEDEW (*undaunted; none the less positive*) You're 'in' now at any rate. I've *put* you and you've got to *stay!* (*Then as he looks round* 650 *too woefully, throwing up his arms in the expression of that's not suiting him a whit, from the moment she thus takes herself off; allowing for this, attenuating*) I don't mean *all* the while, but (*with a vague gesture*) long enough—!

YULE (*not at all taking it*) Long enough for *what?* 655

MRS GRACEDEW (*finding her answer*) For me to feel you're *here.*

YULE (*unappeased*) And how long will *that* take?

MRS GRACEDEW (*as she considers for him*) Well, I suppose I strike you as very 'fast', but when I'm doing what I really *want* it takes me half a *lifetime!* (*Then further to satisfy him*) I told you just now that I had 660 arranged you *lose* nothing. Shall my very next step then make you lose everything?

YULE (*as too dissatisfied with his own poor part-anxious rebellions*) It isn't a question of what I '*lose*'; it's a question of what I *do!* (*As the situation is thus before him*) What the deuce *have* I done to find it all 665 so *plain?* (*Fairly marvelling at his strange case*) I haven't lifted a *finger.* It's you who have done *all.*

MRS GRACEDEW (*having to recognise it, but doing so as little as possible and speaking as with still superior lucidity and authority*) Yes, but

if you're just where you were *before*, how in the world are you   670
saved?

YULE (*with his hands in his pockets and a movement of his shoulders; as if it's evident*) By my life's being my own again, to do what I *want*!

MRS GRACEDEW (*not disconcerted even with this*) What you 'want' is just to appropriate your house.   675

YULE Ah, but only (*with perfect discrimination*) if you,° as you virtually *engaged* to, find me a *way*.

MRS GRACEDEW (*keeping her own contention not less together*) I *have* 'found you a way'; and there the way *is*: for *me* just simply not to touch the place. (*Then arguing more closely*) What you 'want' is what   680
made you give in to Prodmore. What you 'want' is these walls and these acres and (*as she takes the whole place in again*)—these *feelings*! What you 'want' is the course I first *showed* you!

YULE (*focusing this with an effort; dragging it, with a frown, as from out of a remote past*) Why, the course you first showed me was to marry   685
poor Cora!

MRS GRACEDEW (*having, in rigorous logic, to admit it; but as little as possible*) Practically, yes!

YULE (*as with a point, then gained*) Well, it's just 'practically' what I *can't*!   690

MRS GRACEDEW (*as if this was never her fault; and as for historic truth*) I didn't *know* that then. You didn't *tell* me.

YULE (*rubbing, with an approach to a grimace, the back of his head with his hand*) I felt a delicacy!

MRS GRACEDEW (*as if it's just an illustration of the way she has had to   695
grope*) I didn't know even *that*.

YULE (*as making out for himself a little the possible reproach in this*) It didn't strike you I *might* be shy in naming her?

MRS GRACEDEW (*thinking a moment; reconstituting the past; gravely*) No. (*Giving it further consideration*) No. (*Then as quite to dismiss the   700
point*) But don't quarrel with me about it *now*!

YULE (*surprised; resenting the term*) 'Quarrel' with you?

MRS GRACEDEW (*without sharpness, but with clear distinctness*) Remember I was 'struck', as you call it, right and left. (*Then in the same way, while his eyes are on her*) I was in the thick of the battle.   705
(*After which, with a straight transition; very definite, before he can speak*) Cora, at any rate, felt no delicacy. *Cora* told me.

YULE (*fairly gaping with surprise*) Then she did know?

MRS GRACEDEW (*immediate*) She knew all; and if her father told you she *didn't*—well, he simply told you what was *not*! (*But keeping this   710 *clear and straight; keeping it above all just to Cora*) It was quite right of her. She would have refused you.

YULE (*gaping at this belated news*) Oh! (*Then more humorously and for the question of the personal slight to him represented by it*) Do you call that 'quite right'?   715

MRS GRACEDEW (*as having it well before her*) For her, yes. (*Then after another instant*) Wrongly only, of course, for *Prodmore*.

YULE (*recognising with appreciation the difference*) Ah, the more wrong for Prodmore—

MRS GRACEDEW (*taking him straight up; highly distinct*) The more   720
right for everyone else! (*Then as if this is an exact sequence*) To stay at your post, *that* was the course I enjoined.

YULE (*as on a due understanding at last of this; yet as if the ground so gained opens out more obscure; so that the 'freedom' they have just talked of is after all but a new and painful predicament; though he tries   725
to keep the reasonable tone*) I know it was, dear lady. But how can I follow *any* course—

MRS GRACEDEW (*again quickly anticipating*) If I only stick here on your *path*? (*Making an absolute end*) I won't stick an instant *more*! (*Then as to call his attention, as even for her very dignity, to the way he   730
has headed her and still keeps heading her off*) Haven't I been fighting to escape?°

YULE (*very serious now; passing to left to keep her down, then as she moves right doing the same thing there; consciously opposing her; and speaking with abrupt force*) Why do you surrender your rights?   735

MRS GRACEDEW (*pulled up; with a pang for her pride at having to say; and thereby begging the question*) Weren't you ready to surrender yours?

YULE (*before her; clearer; more dominant now than he has been about anything*) I *hadn't* any, so that was nothing. I hadn't paid for them.   740

MRS GRACEDEW (*while he holds her at bay, though she keeps her distance from him; prompt with her reply*) Your ancestors had 'paid'. It's the same thing! (*Then as the best statement of their case possible*) You're just in a manner my tenant.

YULE (*repeating the word as to test it*) Your 'tenant'? (*Blank*) On what   745
terms?

MRS GRACEDEW (*as if this is but a detail*) Oh, on *any* terms! (*Then moving, as to circumvent him, to right*) You can *write* me about them!

YULE (*who has checked her, right; sceptical*) To Missoura Top?

MRS GRACEDEW (*cheerful and clear, as to put him off his guard*) I go   750
right back. (*Then rapidly gaining L*) Farewell!

YULE (*his rapidity greater; his presence, at* L, *effectual;° his manner still all courteous, but intensely earnest; his idea of what he wants to know now dominant*) Just one little moment, please. (*Then while she's obliged to wait*) If you won't tell me your own terms, you must at least tell me Prodmore's.   755

MRS GRACEDEW (*not facing this; turning away from it; able only unpreparedly to echo it*) 'Prodmore's'?

YULE (*not moving from her path; very emphatic*) Yes, Prodmore's. (*Quite 'categorical'*) How you did it. How you managed it. (*As if he quite expects her to tell him*) You bought him *out*?   760

MRS GRACEDEW (*giving way, turning off, before the barrier he thus erects for her; but with a motion of her arms that makes nothing of what she has done—seems to define it as a case of her having paid ninepence*) I bought him *out*.   765

YULE (*not believing in the ninepence*) For how *much*? (*Then as she now has turned her back; while he watches her move off; though keeping, guardedly, as it were, on a parallel line*) You see I really must *know*!

MRS GRACEDEW (*very determined, keeping away from him*) You shall *never* know!   770

YULE (*equally emphatic; not seeing her face*) I'll get it from *him*!

MRS GRACEDEW (*throwing up and dropping her hands; very firmly but slowly and rather sadly shaking her head while she moves*) Get it if you *can*!

YULE (*struck, with this, while he watches her; sharply affected, but with an intense little pause before he speaks*) He won't say because he *did* you?°   775

MRS GRACEDEW (*who has stopped, at this, in her slow movement, and then, after an instant's thought, turns round to him, shaking her head again in the same way*) He'll never, *never* say!   780

YULE (*held there, the space between them being now considerable, by the expression of her face and voice and by the sharper sense of what the whole thing, her determination not to speak in particular, may mean; then bringing it out with deep resentment*) The scoundrel!

MRS GRACEDEW (*raising her two hands, holding them up, with authority, as if, for reasons of her own, to check that tone, which is in a manner an injustice*) Not a bit a 'scoundrel'. A victim. (*Then while she faces Yule*) I was only too 'smart' for him. (*After which, as with a highly abrupt flare, coming back to her purpose and moving upon him*) So now let me *go*!   790

YULE (*'all there' indeed now; impassable; his arms out, to prevent her, as if all across the hall; immensely protesting*) With this heroic proof of

your power, this barren beauty of your sacrifice? (*Ardent, eloquent*)
You pour out money, you move a mountain, and to let you 'go', to
bow you stupidly *out* and close the door *behind* you, is all my poor   795
wit can think of? (*His emotion trembling out of him like the stammer
of a new language; but of which, in an instant, before her there, he is
already master*) You're the most generous, you're the noblest of
women! (*Breathless*) The wonderful chance that brought you here!

MRS GRACEDEW (*to whom he is now, in his ardour, so near that she has*   800
*but to put her hand straight out, which she does, all beautifully, to grasp
his arm and stay his words*) It brought *you* at the same happy hour!
(*Very simply and sincerely*) I've done what I *liked*, (*with an exquisite,
a satisfied, accepting shrug*) and the only way to 'thank' me is to
believe it.   805

YULE (*in full possession of his powers now*) You've done it for a proud,
poor man, who has nothing, in the light of such a magic as yours,
either to *give* or to *hope*; but whom you've made, in an hour of
mysteries and miracles, think of you as he has thought of no other
woman! (*Then while, under this final, this personal possession of her,*   810
*she has to take it from him, his eloquence, his coherency drop and he can
fall but to pleading*) Mrs Gracedew, don't *leave* me! (*He signalises,
with immense breadth, the whole place, glowing now with the more and
more lovely hour*) If you've made me care—

MRS GRACEDEW (*dropping, sharply, his arm, which she has still been*   815
*holding; interrupting him with a laugh of joy that disengages both of
them; so that, as having got now all she has dreamt of, she can again put
space between them*) It was surely that you had made *me* first!

YULE (*accepting the space now; watching her, as she moves, as if no longer
fearing her flight and completing the words she has launched upon the*   820
air; speaking as with a clear and definite vision gained) Then let us go
on caring! (*Earnestly developing*) When I begged you a while back to
lay for me some simple plank across the dizzy gulf of my so sudden
new source of credit, you merely put off the question; told me I
must trust to time for it. Well (*firmer and firmer*) I've trusted to time 825
so effectually that ten little minutes have *shown* me my wondrous
bridge: made of the finest, firmest, fairest material that ever
spanned a deep predicament. (*Keeping it up; gallant and clear with
his image*) If I've found where to *pass*, and *how*; it's simply because
I've found you. (*Then for his fine climax; immensely definite*) May I   830
keep then, Mrs Gracedew, *everything* I've found? I offer you in
return the only things I have to give; I offer you my hand and my
life.

MRS GRACEDEW (*holding off from him, across the hall, the entire space between them now, she decidedly left and he right; with an intensity of* 835 *suspended response that may almost pass as a plea for further postponement, or even as a plea for mercy, in respect to so immediate a sequel to her deeds; though it is all a rich, deep, full response that comes out as she happily, expressively wails*) Ah, Captain Yule!

Enter Chivers from ante-room°

YULE (*as she drops and they both see Chivers up right, by whom his master* 840 *is much disconcerted; veritably glowering*) What the devil is it?

CHIVERS (*characteristically pained at having to intrude, to nip in the bud, as it were, the fragrance that his fine old sensibility feels in the air; but only knowing his traditional duty*) Another party.

MRS GRACEDEW (*instantly touched by this; in possession again of all her* 845 *resources; delighted*) The party 'up'? (*Resolute, rising to the occasion*) Show them *in*!

Exit Chivers to ante-room

YULE (*astonished, alarmed; wailing across at her*) You'll *have* them?

MRS GRACEDEW (*sublime; tossing it back at him for all it's worth*) Mayn't I be proud of my house? 850

YULE (*radiant at this speech, raising up his arms from where he stands*) Then you *accept*?

MRS GRACEDEW (*her arms, down at left, raised higher still, but with the fine spread, commanding, controlling movement by which a leader holds his big orchestra in check before the first note*) Hush! 855

Enter Chivers in conduct again of a party, ushering them down centre as he has ushered the previous, but making the most, this time, of more scanty material as to number, though more important and showy as to appearance and class: four or five persons of the eye-glassed, satchelled, shawled and hand-booked order° that suggests a preponderantly American origin and a tourist habit; the appearance of a greater familiarity with remarkable houses and the general practice of behaving in them, when on view, rather as in the halls of big hotels, looking about with expert eyes and free sounds while they wait for rooms to be assigned. Yule gives way before them, instinctively edging off and, as he has been at right, passing impatiently behind them to get round and up to left and toward door of garden where he is furthest removed from them. Mrs Gracedew, on the other hand, instinctively does the opposite; awaiting them serenely in front of great chimney-place, whence she commands the clustered group, for which Chivers has had his various immemorial motions and

arrangements; several of which, as the taking from them of
pointed instruments, sticks and umbrellas that they may
dangerously poke at things, and the offering them of old
catalogue-cards, on handles, like stiff fans, constitutes here a
sufficient by-play. In these proceedings, though they are not too
prolonged, but rapid, direct and business-like, expressive of
perfect expertness, detachment and world-weary automatism on
Chivers's part, Mrs Gracedew frankly and unshrinkingly loses
herself; the little business making a vivid interval during which
the tourists consider unreservedly the beautiful unperturbed lady,
her person and her wonderful clothes, very much as if she's a part
of the show, one of the highly interesting features; and she on her
side returning their regard with a placid relish that expresses all
the interest she promises herself now to extract from a future of
these processions. It is after they have well taken her in, though
glancing at their catalogues first as if she may really be
mentioned in them, that, not finding her apparently 'down' there,
they address themselves to a reference to other objects; Chivers
having, when he has marshalled them in row and properly
supplied them, given them their cue by pointing, with a now-
assumed wand of office, to the first in order of the dark pictures
ranged on the most advantageous wall. The cue is immediately
taken by one of the American gentlemen

TOURIST (*catching° in hand; very loud and familiar*) The regular thing;
fine old family portraits?

CHIVERS (*highly superior, ignoring familiarity and beginning, with a*
flourish of his wand, in the right place) Dame Dorothy Yule, who
lived to a hundred and five.   860

TOURISTS (*together; much impressed*) A hundred and five! Is that so?

TOURIST (*with the habit of jocose comment*) You must have a fine old
healthy place!

MRS GRACEDEW (*from her position; uncontrollably; with the highest*
geniality and very rapidly) Yes, it's fine and it's old and it's healthy,   865
and it's perfectly lovely!

CHATTY AMERICAN LADY You tried it long?

MRS GRACEDEW (*prompt*) No, but I'm trying it now! (*Smiling at them*
sociably) You see we're not *all* a hundred and five. (*Then as Chivers*
in his regular way has raised his wand to the next portrait in order, her   870
pointing arm directs their heads to it at the same time) John Anthony
Yule; who passed away, poor duck,° in his flower!

Captain Clement Yule has during this passage reached the garden

*door where he has restlessly turned about again, watching the
scene and coming down, toward the chimney-place, left of
Chivers and the party; so that, irresistibly drawn back, he has
approached Mrs Gracedew when the same inquirer speaks again*

CHATTY LADY (*indicating the portrait of the gentleman in the white
trunk-hose, with the long legs, hung over door of garden; to whom
Chivers has already raised his wand*) And this *funny* one?   875

MRS GRACEDEW (*who, with Yule close upon her now, is conscious only of
him and who takes his arm, drawing him beside her, as to present him,
while she answers the Chatty Lady*) Oh, this funny one's my
husband!

CHATTY LADY (*whose place is such that she is the first all sympathetically   880
to take it, while she immediately imparts it to the others, who stand in
line down to right, each passing it to next, as in confidential discretion
and interest*) Her husband. Her husband. Her husband.

YULE (*beside her, her arm in his, opposite to the party, which he now
addresses, while they smilingly and admiringly accept the presentation;   885
while Chivers, centre, staring at this announcement, yet instinctively
straightens himself, his wand upright, his posture erect and official, his
expression inscrutable; and while the curtain is about to fall*) And *this*
funny one's my wife!

Curtain

EXPLANATORY NOTES

ABBREVIATIONS

Edel
: *The Complete Plays of Henry James*, ed. Leon Edel (New York and Oxford: Oxford University Press, 1996)

LC
: Lord Chamberlain's Manuscripts

London Encyclopaedia
: Ben Weinreb and Christopher Hibbert (eds.), *The London Encyclopaedia* (London and Basingstoke: Macmillan, 1983).

OED
: *The Oxford English Dictionary* (Second Edition) (Oxford: Oxford University Press, 1989)

Smith
: James L. Smith (ed. and introd.), *London Assurance*, New Mermaids (London: A. & C. Black, New York: W. W. Norton & Co., 1984)

TYP
: Typescript version of Henry James, 'The High Bid' (for further details see Note on the Texts, p. li).

Money

DEDICATION

John Forster, Esq.: John Forster (1812–76) established his reputation as a journalist and biographer, most famously and lastingly perhaps through his biography, *The Life of Charles Dickens*, 3 vols. (London, 1872–4). Bulwer-Lytton had formed a friendship with him when Forster approached him to help his friend Leigh Hunt in 1831 and started contributing to the *New Monthly Magazine* in 1832, of which Bulwer was the editor at the time. Seldom stalling, their friendship lasted right up to Bulwer's death in 1873. See James A. Davies, *John Forster: A Literary Life* (Leicester: Leicester University Press, 1983), 37–56 and *passim*.

The Lives ... Commonwealth: John Forster had first entitled the five volumes *Lives of Eminent British Statesmen* (London, 1836–9), publishing one volume a year, except for the two volumes on Cromwell in 1839; the set was reprinted under the title *The Statesmen of the Commonwealth of England. With a treatise on the popular progress in English history*, 5 vols. (London, 1840).

although ... 'Money'!: Bulwer's polite pun turns on the double meaning of money in both the literal sense of the word and as the title of his play, implying (*a*) the compliment to his friend that he always considered his motives and critical judgment to be of a noble, non-mercenary nature and (*b*) that he was flattered by his favourable comments on the play where the author modestly assumes that the critic's judgement must have been misled (by 'Money'). Forster had indeed written a highly laudatory review of the play in *The Examiner*, 13 December 1840, 790.

CHARACTERS OF THE PLAY

Glossmore: several of the characters have more or less obviously telling names; Glossmore's alludes to the superficial lustre and threadbare pretentiousness of his financial and possibly also his moral standing.

Bart., Knight of the Guelph; F.R.S., F.S.A.: Sir John has collected an impressive array of titles and memberships. A baronetcy ('Bart.'), identified by the prefix 'Sir' to Christian and surname, is a hereditary honour descending from father to son. The Royal Guelphic Order was instituted, originally as an order of the House of Hanover, by George, prince regent, afterwards George IV of Great Britain, in 1815; it ceased to be bestowed after the death of William IV in 1837. 'F.R.S.' indentifies Sir John as a Fellow of the Royal Society for the Improvement of Natural Knowledge, as its name runs in full, which time-honoured institution obtained its Royal charters in 1662 and 1663. 'F.S.A.' shows him to be a Fellow of the Society of Antiquaries, which was founded in 1572, suppressed under James I, and refounded in 1717/18. As indicated by the 'etc.' in 1.426, the list of his honours is actually longer than this and shows his eagerness to impress by outward marks of his pretended social importance and wealth.

Graves: the name alludes to his grave and melancholy disposition.

Smooth: the name points to the smoothness of his play at cards.

Sharp: a lawyer with a 'sharp' wit.

Tabouret: the name refers to his profession, a tabouret being a low seat or stool, without back or arms, for one person.

MacStucco: direct reference to his occupation in the building business, where stucco is applied.

Kite: the name implies that he is disingenuous in his horse-dealing, a sharper.

Crimson: obvious allusion to his profession, with the ironic undertone that he may be very generous with crimson to touch up the colour of lips and cheeks in his portraits.

Grab: the name suggests this publisher's tendency to snatch up any manuscript for publication which he thinks will bring him profit, regardless of its poetic or literary quality.

*** *Club*: Bulwer does not give the name of the club, but replaces it by asterisks; the suggestion that any existing club in London favoured gambling for such high stakes might have tainted its respectability. Cards were, however, a common feature in the clubs. It seems likely that Bulwer specifically thought of the Crockford's Club, as he asked Macready to inquire whether playing cards was at all common in it, so as not to make his plot sound unrealistic (see Introduction, n. 13). Crockford's was a private club and gambling house, opened in 1828 at 50 St James's Street; see *London Encyclopaedia*, 212.

Franklin: the name alludes to her 'frankness' and plaindealing.

1 S.D. *sofa writing-table*: a small table placed beside a sofa with the right height for writing while sitting on the sofa.

6 *living in chambers*: as a widower with no children in the household, Graves lives in a modest apartment and hence lacks vital facilities for the reception of ladies.

18 *surfeit*: digestive disorder caused by unwholesome food.

19 *pilaus*: an oriental dish of rice boiled with fowl, meat or fish, and spices.

20 *hookah*: a pipe used especially in Arab countries for smoking tobacco. It has a long, flexible tube, which passes through a container of water which cools the smoke as it is drawn in.

26 *like a kangaroo in a jaundice*: not a generally recognized or proverbial saying; here obviously used as Sir John's humorous and confirming paraphrase of Georgina's 'ugly'.

30 *Freemasons' Tavern*: in Great Queen Street, WC2; one of London's most celebrated taverns, replaced by the grand Connaught Rooms in 1905; it had been built as an extension to the new masonic hall, which was designed by Thomas Sandy and opened in 1776, but subsequently proved inadequate, so that, at Sandy's suggestion, the Freemason's Tavern was built in the 1780s; see *London Encyclopaedia*, 193 and 293. Sir John need not necessarily have been a freemason himself to be invited to speak there, but his speech on 'the great Chimney-sweep Question' (see following note) would have been of a reformist bent, as there existed a close link between freemasons and radicalism, many freemasons joining the radical corresponding societies from the 1790s onwards; for this link see the contemporary account of W. H. Reid, *The Rise and Fall of the Infidel Societies in this Metropolis* (London, 1800), and for a good summary, the article on 'freemasonry' in Iain McCalman (ed.), *An Oxford Companion to the Romantic Age: British Culture 1776–1832* (Oxford and New York: Oxford University Press, 1999), 513.

Chimney-sweep Question: young boys employed as chimney-sweepers had frequently been subjected with reckless cruelty to the most appalling working conditions by their masters. Their life expectancy was minimal because of malnutrition and lung disease caused by the soot. The matter was brought before parliament and Acts were passed regulating the employment of chimney-sweepers in 1840, 1864, 1875, and 1894, effectively banning child labour in the trade.

39 *with address*: with proper skill, dexterity.

56 *wheedled a constituency*: until the Corrupt Practices Act of 1883 which set strict expenditure limits for an election, contested elections for the House of Commons could be extremely expensive for the candidates; Sir John, however, implies that he managed to gain his seat on the strength of pre-election promises which he did not need to pay after winning the election because he gave up his seat to a minister—for a handsome reward. Charles Dickens gives a humorous example of the 'wheedling' of the Eatanswill constituency in *The Pickwick Papers* ch. xiii (1837, Oxford: Oxford University Press, 1987), 173 f: 'The speeches of the two candidates, though differing in every other respect, afforded a beautiful tribute to the merit and high worth of the electors of Eatanswill. Both expressed their opinion that a more independent, a more enlightened, a more public-spirited, a more noble-minded, a more disinterested set of men than those who had promised to vote for him, never existed on earth; each darkly hinted his suspicions that the electors in the opposite interest had certain swinish and besotted infirmities which rendered them unfit for the exercise of the important duties they were called upon to discharge.'

58 *a patent office*: an office so called because it is conferred, usually by the Crown, by a 'letter patent' or 'letter overt'.

76 *Where the deuce*: a question expressing annoyance, with 'deuce' here in the sense of 'devil'.

79 *humorist*: here, in the older sense of the word, meaning a whimsical person; someone given to 'humours'.

86 *Commission*: generally, a body of persons empowered to act in a certain capacity. In the nineteenth century many Commissions of inquiry, usually set up by Parliament, preceded major legislation; their findings were published in reports; an early and very prominent example is the Poor Law Commission, set up under Edwin Chadwick's encouragement and stimulus, whose famous report of 1834 formed the basis of the Poor Law Act passed in the same year.

144 *Exeter Hall*: situated in the Strand and built in 1829–31, this was a nonsectarian hall for religious and scientific gatherings and for the meetings of various philanthropic societies. It was demolished in 1907.

debates on the Customs: conservative-minded landowners had an interest in high custom duties to protect their income from cheap imports of raw materials, and therefore championed protective laws, such as the Corn Laws of 1815. These were fiercely opposed by both liberal free traders, who were in favour of unhindered imports and exports, drawing their arguments from David Ricardo's *On the Principles of Political Economy and Taxation* (1817), and on the other hand by the Radicals whose priority was a low price for raw materials and basic food, especially corn, to secure a sufficient food supply for the poor. The fierce debates of the 1830s and 1840s led to a gradual liberalization, notably in the repeal of the Corn Laws in 1846 and in the free trade budgets under Gladstone's premiership in 1853 and 1860.

146 *floss silk*: untwisted filaments of silk used in embroidery and crewel-work (*OED*).

147 *Storr's*: Paul Storr was a famous London goldsmith who started his career by working for the firm Rundell & Bridge (1792–1821), but from 1821 had his own shop in partnership with John Mortimer, which continued to exist under that name for two more years after Storr's death in 1837. The shop appears under both partners' names in 3.1.36.

148 *Hookham's*: Hookham's and Sons, booksellers and stationers, at 15 Bond Street, Piccadilly.

last H.B.: i.e. the latest issue of 'H.B.', possibly an abbreviation of *Heath's Book of Beauty* (1833–47), ed. L. E. L[andon], Countess of Blessington.

149 *Comic Annual*: *The Comic Annual* was edited by Thomas Hood (1799–1845); it ran, under varying titles, from 1830 to 1842.

152 *peg-top*: a pear-shaped wooden spinning-top, with a metal pin or peg forming the point, spun by the rapid uncoiling of a string wound about it (*OED*).

153 *Paley*: William Paley (1743–1845), English theologian and philosopher; mainly remembered for his *Evidences of Christianity* (1794) and *Natural Theology* (1802). By making Evelyn read Paley at his first appearance on stage, his attitude of frustrated, philosophical withdrawal from society is emphasized, but Bulwer may also suggest, through Paley's scientific, logocentric approach to Christianity as expressed in Evelyn's quotation, the way Evelyn tries to come to terms with his situation. This strictly logical, reasoned approach characterizes his love to Clara, but also Clara's own opinions on the subject.

197 S.D. *converse in dumb show*: mime a conversation which is not actually audible to the audience.

213 *Panorama*: the most famous of London panoramas was Barker's (after a change of proprietor called Burford's from about 1826) in Leicester Place, which opened in 1794. It presented in its 90-ft. rotunda many spectacular views and scenes. In 1863 it was converted into a French church. See also Blount's reference, l. 224 below, which suggests that a view of Naples was the current presentation of the panorama they had visited. Naples was a favourite among the topographical subjects of the

early panoramas; the *Illustrated London News*, 11 January 1845, has an engraving of 'Naples by Moonlight', painted by Robert Burford and H. C. Selous and shown at Burford's Panorama at the time. For a reprint of the engraving and for a cross-section and description of Burford's Panorama, see Richard A. Altick, *The Shows of London* (Cambridge, Mass., and London: Harvard University Press, 1978), 138, 132–6, and *passim*.

216   *civet*: a strong-smelling essence obtained from the civet cat, and used in the production of perfume.

216–17   '*I cannot . . . perfume!*': lines from William Cowper's 'Conversation' (1781), ll. 283 f.

230–1   '*How much . . . home*': lines from William Cowper's 'The Progress of Error' (1782), ll. 415 f.

236   *cuwicle*: curricle; a light two-wheeled carriage, usually drawn by two horses abreast.

248   *Au plaisir!*: (French) short for *au plaisir de vous revoir*; good-bye.

255   *cashmere*: soft wool obtained from the Cashmere goat and the wild goat of Tibet; often used for expensive shawls.

323–4   *East . . . wise men*: allusion to Matthew 2: 1–12.

329   *vestry*: here a parochial board meeting of elected members of the congregation charged with the administrative and economic affairs of the parish; this assembly in an English parish takes its name from the fact that it originally met in the vestry, i.e. the small room adjacent to the main building of a church where priest and choir robe and prepare for service and where the necessary utensils are kept.

361   *Cheltenham waters*: bottles of water from Cheltenham; a well with medicinal waters was discovered in Cheltenham in the early eighteenth century and the town became a fashionable spa.

363   *Parliamentary Debates*: there were various publications of the proceedings and debates of both Houses; Stout's title reference fits *Cobbett's Parliamentary Debates*, 22 vols., 22 November 1803–4 May 1812 (London, 1804–12), continued as *(Hansard's) Parliamentary Debates*, published in London by Thomas Curson Hansard and others. The reports on the parliamentary session of 1839 for example consist of six substantial volumes, which, bound in calf and posted to India, would have meant a considerable expense annually incurred by Stout.

365   *Malthus*: Thomas Robert Malthus (1766–1834), English social theorist, whose *Essay on Population* (1798) subverted the Enlightenment belief in unlimited progress. Malthus maintained that population growth was geometrical and hence always faster than the growth of resources. Population growth must, thus Malthus's reasoning, be kept in check, if possible not through famine and disease, but by 'preventive check'. The passage to which Stout most likely alludes reads: 'The preventive check

appears to operate in some degree through all the ranks of society in England. There are some men, even in the highest rank, who are prevented from marrying by the idea of the expenses that they must retrench, and the fancied pleasures they must deprive themselves of, on the supposition of having a family' (*Essay on the Principle of Population*, Oxford World's Classics, Oxford: Oxford University Press, 1993, 31 f.).

399 S.D. *Chorus*: here, and in the following instances, the members of the chorus naturally vary, always excluding the person who is just being addressed by the reading of the will.

402 *imprimis*: in the first place.

403 *Pall Mall*: fashionable street in London which takes its name from a game similar to croquet which originated in Italy under the name of *pallo a maglio* (ball to mallet).

433 *Albany*: house in Piccadilly, originally built in 1770–4 for the Viscount of Melbourne, but converted into chambers for bachelors to the design of Henry Holland in the early nineteenth century.

435 *three per cents*: the government securities of Great Britain, consolidated in 1751 into a single stock paying three per cent interest (*OED*); in his pessimistic vein, Graves does not consider government securities a safe asset as their returns are of course tied to the financial development of the national economy, whereas he sees land as the property with the most enduring value.

441 *India stock*: a share in the subscribed capital of the East India Company.

448 *bonds*: certificate for money lent to a company, or indeed the government, which is to be paid back with interest.

449 *exchequer bills*: bills of credit issued by authority of parliament, bearing interest at the current rate.

  consols: abbreviation of 'consolidated annuities', i.e. the government securities of Great Britain.

450 *in the Bank of Calcutta*: this can either refer to money deposited in the Bank of Calcutta or, more probably, to shares held in that bank.

467 *put you up at the clubs*: introduce you as a new member to the fashionable London clubs. To be admitted to the membership of London's traditional clubs, the name of the candidate had to be put forward by an old member; the London clubs were (some of them still are) exclusively male clubs, whose usually substantial entrance fee and high annual subscription Evelyn now can easily afford to pay.

473 S.D. *[Curtain]*: for scene changes, the front-of-stage curtain would be lowered.

2.1.3 *Money makes the man*: proverbial; a person's wealth determines his or her claim to high social esteem.

4 *schneider*: German for 'tailor'.

5 *St James's*: probably refers to St James's Square, SW1 (there is also a St James's Place nearby); building had started in the seventeenth century, and St James's Square had remained one of London's most fashionable addresses through to the end of the eighteenth century. When in the early nineteenth century the fashionable circles moved to Belgravia, clubs and tradesmen, like Mr Frantz, moved in and the Square's air of nobility disappeared.

15 *Scraitch me and I'll scraitch you!*: variant of the proverbial 'scratch my back and I'll scratch yours', also current in the form 'claw me and I'll claw thee'.

16 *levee*: in aristocratic circles, a reception of visitors on rising from bed; hence, referring also to the assembly of people for the purpose of meeting a prince or nobleman.

22 *Correggio*: Antonio Allegri, called 'il Correggio' (1489–1534), famous Italian painter.

36–7 *'Now I am . . . refines!'*: Evelyn is probably thinking of Alexander Pope's *Essay on Criticism* (1711), ll. 420 f: 'But let a Lord once own the happy Lines, | How the Wit brightens! how the Style refines!'

47 *Groginhole*: probably meaning spirits or booze (grog) in the mouth (hole), and referring to the practice of bribing voters by buying them drinks.

51 *patriot*: the appeal to patriotism had already been an instrument of opposition to the Walpole government in the eighteenth century, but had more specifically become associated with radicalism in the early decades of the nineteenth century. The attribute 'patriot' here consequently indicates Popkins's radical political convictions. Later, in the last quarter of the nineteenth century, the language of patriotism was, however, increasingly appropriated by the political right. See Hugh Cunningham, 'The Language of Patriotism', in Raphael Samuel (ed.), *Patriotism: The Making and Unmaking of British National Identity*, i: *History and Politics* (London and New York: Routledge, 1989), 57–89.

boro': short form of 'borough', that is, the electoral district of a Member of Parliament.

52 *the instant Hopkins is dead*: when a Member of Parliament dies, his or her seat does not remain vacant until the next General Election, but a by-election is held to fill the seat again as quickly as possible.

Your interest: your (financial) support of his election.

62 *Enlightenment . . . Constitution!*: Popkins the brewer is obviously campaigning for the Whigs who advocated constitutional reform, while Lord Cipher, identified as a member of the nobility by his title, is to stand for the Conservative Party campaigning for the preservation of the constitutional *status quo*.

68 *turn every man out of his house*: as their landlord, Evelyn could turn his tenants out of their houses at the shortest of notice. Legal protection for tenants was practically non-existent in the nineteenth century.

79 *Speaker*: the Speaker in the House of Commons is chosen from among the MPs to preside over debates.

84 *leveller*: one who would level all differences of position or rank among men. More specifically, 'Levellers' was the name given to a political movement during the civil wars of the 1640s, which advocated universal male adult suffrage, the abolition of the monarchy and the House of Lords, and religious toleration.

87 *battledore*: game for two persons who strike a shuttlecock to and from each other with a small racket, which is itself called a battledore.

110 *yellow earth*: i.e. gold.

113 *excellent in form*: Shakespeare, *Hamlet*, II. ii. 304 ff.: 'What piece of work is a man, how noble in reason, how infinite in faculties, in form and moving how express and admirable . . .'

129 *Have you no bowels?*: the bowels were once considered the seat of the sympathetic, tender emotions, as in the Authorized Version of the English Bible of 1611, which translates Colossians 3: 12 as 'Put on therefore . . . bowels of mercies, kindness, humbleness of mind, meekness, longsuffering.'

145 *sizar*: the lowest kind of undergraduate whose reduction in fees is paid for by menial work, such as waiting at table, etc.

2.2.74 *walk barefoot . . . ordeal*: in this type of ordeal, persons accused of a crime had to walk over a red-hot ploughshare and could prove their innocence if it did not burn them. It was used in medieval Europe especially in cases of the wife's (alleged) adultery; see Robert Bartlett, *Trial by Fire and Water: The Medieval Judicial Ordeal* (Oxford: Clarendon Press, 1986), 10, also 15–18, 33, 46, 74; there is a reference to this ordeal in John Webster's *The Duchess of Malfi*, III. i (1612/13, published 1623).

102 *Pentonville*: one of the earliest planned suburbs in North London, built from 1773 onwards. It deteriorated into a slum in the course of the nineteenth century and was mostly rebuilt.

107 *crises*: the spelling in the text is 'criseses', but it is unlikely that a malapropism is intended here.

109 *eighteen crises, six annihilations . . . entire Constitution*: this was, of course, the apocalyptic tenor of anti-reformist, conservative scare-mongering which painted consequences of the admittedly profound changes in the social and political structure of Britain in the darkest colours; much of its rhetoric was ultimately an offspring of Edmund Burke's *Reflections of the Revolution in France* (1790) which remained a major source of inspiration for the conservative opposition to the movements of popular radicalism

and political reforms. The direct reference in the text is specifically to *The Times*, which Lady Franklin has offered to go and fetch and with which she has just returned.

142 *Almack's*: Almack's Assembly Rooms, King Street, St James's, designed by Robert Mylne in 1765 and named after the first proprietor, William Almack. There was a weekly ball, on which occasion the gentlemen had to wear knee breeches and white cravats. The balls began to go out of fashion after 1835 and were discontinued in 1863. See *London Encyclopaedia*, 20.

146 *écarté*: a game of cards for two persons. One feature is that a player may ask leave to discard, or throw out (French: *écarter*) certain cards from his hand, and replace them with fresh ones from the pack.

piquet: a card-game played by two persons with a pack of 32 cards.

152 *Carlsbad*: Karlsbad, today Karlovy Vary in the Czech Republic; its warm springs were probably known to the Romans; the town developed into a fashionable spa in the eighteenth century.

223 *Tivoli*: Italian city in Latium, 30 km. east of Rome, famous for its Roman antiquities and its villas, esp. the Villa d'Este; therefore a great tourist attraction.

226 *damned*: printed as 'd——d' to prevent censorship in print. However, different standards obtained for the spoken word on stage, where censorship was more difficult to implement, so that there is little doubt that 'd——d' was fully pronounced on stage. In the text of this edition, similar abbreviations are therefore silently replaced by the complete forms.

231 s.d. *Pays . . . in dumb show*: Evelyn and Georgina continue their conversation in the background, their words being inaudible to the audience, while audience attention is now directed to the other pair, Clara and Sir Frederick Blount.

3.1.16 *jointure*: property or money settled in the marriage contract to be at the free disposal of the wife during her marriage but also in the case of widowhood; for details of the historical background see Lee Holcombe, *Wives and Property: Reform of the Married Women's Property Law in Nineteenth-Century England* (Oxford: Martin Robertson, 1983) and Susan Staves, *Married Women's Separate Property in England, 1660–1833* (Cambridge, Mass., and London: Harvard University Press, 1990).

31 *he . . . settlements*: Sir John fears that Evelyn will have to change the terms of the marriage contract and reduce Georgina's jointure.

53 *falling away*: wasting away, becoming thin and weak because of worry.

53–64 *Now, there's . . . I—I—*: In the 1840 edition, these lines are in inverted commas, with the following footnote (p. 67): 'The lines between inverted commas are omitted on the stage.' The omission seems odd, however, as

Sir John's communication with Clara on her authorship of the letter to Evelyn's nurse seems important for Clara's persistent silence on that matter in the following. It is possible that this communication was inserted in a briefer form a few lines down, when Sir John returns to the topic at Clara's departure. With the mere excision of the marked passage, Sir John's reference to 'the letter' in the latter instance would be unintelligible.

80 *like a black cat in the megrims*: a further elaboration of the more common proverbial phrase 'as melancholy as a cat' and a further instance of Sir John's fondness of garishly colourful imagery for emphasis; see his 'kangaroo in a jaundice' in 1.25–6.

101 *Exeter Hall*: see note to 1.144 above.

102 *rehearsal*: here probably in the sense of 'performance'.

Cinderella: the Cinderella story was hugely popular with nineteenth-century playwrights for pantomimes, burlettas, burlesques, or comic operas. A version of Rossini's *La Cenerentola* was first performed at Drury Lane on 9 January 1837, and there was a burletta *Cinderella* by an anonymous author first performed at the City of London Theatre on 21 February 1838.

104 *Garraway's*: Garraway's Coffee House, Cornhill, one of the chief auction houses of the City. It closed down in 1872. See *London Encyclopaedia*, 303.

105 *the Duke of Lofty's card*: a 'calling-card' with its owner's name on it, which would, for instance, have been left as a token that someone has called in a person's absence.

108 *Mr Squab . . . Association*: Mr Squab's name, in reference to a person, means 'short and stout', but may also allude to a penchant for 'squabbling', that is wrangling, disputing, brawling, thus ironizing his reformist activities. As opposed to that Mr Qualm's name also satirizes his conservatism, as he has 'qualms', that is second thoughts or scruples, about any kind of political and social change. They are associated with the newspapers of the corresponding political biases in the following sentence.

110 *Weekly True Sun . . . Morning Post*: the first is probably a misnomer for the *True Sun*, which was a daily, sevenpenny evening paper, politically situated at the more radical wing of the Whigs; it was founded by Patrick Grant in 1832 as a rival to the *Sun*, which he had previously owned, but foundered in 1837, despite having had such illustrious contributors as the young Charles Dickens and John Forster. *The Times* and the *Morning Post* represent the conservative side of the daily press. For the newspaper press in Victorian Britain see Lucy Brown, *Victorian News and Newspapers* (Oxford: Clarendon Press, 1985) and Stephen Koss, *The Rise and*

Fall of the Political Press in Britian, i: *The Nineteenth Century* (London: Hamish Hamilton, 1981).

159 *a long-baffled spirit*: here meaning a spirit that has been oppressed, foiled in unfolding his plans and potentialities for too long.

176 *hyssop and gall*: Christ at his crucifixion was offered 'wine to drink, mixed with gall' (Matthew 27: 34) and, according to John 19: 29, he was offered a sponge filled with sour wine, conveyed to the crucified's mouth by means of a stick of hyssop; thus the phrase indicates the extreme bitterness and utmost desperation of penury.

186 *gaud*: idle, showy display.

288 *gaming*: playing at games of chance, especially cards, for money or other stakes.

316 *absent*: absent-minded.

322 *dog-days*: the days about the heliacal rising of the dog-star; noted from ancient times as the hottest and most unwholesome period of the year.

3.2.2 *Mum!*: Say nothing! Silence!

19 *Jealous Wife*: written by George Colman the Elder, probably with David Garrick's assistance, the play was first performed at Drury Lane in 1761. A central feature of the comedy's plot is the jealous passions with which Mrs Oakly unjustly and continually henpecks her husband. Her suspicions are based on a letter addressed to her husband's ward and nephew, Charles Oakly, by Mr Russet, a country squire, who complains that his daughter Harriot has eloped and that Charles must know about this. Mrs Oakly thinks that the man behind the girl's elopement is not Charles, but her husband. It is thus ironically implied that Mrs Oakly was a fitting part for Graves's wife to play, whose treatment of her husband was very similar to the one displayed by Colman's Mrs Oakly, as Graves actually confesses in his next speech ('she used to practice it on me twice a day').

23 *'Your . . . of me!'*: part of Mrs Oakly's tirades against her husband in the first scene; the speech reads in full: 'I know you hate me; and that your unkindness and barbarity will be the death of me. (*Whining.*)'; George Colman, *The Dramatick Works* (1777, facs. repr. Hildesheim and New York: Georg Olms Verlag, 1976), i/ii. 14.

39 *reel*: a lively dance, usually danced by two couples facing each other, and describing a series of figures of eight.

68 *to you*: followed by footnote in the 1840 edition: 'For the original idea of this scene the author is indebted to a little *proverbe*, never, he believes, acted in public.' *Proverbes dramatiques* were short dramatic pieces illustrating a proverb. In the nineteenth century the most famous plays of the genre were written by Alfred de Musset, frequently translated into English. It is not clear, however, which unpublished *proverbe*, based on which proverb, Bulwer has in mind here.

3.3 S.D. ***'s *Club*: see note to Characters of the Play.

5 *play*: gambling.

6 *'hushed . . . prey'*: from Thomas Gray's 'The Bard. A Pindaric Ode', ii, 3, ll. 73 f.: 'Regardless of the whirlwind's sway, | That, hushed in grim repose, expects his evening-prey.'

10 *Political economy*: 'originally the art or practical science of managing the resources of a nation so as to increase its material prosperity' (*OED*); Evelyn's use of the phrase is, of course, ironic here, subliminally suggesting that the politicians' conduct of the national economy is not conducted in a way which is more honourable than gaming.

12 *Corn Laws, Poor Laws*: the landowners had managed to persuade the Tory government in 1815 to levy, in the form of the notorious Corn Laws, a heavy protective duty against cheap oversea imports of corn; the duty was of course most resented by the poorer part of the population, since they suffered most under the artificially high prices of corn which these laws entailed; the duties were lowered in 1828 and again in 1842, and the Corn Laws were repealed in 1846; the Poor Laws pertinent at the time were mainly those in the Poor Law Amendment Act of 1834, which had stopped out-door relief for the able-bodied poor and their families; under the authority of Poor Law Commissioners, these persons were to be assigned to workhouses by elected Guardians, where they would have a place to live, but where they would also be expected to work, their physical conditions permitting. The way the system developed in practice, with all its shortcomings, has again been vividly portrayed and satirized by Charles Dickens, especially in the first chapters of *Oliver Twist*, where the novel's protagonist is born in a workhouse.

13 *'dot and go one'*: here in the sense of 'dot and carry one', a schoolboy's expression in some processes of elementary arithmetic (addition, subtraction) and hence a name for such a process.

21 *wubber*: 'rubber'; a competition in certain card games (in this case, whist), which here consists of a set of three or five games played between the same players; here the 'rubber' is made up of Blount, Glossmore, Flat, and Green.

29 *repique*: in piquet, 'the winning of thirty points on cards alone before beginning to play (and before the adversary begins to count), entitling the player to begin his score at ninety' (*OED*).

34 *Ce cher Alfred!*: (French) 'This dear Alfred . . .'

50 *consequence*: here in the meaning of social distinction, high standing.

52 *a pony on the odd twick*: Blount bets with Flat for a 'pony' (slang for £25) on winning the final round ('trick') which, in whist, is the thirteenth, being called the 'odd trick' when six tricks have equally been won by each party and the outcome of the final round will decide the game.

62 *seven for his point*: Smooth and Evelyn are playing piquet, a game for two players, using a shortened pack of 32 cards which omits 2 to 6 in each suit; the players compete not only to score more points than their opponent, but also to be the first 'to get over the Rubicon' by scoring more then 100 points. 'Point' is the first category of scoring combinations; here the most numerous suit in a player's hand scores as many points; seven is a very high score in this phase of the game.

64 *throw out four*: discard four cards.

76 *You have . . . king*: Smooth furthermore has a set of four queens, which is called a 'quatorze' and counts fourteen points; and a sequence of five cards ending with a king, which is called a 'quint' and scores fifteen points.

98 *Great happiness of the greatest number*: slightly misquoted key phrase of the nineteenth-century utilitarians ('greatest happiness of the greatest number'), first to be found in the *Inquiry into the Original of our Ideas of Beauty and Virtue* (1725), II. iii. 8 by the Scottish moral and political philosopher Francis Hutcheson (1694–1746): 'That action is best, which procures the greatest happiness for the greatest numbers.'

114 *Grosvenor Square*: built between 1725 and 1731, the second largest square in London (after Lincoln's Inn Fields) and a very fashionable address ever since.

116 *at a valuation*: with the value determined by (usually professional) estimation.

4.1.4 *make hay while the sun shines*: proverbial; strike while the iron is hot, make use of an opportunity while it is there.

36 *in the buiks*: in my account books.

39 *distressed*: his goods and chattels seized in lieu of debts unpaid.

54 *the Belgian minister, Portland Place*: Portland Place, one of London's grandest streets, was (and still is) a favourite location for embassies; the servant's errand there is, obviously, to get a visa for Evelyn to be allowed to enter Belgium.

75 *Donner und Hage!*: (German) literally, 'thunder and hail'; oath expressing Frantz's indignation.

110 *off leg . . . spavin*: the off leg of a horse is on the side opposed to that where the rider mounts; a spavin is a hard bony tumour or excrescence formed at the union of the splint-bone and the shank in a horse's leg.

126 *Wansom's*: (Ransom's), a humorous 'telling name' for a banking house, which, it is implied, holds its debtors to ransom, keeps them as prisoners to their debts.

157 *Hollo*: a shout to excite attention, here still carrying something of one of its former connotations of 'holla', 'stop', as in Shakespeare's *As You Like It*, III. ii. 257: 'Cry holla, to the tongue, I prithee.'

176 *area*: an enclosed, usually sunken court shut off from the pavement by railings, and approached by a flight of steps, which gives access to the basement of dwelling houses, where the kitchen was situated and where servants and tradesmen would call.

178 *abridgments*: here, curtailment of privileges, i.e. Evelyn's freedom.

179 *line the pockets*: pay a bribe.

180 S.D. *note*: banknote.

181 *no claw*: to catch without using claws, i.e. without causing a stir, quietly; as in the French phrases *sans griffe* or *sans ongle*.

4.2. S.D. *Stout*: editorial addition; Stout will be addressed by Evelyn at l. 30, and it seems best to have him on stage with Evelyn and Graves at the opening of the scene.

36 *embarrassed*: having difficulty in meeting financial obligations; short of money.

113 *spinning-jennies*: an early form of spinning-machine, introduced by James Hargreave and patented in 1770.

137 *Hoare's*: business founded by Richard Hoare, goldsmith and banker, in Fleet Street, in about 1672; and banking had displaced the goldsmith business as early as the 1690s; the company still exists today as Hoare and Co. See *London Encyclopaedia*, 384.

144 *Jeremy Diddler*: the protagonist of James Kenney's celebrated farce *Raising the Wind* (Covent Garden, 5 November 1803), whose lack of funds forces him to live on appearances.

194 *Bah!*: an exclamation expressive of contempt; the original reads 'Baugh', which might also suggest the sound of a dog's bark (as in 'bow-wow'), not a likely utterance in this context.

5.1.18 *Bench*: as a Member of Parliament, he would have enjoyed immunity from prosecution for debt, and thus avoided being sentenced by a 'bench', i.e. a court of justice.

32 *of course*: as in the ordinary course of (legal) procedures in a marriage contract.

35 *close*: stingy.

47 *done up*: ruined, finished (here: financially).

78 *expect satisfaction*: Blount challenges Stout to a duel.

5.2.43 *Doctors' Commons*: colloquial name for the College of Advocates and Doctors of Law which was situated near St Paul's Cathedral. A vivid description of the place at work is given in Charles Dickens's *David Copperfield*, ch. 23.

5.3.22 *hobble*: difficulty, perplexing situation.

31 *Sybarites*: the inhabitants of Sybaris in southern Italy were proverbial for

their self-indulgent life style; hence, a self-indulgent, wanton person; therefore, Evelyn's 'Sybarites of sentiment' adhere, as he explains, to the primacy of passionate love and sentiment over reason and, as readers, would prefer the sentimental tradition, as classically portrayed and critically investigated in the figure of Marianne Dashwood in Jane Austen's *Sense and Sensibility* (1811).

37 *What do you tend to?*: What do you intend to do?

54 *hid below!*: followed by author's note: '"Errors, like straws," &c.' The quotation is from the prologue of John Dryden's *All For Love; or, The World Well Lost* (1677) and reads in full: 'Errors, like straws, upon the surface flow; | He who would search for pearls must dive below.'

68 s.d. *Enter Servant*: the original stage direction here reads '*Enter Servant announcing Lady Franklin and Miss Douglas*' without giving the actual announcement and entrance of the two ladies; the servant's announcement has therefore been inserted along the lines of similar entrances.

167 *Mysteries of Udolpho*: title of a novel by Ann Radcliffe, published 1794; one of the major works in the tradition of the Gothic novel. The novel's heroine, Emily St Aubert, is forced to follow her aunt to join that lady's Italian husband, who lives in a castle in the Apennines. To Emily's horror, Castle Udolpho, with its turrets and dark corridors turns out to be full of dark secrets and sombre mysteries, all of which are, however, solved in the end.

187 *the City*: London's historic and financial centre around the Royal Exchange and the Bank of England, extending to about one square mile, marked by the ancient City boundaries.

189 *Blue*: blue is the colour of the Tory party.

192 *closed in the first hour*: Evelyn's majority of the votes given was so great that it could be established within an hour of counting.

Hollow: shout of exultation, akin to holla, or hallo.

265 *on the road to Scotland*: marriage laws were different in Scotland, with fewer legal formalities, allowing for a much simpler and swifter procedure. Much of the plot in Gilbert's *Engaged* turns on these differences; see note to *Engaged*, 1.135.

301 *session*: parliamentary session; period of the year during which parliament convenes, thus the time between the opening of parliament and its prorogation.

307 *flies upon both sides of the wheel*: the reference is to the fable which Francis Bacon quotes in his essay 'Of Vain-Glory': 'The fly sat upon the axle-tree of the chariot wheel, and said, "What dust do I raise!"' Bacon misattributes the quotation to Aesop, while it is really taken from Lorenzo Bevilaqua; see *Notes and Queries*, 202 (1957), 378. The idea of flies on 'both sides of the wheel' is Bulwer's allusion to the political parties

competing in the election, while the implication of faction is already in Bacon's comments on the fable: 'So are there some vain persons, that whatsoever goeth alone or moveth upon greater means, if they have never so little hand in it, they think it is they that carry it. They that are glorious must needs be factious; for all bravery stands upon comparisons', *Francis Bacon: A Critical Edition of the Major Works*, ed. Brian Vickers, The Oxford Authors (Oxford and New York: Oxford University Press, 1996), 443 f.

309 *post-boys*: postilions.

312 *John Bull*: a common personification of England, usually as a stout gentleman; first introduced in John Arbuthnot's pamphlet collection *The History of John Bull* (1712), republished in Alexander Pope's and Jonathan Swift's *Miscellanies* (1727). In the present context, John Bull's position clearly reflects Evelyn's own political stance claiming a place above party politics and serving the interests of society as a whole; but for the ambiguity of this position and the many faces and functions of the John Bull figure, see Jeannine Surel, 'John Bull', in Raphael Samuel (ed.), *Patriotism: The Making and Unmaking of British National Identity*, iii: *National Fictions* (London and New York: Routledge, 1989), 3–25.

314 *trimmer*: one who moves back and forth between opposing parties in politics. Applied originally in this sense to Lord Halifax and those associated with him, but by him accepted in the sense 'one who keeps even the ship of state'; hence 'one who changes sides to balance parties' (*OED*).

329 *GEORGINA . . . tempers*: added in later (4th) edition to give her the opportunity to join in the finale with all the others.

London Assurance

DEDICATION

This dedication, taken from the play's first edition of 1841, is not in Lacy's Acting Edition.

Charles Kemble: Charles Kemble (1775–1854) was a prominent actor-manager. He had retired from the stage in 1832 to become Examiner of Plays and give readings from Shakespeare.

Bourcicault: one of the (earlier) variants of spelling Boucicault's name.

PREFACE

Only the play's first octavo edition of 1841 contained the Preface, which was omitted in subsequent editions.

7 *The management . . . comedy*: see Introduction, pp. xxiv–xxv.

8 *Mathews*: for further information on the persons mentioned in this Preface see the notes to Characters of the Play and the Introduction, pp. xxiv–xxvii.

21 *currente calamo*: (Latin) with the pen running on; i.e. extempore, without deliberation or hesitation.

27 *last November*: i.e. November 1840.

28 *Lee Moreton*: pseudonym used by Boucicault as actor and playwright in London and the provinces, 1838–40.

31 *productions*: i.e. parts of his script, handed in to the management as he finished them, or various versions of the manuscript which were then commented on by the management.

33 *liberality of its appointments*: Smith (p. 6) quotes the *Theatrical Journal*, 13 March 1841, 87: 'The expense of the new scenery, &c. . . . is said to have amounted to 600 pounds.'

36 *my first appearance before the public*: my first play to be staged.

44 *ci-devant jeune homme*: (French) erstwhile young man.

45 *roué*: (French) debauchee, rake.

47 *beau monde*: (French) the fashionable world.

54 *hits*: pointed sayings, telling phrases; with a connotative reference to marksmanship as developed in the following 'loaded, primed and pointed', suggesting the preparations to fire a gun.

66 *Mem.*: (abbreviation of Latin) *memorandum*, 'to be remembered'; 'placed in front of a note of something to be remembered'.

69 *last*: i.e. of the actors who were generally listed before the actresses.

75 *frolic*: frolicsome, sportive.

Momus: Greek god of ridicule.

CHARACTERS OF THE PLAY

Courtly: a telling name, the meaning of which is obvious, indicating his courtly behaviour; Sir Harcourt's first name is an old English family name which, through its French appearance, points back to Norman times, further to suggest Sir Harcourt's particularly ingrained gentility.

Harkaway: Max's surname points to his hunting obsession; it is a shout starting or urging on the hounds in the chase (*OED*).

Spanker: Apart from its connotation of Lady Gay's patronizing treatment of her husband, which, however, stops short of slapping (spanking) him, the main reference of the couple's family name is to their sterling qualities, a 'spanker', in its colloquial sense, being 'anything exceptionally large or fine; a person . . . of superior quality or character' (*OED*).

Dazzle: reference to his dazzling behaviour which takes people off their guard and impresses them so that they can easily be manipulated by his 'London assurance'.

Meddle: a meddling lawyer who gratuitously interferes where his services are not called for.

Solomon Isaacs: the choice of name for, and characterization of, this figure draws on the familiar hostile stereotype of the unrelenting Jewish usurer.

Pert: the 'pert', that is forward and insubordinate, lady's maid.

1 S.D. *Belgrave Square*: named after a Leicestershire village, Belgravia. Its owner, the Earl of Grosvenor, received permission to build on the land in 1826, and the square and surrounding area developed into one of the most fashionable areas in London. Its residents included those of the highest orders, such as the Duke of Bedford and the Earl of Essex. For more information see *London Encyclopaedia*, 53 f.

S.D. *doors . . . and C*: the play's stage directions do not make it quite clear how many doors there are supposed to be. There are probably three doors at the back of the stage (*RC*, *C*, and *LC*) and two at each side, *R1E* and *R2E*, *L1E*, and *L2E*. It is uncertain, however, whether *LUE* and *RUE* are to be taken as synonyms for the second side doors, as the single variant direction '*2RUE*' seems to suggest, or whether there are actually three doors at each side.

S.D. *R*: '*R door*' or '*R*' as a stage direction for an entry does not indicate precisely through which of the doors on the right Cool is supposed to come on stage. The decision is therefore left to directors or actors.

7 *give warning*: announce the intention to quit the employment.

16 *arrests*: i.e. arrest warrants.

26 *Hottentot*: this name of the south-west African ethnic group had come into eponymous usage for a person considered inferior in civilization and intellect, reflecting the widespread European view at the time of the African native population.

28 *Bow Street*: site of the Magistrates' Court, London's metropolitan police-court.

34 *puzzle*: here in the obsolete meaning of 'baffle', 'confound'.

67 S.D. *Greek skull-cap and tassels*: skull-caps were worn either as nightcap or smoking-cap. Smith (p. 12) notes that Tenniel's sketch of 1842 shows Farren in a small rakish fez, with tassels.

73 *commencement of the season*: extending in 1841 from late April to early July (Smith, 13).

85 *no further use . . . dressing-gown*: meaning that Cool can use it now; such cast-offs were an important part of servants' incomes.

93 *paying my devoirs*: visiting and paying my dutiful respects.

96 *made a market of*: profited from, exploited.

103 *heir presumptive or apparent*: the difference between these two types of heirs is that the latter succeeds if he outlives the present holder of the property, title, etc., while the heir presumptive's succession may be broken by the birth of someone nearer akin.

120 *pilot-coated, bearskinned brawling*: a pilot-coat, or pea-jacket, is a short overcoat of coarse woollen cloth; bearskin here refers to a shaggy kind of woollen cloth, used for such overcoats; both refer to clothing typically worn by sailors, who would also be notorious for their readiness to quarrel and fight.

149 *Lady Acid's last reunion*: a social gathering to which the lady invited a select and distinguished company; the italicized spelling suggests Sir Harcourt's French pronunciation of the word, which was not uncommon in the nineteenth century (cp. *OED*).

150 *Apollo*: Greek god of music, poetry, archery, prophecy, and the healing art; the sculpture of Apollo Belvedere, so called from the Belvedere Gallery in the Vatican, discovered at Anzio in 1485, was considered the antique model of male beauty and has been frequently copied.

154 *Ajax, in the Pompeian portrait*: portraits recently excavated in Pompeii were identified to represent Greek gods or heroes, but not Ajax (Smith, 17).

158 *entail*: twofold meaning of 'necessitate' and 'pass down by succession'.

173 *damages*: Sir Harcourt launched a successful action for 'criminal conversation', i.e. for adultery, in the legal aspect of a trespass against the husband (in England until 1857); the husband could sue for damages for another male's illicit use of his property in his wife's person. For a survey of the legal proceedings and cultural background see Lawrence Stone, *Broken Lives: Separation and Divorce in England 1660–1857* (Oxford: Oxford University Press, 1993).

176 *the Derby*: among the most famous English races, instituted by the Earl of Derby in 1780, and taking place every year in May or June at Epsom.

184 *bereaved*: deprived, robbed, but the more specific connotation of 'having lost a near relative' is of course present and adds a comic twist.

185 *object*: target, focus.

191 *'vive la bagatelle!'*: (French) long live frivolity or nonsense.

193 *bon mot*: (French) witticism.

195 *economy*: artful harmony of a carefully arranged make-up.

198 *primâ facie fact*: (Latin) an obvious fact, as it appears 'at first sight'.

200 *like a fox to his own tail*: with the same ingenuity with which a fox tries to evade the hunters who are after his tail for a trophy.

203 *eat fish with a knife*: Smith (p. 19) quotes from *The Gentlemen's Guide to*

Etiquette (1855), 12: 'The fish must be eaten with the fork, aided, if you choose with a piece of the crust cut off your bread . . . Never convey the knife to your mouth.'

209 *one of the faculty*: accepted, as a qualified doctor, by the professional body ('faculty') of one's fellows.

238 *the process of dressing*: another reference to Sir Harcourt's attention to etiquette. Again, Smith (p. 21) aptly quotes *The Gentleman's Guide to Etiquette*, [5]: 'It is from a man's dress that the first impression of his general manner is drawn; and it is therefore, the branch of Etiquette that demands the most serious attention of the student in politeness.'

244 *the manufacture of his person*: the creation of his physical appearance.

249 *gaiters*: were no longer considered fashionable at the time (Smith, p. 21).

250 *governor*: here, colloquial designation of the father of the family.

253 *bailiff*: official who executes writs and warrants on debtors.

280 *no shooting . . . year*: hunting is restricted to certain seasons of the year to protect the game during times of reproduction.

285 *preserves*: woods or other ground set apart for the protection and rearing of game (*OED*).

290 *a blood*: a blood-horse, i.e. a throroughbred, a horse with a pedigree.

295 *forty minutes*: the time needed by Shakespeare's Puck in *A Midsummer Night's Dream* (II. i. 175 f.) for this feat.

296 *Fiddlestrings*: literally, the strings of the bow of a fiddle; here, Max probably uses it synonymously with 'fiddlestick' in its humorous meaning of 'something insignificant or absurd, a mere nothing' (*OED*), but Max's choice of the word may also or in addition be motivated by an allusion to Sir Harcourt's way of wearing very tight-fitting clothes to press his body into shape, since one of the proverbial attributes of fiddlestrings is the tightness of their stretch, as in the adage 'Friends are like fiddlestrings, they must not be screwed too tight'.

299 *get cleared out*: lose his money.

300 *hazard . . . whist*: hazard is a game of dice. In 'French' hazard, the players stake against the bank, in 'English' hazard, against each other (*OED*). Whist is a game of cards for (usually) four players.

301 *state*: social splendour.

303 *deaths*: probably in the sense of 'near-deaths', i.e. dangerous situations for the hunters; the ironic reference to the many 'unheeded' deaths of the hunted animals may also be intended.

312 *its consequences are not entailed*: quibble on the meaning of 'entailed'; while wine does not have any consequences (none are entailed), love has consequences (children) to whom then possessions have to be entailed (bestowed upon as an inheritance or inalienable right).

331 *Yoicks! Tallyho-o-o-o!*: 'yoicks' is a call in fox hunting to urge on the hounds, whereas 'tally-ho' is used on first catching sight of a fox. (*OED*)

337 *at my own proper peril*: by paying for it myself.

338 *flirt with a banquet*: play, trifle with a banquet.

348 *Unattached*: i.e. not attached to a particular regiment.

'Dirty Buffs': Smith (p. 26) suggests that this fictive name is a contraction of the nicknames for the 50th Foot ('The Dirty Half-Hundred') and the 3rd Regiment of Foot ('The Buffs').

356 *retreat . . . Napoleon*: in his later career, Napoleon was noted for his skill in organizing retreats.

362 *road-book*: a book combining a road map and a local guide. Oak Hall is probably a fictive name; there is, for example, the following entry for Oakley Park in *Black's Picturesque Tourist and Road and Railway Guide Book Through England and Wales. With a General Travelling Map; Charts of Roads, Railroads, and Interesting Localities . . .* (Edinburgh, 2nd edn. 1851), 160: 'Oakley Park, (Earl Bathurst) erected by Lord Bathurst, the patron of Pope' at 89¼ miles from London on the route 'London to Gloucester through Maidenhead'.

374 *Curzon Street*: named after Nathaniel Curzon, a Derbyshire baronet who acquired the area in 1715, and built from the 1720s onwards, Curzon Street was a fashionable address at the time.

376 *put a man in*: i.e. send a bailiff to claim the movables to cover Courtly's debts.

380 *acceptance*: formal agreement to pay a bill of exchange when due.

387 *do the polite*: elliptical for 'do the polite thing', i.e. behave in a polite way.

394 *some game*: ironic, punning use of 'game' (which carries both its meanings of 'a competitive play or sport with rules' and 'animals hunted for food or sport'): related to card games by their writing a 'card', but also to their 'making game of' (poking fun at) Mr Solomon Isaacs.

396 *P.P.C.*: i.e. *pour prendre congé*, (French) 'by your leave'; formula used on visiting cards by those calling 'to take leave'.

397 S.D. *Exit Cool, L*: Lacy's Acting Edition adds: '*End of Act 1 (25 Minutes) Change to Travelling Dresses*'.

2 S.D. *discovered*: i.e. as the curtain rises (not subsequently noted). Each of the acts concludes with the drop of the curtain, to allow for changing the scenery on the stage.

8 *stuffed eel-skin*: suggesting a senile constitution in general, and senile impotence in particular.

16 *halter*: Pert's inadvertent use of the common pun on 'altar' and the 'halter', as used to fasten horses, but also referring to the hangman's noose.

27 *Law*: exclamation expressing surprise at being asked a question; connoting 'Christ's Laws' but also coalesced with 'Lor' for 'Lord' as an exclamation.

36 *a great restorer of consumptive estates*: the most frequent motives for a sojourn on the Continent were either failing health and the hope for a cure in a warm climate, or lack of money, which could be alleviated by a less expensive life abroad.

65 *his rival 'contemporary solicitor'*: 'Meddle, an attorney-at-law, conducts litigation in the Courts of Common Law; Jenks, a solicitor, in the Courts of Equity; but by 1835 solicitors were admitted to practise as attorneys in *any* court—hence Meddle's 'contemporary' antagonism' (Smith, p. 32).

69 *character*: reputation, professional standing.

72 *minority*: being under age.

82 *verdict*: favourable judgement.

84 *taken . . . by the button*: detained.

   Mrs: contracted form of 'Mistress', an obsolete form of address to an unmarried lady.

87 *nisi prius*: (Latin) here: an unavoidable first step to; generally: 'a writ directed to a sheriff commanding him to provide a jury at the Court of Westminster on a certain day, unless [*nisi*] the judges of assize previously [*prius*] come to the county' (*OED*).

   on the woolsack: in absolute judgment; Meddle satirically depicts Mrs Pert as a kind of 'Lord Chancellor of the Kitchen', who sits on the woolsack as does the Lord Chancellor in the House of Lords.

88 *pantry . . . kitchen etiquette*: as lady's maid, Mrs Pert would have held one of the highest ranks among the servants, which would, for instance, have included possession of a key to the pantry where the (often precious) victuals were stored.

90 *legal character*: person of legal training and reputation.

   considered: held in consideration or regard.

95 *have a long suit of me*: spend a long time courting me.

101 *dust-hole . . . bad ends*: as pigs rummage through mud or dust-holes with their snouts to find something edible and are given refuse from the kitchen ('bad ends') to eat.

103 *six-and-eightpence*: an attorney at law, whose fee was frequently fixed at the sum of six shillings and eight pence.

105 *butted*: in the threefold sense of (1) 'gainsaid' (as in the phrase 'but me no buts'); (2) pushed around ('to butt'), and (3) 'limited', 'restricted' (butted) in a legal sense (*OED*).

107 *an action will lie*: an action will be permissible or sustainable (*OED*).

112 *ring your nose*: rings are put through noses of swine or cattle to be able to guide or constrain them.

117 *stipendium*: (Latin) fixed payment.

121 *know him*: become acquainted with him; know who he is.

139 *Mud-Puddle*: Meddle continues to be associated with pigs, as Courtly's malformation of his name now suggests the puddles of mud which pigs like to rout in.

140 *show . . . lions*: show the (tourist) sights, as one would be shown the lions in the Tower of London.

175 *Crim. con.*: criminal conversation; see note to 1.173.

190 *sweetmeat*: sweet, sugary food.

191 *Pythagorean silence*: the avoidance of idle talk was part of the ascetic teachings of the Greek philosopher Pythagoras (sixth century BC).

200 *Ascot*: Royal Ascot, named after a village near Windsor which is the venue, is, with Epsom, the most famous annual English race meeting.

218 *situation*: position, employment.

220 *previous to*: before.

226 *until a seat . . . in the face*: until their financial situation becomes so critical that becoming a Member of Parliament (and thus enjoying an MP's immunity to prosecution for bancruptcy) or flight to the safety of the Continent is all that remains to them.

236 *shopman*: the owner of, or the assistant in, a shop.

241 *literary dandyisms and dandy literature*: foppish and over-exquisite behaviour and literature as popularized by the so-called 'fashionable novel' or 'silver-fork school' of the mid-1820s and 1830s, such as Bulwer-Lytton's *Pelham* (1828); see William Hazlitt's criticism of this vogue in his essay 'The Dandy School' in *The Examiner* (1827). Smith (p. 41) points out that it was actually a British phenomenon which was exported to France, rather than the other way round as Grace seems to suggest.

245 *plays off*: plays.

249 *lay out*: expend.

253 *intended*: (colloquial) prospective husband, fiancé.

257 *the West End mint*: the Royal Mint, near the Tower of London.

issue: put into circulation.

259 *sovereign*: supreme; with a pun on the gold coin called a sovereign.

260 *fashion's head upon its side*: 'fashion on its side' with a double meaning referring to the king's or queen's head stamped on one side of the gold coin (hence its name).

stamps it current: makes it legal and acceptable.

270 *forsooth*: in truth.

271 *coxcombs*: fops.

273 *pelisse*: women's long mantle, made of silk or velvet, reaching down to the ankle.

279 *Euclid*: Greek geometer (*c*.300 BC). His *Elements* were, even in the nineteenth century, the archetypal textbook of geometry.

281 S.D. *down*: downstage, i.e. to the front of the stage, towards the audience.

286 *Counsel . . . off*: (legal language) a barrister (counsel) is engaged (retained) and the suit (cause) is about to go to court (come off).

301 *Oldborough*: There is a place of that name in Devon, north-west of Exeter.

310 S.D. *up*: upstage, i.e. towards the back of the stage, away from the audience.

311 *give ye welcome*: [may God] give you welcome.

321 *steam carriage*: steam-powered road coach.

325 *essences*: perfumes.

347 *dine at half past one p.m.*: be found in the unfashionble habit of having her main meal so early and not, as was *de rigueur* at the time, in the early evening.

355 *Full of blood*: full of vigour (a hunting term).

363 *consistorial court*: a bishop's court held for causes and offences dealt with by ecclesiastical law, here especially matrimonial disputes and divorce.

369 *jade*: minx, hussy; otherwise a contemptuous, sometimes only playful name for a horse.

370 *Oh dear!*: here an exclamation of surprise.

373 *N'importe!*: (French) No matter.

379 *May I be permitted?*: Sir Harcourt formally asks permission to be introduced to the lady.

391 *Here, . . . permit me*: Here, Sir Harcourt, as the socially superior ranking, is asked permission for an introduction.

412 *Newman's best fours*: 'a carriage with four horses hired from J. Newman, who operated a coach service from Bishopsgate Street' (Smith, p. 51).

436 *Bring an action*: take him to court.

441 *love and cherish*: part of the husband's oath in the marriage ceremony.

446 *'no effects!'*: written by bankers on dishonoured cheques when the drawer has no funds in the bank.

457 *census*: in Great Britain, a census has been taken every tenth year since 1801.

462 *board wages*: 'wages allowed to servants to keep themselves in victuals' (*OED*).

466 *are actionable*: are vulnerable to being prosecuted legally.

479 S.D. *Exit . . . L*: Lacy's Acting Edition adds '*End of Act 2 (39 Minutes) Change to Dinner Dresses*'.

3.7 *written to town for*: sent a letter to London summoning.

22 *long-headed*: wily, shrewd and well informed.

29 *domestic economy*: the art or science of managing a household.

33 *con amore*: (Italian) with love, zeal, or delight.

36 *bachelor*: plays on the word's double meaning of (1) an unmarried man and (2) a person holding a first university degree.

44 *during the summer months*: 'i.e. before the game season opens in August' (Smith, p. 58).

52 *hand gallop*: an easy gallop, in which the horse is kept well in hand to prevent excess of speed.

55 *seat*: riding posture, sitting firm in the saddle.

66 *thrill her laugh*: modulate her laugh with a tremolo.

67 *in the field*: among the other huntsmen.

73 *Mr Adolphus . . . Spanker*: as the daughter of an earl, Lady Gay retains her title on marriage, though she changes her name (Smith, p. 60).

75 *climbing up your stairs*: 'This suggests an upper room, which is contradicted by its "*French windows opening to the lawn*"; perhaps they give onto a terrace with *steps* down to the grass' (Smith, p. 60).

   long clothes: Smith (p. 60) gives an example of the illustration of a riding habit including 'a close-fitted jacket with tight sleeves and a fully pleated skirt with a long train'.

105 *stays*: support, grip.

118 *Bucephalus-tamer*: Bucephalus was the charger of Alexander the Great, said to be unmanageable, but tamed by the king.

128 *thrilly*: vibrant.

136 *waits*: street musicians soliciting gifts of money by playing under windows.

145 *view-halloo*: the shout given by a huntsman on seeing the fox break cover.

152 *had a chance*: 'i.e. with a second horse, Kitty, ridden by a friend' (Smith, p. 62).

160 *tug*: hard fight.

167 *Walked the steeple*: easily won the steeplechase as in a leisurely walk.

174 *whoo-whoop*: the shout of huntsmen at the death of the game.

207 *I always dine—*: presumably, Spanker is about to say 'at home'.

268 *address*: courteous attention.

269 *laid herself out for display*: did all she could to show herself to advantage.

282 *acceptance*: bill of exchange. Smith (p. 70) succinctly summarizes the trickery: 'Dazzle tells Sir Harcourt he lent Charles £100. To support the lie, he takes from his wallet (*pocket-book*) a blank bill already drafted (*drawn*) for this amount (*pattern*) and with the appropriate revenue *stamp* affixed. Charles signs his name across the bill (thus *accepting* the debt). Dazzle takes it to Sir Harcourt and collects the money.'

304 *date it back*: give it an earlier date.

404 *indifferent*: (obsolete) of no interest or concern.

412 S.D. *runs off . . . R*: in some editions (cf. Smith, 76), this stage direction reads '*Snatches a kiss from her, and runs off through window*', implying that it is Courtly who leaves, which is not logical as he has a dialogue with Lady Gay immediately following this.

413 *Fizgig!*: What a flighty person!

419 *in at the death*: present when the hunted animal is killed.

    drop your ears: be discouraged.

420 *a little fresh*: too brisk or eager.

421 *outrun herself*: tire herself out.

438 *distance*: outstrip and defeat. Smith (p. 78) explains: 'Stragglers in a horse race were compulsorily withdrawn if the leaders outstripped them by a fixed distance.'

456 S.D. *take it*: Lacy's Acting Edition adds '*End of Act 3 (28 Minutes)*'.

4.5 *contemplation*: thought, prospect.

17 *pleasant*: tipsy.

21 S.D. *'A southerly . . . sky'*: very likely a hunting song, which continues, according to a friend's recollection, '. . . proclaim a hunting morning'; source unidentified.

42 *Pull up*: (as when drawing up the reins of a horse to slow it down or bring it to a standstill) Steady!

55 *distingué*: (French) distinguished.

67 *consider . . . constitution*: Smith (p. 83) aptly quotes from *The Gentlemen's Guide to Etiquette* (1855), 22: 'Politics and all other matters involving strong differences of opinion, must be carefully avoided in the presence of ladies.'

80 *discuss that to me*: discuss that with me.

    S.D. *gaucherie*: (French) awkwardness.

83 *sponsorial appellation*: baptismal name.

84 *amour propre*: (French) self-esteem.

91 *whipper-in*: a huntsman's assistant who keeps the hounds from straying and drives those who have strayed back into the pack.

122 *pipe*: a large cask (holding 92 imperial gallons).

123 *magnum*: a bottle containing two quarts of wine.

   meerschaum: expensive tobacco-pipe, the bowl of which is made of meerschaum.

124 *Canaster*: supreme brand of tobacco, made of the dried leaves coarsely broken.

   the ultimatum: the very best.

126 *Olympus*: the Greek mountain where the gods were said to have their dwelling place.

144 *love, honour and obey*: the words of the promise given by the bride in the Anglican marriage service.

148 s.d. *Exit . . . [and Servants]*: Smith's decision (p. 87) to make the other servants exit at this point seems convincing.

151 *Sir Roger de Coverly*: a country dance of that name (or, more precisely, *Roger of Coverly*) was known before 1800; in Addison and Steele's *Spectator* a character of that name appears in several numbers, whose great-grandfather is said to have invented a country dance named after him. Addison and Steele's Sir Roger epitomizes the characteristics of the Tory backwoods squire.

152 *whoo-whoop*: see note to 3.174 above.

164 *I never dance*: Smith (p. 88) quotes from *The Gentleman's Guide to Etiquette* (1855), 14: 'In all civilized countries dancing is considered to be the first element in the Art of True Etiquette, and without a perfect knowledge of which, no person can be allowed to mix in the society of cultivated people of rank or station.'

166 *do the gallant*: act as cavalier or escort (to a lady).

168 *prize essay . . . subject*: again, Smith (p. 88) quotes *The Gentleman's Guide to Etiquette*, 21: 'A well-bred man, if called upon by circumstances to lead the discourse, will be careful to adapt the topics to what he conceives to be the taste or capacities of those present.'

169 *Corpus Christi*: both Oxford and Cambridge have a college of this name.

174 *proved*: (1) demonstrated, but also (2) tested, probed.

   concoct: improvise, invent.

178 *'The labour . . . pain'*: Shakespeare, *Macbeth*, II. iii. 54.

180 *Ben Jonson*: (1573–1637) dramatist and poet, well-known for his conviviality. His 'Leges Conviviales', in Alexander Brome's translation, contain the rule 'And let our only emulation be | Not drinking much, but talking

wittily.' See *Ben Jonson*, ed. Ian Donaldson, The Oxford Authors (Oxford and New York: Oxford University Press, 1985), 510f. (and nn.).

perplexion: perplexity.

intellects: (archaic) mental faculties.

181 *spirituous*: alcoholic.

182 *evidence*: (here) example, instance.

225 *rolls*: official list of attorneys.

226 *pleadings*: formal allegations for both parties in a legal action.

229 *worked*: proceeded.

238 *paradise is regained*: echoes the title of John Milton's second great epic poem, *Paradise Regained* (1671), sequel to his earlier *Paradise Lost* (1667).

244 *express accommodation*: particular convenience.

246 *What . . . there!*: Shakespeare, *Macbeth*, V. i. 59.

253 *interested*: here: strongly concerned, (an understating expression for) impassioned.

254 *verdure*: green vegetation, plants or trees.

264 *out-Heroded*: King Herod, who, according to Matthew 2: 16, ordered the massacre of the infants of Bethlehem, was acted as a blustering tyrant on the medieval stage. As such he is referrred to in Shakespeare's phrase, 'it out-Herods Herod' (*Hamlet*, III. ii. 14), which became a popular saying in the nineteenth century. In the present context, 'out-Heroded' means 'surpassed'.

294 *Pug*: (hunting vocabulary) a *quasi*-proper name for a fox; *OED* gives an example from Maria Edgeworth's tale *The Absentee* (1809), ch. viii: 'There is a dead silence till pug is well out of cover . . .' The reference is, of course, to Sir Harcourt, as Lady Gay is not supposed to see Meddle who is hiding to overhear the conversation.

312 *fall*: straightness, upright posture.

328 *Veni, vidi, vici!*: according to Plutarch, this was Julius Caesar's concise report to his friend Amintius of his victory at Zela (47 BC).

336 *'There is a . . . to fortune'*: Shakespeare, *Julius Caesar*, IV. iii. 218f.

337 *'Virtue . . . reward'*: old proverb going back to Roman times.

341 *decimate your hopes*: pass verdicts drastically below the plaintiff's expectations in damages (which is why Meddle goes in for such a large sum to start with).

343 *The plaintiff . . . action*: Meddle hopes to persuade Spanker to bring a legal suit of adultery against Sir Harcourt.

354 *bona fide*: (Latin) in good faith; hence, genuine, sincere.

368 *run away with me*: spend all I have.

398 *element*: water as one of the four elements: earth, wind, fire, and water.

408 *say Grace*: punning on Grace Harkaway's name and the saying of prayers (*grace*) before meals.

415 *prevent*: precede, anticipate.

421 *severally*: separately, by different exits.

422 S.D. *Act drop quickly*: Lacy's Acting Edition adds: '*End of Act 4 (36 Minutes)*'.

5.1 *affair*: love intrigue.

4 *encumbrance*: dependant.

10 *wicket*: small door in the wall or fence for use when the main gates are closed.

14 *faux pas*: (French) false step; compromising act.

22 *Morning Post . . . Herald . . . Chronicle*: all three of the newspapers mentioned are London morning papers: the *Morning Post* (founded in 1772), the *Morning Herald and Public Advertiser* (founded in 1780), and the *Morning Chronicle* (founded in 1769).

23 *Boulogne*: fashionable bathing resort on the coast of France and the usual port of arrival on crossing the Channel for the Continent. Smith (p. 103) notes that, in 1840, on a venture similar to Sir Harcourt's project, Boucicault's guardian Dr Lardner went on to Paris with Mrs Richard Heaviside.

31 *defalcation*: defection.

33 *bruited*: noised abroad.

43 *procured disguises*: Sir Harcourt would here need to produce some clothes such as a cape or a veil for the lady; some kind of mask or half mask would also be possible.

64 *subpoena*: (Latin) under a penalty; serve you with 'a writ issued from a court of justice commanding the presence of a witness under a penalty for failure' (*OED*). Since Meddle already has these writs at the ready as the occasion arises, we are to conclude that he has procured himself a collection of blank forms which he can fill in as the case may be. Whether this practice was possible, or indeed legal, remains uncertain.

65 *a shilling apiece*: 'given as a token payment of expenses to ensure a witness's attendance at court' (Smith, 105).

73 *book*: i.e. a Bible on which to swear an oath.

76 *Lothario*: this type-name for a rakish lover has its original in a character of that name in Rowe's tragedy *The Fair Penitent* (1703), which in turn is based on Massinger and Field's *The Fatal Dowry*.

94 *imperative, indicative, injunctive*: pseudo-legal jargon suggesting declining degrees of peremptoriness.

96 *ribbons*: reins.

    box-seat: seat where the coach driver sits.

101 *end in smoke*: come to nothing; Lady Gay takes up Dazzle's powder imagery to deflate the high talk of honour and duelling, but, as events then show, almost produces a dramatic irony here, since there will be real gunpowder smoke later on.

108 *Compromise the question!*: pull his nose, instead of duelling with him, as a compromise.

163 S.D. *seal*: usually an engraved stone or other hard material, worn in a ring or a trinket on a pocket-watch chain, to authorize transactions as with a signature. By giving Meddle his seal, Spanker has authorized him to act as his legal representative in the affair.

167 *come off*: take place.

171 *irons*: guns.

    string: as in billiards, to decide who has the first shot. In billiards, this is done by a preliminary stroke, whose winner is the first to start the game proper; so presumably the duel's first shot would be decided by a preliminary contest of marksmanship between the opponents.

174 *object*: person in view, target.

181 *weeds*: i.e. widow's weeds; the kind of clothes worn by widows.

196 *revert the joke*: turn the joke against them.

207 *en règle*: (French) according to rule.

208 *couching*: phrasing.

218 *hair-triggered*: 'fitted with a delicate spring mechanism (*hair*) which releases the main trigger at the slightest touch' (Smith, 113).

    saw grip: saw-handled, i.e. having a handle shaped like a saw to ensure a firmer and more secure grasp.

221 *hereditaments*: inherited properties.

240 *entailed*: legally settled on a succession of heirs who cannot bequeath them at pleasure.

246 *What's to do now?*: (here) What's all the fuss.

262 *linch-pin*: pin or peg passed through an axle's end to keep the wheel in place.

269 S.D. *Two shots heard*: the editorial addition of this stage direction is necessitated by Sir Harcourt's reference to the discharging of the guns in his following explanation at l.275.

289 *played upon by her*: Smith (p. 116) notes that this allegation is unjustified: Grace has not been 'played upon' by Lady Gay; the passage may reflect an earlier, undocumented version of the play, where Lady Gay could have played a more active part in helping Courtly win Grace.

311 *common acceptation*: usual meaning.

367 *particular*: especially concerned.

393 *'Requiescat in pace'*: (Latin) May he (or she) rest in peace; common inscription on tombstones.

404 *cozening*: cheating, deceitful.

406 *under age*: Smith (p. 123) notes: 'A debtor under twenty-one was immune from prosecution; Boucicault used this defence when his tailor sued in 1842.'

429 *under the rose*: in secret.

467 *oblige*: gratify (ironic).

468 *I am always thick on*: I always have a large stake on.

470 *attest your title*: validate your claim.

478 *engrossed*: written out or expressed in legal form.

480 *Mr Spanker . . . L*: the names of the characters are printed in this order in Lacy's Acting Edition to indicate their relative position on the stage when the dialogue ends. They hold these final positions in a tableau to take the first applause. Thereafter, they take curtain calls individually or in groups.

Engaged

NOTE

actions.: in French's Acting Edition (London, n.d.), one further sentence follows at this point: 'Directly the characters show that they are conscious of the absurdity of their utterances the piece begins to drag.'

The Boltons: two facing crescents in South Kensington, SW1; a very fashionable address, where Gilbert moved after his marriage in 1867, to no. 24 which he had bought that year.

1.1 *Wha*: (Scottish dialect for) What. Subsequent uses of Scottish dialect will be explained in the Glossary.

3 *scribbled*: carded or teased coarsely.

8 *glowerin'*: gazing intently.

25 *nor any woman neither*: cf. Shakespeare, *Hamlet*, II. ii. 309 f.: 'Man delights not me—nor woman neither, though by your smiling you seem to say so.'

48 *illicit whusky still*: the word form 'whisky' (here in the Scottish dialect 'whusky') came into use in the eighteenth century as a short form of the Gaelic original *uisge beatha* ('water of life'). After extensive legislation in

the early ninteeenth century, the black market for illicit whisky more or less disappeared. Angus's practice of an illegal still can therefore no longer be associated with the highly symbolic value it would have had a hundred years earlier, when the evading of taxes imposed by the English would also have been a politically significant action.

49 *distracted*: (obsolete) agitated, troubled.

50 *cot*: small house, cottage.

79 *the red-headed exciseman*: that excisemen were traditionally unpopular in general (see note above on whisky), and with people like Angus who had their own 'illicit whusky still' in particular, is obvious. The saying 'to wed the red-headed exciseman' is therefore a fitting phrase, especially coming from Angus, to describe the worst thing for a girl to do. Red hair ('red-headed'), albeit a common stereotype for the Irish and Scots (e.g. Sir Walter Scott, *Marmion* (1808), vi. 19: 'While wildly loose their red locks fly . . .'), is here used as the symbol of lasciviousness, hence also moral depravity and so prone to the devil, as Robert Burns's 'The De'il's Awa wi' the Exciseman' celebrates: 'The De'il cam fiddling thro' the town, | And danced awa wi' the Exciseman; | . . . | We'll mak our maut [malt], and brew our drink, | We'll dance and sing, and rejoice, man; . . .'; red hair was also traditionally ascribed to Judas Iscariot; cf. Shakespeare's *As You Like It*, III. iv. 7.

134 *without delay*: while English marriage law since 1573 required banns, a licence, and marriage in a church, Scottish law, at least until 1856, did not. Anyone could act as witness and immediate marriages by declaration were possible. This is why English couples seeking a secret marriage went across the Scottish border, where at Gretna, directly on a main road north, the first house in Scotland was the Old Toll Bar. Together with the Old Blacksmith's Shop somewhat further on at Gretna Green where the blacksmith presided over the marriage at his anvil, this was among the popular venues for such 'ceremonies'. Today, both places have become much-frequented tourist attractions for this reason. For a general survey see, for example, John R. Giles, *For Better, For Worse, British Marriages, 1600 to the Present* (New York and Oxford: Oxford University Press, 1985).

159 *the Cheviot Hills*: the Cheviot Hills are a range of hills on both sides of the border between Northumbria and southern Scotland, their highest elevation being the Cheviot (816 m.).

160 *the Conquest*: i.e. the Norman Conquest of Anglo-Saxon England in 1066.

351 *We see . . . fair*: the cadences of Maggie's speech clearly echo the New Testament, Luke 12: 54 ff. (in the Authorized Version of 1611): 'And he [Jesus] said to the people, When ye see a cloud rise out of the West, straightway ye say, There cometh a shower, and so it is, And when ye

see the South wind blow, ye say, There will be heat, and it cometh to pass . . .'

414 *thirty shillings*: one pound fifty pence in modern currency; possibly an allusion to the thirty pieces of silver which Judas was paid for betraying Christ, see Matthew 26: 15.

564 *fire-eater*: one fond of fighting, a duellist.

584 s.d. *favours*: ribbons or cockades worn at a wedding in evidence of goodwill.

2 s.d. *flat*: i.e. the stage 'wall' formed by wooden frames (*flats*) covered with painted canvas.

89 *devoted*: (here) surely consigned to evil or destruction; doomed.

99 *tarts*: *OED* gives 1887 for the first use of this word in the colloquial sense of 'prostitute', so that audiences at the play's early performances probably did not identify the same pun here that modern audiences see in this double meaning with the word's primary sense of a piece of baked pastry (at that time not necessarily sweet). The pun Gilbert probably had in mind rests perhaps on a third meaning of the word, current at the time of its first performance, which *OED* quotes from John C. Hotten, *A Dictionary of Modern Slang* (London, 1864), 254: '*Tart*, a term of approval applied by the London lower orders to a young woman for whom some affection is felt. The expression is not generally employed by the young men, unless the female is "in her best".'

103 *darksome*: gloomy, cheerless.

153 *dross*: (here) money, wealth.

190 *like chancery . . . enormous*: until the Judicature Act of 1873, the Court of Chancery, presided over by the Lord Chancellor, was the highest court of judicature next to the House of Lords; in the nineteenth century it was notorious for its long, exhausting, and hence expensive, suits. Charles Dickens variously and famously satirized it in his novels, most notably perhaps in *Bleak House*, ch. i.

270 *going it*: engaged recklessly in the spending of money.

283 *I've stuck to it.*: Here a long description of the breakfast has been cut out in the printed texts. It is, however, preserved in LC and is given in Additional Passages, A (p. 193). It seems likely that the passage was left out in performance as an overlong diversion which, for all its vividness, contributes nothing to the developemnt of the plot.

308 *floury*: mealy (spelt 'flowery' in LC and the nineteenth-century editions).

319 *particular*: exacting in regard to details, fastidious.

333 *looking after*: (obsolete) looking for, searching for.

433 *flys*: one-horse covered carriages.

434 *second-class Cook's tourists' tickets*: Thomas Cook (1808–92), a Baptist

missionary, persuaded the Midland Counties Railway Company in 1841 to run a special train for a temperance meeting; this was the first publicly advertised excursion train in England; it became a fixed institution, and Cook went on to organize many others in the following years and founded the firm Thomas Cook and Son; from the 1860s onwards Cook gave up organizing the tours himself and became an agent for sales of domestic and overseas travel tickets. Cheviot bought two of these for a railway journey to Devon in a second-class carriage.

435 *Ilfracombe*: one of the most popular seaside resorts in Devon, famous for its sandy beach and spectacular cliff scenery.

Westward Ho!: coastal resort in Devon which gave its name to a novel (1855) by Charles Kingsley.

436 *Bideford Bay*: bay around the port town of Bideford on the northern coast of Devon.

451 *Patagonia*: the southernmost part of South America (south of the Río Colorado): Although emigration did occur to Patagonia, it is not the most likely destination of a Scottish emigrant at the time, but, as serves the purpose of the plot, it has the connotation of 'beyond the limits of easy reach', 'exotically far away'.

494 *I plighted my troth to*: (archaic) to whom I made a promise of marriage.

3.6 *Says the old . . . on fire*: the song is quite possibly Gilbert's own invention; no source has been identified.

90 *rattletrap*: one who constantly talks in a lively and thoughtless fashion.

121 *the Statute of Limitations*: any of the statutes (esp. 3 & 4 Will. IV c. 25) fixing a period of limitation for actions of certain kinds; here obviously one limiting to six years the time for an action for breach of promise (to marry). Maggie will later bring such an action against Cheviot.

133 *all I can.*: LC has a long recapitulation of Cheviot's situation at this place. It was cut out in the printed versions and may indeed be considered tedious by some, while others might find it a help to keep track of the complications. It is given in Additional Passages, B (pp. 193–4).

177 *Joint Stock . . . '62*: the Act limited the liability of the shareholders (i.e. stock holders) in joint stock companies, i.e. companies set up with more than one shareholder. The Act established that the liability of each share-holder in the event of insolvency was limited to the nominal or face value of the shares that he held. So a shareholder with two shares had twice the liability as a shareholder with one share (and also twice the dividends and votes, etc.). Also, the liability was no greater than this. Before the Act or, as is the case here, where a stock company was not registered under this regulation, there could be unlimited liability in the event of insolvency and the division of liabilities between different shareholders was not clear.

388 *'bouncers'*: (colloquial) 'bouncing' or 'thumping' lies.

390 *bangers*: (colloquial) astounding lies; (synonymous with) bouncers.

416 *an action for breach*: a law suit for breach of promise to marry; promising to marry someone entailed legal obligations; a breach of this promise was (and under certain conditions still is) actionable.

ADDITIONAL PASSAGES

2 *Gunter's*: James and Robert Gunter, confectioners, at 7 Berkeley Square, Piccadilly.

7 *Abernethys*: a kind of hard bisuits flavoured with caraway seeds.

captains: captain's biscuits, of the type Tom Pinch is offered by Mr Pecksniff at the end of ch. v in Charles Dickens's *Martin Chuzzlewit*.

16 *generous wine*: wine rich and full of strength; the pun developed in the following sentence draws on further meanings of the word 'generous', i.e. liberal, giving without expecting rewards or profits, when taken as an attribute to the, admittedly somewhat strained, personification of the wine itself.

20 *epergne*: a centre-dish for the dinner-table.

The High Bid

CHARACTERS OF THE PLAY

Young Man: the part of the Young Man is not included in LC. Cf. Note on the Texts, p. li.

English Tourists . . . Whitaker: the names of the 'tourists' are given in the programme of the performance, a copy of which is kept in the Theatre Museum, London. In the printed text, they are summarily indicated as 'Tourists, Visitors, etc.'

1 S.D. *flagged*: paved with slabs of marble or stone.

S.D. *old garden*: the 'old garden', often walled in, would be on a formal design, perhaps dating from the seventeenth century or even earlier, such as the 'Old Garden' at Rousham, while what is called the 'Park', to which the main entrance is described to open, would be laid out on a more modern plan.

4 *mum*: (abbreviation of) ma'am, madam.

40–2 S.D. *(two-and-twenty . . . good 'sort')*: in LC, Cora's first appearance on stage is her meeting with Prodmore, l. 164 below. This is also the place where her description is located in LC. When James moved her entry forward in TYP, followed in this edition, Cora's description remained—

obviously an oversight, as Edel, 556 n. 1, remarks—unchanged and hence comes too late in TYP. It has here been moved to its evidently correct location at Cora's first entry, following Edel's decision in his edition. Cf. also Note on the Texts, p. li.

63 *sunk fences*: this type of fence, also called a ha-ha, consists of a trench, the inner side of which is perpendicular and faced with stone, the outer sloping and turfed; it thus does not obstruct the view.

82 *Bellborough*: evidently a fictitious English town.

35–110 *[CHIVERS] Poor dear old bell, broken . . . CHIVERS What does come over them?*: This long passage is not in LC, which has instead the following continuation of Chivers's lines before Prodmore's entry: '(*Then as he seems to have his eye up to where it may tinkle in its dusky corner*) The poor dear old broken-down bell! Broken-down, broken-down—(*He exhales it nervously, and with a murmur of great patience, which is taken up the next instant by the husky plaint of the signal itself. The old bell hoarsely but limply sounds, and he starts for the door to the park as if he has been sleeping at his post*) Mercy, if I *didn't* watch—! (*He breathlessly shuffles up and under the dusky arch of the entrance front, opens wide the house-door into the outer brightness, against which the figure of Mr Prodmore looms large*)'.

134 *the most convenient of my seats*: the one of my several places of residence that lay closest to Covering End.

222–4 *and who is also going . . . her here*: replaced by, 'a wonderful American widow.' in TYP.

231 S.D. *lighting*: growing light, cheerful.

231–45 *CORA So I suggested. . . . PRODMORE (reviewing the affair) . . . won't do*: not in TYP.

272 *a show-house*: a house that can be visited by the public.

324 *come down on him*: descend on him with severity; put him under pressure.

335 *shuffling*: shifting or evasive.

329–36 *CORA (moving a little . . .) . . . PRODMORE (slightly impatient) . . . mean by it?*: not in TYP.

376–7 *, and—to be so many . . . young*: not in TYP.

398–404 *CORA (with a nervous . . .) . . . PRODMORE . . . (Then both . . . business)*: omitted in TYP, which then begins the next sentence with 'Cora, . . .'.

411 *temper*: temperament.

432 *'radical . . . revolution'*: The term 'radicalism' was used from the late eighteenth century onwards for those who worked for fundamental ('radical') political and social change, such as parliamentary reform, extensions of the franchise, reform of the land law, better care for the poor. Radicalism, which continued as an influential movement throughout the nineteenth century, was no homogeneous force. It was not only a

325

working-class phenomenon, but had also a strong middle-class basis among professionals and manufacturers. For all their variety, however, radicals generally were united in their opposition to aristocratic ideals and the notion of an oligarchic rule of the nation, both in political and economic terms. For the middle-class environment of radicalism, to which Captain Yule obviously belonged, see further for example Paul Adelman, *Victorian Radicalism: The Middle Class Experience 1830–1914* (London: Longman, 1984).

447 S.D. *wheels in the park*: replaced by '*the bell*' in TYP.

448 *A fly?*: replaced by 'It must be *he*!' in TYP.

465 S.D. *The house-bell . . . leaving door open*: not in TYP.

466 S.D. *was*: editorial emendation to give the sentence, which otherwise lacks a verb in the main clause, grammatical coherence.

529 S.D. '*off*': distant.

550–5 *PRODMORE (interrupting in turn) . . . PRODMORE (abounding . . . all other thoughts)*: not in TYP.

607 *fancy-values*: estimated by caprice rather than actual value.

623 *fancies*: strange ideas.

680–3 *(after watching . . .) . . . with abuse for!*: not in TYP.

688 *You come high*: Your price is high.

713 *corpus delicti*: (Latin) literally, the body of the crime; in strictly legal terms, the sum of all elements (corpus) that, together, constitute a breach of law; generally, the concrete evidence of a crime, e.g. the body of a murdered person; by his use of the word corpus (body) with reference to Cora, Yule wittily evokes the idea of a barter over an inanimate merchandise.

751–2 [*CHIVERS*] *a kind of brilliant— YULE . . . Oh, a 'brilliant'—*: Chivers probably wanted to say 'brilliant, i.e. shining, red', but Yule takes up his word and turns it into the noun 'brilliant', i.e. a diamond of the finest cut and 'brilliancy'.

828–9 *snapped down . . . celebrated poem*: the poem referred to is 'Ginevra' by Samuel Rogers (1763–1855), published in *Poems* (London, 1836), ii. 92–6. See also 'The Mistletoe Bow' by Nathaniel Thomas Haynes Bayly (1797–1839), set to music by H. R. Bishop. Rogers's poem tells the story of Ginevra, a young lady from Modena, who went missing on her wedding-day. Her body was discovered years later in an oaken chest, in which she had apparently been locked while hiding as a prank.

829–32 S.D. *(Her manner . . . range)*: not in TYP; *gave her the range*: allowed her to go freely around the house.

851 '*The good . . . van Rhyn*': the title of the painting alludes to the Parable of the Talents in Matthew 24, in which, in the version of the King James's

Bible, the returning master says to the servant who has increased his five talents to ten in the master's absence: 'Well done, thou good and faithful servant'. There is, however, no painting of this title in the currently recognized Rembrandt canon; there is a Rembrandt painting entitled *The Good Samaritan* and James could have seen a copy of it by Drost in the Wallace Collection in London. That Collection also contains a painting entitled *The Unmerciful Servant*, which was then attributed to Rembrandt but has since been identified as painted by Jacob Backer. By her reference to Rembrandt, Mrs Gracedew is of course suggesting that Chivers, in his traditional, faithful servant's role, fits in with the gilt-edged old master paintings in the house.

Baedeker: not in LC. Founded by Karl Baedeker (1801–59), the German publishing house of his name became famous for its guidebooks. The first English 'Baedeker' appeared in 1861.

869 *royal . . . guns*: the royal salute for Queen Victoria, as Empress of India, was 100 guns. Cf. 'royal salute' in George E. Voyle and G. de Saint-Clair Stevenson, *Military Dictionary. Supplement* (3rd edn. 1877–81).

889 *put up in paper and bran*: packed with paper wrapped round the object, and bran (husks left when the flour is taken from cereals in the mill) used as a protective fill-in in the box.

896 *Chelsea*: the Chelsea Porcelain Works in Lawrence Street, Chelsea, London, were founded in 1745 and operated until 1784. They were particularly famous for their vases, snuff-boxes, and smelling-bottles and other similar items.

901 *pew-opener*: beadle; official in a church who directs the members of the congregation to their seats and may open the pew-doors for them.

921 *type*: model, pattern.

926 *'simple . . . flower'*: quotation from Alfred Lord Tennyson's poem 'Lady Clara Vere de Vere', stanza 2 (ll. 15 f.): 'A simple maiden in her flower | Is worth a hundred coats of arms.'

957 *a-taking*: in the process of taking.

991 *Limoges*: Henry James most probably had in mind one of the famous Limoges painted enamels, manufactured only in a few family businesses, with the finest work being produced in the sixteenth century, rather than the simpler Limoges porcelain of a later date.

1013 *upstairs . . . chamber*: quotation from the nursery rhyme 'Goosey Gander': 'Goosey, goosey gander, | Whither shall I wander? | Upstairs and downstairs | And in my lady's chamber. | There I met an old man | Who would not say his prayers, | I took him by the left leg | And threw him down the stairs.' See Iona and Peter Opie, *The Oxford Nursery Rhyme Book* (Oxford and New York: Oxford University Press, 1955, 7th impr. 1998), 26.

1063 *for the more . . . the better!*: the more often, more intensely we look at the interior of the house and the more of it we see the better; not in TYP.

1074 *Lady*: replaced by 'madam' in TYP.

1115 *Gothic roof*: suggesting that the main hall does not have a ceiling but has the full height of the house and is covered by its roof which, in the Gothic style, might be decorated by (originally colourful) wood carvings.

1117 *Methuselah*: according to Genesis 5: 27, Methusela, the son of Enoch and father of Lamech, lived to the age of 969 years. Hence he became eponymous for extreme longevity.

1118–19 *It was here . . . 1611*: in a letter to the Countess of Jersey (quoted Edel, 520) James identifies the mansion inspiring his fictional 'Summersoft' in his tale *The Lesson of the Master* as Osterley Park House near Heston, Middlesex. Here, an original Elizabethan building was remodelled to the design of Robert Adams between 1761 and 1780, which included a long gallery along the entire west front. Whether this archetype was retained in James's mind when the 'Summersoft' of the tale was used as the name of the country house in the one-act play for Ellen Terry, and then became the Covering End of the short story and the three-act *High Bid* is a question difficult to assess. Osterley does not have a particularly striking staircase, and it lacks the medieval origins referred to in the plays. Designs of other houses may therefore have intermingled in James's mind. To venture one suggestion, Hatfield House in Herfordshire would perhaps come closest to the play's model. Begun in 1607, the house was built next to an older Tudor palace (where the young princess Elizabeth received the news, in 1558, of the death of her half-sister and her consequent rise to the throne). It had been given in an exchange to Robert Cecil, Earl of Salisbury, by James I, who may have visited his minister here. The house certainly was built for such noble guests. Its spacious design by Robert Lyminge includes James I's drawing room with a statue of the King and a splendid chimneypiece by Maximilian Colt. It has a lavish oak staircase and a famous wooden screened gallery, all features which Mrs Gracedew is 'raving' about. Its large collection of paintings, and impressive Brussels tapestries in the hall also fit the play's design. However, there is no grotto in the park of either Osterley or Hatfield.

1122 *fourteenth century*: the obvious anachronism is replaced by 'exactly Jacobean' in TYP.

1123 S.D. *takes it from her*: takes over again, continues.

1133 S.D. *in fine*: in short.

1135 *Castle Gaunt*: 'Gaunt House, a moated dwelling of the fifteenth century, near Oxford' (Edel). 'The house was fortified and besieged in the Civil War. A large chimney breast at the rear may be C15, but the rest is a rebuilding of *c.*1660' (Jennifer Sherwood, Nikolaus Pevsner, *Oxford-*

shire, The Buildings of England (Harmondsworth: Penguin Books, 1974), 778).

1141 *puss-in-the-corner*: a game played by children, of whom one stands in the centre and tries to capture one of the 'dens' or 'bases' as the others change places.

1153 S.D. *trunk-hose*: 'Full bag-like breeches covering the hips and upper thighs, and sometimes stuffed with wool or the like, worn in the 16th and early 17th centuries' (*OED*).

1156 *Tewkesbury . . . Blenheim*: in the War of Roses, the Yorkist army led by King Edward IV won a decisive victory in the Battle of Tewkesbury (1471) over the Lancastrians, capturing Queen Margaret, while her son, Edward Prince of Wales, was killed in action. In the War of Spanish Succession, the British army under the Duke of Marlborough in alliance with Prince Eugen of Savoy defeated the French at Blenheim (Blindheim on the Danube in Germany) on 13 August 1704. In recognition of this victory, Queen and Parliament granted Marlborough funds to build Blenheim Palace at Woodstock, Oxfordshire.

1256 *Staircase*: replaced by 'Gallery' in TYP.

1315 S.D. *him*: the copytexts read 'her'; here replaced by the more logical 'him' referring to Yule.

2.9–22 *[MRS GRACEDEW] (showing by her . . .) . . . (Then with curiosity)*: not in TYP.

40–57 *[MRS GRACEDEW] . . . (Then as it strikes her . . .) . . . taken a line today!*: replaced by 'When I've taken a line I stick to it as you certainly must think I've done today.' in TYP.

78 *let me put you up*: allow me to provide all the information required.

86 S.D. *diverted at*: amused by.

89–95 S.D. *[MRS GRACEDEW] . . . (Then as, for the house . . .) . . . (Then . . . showing it)*: replaced by 'But now for the long gallery.' in TYP.

133 *got you up*: learned about you.

141 *East End of London*: the eastern districts of London used to be (and still are) synonymous with its poorer, working-class areas.

234 *Dead Sea fruit*: Dead Sea fruit, Dead Sea apple, or Apple of Sodom is described as of fair appearance externally, but dissolving when grasped, into smoke and ashes; a 'traveller's tale', supposed by some to refer to the fruit of *Solanum Sodomeum* (allied to the tomato), by others to the *Calotropis procera*; hence any hollow disappointing appearance (*OED*).

235–7 *If by a miracle . . . luck!*: not in TYP.

312–14 *MRS GRACEDEW (as demuring . . .) YULE Well, sacrifice them*: not in TYP.

317 *fire-back*: back wall of the fireplace.

319–34 *[YULE (while his spirit ...]* ... *my reserves.*: replaced by 'You don't know what's behind the awkwardness—' in TYP.

369–79 *YULE (as, rather decently ...)* ... *MRS GRACEDEW* ... *(... all the way)*: not in TYP.

381–3 *MRS GRACEDEW Not even* ... *YULE* ... *to everyone.*: not in TYP.

395–416 *[YULE Yes, (so far assenting) ...]* ... *part of the Property.*: not in TYP.

428 *close with*: come to terms or an agreement with.

465 S.D. *chaffingly*: teasingly.

525–34 *[YULE] (who, all this strongly ...)* ... *deal with*: not in TYP.

703 *I burnt my ships*: cut off all means of retreat; after the common practice of generals who, invading a foreign land, ordered the ships to be burnt after landing to show their soldiers that, retreat being impossible, they must conquer or die.

759 *as Chicago does*: completely, utterly; according to Mitford M. Mathews, *A Dictionary of Americanisms on Historical Principles* (Chicago: University of Chicago Press, 1951, repr. 1966), 307, a 'Chicago' is 'In baseball, a defeat in which the losing team fails to score'. The first use of the word in this sense is given in the *New York Herald*, 5 July 1871; subsequently the word was also in use as a verb, 'to Chicago', in that sense.

792–842 *[MRS GRACEDEW (this manner from him ...)]* ... *(... absolute)*: not in TYP.

849 S.D. *, even yet*: not in TYP; inserted in pencil in LC.

924 *bundle out*: leave precipitately.

1094–1109 *CORA (reassured again ...)* ... *MRS GRACEDEW* ... *But your*: replaced by 'Your' in TYP.

1115 *from the point of view of things he's in*: considering his circumstances, important connections, and business interests.

1126–36 *[MRS GRACEDEW (reasonably assenting) ...]* ... *(who stands*: replaced by '(*stands*' in TYP.

1174 S.D. *Consciously dropping*: deliberately abandoning.

3.3 S.D. *blown*: out of breath.

51 *treat*: (here in the archaic meaning of) negotiate, come to a bargain.

106–7 *PRODMORE Oh!* / *MRS GRACEDEW*: not in LC.

110–11 *PRODMORE Pegg?* / *MRS GRACEDEW*: not in LC.

116 *—as he is ... and to her*: not in TYP.

164–8 S.D. *, where, on the opposite ... confess to*: not in TYP.

191–201 *PRODMORE (slowly turning round ...)* ... *MRS GRACEDEW (her laugh nervous ... smoothness)*: not in TYP.

216 S.D. *cross-barred*: with a pattern of bars or stripes drawn across it.

221–41 *[PRODMORE (in whom this question ...)]* ... *(... happy advantage)*: not in TYP.

242 *already dealt ... lumps!*: replaced by '*yourself* given me the benefit of an estimate.' in TYP.

247–50 MRS GRACEDEW *(shut up ...)* ... PRODMORE ... *(... fine free laugh)*: not in TYP.

251–3 ! / MRS GRACEDEW *(embarrassed ...)* / PRODMORE *(taking her up; derisive 'Charming'?*: not in TYP.

258–85 MRS GRACEDEW *(as if it's indeed an indictment ...)* ... PRODMORE ... *an hour ago!*: not in TYP.

299–326 PRODMORE *(as proof not only against ...)* ... *didn't believe?*: replaced by 'I raved just to please you. / PRODMORE You said what you didn't *believe?*' in TYP.

334–8 *do. ... Well—I*: do—I in TYP.

345 *thousand*: not in LC.

381 S.D. *Exit ... park*: in LC and TYP, Chivers's exit direction is in the stage directions in Prodmore's preceding speech, after '... *to the door to park.*' According to series conventions, it is here printed on its own line.

405–7 MRS GRACEDEW *(bringing it ...)* / PRODMORE ... *call the same?*: not in TYP.

460–2 MRS GRACEDEW *(while she waits ...)* / YULE *(in darkness)*: not in TYP.

465–74 YULE *(assenting as if ...)* ... MRS GRACEDEW ... *any engagement*: replaced by 'You don't perform it.' in TYP.

481 *Dear no*: elliptical for 'Oh dear, no', 'dear' being an exclamation not a vocative in this context.

502–10 *[YULE] (breaking, under ...)* ... *(completing ... his explanation)*: not in TYP.

515–17 MRS GRACEDEW *(just impenetrable ... YULE ... trying.*: not in TYP.

585–628 MRS GRACEDEW *(a little impatient ...)* ... / YULE No, but even ... *(... to her stay;*: replaced by 'MRS GRACEDEW Well, enough for inspiration. So now—! *(Goes to him and shakes his hand)* / YULE ' in TYP.

676 *you*: editorial emendation to furnish a subject for 'find' in the original phrase 'if, as you virtually *engaged* to, find me a *way*', ll. 676–7.

663–732 YULE *(as too dissatisfied ... | ... MRS GRACEDEW (again quickly ...)* ... *to escape?*: not in TYP.

752 S.D. *effectual*: i.e. in preventing Mrs Gracedew from leaving.

777 *did you*: took you in, cheated you.

839 S.D. *Enter ... ante-room*: editorial for 're-enter Chivers from ante-room',

originally placed after '. . . *they both see Chivers up right*' (l. 840) in LC and TYP.

855 *hand-booked order*: type of tourists equipped with guidebooks.

856 S.D. *catching*: catching stick or hook used by shepherds to catch their sheep; here: a walking stick.

872 *duck*: term of endearment, such as 'darling' or 'dear'.

GLOSSARY

a' (Scottish dialect) all

abun' (Scottish dialect) about

ain (Scottish dialect) own

amang (Scottish dialect) among

anither (Scottish dialect) another

apostrophise to address with an apostrophe (an exclamatory address)

apropos (French) with reference to, concerning

auld (Scottish dialect) old

au revoir (French) goodbye

bairn (Scottish dialect) child

bannock (Scottish dialect) in Scotland, bread made from barley- or pease-meal, usually unleavened, of large size, round or oval form

blathering blethering, talking foolishly

blent mingled

bluid (Scottish dialect) blood

bodie (Scottish dialect) person

bonnie (Scottish dialect) beautiful, pretty

braw (Scottish dialect) brave, fine, splendid

broil to cook meat on a fire or over metal bars

brose (Scottish dialect) a dish of oat- or pease-meal mixed with boiling water or milk, with salt and butter added

burn (Scottish dialect) brook, stream

ca' (Scottish dialect) call

canna (Scottish dialect) cannot

carol (v.) dance and sing, make merry

coom (Scottish dialect) come

coummerce (Scottish dialect) commerce

damme abbr. of 'damn me'; used as a profane imprecation

dang (euphemistic substitute for) damn

dee (Scottish dialect) die

deevil (Scottish dialect) devil

deuced devilish, confounded

devoir dutiful act of civility or respect

dinna (Scottish dialect) do not

doun (Scottish dialect) down

dra's (Scottish dialect) draws

dressing-case a case of toilet utensils

dun (n.) an importunate creditor; an agent employed to collects debts; (v.) to pester, plague constantly, esp. with demands for money

ebullition a sudden outburst

ee, een (Scottish dialect) eye, eyes

fane temple

fasht (Scottish dialect) angry

flacon (French) small stoppered bottle

fra (Scottish dialect) from

fulishly (Scottish dialect) foolishly

galloway a small-sized horse, especially for riding

gang (Scottish dialect) go

gaun (Scottish dialect) gone

geeming (Scottish dialect) gaming

gie (Scottish dialect) give

gillie (Scottish dialect) a sportsman's attendant, usually in deerstalking or angling in the Highlands

gin (Scottish dialect) if

Glaisgie (Scottish dialect) Glasgow

glower (Scottish dialect) stare, gaze intently; gleam, shine brightly

go to! (obsolete) come, come! (expressing disapprobation, remonstrance, protest)

gratis (Latin) without payment, free of charge

gude, guid (Scottish dialect) good

hairt (Scottish dialect) heart

hairtily (Scottish dialect) heartily

heed (Scottish dialect) mind, bother

heerd (Scottish dialect) heard

hie (Scottish dialect) hurry, go quickly

housie (Scottish dialect) house

hydrostatic relating to the equilibrium of liquids

impassionable excitable, easily roused to passion

imprimis (Latin) in the first place

in propria persona (Latin) him- or herself, in his or her own person

ither (Scottish dialect) other

ken (Scottish dialect) know, understand, perceive

kirk (Scottish dialect) church

lang (Scottish dialect) long

lass, lassie (Scottish dialect) girl, (unmarried) woman, maiden

law, laws (clipped form of) Lord, used as interjection or exclamation

law-a-mercy (corrupted form of) may the Lord have mercy (expressing surprise or fear)

leetle (Scottish dialect) little

legion a vast host or multitude

lor (clipped form of) Lord, used as an interjection or exclamation

mair (Scottish dialect) more

mebbe (Scottish dialect) maybe

ministrant one who ministers, attends to the comforts or wants of another

mither (Scottish dialect) mother

mon (Scottish dialect) man

mony (Scottish dialect) many

mousie (Scottish dialect) mouse

muckle (Scottish dialect) much

mun (Scottish dialect) must

na, nae (Scottish dialect) not; no

nicht (Scottish dialect) night

no (Scottish dialect) not

noo (Scottish dialect) now

ottoman a cushioned seat like a sofa, but without back or arms

ower (Scottish dialect) over; too (as in 'too late')

pairt (Scottish dialect) place, area, neighbourhood

parritch (Scottish dialect) porridge

peetience (Scottish dialect) patience

pettifogging (of a person) paying too much attention to unimportant detail

pier-glass a large tall mirror

pleete (Scottish dialect) plate

plume (of a bird) to dress its feathers (so as to prepare for flight, etc.)

pool (Scottish dialect) pull

precautional precautionary

preceptor teacher, instructor

pshaw exclamation expressing contempt, impatience, or disgust

puir (Scottish dialect) poor

purl (Scottish dialect) (of a brook) flow with whirling motions, twisting round little obstacles

richt, richtly (Scottish dialect) right, rightly

sae (Scottish dialect) so

sair (Scottish dialect) sore

Sassenach (Scottish dialect) Englishman or -woman

saut (Scottish dialect) salt

sax (Scottish dialect) six

scrappie (Scottish dialect) bit

'sdeath (obsolete) euphemistic abbreviation of 'God's death' used in oaths and asseverations

sheam (Scottish dialect) shame

sic (Scottish dialect) such

siller (Scottish dialect) silver; silver coin, money

smallclothes breeches

sough (Scottish dialect) sigh

spake (Scottish dialect) spoke

squeam (or 'squean') (of swine, and figuratively) to make a restless, fretful noise

stane (Scottish dialect) stone

suspeecious (Scottish dialect) suspicious

taulk (Scottish dialect) talk

teeste (Scottish dialect) taste

toun (Scottish dialect) town

trimmer a stiff competitor, fighter

twa (Scottish dialect) two

unco (Scottish dialect) very, exeedingly, extremely

var(r)a (Scottish dialect) very

vis-à-vis (French) opposite, so as to face (one another)

wad (Scottish dialect) would

wadna (Scottish dialect) would not

weal welfare, happiness

wee (Scottish dialect) small, tiny, little

weel (Scottish dialect) well

wha (Scottish dialect) who

whusky (Scottish dialect) whisky

wifie (Scottish dialect) wife

winsome (Scottish dialect) attractive in
appearance, manner, or nature;
charming

wrang (Scottish dialect) wrong

writ (Scottish dialect) a formal or legal
document of writing; a written record
or document of any transaction,
especially of a legal or formal nature

wuish (Scottish dialect) wish

ye you

yon (Scottish dialect) that (one)

zounds abbr. of 'by God's wounds', used
in oaths and asseverations

	Oriental Tales
WILLIAM BECKFORD	Vathek
JAMES BOSWELL	Boswell's Life of Johnson
FRANCES BURNEY	Camilla
	Cecilia
	Evelina
	The Wanderer
LORD CHESTERFIELD	Lord Chesterfield's Letters
JOHN CLELAND	Memoirs of a Woman of Pleasure
DANIEL DEFOE	Captain Singleton
	A Journal of the Plague Year
	Memoirs of a Cavalier
	Moll Flanders
	Robinson Crusoe
	Roxana
HENRY FIELDING	Joseph Andrews and Shamela
	A Journey from This World to the Next and The Journal of a Voyage to Lisbon
	Tom Jones
	The Adventures of David Simple
WILLIAM GODWIN	Caleb Williams
	St Leon
OLIVER GOLDSMITH	The Vicar of Wakefield
MARY HAYS	Memoirs of Emma Courtney
ELIZABETH HAYWOOD	The History of Miss Betsy Thoughtless
ELIZABETH INCHBALD	A Simple Story
SAMUEL JOHNSON	The History of Rasselas
CHARLOTTE LENNOX	The Female Quixote
MATTHEW LEWIS	The Monk

The Oxford World's Classics Website

www.worldsclassics.co.uk

- Information about new titles
- Explore the full range of Oxford World's Classics
- Links to other literary sites and the main OUP webpage
- Imaginative competitions, with bookish prizes
- Peruse *Compass*, the Oxford World's Classics magazine
- Articles by editors
- Extracts from Introductions
- A forum for discussion and feedback on the series
- Special information for teachers and lecturers

www.worldsclassics.co.uk

American Literature

British and Irish Literature

Children's Literature

Classics and Ancient Literature

Colonial Literature

Eastern Literature

European Literature

History

Medieval Literature

Oxford English Drama

Poetry

Philosophy

Politics

Religion

The Oxford Shakespeare

A complete list of Oxford Paperbacks, including Oxford World's Classics, OPUS, Past Masters, Oxford Authors, Oxford Shakespeare, Oxford Drama, and Oxford Paperback Reference, is available in the UK from the Academic Division Publicity Department, Oxford University Press, Great Clarendon Street, Oxford OX2 6DP.

In the USA, complete lists are available from the Paperbacks Marketing Manager, Oxford University Press, 198 Madison Avenue, New York, NY 10016.

Oxford Paperbacks are available from all good bookshops. In case of difficulty, customers in the UK can order direct from Oxford University Press Bookshop, Freepost, 116 High Street, Oxford OX1 4BR, enclosing full payment. Please add 10 per cent of published price for postage and packing.